www.ingramcontent.com/pod-product-compliance
Lightning Source LLC
Chambersburg PA
CBHW070808300326
41914CB00078B/1908/J

Abbreviated Criminal Procedures for Core International Crimes

Morten Bergsmo (editor)

2017
Torkel Opsahl Academic EPublisher
Brussels

This and other books in the *FICHL Publication Series* may be openly accessed and downloaded through CILRAP's web sites which use Persistent URLs for all publications it makes available (such PURLs will not be changed). Printed copies may be ordered through online and other distributors, including https://www. amazon.co.uk/. This book was published on 29 April 2017.

ISBNs: 978-82-93081-20-3 (print) and 978-82-8348-104-4 (e-book).

Dedicated to the memory of Marius Bergsmo,
my brother and childhood friend

EDITOR'S PREFACE

This book invites reflection on the difficult issue of 'abbreviated criminal procedures for core international crimes cases'. The Forum for International Criminal and Humanitarian Law (FICHL) – a department of the Centre for International Law Research and Policy (CILRAP) – pioneered the topic when convening a conference on 9 October 2009 in Sarajevo on what was then a new subject-matter in the international criminal law discourse. It brought together a group of experts to shed light on issues such as national abbreviated criminal procedures for ordinary crimes, early experiments with such procedures for core international crimes cases in Colombia and Rwanda, arguments for and against such procedures, and perspectives from human rights and victims' perspectives.

This book contains edited papers prepared in connection with that conference, varying in length and the extent of detail in the analyses. It is hoped that the book will encourage and enable lawyers and legal researchers in different parts of the world to gradually explore the topic of abbreviated criminal procedures for core international crimes further.

The venue of Sarajevo was chosen deliberately. Not primarily because Bosnia and Herzegovina is the chief laboratory of accountability for core international crimes after Nuremberg and Tokyo. But because the country's wars in the 1990s led to the opening of many more war crimes case files than its criminal justice system could process through regular criminal procedures. The conference therefore attracted much attention in the legal community of Bosnia and Herzegovina, with some of the country's leading jurists speaking at the event.

The conference and publication are made possible through financial support from the Norwegian Ministry of Foreign Affairs and the International Nuremberg Principles Academy. We received other assistance from the Norwegian Embassy in Sarajevo as well as the High Judicial and Prosecutorial Council of Bosnia and Herzegovina. Ambassador Jan Braathu and Sven Marius Urke made particularly valuable contributions. We also thank Gareth Richards, TOAEP Senior Editor, for his excellent copy-editing, and SONG Tianying and Peter Mitchell.

Morten Bergsmo

i

PREFACE BY AMBASSADOR JAN BRAATHU

I had the privilege of opening the seminar on 'Abbreviated Criminal Procedures for Core International Crimes' in Sarajevo on 9 October 2009. This is a topic of great professional and – I dare say – political importance. It was a pleasure for me to welcome a large number of seminar participants, including a number of international experts who had travelled to Bosnia and Herzegovina, this beautiful but troubled country. When extending my warm greetings to the many participants from Bosnia and Herzegovina at the seminar, I expressed my recognition of the difficult work that they deal with professionally on a daily basis.

The seminar and this publication amount to an attempt to gauge the challenges confronting the judicial systems at both international and state levels in dealing with crimes committed as part of war. This is an effort at the cutting edge of international justice. It is an effort where Bosnia and Herzegovina can contribute with its experiences and expertise to the further development of international justice. I would therefore like to thank Morten Bergsmo, the Director of the Centre for International Law Research and Policy, for his personal initiative and professional dedication that led to the convening of the seminar and this publication.

I believe that we all share a common interest in working towards the objective of fighting impunity and bringing justice to victims of gross violations of international law. In saying this, I am quoting from the address by a former International Criminal Tribunal for the former Yugoslavia ('ICTY') President, Judge Patrick Robinson, before the United Nations General Assembly the day prior to the seminar in Sarajevo. In presenting the ICTY's sixteenth annual report to the General Assembly, President Robinson also pointed out the danger that victims feel forgotten and that their rights are disregarded, not only by the international community but also by their own state justice authorities. President Robinson reminded his listeners that the torch is being passed from the Tribunal to judges, prosecutors and defence counsel in the affected states of the western Balkans.

There is still a large number of pending cases that challenge the capacity of the justice system in Bosnia and Herzegovina. Without entering into a discussion on precise numbers, it nonetheless seems clear that the caseload represents a significant challenge to the capacity of the justice system in this country. We of course applaud and support the efforts made

by Bosnia and Herzegovina institutions and authorities to deal with this issue. Not least do we welcome and support the National Strategy for Processing War Crimes Cases that was adopted by the Bosnia and Herzegovina Council of Ministers in December 2008. This strategy directs the competent authorities to "prosecute as a priority the most responsible perpetrators before the Court of Bosnia and Herzegovina, with the help of agreed upon case selection and prioritisation criteria". However, behind the queue of prioritised cases there will be a large number of other cases of less 'global' importance, but which are nonetheless of huge personal importance for the victims and their families. Such cases may risk never coming to court due to the capacity restrictions of the system.

So, what is to be done? Should such cases be relegated to non-judicial – perhaps political – mechanisms? Are truth commissions an answer to the problem? I believe that the value of truth commissions should not be underestimated. Nor should they be overestimated. Recent studies point to pitfalls and limitations in the truth commission mechanism. What is more, this approach is highly dependent on contextual circumstances that may not apply in all relevant situations or countries.

We support criminal justice accountability for core international crimes, based on international and state law. We must also see war crimes processes in a broader social context. Such processes must meet the objectives determined by law. But they should also answer – however fully – reasonable expectations based on the law. We must not neglect the expectations of victims and their families. We do so at the peril of the very legitimacy of international and national justice in the mind of public opinion.

That is why I believe that there is a case to be made for looking into the possibility of developing a faster judicial procedure for dealing with certain categories of war crimes. No stone should be left unturned before we allow ourselves to conclude that criminal justice systems are unable to deal with large backlogs of core international crimes cases. Certainly, it is reasonable to discuss the merits and demerits of such an approach. And that, of course, is the purpose of this publication.

I am pleased that such a large number of eminent experts from throughout Bosnia and Herzegovina and abroad allocated time to participate in the seminar. I hope the seminar and this book will lead to a professionally stimulating and satisfying process of reflection.

FOREWORD BY JUDGE MEDDŽIDA KRESO[*]

In the first part of the seminar in Sarajevo on 9 October 2009 organised by the Forum for International Criminal and Humanitarian Law (FICHL), we heard very useful information and thoughts about the possible modalities and effects of abbreviated criminal procedures. I would like to thank the organisers for the seminar, during which we had the opportunity to hear such an abundance of new information and ideas.

The arguments presented were generally in favour of the need to seek different mechanisms aimed at reducing the duration and costs of regular criminal proceedings. I will not repeat the data on the number of pending war crimes cases in Bosnia and Herzegovina, which we came to during our work on the National Strategy for Processing War Crimes Cases. However, I wish to mention the data which I presented at the seminar as an additional illustration of this problem. Specifically, in the State Court of Bosnia and Herzegovina we have conducted an analysis to determine the average duration of main trials in war crimes cases. Based on a sample of eight cases that qualify as non-complex cases (with one or possibly two accused persons), it was established that main trials on average lasted for seven and a half months. Within those seven and a half months, there were approximately 23.3 hearings per case, in which one hearing took three and a half hours on average. Therefore, around 80 hours per case were spent in the courtroom alone.

These data, however, pertain to first instance proceedings only, and as regards the Court of Bosnia and Herzegovina the cases are appealed after the first instance verdict (with the exception of cases involving plea agreements). Following the filing of an appeal against the first instance verdict,

---

[*]   **Meddžida Kreso** is President of the State Court of Bosnia and Herzegovina. She graduated from the Law Faculty of the University of Sarajevo in 1970. Having passed the bar exam in 1973, she was appointed Municipal Prosecutor in Mostar where she worked until 1978 when she was appointed District Court Judge there. She served as President of the Labour Court in Mostar from 1989 to 1992. From 1996 to 1998 she worked as an attorney, and from 1998 to 2001 in the legal department of a bank. In 2001 she was appointed as the Deputy Prosecutor of the Federation of Bosnia and Herzegovina and served until the end of 2002. When the Prosecutor's Office of Bosnia and Herzegovina was established in 2003, she was appointed Deputy Chief Prosecutor of Bosnia and Herzegovina in January 2003. On 10 October 2004, Judge Kreso was appointed Judge and President of the Court of Bosnia and Herzegovina.

proceedings continue before the Appellate Panel. This means that the actual duration of the cases is far longer, because they include appellate proceedings, involvement of the Appellate Panel in the proceedings, possible revocation of the first instance verdict and a retrial before the Appellate Panel, and so on. This clearly shows that even a significant increase in the number of prosecutors and judges cannot lead to the expectations of a significant increase in efficiency in trying this type of case. One should also not disregard all other limitations that the courts face, such as staffing, technical and, particularly, space-related limitations.

The statistics presented inevitably lead us to think about ways to improve the trial process in war crimes cases, that is, to find a model to speed up the proceedings and bring to trial as many war crimes cases as possible, and, in that way, contribute not only to strengthening of the rule of law but also to the entire reconciliation process in the region.

In any event, one should keep in mind that Bosnia and Herzegovina legislation provides for the possibility of summary proceedings, but only in cases of minor violations of the Criminal Code, carrying milder penalties. Within the Special Procedures section, the Criminal Procedure Code of Bosnia and Herzegovina, just like the laws of the entities and of the Brčko District, provides for the possibility of issuing a sentencing warrant if the case involves criminal offences carrying a principal punishment in the form of a fine or a prison sentence of up to five years. Similar options exist in other European states whose procedural law recognises summary proceedings of some sort. In view of the punishments prescribed for criminal offences that fall in the category of war crimes, it is clear that at present this option cannot be applied in those cases. It certainly needs to be highlighted that, since all abbreviated procedures in some way impose limitations on certain rights of the accused person, introducing such procedures in complex war crimes cases may carry a certain amount of risk. More specifically, although the introduction of abbreviated procedures in war crimes cases might accelerate the criminal procedures to the maximum, and thus contribute to efficiency in such cases, care must be taken of all aspects and standards of a fair trial that must be satisfied in such complex cases.

However, I would use the opportunity to draw attention to the fact that the existing legal framework in Bosnia and Herzegovina recognises other institutions that may be said to serve not only to the acceleration of the criminal proceedings and greater effectiveness and efficiency in the operation of courts but also the observance of the right to a trial without delay and within a reasonable time, particularly when the parties do not dispute the facts. Here we should primarily highlight the notion of *plea*

agreement, which provides for the possibility of entering into such agreements in war crimes cases too. Unfortunately, even though that option has been in existence since 2003, the first plea agreement in a war crimes case was concluded as late as February 2008, and the Court of Bosnia and Herzegovina has not had many plea agreements concluded to date. If one knows that in general crime and organised crime cases, in the period from 2005 to 2007 only, 204 plea agreements were concluded, it becomes clear how underutilised the potential of plea agreements is. Not only do they reduce the duration and costs of regular criminal proceedings, they also have another important function. That function is reflected in the fact that possible co-operation of one of the accomplices to the criminal offence may be an extremely useful way of obtaining information and secure testimonies with regard to the other suspects or accused in solving serious criminal cases. The nature of a substantial number of criminal cases involving war crimes is such that they incorporate a large number of participants, and without co-operation between the Prosecutor's Office and some of the participants, it is often difficult to establish with certainty the exact division of roles and prove the degree of individuals' responsibility. That is why I believe that this option has not been fully used, particularly because it appears that the initial resistance and distrust on the part of the public and judicial officials towards this institution have been overcome.

The FICHL has developed a very useful practice, which is to put together and publish through the Torkel Opsahl Academic EPublisher an open access publication of all the materials from the seminars it organises. Having in mind the tradition of the criminal justice system in Bosnia and Herzegovina and the region on the issue of abbreviated procedures, as well as the need to open a broader discussion on that matter in relation to war crimes cases, I welcome that the organisers have edited this anthology.

In 2003 Bosnia and Herzegovina got new criminal codes – substantive and procedural law – which abandoned some of the traditional legal approaches and introduced a significant number of new provisions and notions. Bearing that in mind, soon after the laws were passed, a special team for monitoring the application of the criminal laws was formed, comprising prominent lawyers, judges, prosecutors and university professors of law. The team is still active and its task is to continuously monitor the application of the criminal laws, identify the problems in their application, identify the possibility of further improvements of the current provisions, as well as to make proposals of necessary amendments to the criminal laws.

In view of the above, I think that it would be very useful if the team members would be able to acquaint themselves with the subject matter of

this publication, so that this professional and qualified forum could initiate a discussion on these matters and offer possible provisions.

One thing is sure: states on whose territories large-scale violations of international humanitarian law happened must keep seeking new procedural arrangements. In that respect, I stand in support of the FICHL seminar on 'Abbreviated Criminal Procedures for Core International Crimes'. I thank the Forum for its courage in initiating the discussion on this very delicate issue.

FOREWORD BY JUDGE MILORAD NOVKOVIĆ[*]

It was a pleasure to address the 9 October 2009 seminar in Sarajevo organised by the Forum for International Criminal and Humanitarian Law (FICHL) on abbreviated criminal procedures for international crimes, and to introduce this anthology of seminar papers. The event underlined the significance and challenging nature of the effective processing of war crimes cases. I believe the seminar and this volume answer numerous questions that judges and prosecutors face in their day-to-day work when dealing with war crimes cases and, through the exchange of knowledge and experiences, offer new solutions for quicker and more efficient case processing. I would like to thank the organiser of the FICHL for recognising the significance of the topic and for gathering the relevant national and international experts for the questions raised.

I have several times observed that too much time has elapsed since the end of the wars in Bosnia and Herzegovina with large numbers of war crimes cases unprocessed. Let me underline the personal and above all human factor from the perspective of individuals who were direct victims of the war as well as the family members who have been waiting for justice for years. The question is whether after so many years we can even speak of justice. Or is it an injustice to the victims, their families, to generations who are arriving and should go forward in life unburdened by the weight of the past?

Viewed from a professional standpoint, we have problems such as witnesses who are not motivated to give testimony on war crimes. Aside from time-related reasons, other reasons would be of a territorial nature. Many people have become displaced in the region and have become less and less available or willing to testify. Many witnesses have unfortunately died during the past years and thus their testimonies cannot contribute towards uncovering war crimes or towards the just processing of the perpetrators of such crimes.

---

[*]   **Milorad Novković**, President, Supreme Court of the Federation of Bosnia and Herzegovina. He was President of the High Judicial and Prosecutorial Council of Bosnia and Herzegovina when this text was prepared. Views expressed here do not necessarily represent the views of his present or former employers.

Bosnia and Herzegovina has made many efforts towards resolving the issue of processing war crimes. On 28 December 2008, the Council of Ministers adopted a National Strategy for Processing War Crimes Cases, and subsequently on 19 March 2009 rendered a Decision on the Establishment of a Steering Board for Overseeing the Implementation of the National Strategy for Processing War Crimes Cases of which I served as a member. The Strategy contained a section on criteria to select and prioritise cases, with a view to providing for better processing of cases.

The Steering Board was established with the objective of monitoring efficiency and quality in the execution of measures included in the National Strategy and to evaluate the results achieved in correlation to those expected. Among the challenges raised by the Steering Board was the absence of a common database regarding the number of cases and persons reported with reference to committed war crimes. In order to determine the true number of cases and the names of persons reported for war crimes, the Prosecutor's Office of Bosnia and Herzegovina was tasked to determine precise information both as per each prosecutor's office and for all prosecutor's offices combined. This is a prerequisite for all rational management of portfolios of war crimes cases. Without such a common database and overview one cannot design effective strategies for selection and prioritisation of cases, and meaningfully consider possible introduction of abbreviated criminal procedures for already opened case files, the subject of this anthology. This is also a prerequisite for the effective co-operation between all prosecution offices in the country seized with war crimes cases.

TABLE OF CONTENTS

1

More Opened Case Files Than Trial Capacity

Morten Bergsmo[*]

1.1. A Question of Legal Policy, Not Only Criminal Procedure

This book concerns the situation where a country has opened more case files on core international crimes[1] than its criminal justice system can process through regular trials. Armed conflicts and attacks against civilian populations tend to generate more war crimes and crimes against humanity than the criminal justice systems of the directly affected states (territorial states) are able to investigate and prosecute. This is regrettably commonplace in situations where mass atrocity occurs. Only a few countries open a high number of war crimes case files. Recent examples include Argentina, Bosnia and Herzegovina and Colombia, as described in several of the following chapters. When the criminal justice system of such jurisdictions does not have capacity to process all the case files it has opened, we face the dilemma which this volume is about.

The problem that the book deals with is primarily one of legal policy: should legal systems provide for abbreviated criminal procedures for core international crimes? If the answer is yes, a number of technical legal questions arise regarding the abbreviated mechanism, such as which types of crimes it shall apply to, how it will respect constitutional and international human rights guarantees, and how it will facilitate judicial economy in practice. The legal policy question goes wider than a discussion on criminal

---

[*] **Morten Bergsmo** is Director, Centre for International Law Research and Policy (CIL-RAP), and Visiting Professor, Peking University Law School. He was Senior Researcher, Peace Research Institute Oslo ('PRIO'), at the time he conceptualised the FICHL-conference on the topic of this book in Sarajevo in October 2009. CILRAP's department FICHL was then a PRIO project. The author is grateful for the support of PRIO and the Norwegian Ministry of Foreign Affairs for the first part of this project, and of the International Nuremberg Principles Academy for its finalisation. He also thanks the authors for their co-operation and patience during the project.

[1] By 'core international crimes' in this book is meant war crimes, crimes against humanity and genocide, corresponding to Articles 6, 7 and 8 in the Statute of the International Criminal Court (http://www.legal-tools.org/doc/7b9af9/). 'War crimes' or 'mass atrocity' are sometimes used synonymously with 'core international crimes'.

---

procedure, and includes arguments and considerations from legal philosophy to administration of criminal justice.

It should not be principally classified as a 'transitional justice' problem. Several chapters in the book do consider practice in Colombia and Rwanda under the umbrella of 'abbreviated criminal procedures'. It is indeed useful to inform the consideration of the topic at hand with information on relevant practice. But as Chapter 3 makes clear, abbreviated criminal procedure is primarily developed in national legal systems. Some countries have invested considerable innovative, analytical capacity in designing and implementing procedures, not with core international crimes in mind. It is important that an ensuing discourse on abbreviated criminal procedures for core international crimes fully explores such national procedures, also by involving national experts on those procedures. Discourse actors should not restrict the analysis to the limited transitional justice practice in countries such as Colombia and Rwanda.

The question raised by the book does not lend itself well to the kind of exceptionalist thinking about core international crimes that we sometimes come across: treating war crimes and crimes against humanity as if they are fundamentally different from all other crimes. Rather, as described by Chapters 8 and 10 below, the problem of backlogs of open criminal case files is now a widespread problem in countries around the globe. Questions on the length of proceedings, expedited trials and judicial economy are contested, mainstream political issues in many states. Some countries have made significant legal reforms to alleviate the problem, such as Italy's 1988 Code of Criminal Procedure,[2] as detailed by Kai Ambos and Alexander Heinze in Chapter 3. These reforms are important to understand the direction in which this research project seeks to move the discourse.

Foreign criminal jurisdictions – international(ised) or third state – may exceptionally process a few war crimes cases originating in a territorial state. But it is not realistic to expect that external jurisdictions will be able to handle many such cases in the foreseeable future. There are simply too many constraints, including limited resources available for their prosecution, weak connection between the cases and the forum state in question, inadequate access for the forum state's criminal justice system to evidence of the alleged crimes, and political pressures on exercising universal juris-

---

[2]   Italy, Codice di Procedura Penal, 22 September 1988 (http://www.legal-tools.org/doc/77d222/).

diction. Civil society has been trying to address these problems in several countries, but there is a ceiling to what non-governmental organisations can do in this regard. Our earlier anthology *Complementarity and the Exercise of Universal Jurisdiction* contains several analytical chapters on the contemporary role of universal jurisdiction, a discussion that is separate from this book.[3]

Most perpetrators, victims, witnesses and other evidence can normally be found in the territorial states where core international crimes occur. The criminal justice system in some of these states open core international crimes case files that involve many identified suspects. As mentioned above, this is the situation in, for example, Colombia and Bosnia and Herzegovina, where there are thousands of suspects named in open case files involving allegations of core international crimes in various prosecutors' offices around the country. This is in itself a welcome response to the occurrence of core international crimes, under the applicable laws of the two countries.[4] The problem is that the criminal procedure regimes in place and available capacity do not allow for the processing of more than a relatively low number of cases per year. These cases concern only a small fraction of suspects in the opened files. There is, in other words, a queue or backlog of open case files that cannot be dealt with through regular prosecution and trial. The will to prosecute is not matched by adequate systemic ability.

1.2. Beyond Mapping, Prioritisation or Non-Judicial Mechanisms

This tension between the overall number of suspects in case files on the one hand, and the capacity of criminal justice systems on the other, entails several fundamental challenges, the resolution of which can affect the credibility of the very idea of criminal justice for atrocities. First, it has proven difficult for some jurisdictions with backlogs of war crimes cases to develop adequate overviews of pending case files. The exact nature of the queue of cases is unclear. This has been the situation in Bosnia and Herzegovina, as exemplified by the two forewords above and Chapter 4 below. Such *mapping* or setting up of inventories clarify the dimensions of the workload

---

[3] See Morten Bergsmo (ed.), *Complementarity and the Exercise of Universal Jurisdiction*, Torkel Opsahl Academic EPublisher, Oslo, 2010 (http://www.legal-tools.org/doc/d3f01a/).

[4] That may not always be the case. In Chapter 10, Judge Hanne Sophie Greve expresses reservation about the merit of opening a large number of war crimes case files in jurisdictions where it is abundantly clear, at the time the files are opened, that only a small number of them can be processed by the criminal justice system.

to all legitimate stakeholders in the process. The inventory makes it easier to categorise the case files for prioritisation in a professional and consistent manner. It creates a measure of rational transparency that can serve as a buffer against the inherent problem of selectivity in criminal justice for atrocities. Our book *The Backlog of Core International Crimes Case Files in Bosnia and Herzegovina*[5] deals with this aspect of the tension. The present anthology does not. The speech at the October 2009 FICHL-conference by Judge Milorad Novković[6] did, however, explain how the Prosecutor's Office of Bosnia and Herzegovina had failed to produce an adequate overview of existing core international crimes cases as called for by the Council of Ministers.[7] The authors of *The Backlog of Core International Crimes Case Files in Bosnia and Herzegovina* had called for the development of such an inventory in 2008, leading to the request by the Council of Ministers in December 2008 as a key element of the National War Crimes Strategy of Bosnia and Herzegovina.

Second, in addition to mapping, *prioritisation* of the cases that will go to trial first is essential when there is a large backlog of open war crimes case files. If a criminal jurisdiction prioritises cases that are not considered particularly grave or otherwise representative of the overall criminal victim-isation, trust in the war crimes process will necessarily diminish, especially among the victims. Reasonable expectations of justice will not be satisfied by the random, arbitrary or selective nature of the justice that is offered by the state in question. This is not a mere academic problem. It is a standing challenge in jurisdictions that have a backlog of cases. The criminal justice system in these countries need to prioritise their cases. And the prioritisa-tion must be based on criteria that are legal rather than political in nature. Prioritisation is the topic of the book *Criteria for Prioritizing and Selecting Core International Crimes Cases*[8] – not of the present volume. A new, con-siderably expanded edition of the book will be published shortly after the

---

[5] See Morten Bergsmo, Kjetil Helvig, Ilia Utmelidze and Gorana Žagovec, *The Backlog of Core International Crimes Case Files in Bosnia and Herzegovina*, 2nd ed., Torkel Opsahl Academic EPublisher, Oslo, 2010 (http://www.legal-tools.org/doc/688146/).

[6] He was President of the High Judicial and Prosecutorial Council of Bosnia and Herze-govina at the time.

[7] As reiterated in his Foreword above.

[8] See Morten Bergsmo (ed.), *Criteria for Prioritizing and Selecting Core International Crimes Cases*, 2nd ed., Torkel Opsahl Academic EPublisher, Oslo, 2010 (http://www.legal-tools.org/doc/f5abed/).

---

present volume, taking into account the growing practice on criteria since the publication of the first edition. The Office of the Prosecutor of the International Criminal Court issued a policy paper on criteria in 2016.[9]

Third, proper mapping and prioritisation do not alone resolve the problem of large backlogs of core international crimes cases, far from it. In some jurisdictions, the annual capacity to process such cases is so low compared to the total number of open case files that most suspects and witnesses will die before their cases come to trial. This seems to be the situation in, for example, Bosnia and Herzegovina, where the Council of Ministers in the above-mentioned National War Crimes Strategy limits the process of war crimes prosecutions to 15 years from the time of adoption of the strategy.[10] This official cut-off date makes it easier to calculate the contrast between case capacity and caseload. But the problem can be the same or worse in other backlog states that have not set a deadline for war crimes prosecutions.

In these situations – whether there is a cut-off date or not – the cases against the majority of the core international crimes suspects are likely not to be prioritised for trial. The system is simply unable to process all cases under the existing criminal procedures, despite the best intentions and efforts of the criminal justice professionals concerned. What should be done with the open case files that are left unprocessed? In some countries, these may at the end of the day constitute the overwhelming majority of the opened case files. Should they just linger and be closed when suspects die or become too frail to stand trial? The comfort of not having to make a difficult decision may have a certain political appeal, although it amounts to passive decision-making by omission.

Or should the unprocessed case files be transferred out of the criminal justice system to alternative, non-judicial mechanisms, despite the fact that they already have an established case file name or number? Then they would no longer be criminal justice files, but files of some other mechanism. Although it may be within technical reach, moving open case files out of the criminal justice system could significantly undermine trust in criminal justice in the country concerned. It could be seen as an official statement of lack of ability on the part of the criminal justice authorities.

---

[9] ICC Office of the Prosecutor, Policy Paper on Case Selection and Prioritisation, 15 September 2016 (http://www.legal-tools.org/doc/182205/).

[10] The document appears as Annex 2 in Bergsmo et al., 2010, see *supra* note 5.

The government of the same country and, in some cases, the international community may well have invested considerable effort in constructing public trust in the criminal justice system in question, a trust that could be eroded.

This volume is *not* about alternatives to the processing of core international crimes cases within the criminal justice system, for example truth and reconciliation mechanisms. Such alternatives have their merits, extensively explored in what has become a considerable transitional justice literature. There are empirical deficiencies and other lacunae in this literature, to which CILRAP is committed to making further foundational contributions,[11] but this falls outside the focused scope of the present book.

1.3.   Within the Criminal Justice System

The present concern is whether abbreviated criminal procedures can be designed to process more core international crimes cases within the criminal justice system in ways that deal more effectively with large backlogs of opened case files, especially cases involving less serious core international crimes. Is innovation required to ensure that already opened core international crimes cases are processed by prosecutors and judges, rather than by non-judicial staff in alternative mechanisms? This was the project focus that was carefully explained in advance to the contributors at the FICHL-conference in Sarajevo in October 2009, whose papers make up this anthology. The research project does not advocate that abbreviated criminal procedures are generally required. It takes no position on the definition of such procedures.

The book is not directly concerned with the situation in those territorial states (such as, for example, South Africa) where many core international crimes have indeed been committed, but no or very few case files are opened. There is obviously a considerable potential for cases in such countries, but the criminal justice case files have not yet been opened for one reason or another. The problem of backlog of opened case files does not arise in this situation. The formal files are simply not there. That does not mean that there is not a serious backlog of potential cases in these countries

---

[11]   A number of texts on whether criminal justice for core international crimes can lead to reconciliation have been published in the FICHL Policy Brief Series, see, for example, Nos. 30–36, 40–42 and 75.

– not to mention the overall problem of impunity facilitated by the authorities. But these issues fall outside the scope of this book.

1.4. Compliance with Human Rights Requirements

Both the Sarajevo conference and this book assume that abbreviated criminal procedures to be considered must comply with constitutional and international human rights standards. The rights of the accused and the right to equal treatment of similar cases are therefore not barriers to the discussion which we are calling for. These fundamental rights must be respected, or there will not be support for abbreviated criminal procedures or they will not produce a fair justice that holds. The argument of Marieke Wierda in Chapter 9 – and other authors – is therefore appropriate, but the project concept note was already based on this premise from the start. Judge Hanne Sophie Greve sums this up concisely when she writes:

> For the purpose of this discussion, it is presupposed that abbreviated criminal procedures are so construed as to meet fair trial standards. Abbreviated criminal procedures will furthermore have to comply with the principle of legality. It is also taken as given that the abbreviated criminal procedures are prescribed by law and made an integral part of the state's criminal justice system.[12]

She helps to lift the initial discourse to a level of broad perspective:

> Abbreviated criminal procedures can thus have a very significant role to play by helping states to maintain the rule of law and protect fundamental human rights by also being able to prosecute large numbers of core international crimes within their national criminal justice system and with full respect for fair trail principles. The core of the matter is to simplify without compromising due process.[13]

It is a human rights problem that so many of the opened war crimes case files in situations such as Bosnia and Herzegovina and Colombia will never lead to trial, accountability or closure. There are two sides to the human rights argument.

---

[12] See Hanne Sophie Greve, Chapter 10, p. 265.
[13] *Ibid.*

1.5.   Victim of Its Own Success

There has been a significant increase in the public expectation of criminal justice accountability for mass atrocity crimes since the United Nations Security Council decided in May 1993 to establish the ex-Yugoslavia Tribunal. The ability of the international community to respond with criminal justice has also increased. Nowhere has this been more visible than in Bosnia and Herzegovina where an extraordinary effort of the international Tribunal has been supplemented by a comprehensive national war crimes prosecution programme, both operating at a high level of justice. And this is precisely where we have become a victim of our own success with criminal justice for core international crimes. Even where a national machinery has been put in place, funding is available, sufficient political will has been mobilised, and case files have been opened, we realise that the criminal justice system can only bring a relatively small number of alleged perpetrators to trial.

The acceptance of war crimes justice has grown faster than its structural ability to deliver. Or, the tree of war crimes justice has grown faster than its bark can absorb, so it shows cracks, as does the beautiful tree on the Kyoto Imperial Palace grounds depicted on the front cover of the dust jacket of this book. This captures the dilemma we now face in some situations with backlogs of opened war crimes case files.

1.6.   Subsequent Chapters

The authors of the following chapters of the present volume were asked to address one or more of four specific topics: 1) the need for abbreviated criminal procedures for core international crimes, in particular in territorial states directly affected by crimes; 2) an overview of some existing abbreviated criminal procedures; 3) key elements of possible abbreviated criminal procedures for core international crimes; and 4) a tentative discussion on abbreviated criminal procedures for core international crimes in Bosnia and Herzegovina, the chief laboratory for criminal justice for atrocities since 1993.

Ambassador Dr. *Jan Braathu* – then Ambassador of Norway to Bosnia and Herzegovina, now Head of the Organization for Security and Co-operation in Europe ('OSCE') Mission in Kosovo – sets the stage in his Preface to the book where he cautions that if we neglect the justice expectations of victims, we "do so at the peril of the very legitimacy of interna-

tional and national justice in the mind of public opinion".[14] He believes that "there is a case to be made for looking into the possibility of developing a faster judicial procedure for dealing with certain categories of war crimes. No stone should be left unturned before we allow ourselves to conclude that criminal justice systems are unable to deal with large backlogs of core international crimes cases".[15] He rightly observes that the purpose of this book is exactly to discuss the "merits and demerits of such an approach",[16] an "effort at the cutting edge of international justice"[17] and an "effort where Bosnia and Herzegovina can contribute with its experiences and expertise to the further development of international justice",[18] a country where "the caseload represents a significant challenge to the capacity of the justice system".[19] "Behind the queue of prioritised cases", he observes insightfully, there will be "a large number of other cases of less 'global' importance, but which are nonetheless of huge personal importance for the victims and their families. Such cases may risk never coming to court due to the capacity restrictions of the system".[20]

In her Foreword, Judge *Meddžida Kreso* – the President of the State Court of Bosnia and Herzegovina – authoritatively describes the limitations of the criminal justice system in Bosnia and Herzegovina to process a high number of war crimes cases. The statistics "inevitably lead us to think about ways to improve the trial process in war crimes cases, that is, to find a model to speed up the proceedings and bring to trial as many war crimes cases as possible, and in that way, contribute not only to strengthening of the rule of law but also to the entire reconciliation process in the region".[21] She recognises that "states on whose territories large-scale violations of international humanitarian law happened must keep seeking new procedural arrangements",[22] and that "even a significant increase in the number of

---

[14]   Jan Braathu, Preface, p. iv.
[15]   *Ibid.*
[16]   *Ibid.*
[17]   *Ibid.*, p. iii.
[18]   *Ibid.*
[19]   *Ibid.*, p. iv.
[20]   *Ibid.*
[21]   Meddžida Kreso, Foreword, p. vi.
[22]   *Ibid.*, p. viii.

prosecutors and judges cannot lead to the expectations of a significant increase in efficiency in trying this type of case".[23]

To these considerations, Judge *Milorad Novković* – President of the Supreme Court of the Federation of Bosnia and Herzegovina – describes the Steering Board for Overseeing the Implementation of the National Strategy for Processing War Crimes Cases in Bosnia and Herzegovina, which contains a section on criteria to select and prioritise cases. He observes that without a common database and overview of open case files, "one cannot design effective strategies for selection and prioritisation of cases, and meaningfully consider possible introduction of abbreviated criminal procedures for already opened case files".[24] Developing such a database in Bosnia and Herzegovina had been a problem, until the OSCE Mission to Bosnia and Herzegovina, in co-operation with the Government of Norway, made an important contribution.[25]

Chapter 2 ("The Two Illusions of All-Embracing Criminal Justice and Exclusively Extrajudicial Responses to Mass Atrocity") by *Mark A. Drumbl* sets the stage by broadly surveying some challenges and justifications for abbreviated criminal proceedings for core international crimes. Although he "support[s] abbreviated proceedings as a tool in the toolbox of transitional justice", he also "urge[s] caution, circumspection and deliberation in their design and implementation".[26] He writes that unduly high expectations may be the biggest danger for abbreviated criminal procedures. He also predicts that defendants will challenge the application of abbreviated criminal procedures on the grounds of constitutional or international human rights grounds, by that reminding us that the concept of abbreviated criminal procedures in the project of which this book is part, presupposes that they are in accordance with international human rights standards. He concludes by saying that the "challenges are far from insurmountable. In fact, they can be harnessed and converted into bold justifications for the idea of abbreviated criminal procedures".[27]

Chapter 3 by *Kai Ambos* and *Alexander Heinze* ("Abbreviated Procedures in Comparative Criminal Procedure: A Structural Approach with a

---

[23] *Ibid.*, p. vi.

[24] Milorad Novković, Foreword, p. x.

[25] See *supra* note 3.

[26] Mark A. Drumbl, Chapter 2, p. 19.

[27] *Ibid.*, p. 25.

View to International Criminal Procedure") provides a comprehensive overview of abbreviated criminal procedures in a number of national juris-dictions, showing how widespread are such procedures, how many diverse expressions they take, and how important it is to look beyond English-language jurisdictions when seeking to develop new abbreviated criminal procedures for core international crimes. With its 74 pages and detailed references, it forms a backbone of this volume and the further discourse on the topic. The authors start by recognising that overloaded criminal justice systems are common phenomena in almost every country. As a result, countries have developed proceedings to expedite the trial referred to as special proceedings. The refer to Italy as "a paradigmatic example", insofar as its "new *Codice di procedura penale* ('CPP') was introduced in 1988 to provide for the possibility of special forms of procedure (*procedimenti speciali*) aimed at replacing the ordinary proceedings with a faster summary proceeding":[28]

> The summary trial (*giudizio abbreviato*) waives the trial itself. Punishment can also be waived upon request by the parties (*patteggiamento*). A penal order (*decreto penale*) or a settle-ment (*oblazione*) waives the preliminary investigations (*indagini preliminari*). In all cases, however, it is necessary that the accused co-operates, that is, waives his right to an or-dinary proceeding and thus accepts the use of *procedimenti speciali*. In exchange, his sentence may be reduced, the trial may not be publicised and the conviction will not be registered on the defendant's criminal record.[29]

Section 3.4. deals with summary trial proceedings in detail.

In Chapter 4 ("Abbreviated Criminal Procedures for Core Interna-tional Crimes: The Statistical and Capacity Arguments"), *Ilia Utmelidze* shows – based on the case study of Bosnia and Herzegovina – that many contemporary armed conflicts produce too many incidents, crimes and vic-tims for national criminal justice to have the capacity to process them through traditional criminal trials. He draws on his work on war crimes prosecution strategy in Bosnia and Herzegovina, and advisory work for national criminal justice systems in a number of countries. He argues that innovative approaches are required, and that "abbreviated criminal proce-dures can definitely be an integral part of such innovative mechanisms.

---

[28] Kai Ambos and Alexander Heinze, Chapter 3, p. 36.
[29] *Ibid.*, p. 37 (footnotes omitted here).

Such procedures can provide expeditious ways of resolving certain types of core international crimes cases that can accelerate overall accountability processes".[30]

Chapter 5 ("Abbreviated Criminal Procedures for Serious Human Rights Violations Which May Amount to Core International Crimes") by *Gorana Žagovec Kustura* offers the book's most detailed discussion of arguments for and against abbreviated criminal procedures for core international crimes, and a list of preconditions for such procedures to be acceptable. Section 5.3.6. articulates some basic features that a potential abbreviated criminal procedure for core international crimes should have. She summarises these features in these six points:

> 1) be prescribed by law and an integral part of the criminal justice system, administered by regular courts without creating extrajudicial mechanisms and additional institutional layers; 2) increase the ability to resolve the large numbers of cases that create backlogs; 3) apply on a voluntary basis and respect basic fair trial principles that cannot be compromised; 4) be transparent and open; 5) be designed as part of the wider transitional justice process which is sensitive to victims' interests; and 6) provide for the variety of sanctions with the necessary degree of flexibility.[31]

She concludes her chapter by expressing the following views:

> Perhaps the overarching principle is that the procedure must be flexible and tailored to meet the requirements of each particular case for the purpose of resolving backlogs of cases expeditiously, yet not ignore the rights of defendants or the interests of victims or the society at large. It must garner support of the stakeholders within the criminal justice system and other interested parties, and be seen as a reliable tool of the criminal justice system.[32]

Chapter 6 ("The Colombian Peace and Justice Law: An Adequate Abbreviated Procedure for Core International Crimes?") *Maria Paula Saffon* discusses further the Colombian Peace and Justice Law and its early implementation, beyond its treatment in Chapter 5. She explains that the framework of the much-discussed law establishes a special criminal proce-

---

[30]   Ilia Utmelidze, Chapter 4, p. 116–17.
[31]   Gorana Žagovec Kustura, Chapter 5, p. 121.
[32]   *Ibid.*, p. 168.

dure for dealing with core international crimes, known as the justice and peace procedure:

> The main objective of the procedure is to grant a substantial reduction of the criminal sentence (a minimum of five and a maximum of eight years, regardless of the quantity and gravity of the crimes committed) to those demobilised individuals who cease their illegal activities, fully and trustworthily confess the crimes in which they participated, and offer assets for the reparation of their victims.[33]

She discusses whether the mechanism under the law should be seen as a *de facto* amnesty procedure. It is not clear how the Colombian procedures should be classified under the theme of this book.

Chapter 7 ("The Gacaca Courts and Abbreviated Criminal Procedure for Genocide Crimes in Rwanda") by *Phil Clark*, a leading expert on the topic, discusses the unique procedures used in Rwanda to process a very high number of cases in the aftermath of the 1994 genocide in the country. He informs us that the *gacaca* mechanism has prosecuted around 400,000 suspects. It uses a plea-bargaining scheme, so "the vast majority of those convicted by *gacaca* have either had their sentences commuted to community service or, if they were imprisoned, have now been reintegrated into the same communities where they committed crimes during the genocide".[34] He argues that *gacaca* has produced "variable results, especially in terms of justice and truth",[35] although by "mid-2010, *gacaca* had completed the backlog of genocide cases, including the multitude of new suspects that the population has identified since *gacaca* began and the tens of thousands of first category cases transferred from the national courts to *gacaca* since 2008".[36]

Chapter 9 ("How to Deal with Backlog in Trials of International Crimes: Are Abbreviated Criminal Proceedings the Answer?") by *Marieke Wierda* continues the consideration of Colombia in earlier chapters, but adds analyses of Argentina and East Timor. The author draws on her outstanding overview of the transitional justice field as a whole. She acknowledges the problem of backlog of cases in diverse situations such as Argen-

---

[33] Maria Paula Saffon, Chapter 6, p. 178.
[34] Phil Clark, Chapter 7, p. 189.
[35] *Ibid.*
[36] *Ibid.*, p. 202.

tina, Colombia and Bosnia and Herzegovina, where trials have been taking place in the aftermath of mass atrocities. She says that "a range of measures must be taken to deal with the problem of backlog in international criminal proceedings".[37] She discusses measures that fall outside the scope of the notion of abbreviated criminal procedures advanced by this project, including expediting trials (in section 9.2. below), prioritising cases (section 9.3.), and sending cases to other mechanisms (section 9.4.). She recognises that "it is doubtful to what extent one can truly abbreviate criminal proceedings for serious crimes".[38] She proposes five parameters within which such abbreviated procedures must exist:

> First, trials should form part of a comprehensive approach and should not be expected to deal with all, or even the vast majority, of perpetrators. Second, any criminal trials must respect international standards of fairness as provided for in international human rights law. [...] Third, sufficient resources should be devoted to investigations. [...] Fourth, abbreviated criminal proceedings may be possible where the accused agrees to co-operate. [...] Lastly, public trust is vital to any such strategy.[39]

Chapter 8 ("Key Elements of Possible Abbreviated Criminal Procedures for Core International Crimes") by *Gilbert Bitti* suggests that abbreviated criminal procedures could "rejudiciarise" criminality, after overwhelmed criminal justice systems in many countries have by default dejudiciarised crime, effectively allowing crimes to escape the judicial arena. He proceeds to discuss how abbreviated criminal procedures could satisfy victims' rights (see section 8.1. below) and which could be the elements of such a process (section 8.2.). He focuses on the incentives for a suspect to agree to abbreviated procedures, their scope and some procedural aspects. He suggests that abbreviated criminal procedures may be more easily accepted for crimes against property and personal liberty, when the latter is of limited duration and is not accompanied by other crimes against personal integrity.

The final Chapter 10 ("The Role of Abbreviated Criminal Procedures") is written by Judge *Hanne Sophie Greve*, a former Judge of the European Court of Human Rights. Her chapter asks what is the role (pur-

---

[37] Marieke Wierda, Chapter 9, p. 238.
[38] *Ibid.*, p. 224.
[39] *Ibid.*, pp. 238–39.

pose, reason, rationale, motivation) for abbreviated criminal procedures in cases concerning core international crimes. She starts with an analysis of the rule of law principle, the consequences of the commission of core international crimes, and which options societies may have after such crimes have been committed. Reminding us that backlogs of criminal cases are in no way limited to situations after armed conflict, she observes that it is "highly unfortunate when many core international crime case files have already been opened within a criminal justice system that is unable to process the cases within a reasonable time. It is equally unfortunate when many core international crimes have been committed but hardly any case files opened".[40]

She recognises that the "idea of utilising abbreviated criminal procedures for core international crimes is new", and observes that "[m]ost national criminal justice systems will have room for the possibility of elaborating and enacting abbreviated criminal procedures – entirely within the due process of law requirements – significantly more time- and cost-efficient than regular full criminal procedures".[41] Importantly, she makes the following statement:

> The use of abbreviated criminal procedures should reflect the different levels of gravity of the core international crimes. For example, property offences and minor unlawful detention prior to large-scale transfers of whole population groups are offences committed on an immense scale in many armed conflicts. These offences do not as such violate the interests of life or personal integrity and may thus suitably be addressed in abbreviated criminal procedures.[42]

1.7. A Challenge of Innovation and Perspective

Both Judge Greve and Gilbert Bitti refer in their chapters to the fact that some core international crimes occur in larger numbers than others, and also seem to be less serious. They mention the examples "property offences and minor unlawful detention".[43] There need not be a statutory or agreed hierarchy of core international crimes to see merit in this common-sense

---

[40] Grieve, pp. 263, see *supra* note 12.
[41] *Ibid.*, pp. 263–64.
[42] *Ibid.*, p. 264.
[43] *Ibid.*

distinction. It is beyond dispute that violations against property and temporary unlawful detention are less serious than murder, rape and torture. This is where a consideration of abbreviated criminal procedures should start. An example would be the thousands of soldiers and policemen who were involved in detaining persons for a short time in large parts of Bosnia and Herzegovina in 1992–1993, before they were internally displaced, deported or let go. As Ilia Utmelidze shows in Chapter 4, it would simply not be possible to prosecute everyone suspected of this violation prior to suspects and witnesses dying. Abbreviated criminal procedures may be a relevant tool when such situations arise in the future.

But more analysis should be undertaken before embarking on legislative reform. This topic lends itself well for legal research. Articles and a monograph could be invaluable for legislators who may wish to develop reform proposals. This book seeks to help this discussion along. It is not a pleasant invitation to extend, as the immediate reaction of many actors in international criminal justice or transitional justice will be to ask: but this would violate human rights, no? What exactly would these procedures be? If this were possible, why has anyone not thought about that already? And do you really think the abbreviated procedures in Colombia and Rwanda have worked well? The book is nevertheless in keeping with CILRAP's commitment to also raise real, practice-orientated issues for more in-depth academic discussion, even when they are among the more problematic aspects of transitional criminal justice. This is why we have pioneered issues such as old evidence,[44] criteria for prioritisation of cases,[45] and thematic prosecution.[46]

Even some participants at the FICHL-conference in Sarajevo 2009 had not registered the concept paper's explanation that only abbreviated procedures that are in accord with applicable human rights standards fall within the scope of this project. It means that such procedures need to be consensual as far as the suspects are concerned. And there needs to be an adequate incentive for suspects to opt out of a full trial.

---

[44] See Morten Bergsmo and CHEAH Wui Ling (eds.), *Old Evidence and Core International Crimes*, Torkel Opsahl Academic EPublisher, Beijing, 2012, 313 pp. (http://www.legal-tools.org/doc/f130e1/).

[45] See Bergsmo, 2012, *supra* note 8.

[46] See Morten Bergsmo (ed.), *Thematic Prosecution of International Sex Crimes*, Torkel Opsahl Academic EPublisher, Beijing, 2012, 452 pp. (http://www.legal-tools.org/doc/397b61/).

As other discourse actors take this forward, I hope they will turn their attention to the different technical solutions that have been devised in national criminal procedure, for example in Italian law. There is really no need to try to reinvent the wheel in criminal justice for core international crimes, which is a marginal field compared with the main streams of national criminal law and justice. It is national law we need to first turn to for inspiration and guidance, not the limited experimentation with abbreviated procedures in international criminal justice. We should not be deluded into thinking that international criminal justice has attracted more talented lawyers or thinkers than national criminal justice. Quite the opposite, the practice of international criminal law is a young discipline in comparison, and it needs to be closely tuned to developments and innovations in mainstream criminal procedure and administration. This means that proper research on abbreviated criminal procedures requires the deployment of wider language skills than English and French, and a basic humility towards what has been developed in national jurisdictions that we may not normally refer to in our legal writing on core international crimes. Serious research will also involve consultation with leading experts on the national codes of procedure in question.

There is a public interest in turning every stone to ensure that the criminal justice response to core international crimes – in both international and national jurisdictions – be as cost-effective and credible as possible. If national war crimes justice becomes as expensive as international criminal justice has been since 1995, it will not be sustainable. Prosecuting every suspected war criminal in Bosnia and Herzegovina in the manner of the ex-Yugoslavia Tribunal is neither affordable nor practicable, whether before the Tribunal or the State Court of Bosnia and Herzegovina. Sending opened case files out of a criminal justice system is an option fraught with unwanted consequences. Waiting to let case files die when the suspects and witnesses do is a silent impunity practice. It also comes at a cost for the society concerned.

Governments need to be aware of these constraints when they open a large number of case files on suspected core international crimes. But at the same time, deliberately avoiding opening case files when criminal justice is in possession of strong evidence of such crimes is the hallmark of impunity. Abbreviated criminal procedures are therefore a tool that should be explored for less serious core international crimes. This is necessary in some situations if criminal law shall continue to play a role in

"the impossible balancing act required in the post-genocide society – namely, the need for acknowledgement of crimes and for justice alongside the need to reintegrate perpetrators into their towns and villages to help rebuild the social and economic foundations of the country".[47] At the same time, this reminds us of the clear limits of criminal justice for core international crimes.

---

[47] See Clark, p. 207, *supra* note 34.

2

The Two Illusions of All-Embracing Criminal Justice and Exclusively Extrajudicial Responses to Mass Atrocity

Mark A. Drumbl[*]

This chapter surveys, broadly and briefly, the challenges and justifications for abbreviated (expedited) criminal proceedings as part of the transitional *jus post bellum*. My goal is to situate a need for abbreviated criminal procedures as staking out a middle ground between two illusions. The two illusions are all-embracing criminal justice, on the one hand, and exclusively extrajudicial responses, on the other. Although I support abbreviated proceedings as a tool in the toolbox of transitional justice, I also urge caution, circumspection and deliberation in their design and implementation. Participants and observers should try to elaborate a *raison d'être* for abbreviated criminal proceedings, instead of relying on assumptions and conclusory findings. Obversely, I also hope that those who are doubtful about abbreviated criminal proceedings will avoid grounding their sentiments in different assumptions and conclusory findings.

I proceed through four steps: first, to describe the illusions I identify; second, to underscore why we need to consider abbreviated criminal proceedings; third, to explain challenges that befall any such proceedings; and fourth, to conclude on an optimistic note, although one that underscores that much work remains to be done.

---

[*] **Mark A. Drumbl** is the Class of 1975 Alumni Chair Professor at Washington and Lee University, School of Law, where he also serves as Director of the Transnational Law Institute. He has held visiting appointments on several law faculties, including Oxford University, Université de Paris II (Panthéon–Assas), University of Ottawa, Free University of Amsterdam, University of Melbourne, Monash University and Trinity College Dublin. His research and teaching interests include public international law, international criminal law and transitional justice. His book, *Atrocity, Punishment, and International Law* (Cambridge University Press, 2007) has been widely reviewed and has won awards from the International Association of Criminal Law (US national section) and the American Society of International Law. In 2012, he published *Reimagining Child Soldiers in International Law and Policy* (Oxford University Press).

2.1. Illusions

Let me begin with the illusions. All-embracing criminal justice is an illusion because the atrocity trial as it has been judicialised internationally is unaffordable, extremely selective, externalised from afflicted communities, and is only capable of skimming the surface of the pursuit of justice. Accordingly, it is illusory to suggest it can constitute an all-embracing approach to justice. At best, it offers only a partial print thereof. The dominant model of international criminal law emphasises a handful of spectacular trials, generally of high-level or notorious offenders – although these often are spectacular only in their tedium. In any event, they all are spectacularly expensive. To suggest that the way the International Criminal Tribunal for the former Yugoslavia ('ICTY') and the International Criminal Court ('ICC') do business can be replicated nationally is an absurdity. Moreover, I argue that, even when effectively implemented, international criminal trials are incapable of attaining their self-avowed goals, which include retribution, deterrence, rehabilitation, reconciliation and truth-telling.[1]

Why are exclusively extrajudicial responses to mass atrocity an illusion? This is so for three reasons. First, international duties to prosecute have, for better or for worse, contoured what kinds of policy responses are permissible in cases of atrocity. Second, atrocity trials have emerged in the public imagination as the reflexive image of justice. Buoyed by doctrines such as complementarity or primacy, the atrocity trial with all its formal trappings constitutes the first-best form of justice. It has acquired considerable iconic value in the struggle against impunity. And, third, now that their value is marketised, international criminal lawyers simply will not permit post-conflict transitions to move forward without some element of liberal judicial responses. There can no longer be a transition from massive human rights abuses without courtrooms and jailhouses. There is no excluding the lawyers anymore.

In light of the practical and theoretical limitations to international criminal law, on the one hand, and the operational inevitability of international criminal law, on the other, the only way forward seems to be to diversify the number, type and range of available accountability modalities. I have elsewhere written about why justice mechanisms, such as truth commissions, neo-traditional dispute resolution, civil sanctions and col-

---

[1] See generally Mark A. Drumbl, *Atrocity, Punishment, and International Law*, Cambridge University Press, Cambridge, 2007.

lective forms of responsibility, should form part of the constellation of transitional justice policymaking. In this chapter, I hope to offer some brief comments, responses and reactions to abbreviated criminal procedures as specific transitional justice mechanisms. My purpose is to paint broad brushstrokes that others will be able to refine over time.

2.2. An Integral Part of the Transitional Justice Toolbox

Why do I believe abbreviated criminal proceedings need to be part of the transitional justice toolbox?

Breadth. The international atrocity trial model emphasises depth – a small number of perpetrators are brought to account, in very detailed fashion, for mass crimes. The atrocity trial adopts the individual as its subject and assumes (if the individual is an adult) that individual participation in atrocity is a product of the exercise of free will and disposition. This approach belies the reality that atrocity also is a deeply collective and situational endeavour. Atrocities are group crimes that implicate huge numbers of perpetrators and victims, not to mention acquiescent and passive bystanders. I believe there is value in expanding the lens of implication, even if doing so hinges on proceeding in a more cursory fashion in each individual case. Having more people brought to account better reflects the systematic nature of atrocity. We cannot be purists in search for perfect justice. Doing so would lead to wildly imperfect outcomes.

Backlogs. Even if we did not want to expand the range of defendants much international criminal law's focus on depth still creates burdensome backlogs. Indications are that on the subject of core international crimes there are at the time of writing about 10,000 pending cases in Bosnia alone. What is more, the backlogs are not time insensitive. As time passes, memories dim, witnesses or accused pass away, or fade into obscurity. Due process concerns arise in cases of excessive pre-trial waiting periods. In short, time is of the essence. Abbreviated criminal proceedings recognise this. In this regard, they synergise with the due process right of speedily being brought to account. Abbreviated criminal proceedings could promote breadth of justice while still addressing backlogs and delays.

Incorporating the local. Abbreviated criminal proceedings can involve and embellish local capacity, personnel and infrastructure. Even in our era of transnationalism, for most people in most places local understandings of justice resonate the deepest and, in short, remain the most ac-

cessible. Abbreviated proceedings can cultivate the local, especially if they are not forced to conform to an internationalist agenda. Accordingly, it would be sensible for internationalists to approach bottom-up abbreviated ventures with a light touch and accord them qualified deference.

Flexibility. Abbreviated criminal proceedings need not be holistic. They can be tailored, for example to certain kinds of offenders (that is, youth, militia members or employees of a specific ministry), or certain types of crimes (that is, property crimes, commercial crimes). Beginning with specific categories of offenders or crime might be a wise way to incrementally build up some experience and faith in the system. In turn, good works and the perception of good works could ward off scepticism. Proceeding gradually in an *étapiste* fashion contrasts with splashy and cure-all approaches that seek to develop overarching – and perhaps inevitably controversial – criteria for gravity and case selection.

Some justice is better than none. I caution against the path dependency of becoming cycloptic in our focus on international criminal process. I worry that our seeming obsession with full due process may intentionally or inadvertently lead to inaction on the transitional justice front, or may even become a proxy for stasis. It is not clear to me that formal due process is necessarily superior or inferior to other modalities of securing justice. It may be required for law, but only to the extent that we imagine its singular relevance. Law, as the American jurist Benjamin Cardozo noted, is a process of creation, not discovery. We have positivistically established the centrality of due process to the legitimacy of transitional justice. Although due process does assist in promoting the legitimacy of transitional justice interventions, too much due process also can undermine the legitimacy of those very same interventions.

Storytelling. Implicating followers along with leaders relates a much broader narrative about who did what in times of atrocity. Massive numbers of followers, and an even greater number of benefiting bystanders, are a condition precedent to mass violence. In placing a greater number of these individuals within the narrative of accountability, abbreviated criminal proceedings may weave a more reflective historical record than a handful of spectacular trials. They may permit an authentication of the painful fact that participation in extraordinary international crimes is a product of both situation and disposition. Atrocity would not be possible without many people doing many different things in the name of the group.

2.3. Concerns, Cautions and Challenges

Let us turn to concerns, cautions and challenges to abbreviated criminal proceedings as a tool in the toolkit of transitional justice.

Disappointment. The biggest danger I see for abbreviated criminal procedures takes the form of unduly high expectations. My impression is that proponents of abbreviated criminal procedures wish the best of both worlds. They seek the expediency that international criminal trials lack, but they also crave the authenticity and authority that international criminal trials obtain. They seek cost effectiveness, but then request comprehensive judgments. They wish fairness without much due process. In short, they want it all. For example, Gorana Žagovec Kustura concludes:

> [T]he system should effectively process large backlogs of cases without violating precepts of due process. It must indeed provide more cost-effective and faster justice than the normal procedure while also allowing for the interests of victims to be respected and the historical record to be preserved by detailed, reasoned judicial decisions.[2]

In my opinion, this is simply not possible. It is a pipe dream to have it all. Something has to give way. Accordingly, I think the better question is whether rigid adherence to Article 14 of the International Covenant on Civil and Political Rights is necessarily desirable, or whether some contextualisation or margin of appreciation for national deviation therefrom should be considered. That would open up the debate in an honest and forthright fashion. As I mentioned earlier, there is no actual proof that rigid adherence to due process necessarily furthers transitional justice interests. We assume, with good reason, that this is the case. For us lawyers, it seems so intuitive. But perhaps those intuitions should be tested or, at least, their orthodoxy subject to some scrutiny.

Constitutionalisation of rights. Practically speaking, once a person becomes a criminal defendant, regardless of whether the proceeding is abridged or lengthy, he or she ordinarily becomes entitled to the highest level of due process protections available under national human rights law. Moreover, in some jurisdictions considerations of constitutionalisation involve supranational law: in these instances, defendants may avail them-

---

2   Gorana Žagovec Kustura, "Abbreviated Criminal Procedures for Serious Human Rights Violations which May Amount to Core International Crimes", see Chapter 5 of this volume.

selves of these supranational rights – for example, the European Convention on Human Rights. Accordingly, one can expect that defendants will challenge the application of abbreviated criminal procedures as against them. The result might be extensive litigation, which would decelerate the process and perpetrate the backlogs.

Definition by exclusion. In terms of defining abbreviated criminal proceedings, I base myself on Žagovec Kustura's excellent chapter and Morten Bergsmo's comments in the concept note of and at the CILRAP conference on the topic in Sarajevo on 9 October 2009.[3] Notwithstanding their discussion of these proceedings, I see a persistent need to develop a clearer definition of the concept. Much of the existing understanding is couched in the negative. For example, Žagovec Kustura notes that an abbreviated criminal proceeding is not a plea bargain, nor truth commission, nor a neo-traditional form of dispute resolution such as Rwanda's *gacaca*. But, in an affirmative sense, what exactly is it? What does it look like? How would one describe it?

Moving beyond expedience and pragmatics. Assuredly, there are important utilitarian reasons for considering abbreviated criminal proceedings – that is, dealing with backlogs in a cost-effective fashion. That said, the proposal will gain more traction if, in addition to these utilitarian justifications, proponents can also point to a normative or deontological basis that supports processing perpetrators through abbreviated criminal proceedings. This is something that proponents of truth commissions, who often come at transitional justice debates from the perspective of social psychology, have done well. They have laid out normative reasons why the approach works, what is distinctive about the approach, the kind of justice it can achieve and the place of that kind of justice in post-conflict reconstruction. To a lesser degree, proponents of traditional forms of dispute resolution, cleansing ceremonies and ritualistic ceremonies – often coming from anthropology, area studies and ethnography – have also propounded a coherent normative vision for why these mechanisms should form part of post-conflict justice. I have yet to hear this from proponents of abbreviated criminal proceedings. I think such proponents need to either justify why they want to keep things within the criminal justice apparatus or more radically move beyond this preference for the criminal law. Might there be a penological or criminolog-

---

[3]   For the concept note and programme, see https://www.fichl.org/activities/abbreviated-criminal-procedures-for-core-international-crimes/.

ical rationale for abbreviated criminal procedures? If so, what is it? A burden of proof arises. There is considerable cause to debate the effectiveness of the criminal law generally as a post-conflict accountability mechanism. I view the structural frailties particularly acute at the level of international criminal law, but they also arise in the context of domestic initiatives as well.

Drawing from ordinary common crimes. I remain sceptical that drawing from examples in national criminal law for very routine ordinary common crimes is a useful or relevant analogue. The nature of serious international crimes is so different. What I have seen so far about abbreviated criminal procedures relies on assumptions of individual action and autonomy that fail to recognise the group nature of much of international criminality, particularly in the case of lower-level cadres. Hence, my return to the earlier point about more radical reform that pivots toward institutions that actually recognise the collective nature of collective violence.

Linkages. In a situation where justice is multi-tiered, would participating in an abbreviated criminal proceeding immunise a person from appearing before a truth commission or civil proceeding? Would immunity for other forms of justice attach? If so, then a significant justice cost to the reduced cost of participating in an abbreviated proceeding would arise. I have considerable faith in the relevance of alternate justice mechanisms such as truth commissions, traditional ceremonial rites, collective responsibility, civil sanctions and lustration as post-conflict transitional mechanisms. Even if conducted outside of such institutions, failing to synergistically link abbreviated criminal proceedings to these kinds of polycentric justice initiatives would, I believe, amount to a net loss.

2.4. Conclusion

In the end, the challenges are far from insurmountable. In fact, they can be harnessed and converted into bold justifications for the idea of abbreviated criminal procedures. The dominant justice narrative – that of the internationalised atrocity trial – is incapable of replication fiscally by any state nationally, impractical and not too effective. We need to look beyond. Abbreviated criminal procedures have a place in the transitional justice toolkit. They are no panacea. But no justice mechanism can serve as a cure-all. Rather, the most effective instantiation of justice probably lies in a polycentric amalgam of many different ap-

proaches, situated non-competitively, and operating synergistically. That requires the proponents of each individual accountability mechanism to cede their expertise and the purported curative effects of that expertise. This includes proponents of abbreviated criminal proceedings.

3

Abbreviated Procedures in Comparative Criminal Procedure: A Structural Approach with a View to International Criminal Procedure

Kai Ambos and Alexander Heinze[*]

3.1. Introduction

A famous maxim in Germany states: "The machinery of law works slowly but steadily".[1] While at the end of the nineteenth century a well-equipped judiciary, at least in Germany, did not have any problems with the handling of the cases entering the system,[2] nowadays it is generally acknowledged that justice works slowly as there are "simply too many offences, too many offenders, and too few resources to deal with them all",[3] not only in Germany but in almost every country. As a consequence, the population increasingly loses confidence in the criminal justice system and its operators. Critical comments by the media do the rest[4] and, at least in Germany, every report on another case of violent youths is followed by a discussion about

---

[*] Dr. Dr. h.c. **Kai Ambos** is Professor of Criminal Law, Criminal Procedure, Comparative Law, and International Criminal Law at the Georg-August Universität Göttingen, Germany, and Judge at the District Court (Landgericht) Göttingen. Dr. **Alexander Heinze**, LL.M. (TCD) is Assistant Professor at the Department for Foreign and International Criminal Law at the Georg-August Universität Göttingen. The authors thank Szymon Świderski and Dr. Moritz Eckhardt for the assistance in the preparation of this chapter. We also thank Matt Halling for thorough language editing including useful comments on substance. The original contribution was submitted in 2010 and selectively updated in 2016.

[1] *"Die Mühlen der Justiz mahlen langsam, doch stetig"*.

[2] Gerhard Fezer, "Inquisitionsprozess ohne Ende? Zur Struktur des *neuen* Verständigungsgesetzes", in *Neue Zeitschrift für Strafrecht*, 2010, vol. 30, no. 4, p. 178.

[3] Abraham S. Goldstein, "Converging Criminal Justice Systems: Guilty Pleas and the Public Interest", in *Israel Law Review*, 1997, vol. 31, nos. 1/3, p. 169.

[4] See, for example, "Mühlen der Justiz sollen schneller mahlen", in *Badische Zeitung*, 16 April 2010.

---

the overloaded criminal justice system and the call for (more) expedited trials.[5]

One response is the introduction of measures and methods to lower trial costs and expedite criminal trials.[6] One may distinguish between measures that expedite and simplify criminal proceedings and measures that avoid charges or criminal proceedings in the first place. In order to better understand the rationale of these measures, a short and general characterisation of the diverse approaches to criminal procedure appears reasonable.

3.2. Criminal Procedure Systems Compared

When comparing different systems of criminal procedure, the most common and popular characterisation is still the one of "adversarial" versus "inquisitorial" systems. Yet these terms describe only ideal type models that in their pure form hardly exist in any legal system.[7] Generally labelling

---

[5]   The German news magazine *Stern TV* broadcast a report on youth crime ("Versagt die Justiz?", 26 May 2010, 22:15). In an interview, the late Judge Kirsten Heisig said (translated by the authors):

>   The "Neuköllner Modell" sets priorities to speed and consistency instead of strictness. A detailed co-operation between police, prosecution and youth welfare office will avoid taking more than half a year after the commission of a crime to start the main proceeding, which is far too long, and will guarantee that the time period does not exceed three to six weeks.

[6]   As suggested by Jörg-Martin Jehle, "The Function of Public Prosecution within the Criminal Justice System", in Jörg-Martin Jehle and Marianne Wade, *Coping with Overloaded Criminal Justice Systems: The Rise of Prosecutorial Power Across Europe*, Springer, Berlin, 2006, p. 6.

[7]   Kai Ambos, *Treatise on International Criminal Law*, vol. 3, *International Criminal Procedure*, Oxford University Press, Oxford, 2016, pp. 1, 4–6; Alexander Heinze, *International Criminal Procedure and Disclosure*, Duncker & Humblot, Berlin, 2014, pp. 117–32; Albin Eser, "Changing Structures: From the ICTY to the ICC", in Bruce Ackerman, Kai Ambos and Hrvoje Sikirić (eds.), *Visions of Justice – Liber Amicorum Mirjan Damaška*, Duncker & Humblot, Berlin, 2016, pp. 213–14; John D. Jackson, "Re-visiting 'Evidentiary Barriers to Conviction and Models of Criminal Procedure' after Forty Years", in Bruce Ackerman, Kai Ambos and Hrvoje Sikirić (eds.), *Visions of Justice – Liber Amicorum Mirjan Damaška*, Duncker & Humblot, Berlin, 2016, pp. 236, 241 ("When used for clearly ideological purposes, [the terms adversarial/accusatorial and inquisitorial] become mere caricatures of the differences between Anglo-American and continental proceedings".); Paul Roberts and Adrian Zuckerman, *Criminal Evidence*, Oxford University Press, Oxford, 2004, p. 43. See also Jacqueline Hodgson, "Conceptions of the Trial in Inquisitorial and Adversarial Procedure", in Antony Duff, Lindsay Farmer and Sandra Marshall (eds.), *The Trial on Trial*, vol. 2, *Judgment and Calling to Account*, Hart, Oxford, 2006, pp. 229 ff.;

---

a procedure as "inquisitorial" or "adversarial" is inevitably imprecise and ignores the differences between systems within the same legal tradition.[8] In fact, the terms can have both a traditional and a historical meaning and may describe a theoretical model, a procedural type, and an ideal of procedure.[9] Still, one may identify core elements or features of systems with an inquisitorial or adversarial tendency. Their main difference lies in the division and distribution of power between their protagonists, that is prosecutor, defence and judge, with a view to the collection and presentation of evidence. *Adversarial proceedings* are controlled by the prosecutor and defence as adverse parties.[10] They carry out a contest with regard to their respective cases.[11] They are responsible for gathering, selecting and presenting the evi-

---

Mirjan R. Damaška, *The Faces of Justice and State Authority: A Comparative Approach to the Legal Process*, Yale University Press, New Haven, 1986, pp. 3–4.

[8] See Kai Ambos, "International Criminal Procedure: 'Adversarial', 'Inquisitorial' or Mixed?", in *International Criminal Law Review*, 2003, vol. 3, no. 1, p. 4; Roberts and Zuckerman, 2004, pp. 43–44, see *supra* note 7; Teresa Armenta-Deu, "Beyond Accusatorial or Inquisitorial Systems: A Matter of Deliberation and Balance", in Bruce Ackerman, Kai Ambos and Hrvoje Sikirić (eds.), *Visions of Justice – Liber Amicorum Mirjan Damaška*, Duncker & Humblot, Berlin, 2016, p. 57; Jackson, 2016, p. 253, see *supra* note 7; Mitchel de S.-O.-l'E. Lasser, "On the Comparative Autonomy of Forms and Ideas", in Bruce Ackerman, Kai Ambos and Hrvoje Sikirić (eds.), *Visions of Justice – Liber Amicorum Mirjan Damaška*, Duncker & Humblot, Berlin, 2016, pp. 301, 303. Ironically, when scholars and lawyers first used the accusatorial–inquisitorial dichotomy, they were referring to "a distinction within, rather than between, legal systems"; see Máximo Langer, "In the Beginning was Fortescue: On the Intellectual Origins of the Adversarial and Inquisitorial Systems and Common and Civil Law in Comparative Criminal Procedure", in Bruce Ackerman, Kai Ambos and Hrvoje Sikirić (eds.), *Visions of Justice – Liber Amicorum Mirjan Damaška*, Duncker & Humblot, Berlin, 2016, pp. 273, 280.

[9] Ambos, 2016, pp. 4–5, see *supra* note 7; Heinze, 2014, p. 118, see *supra* note 7.

[10] Hodgson, 2006, p. 224, see *supra* note 7; Roberts and Zuckerman, 2004, p. 48, see *supra* note 7; Ambos, 2003, p. 4, see *supra* note 8; Alphons Orie, "Accusatorial v. Inquisitorial Approach in International Criminal Proceedings Prior to the Establishment of the ICC and in the Proceedings before the ICC", in Antonio Cassese, Paola Gaeta and John R.W.D. Jones (eds.), *The Rome Statute of the International Criminal Court: A Commentary*, vol. II, Oxford University Press, New York, 2002, p. 1445. This is what Damaška, 1986, pp. 23 ff., calls the "coordinate ideal", see *supra* note 7. See also Ennio Amodio, "Rethinking Evidence under Damaška's Teaching", in Bruce Ackerman, Kai Ambos and Hrvoje Sikirić (eds.), *Visions of Justice – Liber Amicorum Mirjan Damaška*, Duncker & Humblot, Berlin, 2016, pp. 51, 53.

[11] Damaška, 1986, p. 3, see *supra* note 7; John Jackson, "Finding the Best Epistemic Fit for International Criminal Tribunals: Beyond the Adversarial-Inquisitorial Dichotomy", in *Journal of International Criminal Justice*, 2009, vol. 7, no. 1, p. 19.

---

dence for trial.[12] In contrast, the judge has a rather passive role[13] as an impartial adjudicator.[14] He or she must ensure the observance of the procedural rules but is not engaged in the fact-finding and ascertaining processes.[15] The common law model is most frequently associated with a jury trial in which the judge decides on questions of law and the jury on questions of fact. The involvement of laypersons, however, is not a constitutive element of an adversarial procedure and may be found in inquisitorial systems as well.[16]

Inquisitorial proceedings may best be described as judge-led.[17] The judge controls the proceedings, at least in the trial phase, and is solely responsible for the collection of the evidence necessary to find the truth.[18] The prosecutor has its share in this truth-finding process by investigating the case and presenting the charges in the first place. His responsibility is reduced if – like in the French inquisitorial system – the pre-trial inquiry is carried out by an investigating judge (*juge d'instruction*). It must not be

---

[12] Bartram S. Brown, "The International Criminal Tribunal for the Former Yugoslavia", in M. Cherif Bassiouni (ed.), *International Criminal Law*, vol. III, *International Enforcement*, 3rd ed., Martinus Nijhoff Publishers, Leiden, 2008, p. 92; Hodgson, 2006, p. 223, see *supra* note 7.

[13] Ambos, 2016, p. 6, see *supra* note 7; Heinze, 2014, p. 123, see *supra* note 7; Hodgson, 2006, p. 231, see *supra* note 7; Roberts and Zuckerman, 2004, p. 48, see *supra* note 7; Albin Eser, "Die Vorzugswürdigkeit des adversatorischen Prozesssystems in der internationalen Strafjustiz? Reflektionen eines Richters", in H. Müller-Dietz, Egon Müller, Karl-Ludwig Kunz, Henning Guido Britz, Carsten Mommsen and Heinz Koriath (eds.), *Festschrift für Heike Jung zum 65*, Nomos Verlag, Baden-Baden, 2007, p. 176; Claus Kress, "The Procedural Law of the International Criminal Court in Outline: Anatomy of a Unique Compromise", in *Journal of International Criminal Justice*, 2003, vol. 1, no. 3, p. 604.

[14] Eser, 2007, p. 176, see *supra* note 13; Orie, 2002, p. 1443, see *supra* note 10; Armenta-Deu, 2016, p. 63, see *supra* note 8.

[15] Hodgson, 2006, pp. 223–24, see *supra* note 7; Roberts and Zuckerman, 2004, p. 48, see *supra* note 7; Eser, 2007, pp. 176–77, see *supra* note 13; Christoph J.M. Safferling, *Towards an International Criminal Procedure*, Oxford University Press, New York, 2001, pp. 217–18.

[16] For more detail, see Roberts and Zuckerman, 2004, pp. 59 ff., *supra* note 7.

[17] Ambos, 2003, p. 4, see *supra* note 8; Safferling, 2001, p. 217, see *supra* note 15. According to the terms of Damaška, 1986, pp. 18 ff., the civil law is therefore based on a "hierarchical model", see *supra* note 7; Eser, 2016, p. 215, *supra* note 7.

[18] Ambos, 2016, p. 5, see *supra* note 7; Heinze, 2014, see *supra* note 7, p. 122; Safferling, 2001, p. 217, see *supra* note 15; Brown, 2008, p. 92, see *supra* note 12; Orie, 2002, p. 1444, see *supra* note 10; Daryl A. Mundis, "From 'Common Law' Towards 'Civil Law': The Evolution of the ICTY Rules of Procedure and Evidence", in *Leiden Journal of International Law*, 2001, vol. 14, no. 2, p. 369; Kress, 2003, p. 604, see *supra* note 13.

---

overlooked, however, that even in France only a small number of cases are dealt with by the *juge d'instruction*. Most cases are investigated by the police and the prosecutor using various summary procedures.[19] In addition, recent reforms have further reduced the role of the investigating judge.[20] In the trial phase, the prosecutor yields control to the judge and remains rather passive. The role of the defence is, in any case, limited to the earliest intervention possible at the investigation phase and subsequently to request the production of certain evidence.[21]

The differences in the *organisation* of the proceedings are due to different conceptions regarding the purpose of the trial.[22] While the inquisitorial model is ideally characterised by the search for the objective or material truth to be discovered by the judge-led procedure,[23] the adversarial model rests on a more procedural understanding of truth[24] which results from the adversarial contest of the parties.[25] Be that as it may, the usefulness of the traditional distinction has been increasingly questioned, especially in international criminal procedure. While the distinction may serve as a useful tool of classification and simplification of complex procedural questions,[26] it must not be overstated. Although most international rules can be traced back to a common or civil law origin, they are rendered *sui generis* and unique in their application.[27] It is therefore not important whether a rule is

---

[19] Kai Ambos and Dennis Miller, "Structure and Function of the Confirmation Procedure before the ICC from a Comparative Perspective", in *International Criminal Law Review*, 2007, vol. 7, no. 2, p. 353, with further references.

[20] See Elisabeth Schneider, "Vers la mort annoncée du juge d'instruction en France", in *Eucrim: The European Criminal Law Associations' Forum*, 2009, nos. 1–2, pp. 50–51; Heinze, 2014, p. 159, with further references, see *supra* note 7.

[21] Orie, 2002, p. 1445, see *supra* note 10.

[22] See also Hodgson, 2006, p. 226, *supra* note 7.

[23] Hodgson, 2006, p. 225, see *supra* note 7. See also Safferling, 2001, pp. 217, 221, *supra* note 15; Orie, 2002, p. 1444, *supra* note 10.

[24] Ambos, 2003, p. 4, see *supra* note 8.

[25] Roberts and Zuckerman, 2004, p. 53, see *supra* note 7; Orie, 2002, p. 1443, see *supra* note 10.

[26] Roberts and Zuckerman, 2004, p. 43–44, see *supra* note 7, stressing the usefulness of splitting up a proceeding for classification purposes.

[27] Cf. also Helen McDermott, *Fairness in International Criminal Trials*, Oxford University Press, Oxford, 2016, p. 1; Hanna Kuczyńska, *The Accusation Model before the International Criminal Court: Study of Convergence of Criminal Justice Systems*, Springer, Heidelberg, 2015, pp. 1, 6; Eser, 2016, p. 223, see *supra* note 7; Richard Vogler, *A World*

either adversarial or inquisitorial, but whether it assists the tribunals in accomplishing their tasks and contributes to the guarantee of a fair trial.[28]

3.3. Measures to Abbreviate and Expedite Proceedings

In fact, it is not so much the difference between an adversarial and inquisitorial process that leads to different methods of dealing with the case overload but rather the underlying principles of the respective procedural systems: that is, the search for the objective or material truth, the principle of full judicial clarification of the facts,[29] the principle of legality (mandatory prosecution, *legalité de poursuites*) and the principle of opportunity (prosecutorial discretion, *opportunité des poursuites*). Thus, some legal systems rest on the idea of "legality" or "compulsory/mandatory prosecution", whereby the relevant official agencies are expected to act upon a formal standard when dealing with all breaches of criminal law which come to their knowledge.[30] In some countries, like Italy, the principle of legality (*principio di legalità*) is primarily related to the substantive (material) criminal law, thus prohibiting the punishment of a crime that was not explicitly punishable at the time it was committed.[31]

View of Criminal Justice, Ashgate, Aldershot, 2006, p. 278; Ambos and Miller, 2007, p. 349, see *supra* note 19. Crit. Heinze, 2014, pp. 27–32, see *supra* note 7.

[28] Jackson, 2009, pp. 20 ff., see *supra* note 11; Kai Ambos, "The Structure of International Procedure: 'Adversarial', 'Inquisitorial' or Mixed", in Michael Bohlander (ed.), *International Criminal Justice: A Critical Analysis of Institutions and Procedures*, Cameron May, London, 2007, p. 500; Rodney Dixon, "Developing International Rules of Evidence for the Yugoslav and Rwanda Tribunals", in *Transitional Law and Contemporary Problems*, 1997, vol. 7, p. 98.

[29] See the German Code of Criminal Procedure, StPO § 244(2): "In order to establish the truth, the court shall, *proprio motu*, extend the taking of evidence to all facts and means of proof relevant to the decision" (translated by Brian Duffett and Monika Ebinger, authorised by the German Federal Ministry of Justice).

[30] See generally Kuczyńska, 2015, pp. 94–106, see *supra* note 27; Christopher Harding and Gavin Dingwall, *Diversion in the Criminal Process*, Sweet and Maxwell, London, 1998, p. 1. About the application of the principles of mandatory prosecution and discretion on the level of International Criminal Justice, see Kai Ambos, "The International Criminal Justice System and Prosecutorial Selection Policy", in Bruce Ackerman, Kai Ambos and Hrvoje Sikirić (eds.), *Visions of Justice – Liber Amicorum Mirjan Damaška*, Duncker & Humblot, Berlin, 2016, p. 30; Kuczyńska, *ibid.*, pp. 106–11.

[31] Ferrando Mantovani, *Diritto Penale, Parte Generale*, 6th ed., CEDAM, Padova, 2009, p. 3; however, there are procedural forms of the principle of legality in Italy, namely "the principle of the legitimate judge" and the "principle of legality". On the distinction between legality in substantive and procedural law, see also Michele Caianiello, "Disclosure

Be that as it may, the (procedural) principle of legality is either subject to important exceptions or qualified by prosecutorial discretion.[32] Thus,
most countries operate in practice on both legality and opportunity, tending
either, in normative terms, more to the former (France,[33] Germany,[34] Italy,[35]
Spain,[36] Poland[37]) or to the latter (Belgium,[38] England,[39] Japan,[40] the Neth-

---

before the ICC: The Emergence of a New Form of Policies Implementation in International Criminal Justice?", in *International Criminal Law Review*, 2010, vol. 10, no. 1, p.
98.

[32] Harding and Dingwall, 1998, p. 1, see *supra* note 30.

[33] The legality principle is included in the Constitution (Articles 34 and 37), although criminal proceedings are mainly governed by the opportunity principle (Article 40, Code de
Procedure Penale). See further Éric Mathias, *Les procureurs du droit: de l'impartialité du
ministère public en France et en Allemagne*, CNRS Éditions, Paris, 1999; Sara Sun Baele,
"Prosecutorial Discretion in Three Systems: Balancing Conflicting Goals and Providing
Mechanisms for Control", in Michele Caianiello and Jacqueline S. Hodgson (eds.), *Discretionary Criminal Justice in a Comparative Context*, Carolina Academic Press, Durham,
2015, pp. 27, 42 ("France does not recognise the principle of mandatory prosecution").

[34] Here the principle of legality has even a constitutional status (see Begründung zum Gesetzesentwurf der Bundesregierung, *Bundestagsdrucksache*, a print of draft laws, major
and minor interpellations, opinions and memorials of the German Bundestag that is dis-
tributed among the members of the Bundestag, Bundesrat and the governmental depart-
ments ('BT-Drs') 16/12310, p. 17; Thomas Fischer, "Absprache-Regelung: Problemlösung
oder Problem?", in *Strafverteidiger Forum*, 2009, p. 181, that is, "a prosecutor is under a
duty to commence investigations if there is evidence that an offence has been committed"
(in Richard Vogler and Barbara Huber (eds.), *Criminal Procedure in Europe*, Duncker and
Humblot, Berlin, 2008, p. 25).

[35] Article 112 of the Italian Constitution. Cf. Giuseppe Di Federico, "Prosecutorial Independence and the Democratic Requirement of Accountability in Italy: Analysis of a Deviant
Case in a Comparative Perspective", in *British Journal of Criminology*, 1998, vol. 38, no.
3, pp. 371–87; Michele Panzavolta, "Reforms and Counter-Reforms in the Italian Struggle
for an Accusatorial Criminal Law System", in *North Carolina Journal of International
Law and Commercial Regulation*, 2005, vol. 30, no. 3, p. 591; Stefano Ruggeri, "Investigative and Prosecutorial Discretion in Criminal Matters: The Contribution of the Italian
Experience", in Michele Caianiello and Jacqueline S. Hodgson (eds.), *Discretionary Criminal Justice in a Comparative Context*, Carolina Academic Press, Durham, 2015, pp. 59,
60, 65 ff.

[36] The legality principle is included in Article 124 of the Constitution as well as in the Spanish Ley de Enjuiciamiento Criminal ('LECrim, Art. 198'); Lorena Bachmaier, "The Principle of Legality, Discretionary Justice and Plea Agreements: The Practice in Spain", in
Michele Caianiello and Jacqueline S. Hodgson (eds.), *Discretionary Criminal Justice in a
Comparative Context*, Carolina Academic Press, Durham, 2015, pp. 89, 90–94.

[37] Kuczyńska, 2015, pp. 103–6, see *supra* note 27.

[38] Luc Reydams, "Universal Criminal Jurisdiction: The Belgian State of Affairs", in *Criminal
Law Forum*, 2000, vol. 11, pp. 183–216.

erlands,[41] Norway[42] and the United States[43]). China may be quoted as an example of one of the few legal systems where prosecutors have no discretion whatsoever as to the disposition of a case on the ground of public interest considerations.[44]

Both the opportunity principle and the legality principle have advantages and disadvantages. The opportunity principle "allows prosecutors to target resources for serious offences; it is effective against organised crime by facilitating charge-bargaining and opens up opportunities for diversionary[45] disposal of offenders".[46] On the other hand, there is a danger of "inappropriate government interference" and the risk of "corrupt decision-making".[47] While the legality principle does not share these disadvantages, when considered with the principle of full clarification of the facts the legality principle can be seen as a kind of luxury in an overloaded criminal justice system, generating "a backlog of cases, which can be destructive of the right to a fair and speedy trial"[48] and effectively impeding alternative procedures that may expedite trial proceedings.[49] Consequently, it is said that criminal proceedings "run more speedily in England than they do in

---

[39]   Julia Fionda, *Public Prosecutors and Discretion: A Comparative Study*, Clarendon Press, Oxford, 2003, pp. 14–64.

[40]   Since its first Code of Criminal Procedure in 1880, the Japanese criminal justice system has been governed by the opportunity principle (cf. § 248 of the Japanese Code of Criminal Procedure ('JCCP'); see Morikazu Taguchi, "Der Prozessgegenstand im japanischen Strafprozessrecht", in *Zeitschrift für Internationale Strafrechtsdogmatik*, 2008, vol. 2, p. 72.

[41]   Some even say that the criminal justice system of the Netherlands is "the least adversarial of the trial systems"; see William T. Pizzi, *Trials Without Truth: Why Our System of Criminal Trials Have Become an Expensive Failure and What We Need to Do to Rebuild It*, New York University Press, New York, 1999, p. 94.

[42]   *Ibid.*, p. 102.

[43]   *Ibid.*, p. 104.

[44]   Yu Mou, "Beyond Legitimate Grounds: External Influences and the Discretionary Power Not to Prosecute in the People's Republic of China", in Michele Caianiello and Jacqueline Hodgson (eds), *Discretionary Criminal Justice in a Comparative Context*, Carolina Academic Press, Durham, 2015, p. 119.

[45]   For a detailed analysis of "diversion" see below fn. 63, the main text and below section 3.5.

[46]   Vogler and Huber, 2008, p. 25, see *supra* note 34; see also Kuczyńska, 2015, p. 94, *supra* note 27.

[47]   *Ibid.*

[48]   *Ibid.*

[49]   Fezer, 2010, p. 177, see *supra* note 2.

continental Europe".[50] Notwithstanding this criticism, legality sometimes possesses, especially in Germany, almost a sacred status since it is intimately related to the search for material truth.[51] The "pure" German doctrine would even prefer the "collapse" of the criminal justice system before renouncing this principle,[52] ignoring the fact that other Continental systems are likewise overloaded.[53] On the other hand, it is said that common law countries are forced to deal with a much higher risk of miscarriages of justice, especially wrongful convictions.[54] Some even say that the adversarial system in general, with its feature of discretion in decision-making,[55] contributes to wrongful convictions "either by injecting error because of its inherent features" or by being "inefficient in weeding out errors that arise during the investigation of crimes".[56] Or, even worse: "[M]any false convictions result from the nature of the current adversarial system", whereby a divergence of "enhanced accuracy" designed by the doctrine on the one hand and the reality on the other hand is significant.[57] In the words of

---

[50] John R. Spencer, "Introduction", in Mireille Delmas-Marty and John R. Spencer (eds.), *European Criminal Process*, Cambridge University Press, Cambridge, 2002, p. 33.

[51] Cf. Carl Joseph Anton Mittermaier, *Die Lehre vom Beweise im deutschen Strafprozesse*, Johann Wilhelm Heyer's Verlagshandlung, Darmstadt, 1834, p. 48 (translated by the authors):

> That procedural form shall be preferred which is qualified best for establishing the highest grade of truth; for that reason every legislation that searches for material truth follows the inquisitorial principle in so far as the investigation aims at collecting every material that helps to judge the truth of the charge.

See also Fezer, 2010, p. 177, *supra* note 2.

[52] The point is made by Fezer, 2010, p. 182, see *supra* note 2.

[53] Spencer, 2002, p. 33, see *supra* note 50.

[54] *Ibid.*

[55] Damaška, 1986, p. 4, see *supra* note 7.

[56] See Marvin Zalman, "The Adversary System and Wrongful Conviction", in C. Ronald Huff and Martin Killias (eds.), *Wrongful Conviction: International Perspectives on Miscarriages of Justice*, Temple University Press, Philadelphia, 2008, p. 74.

[57] Daniel Givelber, "Meaningless Acquittals, Meaningful Convictions: Do We Reliably Acquit the Innocent?", in *Rutgers Law Review*, 1997, vol. 49, no. 2, p. 1360; Innocence Commission for Virginia, *A Vision for Justice: Report and Recommendations Regarding Wrongful Convictions in the Commonwealth of Virginia*, Innocence Commission for Virginia, Arlington, 2005, p. xvi. Identified eight factors found to "underlie" the wrongful convictions that preceded 11 exonerations: mistaken eyewitness identification, suggestive identification procedures, police tunnel vision, antiquated forensic testing, inadequate assistance of defence counsel, failure to disclose exculpatory evidence, high pressure interrogation with vulnerable suspects and inconsistent or suspicious statements by the defendant.

Marvin Zalman: "A guilty defendant has a better chance of acquittal in a common law court whereas an innocent would fare better in a continental court".[58]

Be that as it may, the overburdening of our criminal justice systems has led to "a steady movement towards a convergence of legal systems towards borrowing from others those institutions and practices that offer some hope of relief".[59] Together with an increasing convergence between adversarial and non-adversarial procedural systems[60] and the introduction of "consensual" forms in criminal procedure,[61] the principle of procedural economy has taken centre stage.[62] Every legal system has to take recourse to measures that help to unburden the courts. These measures can be grouped together under the headings of "summary trial proceedings" (see section 3.4.) and "diversion" (see section 3.5.). While summary trial proceedings include all those proceedings that may expedite trials ("abbreviated proceedings", "immediate trial", "direct trial", "penal order" and "plea bargaining"), diversion describes all measures that are designed to reduce charges or even avoid a trial in the first place.[63] Thus, diversion in a broad sense also includes the prosecutorial discretion not to charge.

In most countries the proceedings to expedite the trial are called *special proceedings*. A paradigmatic example is Italy. In this country, a new *Codice di procedura penale* ('CPP') was introduced in 1988 to provide for the possibility of special forms of procedure (*procedimenti speciali*) aimed at replacing the ordinary proceedings with a faster summary proceeding.[64]

---

[58] Zalman, 2008, p. 79, see *supra* note 56.

[59] Goldstein, 1997, p. 169, see *supra* note 3.

[60] See generally Diane Marie Amann, "Harmonic Convergence? Constitutional Criminal Procedure in an International Context", in *Indiana Law Journal*, 2000, vol. 75, no. 3, p. 809; Mary C. Daly, "Some Thoughts on the Differences in Criminal Trials in the Civil and Common Law Legal Systems", in *Journal of the Institute for the Study of Legal Ethics*, 1999, vol. 2, pp. 72–73.

[61] See Mirjan R. Damaška, "Models of Criminal Procedure", in *Zbornik Pravnog Fakulleta u Zagrebu*, 2001, vol. 51, p. 485; Richard S. Frase and Thomas Weigend, "German Criminal Justice as a Guide to American Law Reform: Similar Problems, Better Solutions?", in *Boston College International and Comparative Law Review*, 1995, vol. 18, no. 2, p. 345.

[62] Stephen C. Thaman, "Plea-Bargaining, Negotiating Confessions and Consensual Resolution of Criminal Cases", in *Electronic Journal of Comparative Law*, 2007, vol. 11, no. 3, p. 1.

[63] For a detailed analysis of diversion, see section 3.5.

[64] Law No. 81 of 16 February 1987, 1987 Racc.Uff. I 220, Article 2, Clause 1 (*massima semplificazione nello svolgimento del processo*).

Some regard these summary proceedings as being "radical departures from the former system".[65] The direct trial (*guidizio direttissimo*) and the immediate trial (*giudizio immediato*) skip any committal proceedings (*udienza peliminare*). The summary trial (*giudizio abbreviato*) waives the trial itself. Punishment can also be waived upon request by the parties (*patteggiamento*).[66] A penal order (*decreto penale*) or a settlement (*oblazione*) waives the preliminary investigations (*indagini preliminari*).[67] In all cases, however, it is necessary that the accused co-operates, that is, waives his right to an ordinary proceeding and thus accepts the use of *procedimenti speciali*.[68] In exchange, his sentence may be reduced, the trial may not be publicised and the conviction will not be registered on the defendant's criminal record.[69]

Most interestingly, with regard to a change in *system* (from inquisitorial to adversarial or vice versa), it is worth looking at Japan. Already in 1868, which marked the beginning of the Meiji era, Japan turned Westwards and introduced an inquisitorial criminal process.[70] However, between 1928 and 1948, 12-member juries were used to decide factual questions in serious criminal cases and this entailed a move away from the inquisitorial system.[71] This system mixing was continuously pursued by the Japanese legislators, thus awarding either the police or the prosecution a high degree

---

[65] Stephen P. Freccero, "An Introduction to the New Italian Criminal Procedure", in *American Journal of Criminal Law*, 1994, vol. 21, no. 3, p. 372.

[66] See generally Articles 444–48 of the Italian Criminal Procedure Code; Ruggeri, 2015, p. 71, see *supra* note 35; Daniele Vicoli, "Critical Aspects on the Italian Features Concerning 'Negotiated Justice'", in Michele Caianiello and Jacqueline S. Hodgson (eds.), *Discretionary Criminal Justice in a Comparative Context*, Carolina Academic Press, Durham, 2015, pp. 141 ff.; Kyle McCleery, "Guilty Pleas and Plea Bargaining at the Ad Hoc Tribunals: Lessons from Civil Law Systems", in *Journal of International Criminal Justice*, 2016, vol. 14, no. 5, p. 1115 translates *patteggiamento* as "agreement", "understanding" or "a result of negotiations", referring to Sorin-Alexandru Verena and Versavia Brutaru, "Admission of Guilt in the Romanian Criminal Procedure Code: A Comparative Law Perspective", in *Lex ET Scientia International Journal*, 2014, vol. 21, no. 1, p. 97.

[67] See Piermaria Corso, "Italy", in Christine van den Wyngaert (ed.), *Criminal Procedure Systems in the European Community*, 2nd ed., Butterworths, London, 2000, p. 251.

[68] *Ibid.*

[69] *Ibid.*

[70] See Stephan Landsman and Jing Zhang, "A Tale of Two Juries: Lay Participation Comes to Japanese and Chinese Courts", in *UCLA Pacific Basin Law Journal*, 2008, vol. 25, no. 2, p. 181.

[71] Philip L. Reichel and Yumi E. Suzuki, "Japan's Lay Judge System: A Summary of Its Development, Evaluation, and Current Status", in *International Criminal Justice Review*, 2015, vol. 25, no. 3, pp. 247–48.

of discretion.[72] In contrast, the former Japanese criminal process did not concede many rights to the defence counsel, who was, for example, generally barred from access to clients being interrogated by the police.[73] As a consequence, in 1990 Japan introduced several adversarial elements into its criminal process thereby marking a "shift in Japanese procedure towards the common law family".[74] Further, a two-year limit was imposed on the trial[75] and other mechanisms to expedite trials were introduced.[76] Finally, as the most recent step in the system change, the Act Concerning Participation of Lay Assessors in Criminal Trials came into effect in 2009,[77] after the parliament of Japan established the Justice System Reform Council ('JSRC') to review Japan's criminal Justice system.[78] However, this new so-called *saiban-in* (lay judge) law has already been criticised as not being very effective in solving or even addressing the problems encountered by the 1923 jury reform.[79] As of April 2016, 50,603 lay judges have participated in trials and 8,791 defendants have been tried by lay judges.[80]

---

[72] Daniel H. Foote, "Confessions and the Right to Silence in Japan", in *Georgia Journal of International and Comparative Law*, 1991, vol. 21, pp. 429–31.

[73] Daniel H. Foote, "The Benevolent Paternalism of Japanese Criminal Justice", in *California Law Review*, 1992, vol. 80, no. 2, p. 338.

[74] Takeshi Kojima, "Japanese Civil Procedure in Comparative Law Perspective", in *Kansas Law Review*, 1998, vol. 46, p. 718; Reichel and Suzuki, 2015, p. 251, see *supra* note 71.

[75] Carl F. Goodman, "Japan's New Civil Procedure Code: Has It Fostered a Rule of Law Dispute Resolution Mechanism?", in *Brooklyn Journal of International Law*, 2004, vol. 29, no. 2, p. 518.

[76] See Landsman and Zhang, 2008, p. 187, *supra* note 70.

[77] Noboru Yanase, "Deliberative Democracy and the Japanese *Saiban-in* (Lay Judge) Trial System", in *Asian Journal of Law and Society*, 2016, vol. 3, no. 2, p. 327; Kent Anderson and Emma Saint, "Japan's Quasi-jury (*Saiban-in*) Law: An Annotated Translation of the *Act Concerning Participation of Lay Assessors in Criminal Trials*", in *Asian-Pacific Law and Policy Journal*, 2005, vol. 6, no. 1, p. 234. As laid down by the new Act, there are mixed panels of professional judges and lay jurors to determine the guilt and sentences of the accused. Three judges and six laypersons hear contested cases; one judge and four laypersons uncontested ones (Article 2(2)). However, judges retain the exclusive privilege to interpret law and determine procedure (Article 6(2)). Decisions are reached through a majority vote and require that at least one judge and one lay juror assent (Article 67(1)). See further Ingram Weber, "The New Japanese Jury System: Empowering the Public, Preserving Continental Justice", in *East Asia Law Review*, 2009, vol. 4, no. 1, pp. 160–63.

[78] Reichel and Suzuki, 2015, p. 249, see *supra* note 71.

[79] See Landsman and Zhang, 2008, p. 190, see *supra* note 70. Moreover, as of 2013, 97 per cent of the cases appearing before lay judges have resulted in convictions, see Reichel and Suzuki, 2015, p. 252, see *supra* note 71.

[80] Yanase, 2016, p. 328, see *supra* note 77.

3.4. Summary Trial Proceedings

3.4.1. Summary or Abbreviated Proceedings

The term "summary proceedings" encompasses certain procedural mechanisms that are designed to skip the formal preliminary investigation or avoid a full trial (by jury) with all its attendant guarantees. Typical among these are expedited trials, where the defendant is usually arrested *in flagrantia* or the incriminating evidence is otherwise clear, for example due to an unequivocal confession.[81] The trial will often be further accelerated by elements of negotiation if the evidence allows for it.[82]

As will be seen below, most countries with the legality principle introduced abbreviated (summary) proceedings as "special proceedings" into their criminal codes. In contrast, most prosecutions in England are summary in nature, that is summary proceedings have in England nothing "special" about them *per se*.[83]

3.4.1.1. (Non-)Codification of Summary Proceedings

In this section we first refer to predominantly inquisitorial systems that have codified summary proceedings (Italy, Germany, Spain). Then we look at an adversarial system (England) before finishing with inquisitorial systems that do not codify summary proceedings as such (Belgium).

The Italian Code of Criminal Procedure, introduced in 1988, contains the *giudizio abbreviato* in which the defendant may waive the trial by an abbreviated procedure even if both the prosecutor and the judge do not agree.[84] In addition, the defendant may even ask the judge to call additional witnesses or adduce certain types of evidence.[85] In Germany, an amended version of the expedited trial (*beschleunigtes Verfahren*) was introduced in 1994. The aim was to rapidly deal with minor offences[86] and to unburden courts and the prosecution.[87] However, the expedited trial is not allowed in

---

[81] On the meaning of confession, see section 3.4.3.

[82] Thaman, 2007, p. 7, see *supra* note 62.

[83] A.T.H. Smith, "England and Wales", in van den Wyngaert, 2000, p. 97, see *supra* note 67.

[84] See Corso, 2000, p. 252, supra note 67.

[85] Thaman, 2007, p. 39, see *supra* note 62.

[86] BT-Drs. 12/6853, p. 34 ff.

[87] Urs Kindhäuser, *Strafprozessrecht*, 4th ed., Nomos, Baden-Baden, 2016, p. 337.

the case of private prosecutions.[88] In Spain, abbreviated proceedings were amended by way of Law 38/2002 on 24 October 2002.[89] That law, regulating so-called "fast-track trials", was created "with the purpose of overcoming the technical defects of previous legislation, and of providing sufficient material and human resources in order for these objectives to be achieved properly".[90] The objective of the new law was to accelerate the investigation stage and committal proceedings.[91]

The English provisions for summary trials are contained in the Magistrates' Courts Act of 1980 ("MCA"). This act repeals and re-enacts without amendment several earlier statutes, including the Magistrates' Courts Acts of 1952 and 1957, and parts of the Criminal Justice Act of 1976 and the Criminal Law Act of 1977. All summary offences (the least serious offences) are tried in the Magistrate's Court if both the magistrates[92] (who generally resemble lay judges in continental countries such as Germany and Norway)[93] and the accused agree. The more serious offences are tried in the Crown Court.[94] While a case in the Crown Court[95] is tried by a professional judge sitting with a jury, cases in the Magistrates' Court are tried by magistrates or by a judge sitting alone.[96] In the Magistrates' Court there are lay magistrates[97] and stipendiary magistrates.[98] They receive training to per-

---

[88]   *Ibid.*

[89]   See Fernando Gascón Inchausti and Encarnación Aguilera Morales, *La reforma de la Ley de Enjuiciamiento Criminal*, Civitas Madrid, Madrid, 2003, pp. 213–414; Jaime Vegas Torres, *El procedimiento para el enjuiciamiento rapido*, Marcial Pons, Madrid, 2003.

[90]   Fernando Gascón Inchausti and Villamarín López, "Spain", in Vogler and Huber, 2008, p. 623, see *supra* note 34.

[91]   *Ibid.* About the special regulation of the plea agreement in fast-track proceedings, see Bachmaier, 2015, p. 99, *supra* note 36.

[92]   The term "magistrates" is used differently in the United States and England. While in the United States magistrates are legally trained judges of comparatively low rank, in England magistrates are citizens "not formally trained in the law who are appointed to their position and receive no salary for their service"; see Pizzi, 1999, p. 105, *supra* note 41. About the proceedings in the Magistrates Court see also Heinze, 2014, pp. 270–73, *supra* note 7.

[93]   Pizzi, 1999, p. 105, see *supra* note 41.

[94]   Heinze, 2014, p. 270, see *supra* note 7.

[95]   As another difference with the Magistrates' Court is that when a case comes to the Crown Court it must be turned over to a barrister hired by the solicitor; see Pizzi, 1999, p. 108, *supra* note 41.

[96]   See Andrew Ashworth and Mike Redmayne, *The Criminal Process*, 4th ed., Oxford University Press, Oxford, 2010, p. 323.

[97]   Potential lay magistrates are advised that they must be willing to undertake a minimum of 26 half-day court sittings per annum and normally be prepared and able to sit rather more

form specialist functions and remain up-to-date on the law.[99] In fact, the magistrates' work cannot be fully understood without taking into account the clerk, who serves as an important legal adviser of the magistrate and whose role in the conduct of summary proceedings cannot be underestimated.[100] The clerk, *inter alia*, puts the information to the accused, takes note of the evidence, helps an unrepresented accused in the presentation of his or her case and advises the magistrates upon points of law or procedure.[101] A great difference between summary trial and trial on indictment is that in the case of a trial on indictment the accused must be present to plead on the indictment.[102] He should also be in court throughout his trial.[103] By contrast, summary trials often take place in the absence of the accused.[104] According to section 11(1) of the MCA, if the accused does not appear at the time and place fixed for summary trial, the magistrates have discretion to proceed in his absence.

In Belgium, summary proceedings do not exist, but some proposals have been made following the Italian and French example.[105] Sections 452–459 of the Belgium *Code d'instruction criminelle* ('CIC') provide for submission of the case to the prosecutor within 10 days in cases where the suspect does not deny responsibility; the case must then be submitted to the judge who must set trial within five days.

3.4.1.2. Conditions of Summary Proceedings

Generally speaking, the requirements of shortcutting trial proceedings depend very much on the nature of the crime and the clarity of the evidence.

---

frequently – generally between 35 and 45 sittings per annum; see Rod Morgan and Neil Russell, *The Judiciary in the Magistrates' Courts*, Home Office, London, 2000, p. 13.

[98] Stipendiary magistrates are full- or part-time appointees appointed hitherto to a particular commission area on the basis of a request from the Lord Chancellor's Advisory Committee that a stipendiary be appointed; see Morgan and Russell, 2000, p. 23, *supra* note 97. They serve in urban centres and receive a salary.

[99] See *ibid.*, p. 13.

[100] See John Sprack, *Criminal Procedure*, 15th ed., Oxford University Press, Oxford, 2015, pp. 162–63.

[101] *Ibid.*

[102] *Ibid.*, p. 336.

[103] *Ibid.*

[104] See section 11 MCA; see also *ibid.*, p. 167.

[105] Penny Darbyshire, in van den Wyngaert, 2000, p. 43, see *supra* note 67.

While this notion is true for most countries, states differ significantly as to which procedural phases that shall be expedited.

In Germany, the provisions on expedited trial only shorten the trial, not the investigation phase. In fact, it is at the investigation stage that it is to be determined whether the case is suited for an expedited trial.[106] At the latest, it is after the completion of the investigations (§ 169a of the German Code of Criminal Procedure – StPO) that the prosecution may request expedited trial proceedings.[107] This request presupposes two conditions: on the one hand, the facts of the case have to be simple and clear-cut (*einfache Sachlage*) or unquestionable evidence (*klare Beweislage*) must exist; on the other hand, the trial must be suitable for immediate oral trial,[108] that is, "a rapid clarification of the facts during the trial and a short term completion of the trial" must appear to be realistic.[109] Whether those conditions are fulfilled has to be determined by the prosecutor at the time of his request (§ 419 StPO).[110] Furthermore, the prosecutor must expect to finish the trial in one single hearing.[111] Apart from the request for expedited trial, a writ of accusation is necessary, § 200(1) clause 1 StPO. The actual shortcut of the expedited trial is in its renouncing of an intermediate phase (*Zwischenverfahren*).[112] According to § 418(1) clause 1 StPO, the main proceedings have to be commenced immediately or on short notice;[113] the main proceedings themselves are not changed by the expedited trial proceedings.[114] The expedited trial is finished by a judgment. It is disputed whether the provisions on expedited trials are also applicable to an appeal (on question of fact and law, *Berufung*). According to the prevailing view, this is not the case; the expedited trial is completed by the first instance court's judg-

---

[106] Kindhäuser, 2016, p. 337, see *supra* note 87.

[107] *Ibid.*

[108] *Ibid.*, pp. 337–38.

[109] BT-Drs. 12/6853, p. 35 (translation from German).

[110] Lutz Meyer-Goßner, "§ 417 StPO", in Lutz Meyer-Goßner and Bertram Schmitt (eds.), *Strafprozessordnung*, 58th ed., C.H. Beck, München, 2015, mn. 17.

[111] Jürgen-Peter Graf, in Rolf Hannich (ed.), *Karlsruher Kommentar zur Strafprozessordnung*, 7th ed., C.H. Beck, Munich, 2013, § 417, mn. 10.

[112] § 418(1) StPO.

[113] The definition of "short notice" is laid down in § 418(1) clause 2 StPO: "No more than six weeks should lie between receipt of the application by the court and commencement of the main hearing". This is, however, not a peremptory provision but rather directory provision, see Kindhäuser, 2016, p. 338, *supra* note 87.

[114] *Ibid.* The normal provisions of §§ 243 ff. StPO apply.

ment.[115] It is beyond controversy that the same applies for cases of a pure legal appeal (*Revision*).[116]

In Spain, "fast-track trials" may be commenced if several conditions are met (Article 795.1 LECrim). First, the offence should not exceed a maximum punishment of five years[117] (in case of a custodial sentence) or 10 years (non-custodial sentence). Second, there must be a "*delito flagrante*"[118] (Article 795.1 (1) LECrim). Third, the facts of the case must be simple, clear-cut[119] and related to: domestic or gender-related violence (that is assault, coercion, threats or habitual physical or mental violence), committed against those persons referred to in Article 153 of the Criminal Code (*Código Penal*, 'CP'), theft, robbery, theft of or from vehicles, or motoring offences (Article 795.1 (2) LECrim). Additionally, these speedy trials have to be initiated by way of a police report.[120]

Article 796 LECrim provides in detail for a number of activities the police have to undertake prior to the investigation stage, for example informing the suspect, the victim,[121] the witnesses and any other third party

---

[115] OLG Stuttgart, *Strafverteidiger*, 1998, pp. 585, 587; Graf, 2013, Vor § 417 mn. 4, § 420 mn. 2, see *supra* note 111.

[116] Karl Heinz Gössel "Vor § 417", in Ewald Löwe, Werner Rosenberg *et al.* (eds.), *Die Strafprozessordnung und das Gerichtsverfassungsgesetzt: Großkommentar*, vol. 8, 26th ed., De Gruyter, Berlin, 2009, mn. 34.

[117] The same applies in Portugal, where the abbreviated procedure is limited to crimes whose punishment does not exceed five years of imprisonment or which are punished with a fine. However, an exception is provided for cases when the public prosecutor considers in the indictment that the accused shall not be sentenced to prison for more than five years.

[118] Since the English word "flagrant" describes, *inter alia*, an aggravated offence, *delito flagrante* in this context may be translated as "red-handed".

[119] Again, the same applies in Portugal, where the main criterion is the simple and evident proof of the existence of a crime and of the offender. This is especially the case when the accused was detained during the commission of the crime and the judgment could not take place through the summary proceeding.

[120] See Inchausti and López, 2003, p. 623, *supra* note 90.

[121] Article 796 LECrim speaks of the "*ofendido*", which is a synonym for victim (*victima*) or the person harmed by the offence (*sujeto pasivo del delito*); see Gimeno Sendra and José Vicente, *Derecho procesal penal*, 2nd ed., Colex, Madrid, 2007, p. 860; see also Sanz Hermida and Agata Maria, *La situación jurídica de la víctima en el proceso penal*, Tirant Lo Blanch, Valencia, 2008, p. 22:

> *Además es preciso destacar que no siempre se utiliza el término 'víctima' como tal, sino que aparece sustituido por otros términos o expresiones jurídicos no siempre intercambiables como 'sujeto pasivo del delito', 'ofendido' o 'perjudicado' por el delito. [...] De ahí que, con*

about the suspect's appearance before the court. After these measures and the subsequent police report (to be filed according to Article 795.1 LECrim) the court decides whether to initiate proceedings.[122] Once that stage has been concluded, the judge may issue an order transforming the preliminary investigations into abbreviated proceedings if he considers that the measures taken were sufficient.[123] In the course of the trial, after the formulation of the indictment by the prosecution, the accused may file a defence immediately (or within five days on application) and the judge sets down a date for a trial. This trial is completed by a judgment that must be given within three days and which may be appealed.

While the "fast-track trial" may only be commenced where the offence does not exceed a maximum punishment of five or 10 years imprisonment, in Italy, the *giudizio abbreviato*[124] (Articles 438–443 of the CPP) can be used for all offences, regardless of their seriousness, except for offences that carry a life sentence.[125] One may regard *giudizio abbreviato* as a "quasi-trial procedure"[126] since the case is judged not by the trial judge, but by the judge for the preliminary investigations (Article 438 CPP), whose decision rests on the prosecution dossier. Against this decision only a limited appeal is possible (Article 443 CPP). In this context, a case of insufficient evidence with the *giudizio abbreviato* may end with an acquittal.[127] Since both the prosecutor and the defendant must agree to select the simplified procedure,[128] the *giudizio abbreviato* involves an agreement on the

---

    carácter general, la cualidad de víctima u ofendido por el delito sea
    personal e intransmisible y la ostente el titular 'persona física o jurídi-
    ca' del bien jurídico protegido.

  The reason why many authors do not only refer to the victim but also to "persons harmed by the offence" is unclear given that the terms, in substance, are interchangeable. A case where the victim might differ from the person harmed by the offence might be the case where the victim was killed by the offender. In Germany relatives of the victim may then join the public prosecutor in the prosecution of certain offences (§ 395(2) StPO).

[122] See Inchausti and López, 2003, p. 623, *supra* note 90.

[123] *Ibid.*

[124] See Leonardo Suraci, *Il giudizio abbreviato*, Edizioni Scientifiche Italiane, Naples, 2008.

[125] See Elisabetta Grande, "Italian Criminal Justice: Borrowing and Resistance", in *American Journal of Comparative Law*, 2000, vol. 48, no. 2, p. 254.

[126] *Ibid.*

[127] Manfred Maiwald, *Einführung in das italienische Strafrecht und Strafprozessrecht*, Peter Lang, Frankfurt am Main, 2009, p. 226.

[128] Giovanni Conso and Vittorio Grevi, *Prolegomeni a un commentario breve al nuovo Codice di Procedura Penale*, CEDAM, Padova, 1990, p. 353.

form of procedure, not on the verdict. Interestingly, apart from convicting the defendant, the judge may also impose collateral civil orders, Article 442 CPP.

Given the restrictions on the accused's procedural rights, one wonders what incentive the *giudizio abbreviato* may offer to him. In fact, the advantages are considerable. Apart from a reduction of the sentence by a third[129] and the fact that the conviction will not be included in his criminal record, the accused will avoid the publicity of a trial since the proceedings are held *in camera* before the judge for the preliminary investigations. Additionally, the charge cannot be changed, that is, there is no room for a modification of the charges *in peius* as in ordinary proceedings. Yet the *giudizio abbreviato* also places certain disadvantages and risks on the accused. Apart from the fact that the parties cannot ask for the production of additional evidence[130] (unlike at the preliminary hearing in an ordinary trial[131]), the defendant can also never be totally sure of the promised sentencing reduction due to the judge's sentencing discretion.[132]

Given that the one-third reduction laid down by Article 442 is mandatory,[133] it is difficult to understand why the defendant cannot be sure of the reduction. The issue has been well explained by William T. Pizzi and Luca Marafioti: bearing in mind the judge's sentencing discretion in an ordinary trial, the defendant would be tempted to choose an ordinary trial instead of a *giudizio abbreviato*, if the file does not contain all the mitigating evidence that could lower his base sentence, hoping for a reduction of

---

[129] Article 442 CPP. This article also states that, in the case of a life sentence, the sentence shall be reduced to 30 years. However, the Constitutional Court held this provision to be in violation of the specific directives of the 1987 Legge-Delega. Judgment No. 176 of 23 April 1991, Corte Cost., 1991 Foro It. 2318.

[130] See Renzo Orlandi, "Absprachen im italienischen Strafverfahren", in *Zeitschrift für die Gesamte Strafrechtswissenschaft*, 2004, vol. 116, p. 125; see also Grande, 2000, *supra* note 125. This provision was challenged unsuccessfully before the Constitutional Court. Judgment no. 92, 1992, 37 Giur. Cost. 904, 1992.

[131] At the preliminary hearing in an ordinary trial, the judge may ask the parties for additional evidence to decide whether to set the matter for trial. Such a request is not permitted at a *giudizio abbreviato*; see William T. Pizzi and Luca Marafioti, "The New Italian Code of Criminal Procedure: The Difficulties of Building an Adversarial Trial System on a Civil Law Foundation", in *Yale Journal of International Law*, 1992, vol. 17, no. 1, p. 24.

[132] See Grande, 2000, *supra* note 125.

[133] Maiwald, 2009, supra note 127.

---

the sentence by the judge.[134] In other words, the defendant can never be totally sure that the sentence reduced in a *giudizio abbreviato* is indeed lower than the sentence that would have been imposed in an ordinary trial.

Interestingly, it is said that the *giudizio abbreviato* very much resembles the summary trial in England.[135] According to section 2 of the Magistrates' Courts Act, the court has jurisdiction to try any summary offence or offences "triable either way" and the accused has to agree to select summary trial.[136] To a large extent, the course of summary trials is identical to the course of a trial on indictment with the difference that, in a summary trial, the accused cannot plead not guilty as charged but only guilty of some other (lesser) offence.[137] After the defence closing speech, the magistrates must give a unanimous decision.[138] While, on the one hand, a magistrate has the power to impose certain sanctions or conditions (he may imprison or fine and absolutely or conditionally discharge an offender, place probation, order attendance at an attendance centre, order performance of work for the community, or send an offender to a young offenders' institution),[139] this power is, on the other hand, restricted as laid down by section 154 (1) of the Criminal Justice Act 2003:[140] "A magistrates' court does not have power to impose imprisonment for more than 12 months in respect of any one offence". In case the offender committed two or more summary offences, section 133 of the MCA applies: "[W]here a magistrates' court imposes two or more terms of imprisonment [...] to run consecutively the aggregate of such terms shall not, subject to the provisions of this section, exceed 6 months".

---

[134] Pizzi and Marafioti, 1992, p. 28, *supra* note 131.

[135] Paolo Tonini, "I procedimenti semplificati", in Giuffrè (ed.), *Studi in memoria di Pietro Nuvolone*, Vol. 3: *Il nuovo processo penale, studi di diritto straniero e comparato*, A. Giuffrè, Milan, 1991, pp. 476–78.

[136] See Sprack, 2015, p. 141, *supra* note 100.

[137] *Ibid.*, p. 155.

[138] *Ibid.*, p. 158.

[139] *Ibid.*, pp. 160–61.

[140] This Act amends section 78 of the Powers of Criminal Courts (Sentencing) Act 2000: "[A] magistrates' court shall not have power to impose imprisonment [...] for more than six months in respect of any one offence".

3.4.2. Other Forms of Summary Proceedings

As previously mentioned, summary proceedings were designed mainly to accelerate criminal proceedings and, generally speaking, to deliver a judgment more quickly. However, some countries have created proceedings that not only shorten but skip a trial phase, that is, the investigation phase.

3.4.2.1. Immediate Proceedings

In France, immediate proceedings are only available in respect of middle-range offences (*délits*) carrying a penalty of more than two years imprisonment or six months in the case of a "flagrant" offence, Article 395 of the *Code de procédure pénale*[141] ('CPP')[142] up until 10 years.[143] If the prosecutor considers the case to have been sufficiently prepared to be tried at once (Article 395 CPP), the defendant's agreement upon the alleged acts is, similar to the summary proceedings, required (Articles 393–397 CPP).[144] According to Article 394 CPP, the district prosecutor may invite the person brought before him to appear before the court within 10 days to two months ("judicial *rendezvous*" procedure[145]), except where the person concerned waives this time limit in the presence of his advocate.

In Italy, an immediate trial may be conducted when the prosecutor finds that there is no need for a preliminary investigation because there is enough (and clear) evidence against the accused (*quando la prova appare evidente*, Article 453 CPP). This may take place within 90 days since the entry of the *notitia criminis* in the appropriate register (Article 454 CPP). The judge then notifies the non-requesting party of the request, giving the defendant the option of requesting either the abbreviated proceedings or a

---

[141] The *Code de procédure pénale* goes back to 1958, when the preceding *Code d'instruction criminelle* of 1808 was redrafted; see Valérie Dervieux, "The French System", in Delmas-Marty and Spencer, 2002, p. 218, see *supra* note 50.

[142] Richard Vogler, in Vogler and Huber, 2008, p. 204, see *supra* note 34.

[143] Jacqueline Hodgson, *French Criminal Justice: A Comparative Account of the Investigation and Prosecution of Crime in France*, Hart, Oxford, 2005, pp. 51, 130. Interestingly, the previous seven-year threshold was introduced in 2002 because the limitation of the offences to over two years imprisonment was regarded as narrowing the scope of the provision on *comparution immediate*; see Vogler, 2008, p. 204, *supra* note 142.

[144] Hodgson, 2005, p. 59, see *supra* note 143: "[T]he comparution immédiate procedure is designed to deal rapidly with cases where the suspect has admitted involvement".

[145] Richard Vogler, in Vogler and Huber, 2008, p. 204, see *supra* note 34.

negotiated sentence.[146] Apart from the prosecutor's request, *giudizio imme-diato* may be requested by the accused, for example, in cases where the accused does not wish to disclose his case until the trial.

3.4.2.2. Direct Trial

The direct trial exists especially in Italy (*giudizio direttissimo*), constituting a proceeding in which the case is directly brought before the trial judge, without passing through committal proceedings and, very often, even the preliminary investigations.[147] The trial is conducted according to the ordi-nary procedural rules and can be used either when the accused has been arrested while committing the offence (*arresto in flagranza*)[148] or when he has made a confession[149] to the public prosecutor or to the judge. In other words, the direct trial can only be used when there is a strong *prima facie* case against the accused. As an essential condition, both the defendant and the prosecutor can agree to conduct a *giudizio direttissimo*,[150] but the pro-cedure must be conducted no later than 15 days after the defendant was taken into custody.[151] In cases of an *arresto in flagranza* or a confession, the judge must (as in the case of immediate proceedings) notify the defend-ant of the option to seek abbreviated proceedings or a negotiated sen-tence.[152] One may argue that the direct trial resembles the immediate trial, for example with regard to the "obviousness" of the evidence.[153] However, the requirement of *arresto in flagranza* does not exist in an immediate trial.

---

[146] Article 456 CPP.

[147] Articles 449–52. These proceedings also existed under the former CPP. See Articles 502–5 CPP, 1930.

[148] Under Italian law, the judicial police can arrest individuals without prior authorisation when they apprehend them in the act of committing serious crimes. *Ibid.*, Article 380. The individual must then be brought before a judge within forty-eight hours for a hearing rati-fying the arrest. *Ibid.*, Articles 390–91.

[149] Article 449(5) CPP.

[150] Article 449(3) CPP.

[151] Article 449(5) CPP.

[152] Article 451 CPP.

[153] See Grande, 2000, p. 252, *supra* note 125.

3.4.2.3. Penal Orders

A special and indeed very effective form of a summary proceeding[154] is an abbreviated process known as "penal order". According to a general and prefatory definition, a penal order can be seen as a "written proposal by the state to a defendant stipulating the crime committed and the penalty to be levied if the defendant does not object".[155] In countries like Germany,[156] France[157] and Italy[158] the penal order may be used in cases sanctioned by fines, which practically applies to misdemeanours (such as traffic or shop-lifting offences) in most cases.[159] Furthermore the penal order may also be used in cases of imprisonment of up to six months in Italy,[160] up to one year in Germany,[161] up to five years in Luxembourg[162] and up to 10 years in Poland.[163]

---

[154] In fact, the practical impact of a penal order can not be underestimated since a great amount of convictions result in a penal order: two-thirds of all convictions in Germany and 28 per cent in Croatia. In Norway 215,276 cases were resolved by penal orders in 2001. On the other hand, "fixed penalties" are imposed only in 2–3 per cent of all cases in Scotland. In the mid-1990s around 22 per cent of penal orders in Germany were refused by defendants (see Thaman, 2007, pp. 1, 18, fn. 141, *supra* note 62). On the contrary, several defendants did not accept the penal order in France; see Roger Merle and André Vitu, *Traité de droit criminel*, vol. 2: *Procedure pénale*, 5th ed., Cujas, Paris, 2001, pp. 915–18. In addition, any costs assessed as part of the penal order are presumably less than they would be after trial, thus producing, in effect, a lower fine; see Richard S. Frase, "Comparative Criminal Justice as a Guide to American Law Reform: How Do the French Do It, How Can We Find Out, and Why Should We Care?", in *California Law Review*, 1990, vol. 78, no. 3, p. 646.

[155] William L.F. Felstiner, "Plea Contracts in West Germany", in *Law and Society Review*, 1979, vol. 13, no. 2, p. 309.

[156] Claus Roxin and Bernd Schünemann, *Strafverfahrensrecht*, 28th ed., C.H. Beck, Munich, 2014, § 68 mn. 1.

[157] Bernard Bouloc and Haritini Matsopoulou, *Droit pénal général et procédure pénal*, 18th ed., Sirey, Paris, 2011, pp. 439 ff.; Baele, 2015, p. 42, see *supra* note 33.

[158] See Corso, 2000, p. 254, *supra* note 67.

[159] Jörg-Martin Jehle, "Was und wie häufig sind Fehlurteile? – Eine Skizze", in *Forensische Psychiatrie, Psychologie, Kriminologie*, 2013, vol. 7, pp. 220, 224.

[160] Corso, 2000, p. 254, see *supra* note 67; the judge can reduce the sentence to half the minimum laid down by statute.

[161] Roxin and Schünemann, 2014, § 68 mn. 1, see *supra* note 156.

[162] Alphonse Spielmann and Dean Spielmann, in van den Wyngaert, 2000, p. 276, see *supra* note 67.

[163] Stanisław Waltoś, *Proces Karny* [Penal Proceedings], 9th ed., Wydawnictwo Prawnicze Lexis Nexis, Warsaw, 2008, p. 300.

In Germany the prosecutor may submit an application for a penal order at any time, even after the beginning of trial, § 408a StPO. Generally
spoken, this penal order will inform the defendant that he will receive a
specified sentence for a specified crime unless he or she objects within two
weeks,[164] in which case the matter will proceed to a normal trial before the
appropriate court by a single professional judge.[165] The judge must issue
the penal order if he has no substantial objections.[166] In practice this means
that judges grant virtually all applications for a penal order as a matter of
course.[167] The requirement of the defendant's consent entails the possibility
of bargaining over the fine to be imposed between the defence and the
prosecution.[168]

Penal orders are even more significant in France,[169] where the *juge de
police*, without giving any reasons, delivers a judgment without hearing and
even without the presence of a defence lawyer.[170] Nearly the same applies
in Italy, where a penal order (*decreto penale*), regarded as a conviction, is
issued upon request of the prosecutor in the absence of the accused and
without a trial.[171] Last but not least, a prosecutor's request for a penal order
without any hearing or debate can also be made in Luxembourg (*ordonnan-
ce penale*).[172]

Needless to say, a penal order may not always be the appropriate answer to a crime. Thus, in every country there exist decisions against the

---

[164] See Albert Alschuler, "Implementing the Criminal Defendant's Right to Trial: Alternatives
to the Plea Bargaining System", in *University of Chicago Law Review*, 1983, vol. 50, no.
3, pp. 956–57; Gerhard Dannecker and Julian Roberts, "The Law of Criminal Procedure",
in Werner F. Ebke and Matthew W. Finkin (eds.), *An Introduction to German Law*, Kluwer Law Internation, The Hague, 1996, pp. 445–46.

[165] §§ 407, 409 StPO; Nancy Amoury Combs, "Copping a Plea to Genocide: The Plea Bargaining of International Crimes", in *University of Pennsylvania Law Review*, vol. 151, no.
1, 2003, p. 41.

[166] Cf. §§ 408 (3), 408a (2) StPO: "*keine Bedenken*".

[167] Markus Dirk Dubber, "American Plea Bargains, German Lay Judges, and the Crisis of
Criminal Procedure", in *Stanford Law Review*, 1997, vol. 49, no. 3, p. 559.

[168] *Ibid.*, pp. 559–60: "In penal order bargains, the prosecutor may offer to initiate a penal
order proceeding instead of filing the case in the single judge court, thereby limiting the
defendant's maximum exposure to a suspended one year prison sentence".

[169] The penal order procedure in France has existed since 3 January 1972.

[170] Jean Pradel, in van den Wyngaert, 2000, p. 130, *supra* note 67.

[171] Corso, 2000, p. 254, *supra* note 67.

[172] Spielmann and Spielmann, 2000, p. 276, see *supra* note 162.

---

imposition of a penal order. In France, *inter alia*, the public prosecutor may choose ordinary proceedings instead of penal order for three reasons. First, the facts may present certain difficulties which can only be solved in a hearing. Second, a fine is regarded as not sufficient punishment in the respective case.[173] Third, if a case is referred to the *juge de police* by the public prosecutor's department, he could refuse to deal with this case by penal order, taking the view that a more severe sentence should be imposed.[174] Further, once the decision for a penal order is made, the accused is by no means bound to that decision but can apply for a review of the order (*opposition*).[175] If he does so in France, his case will be publicly heard by the *juge de police* in an ordinary proceeding.[176] The accused can also oppose the penal order in Germany,[177] Italy (*opposizione*)[178] and Luxembourg.[179]

3.4.3. Consensual Procedures in a Broad Sense

As pointed out, summary proceedings always require a certain amount of agreement from the accused. In other words, one may say that every form of expediting trials contains an element of negotiated justice to award the accused with a less expensive, faster, more confidential trial that normally comes with a lower sentence. Apart from the different translations in different legal systems, this so-called "negotiated justice", which broadly[180] describes the "negotiation and social interactions involved in the routine production of justice",[181] involves a great amount of notions. Contrary to nego-

---

[173] Pradel, 2000, p. 130, see *supra* note 170.

[174] *Ibid.*, p. 131.

[175] Regarding France, within a month of notification of the order, see *ibid.*

[176] *Ibid.*

[177] See *supra* notes 164 ff. and main text.

[178] But only if filed within 15 days; he may also ask for *patteggiamento*, summary, immediate trial or, if possible, financial settlement; see Corso, 2000, p. 254, *supra* note 67; Ruggeri, 2015, p. 71, see *supra* note 35.

[179] Spielmann and Spielmann, 2000, see *supra* note 162.

[180] Others prefer a narrower interpretation, describing negotiated justice as "a diarchic process of regulation which 'consists in two persons or their representatives themselves seeking a solution to their conflict'"; see Françoise Tulkens, "Negotiated Justice", in Delmas-Marty and Spencer 2002, p. 641, fn. 4, *supra* note 50, taking recourse to (and translating) Jacques Faget, *La médiation: Essai de politique pénale*, Erès, Toulouse, 1997, pp. 12–13.

[181] Eamonn Carrabine, Pamela Cox, Pete Fussey, Dick Hobbs, Nigel South, Darren Thiel and Jackie Turton, *Criminology: A Sociological Introduction*, 3rd ed., Routledge, London, 2014, p. 333.

tiated justice, there exist the notions of procedural justice (referring to procedural safeguards), substantive justice (referring to the substantive outcomes)[182] and consensual justice. For the sake of simplification, we equate "consensual justice" with "negotiated justice" since both are often mentioned in the same breath.[183] However, it should be mentioned that some indeed distinguish between the two: consensual justice describes a "model which leaves room, to greater or lesser extent, for the consent of the parties concerned, whether in a positive form with their acceptance or a negative form in the absence of their refusal",[184] while negotiated justice "does not confine itself to granting individuals the power to accept or refuse proposals over whose content they have no control".[185]

Negotiated justice is found at all stages of criminal procedure: during the police investigation, at the moment of the prosecutorial decision to charge or not to charge, and during trial. In this context, we are only referring to negotiated justice during the latter two stages; the police stage, albeit of great practical importance, will not be subject of our analysis. Interestingly, negotiated justice is always mentioned together with plea bargaining and guilty plea.

3.4.3.1. Plea Bargaining and Guilty Plea

Plea bargaining patterns like the US model have played a great role in the discourse and reforms surrounding negotiated justice in Europe.[186] However, before observing plea bargaining in more detail, some comments on terminology are required. First of all, one has to distinguish between a guilty plea and plea bargaining. Plea bargaining marks the *process* through which a defendant pleads guilty to a criminal charge with the expectation of

---

[182] *Ibid.*

[183] See, for instance, Mirjan R. Damaška, "Negotiated Justice in International Criminal Courts", in *Journal of International Criminal Justice*, 2004, vol. 2, no. 4, p. 1024; and Stefano Maffei, "Negotiations on evidence and negotiations on sentence", in *Journal of International Criminal Justice*, 2004, vol. 2, no. 4, p. 1067, which appear to use both phrases interchangeably.

[184] Examples given by the report of the fifth conference of the European Forum for Restorative Justice, "Building Restorative Justice in Europe: Cooperation between the Public, Policy Makers, Practitioners and Researchers", Verona, 17–19 April 2008, p. 170.

[185] *Ibid.*

[186] Maffei, 2004, p. 1051, see *supra* note 183.

receiving something in return from the state.[187] It generally refers to charge bargaining, that is, the negotiation about the charge,[188] and sentence bargaining, that is the negotiation about the sentence.[189] While charge bargaining may be described as a "horizontal negotiation" which takes place at the prosecution stage between the prosecutor and the person charged, sentence bargaining is regarded as "vertical negotiation", that is, an agreement given by the prosecution that can bind the trial judge.[190] On the contrary, the guilty plea, which is often preceded by plea bargaining,[191] characterises the decision of a defendant to plead guilty to, or not contest, a number of counts on the indictment.[192] Thus, in sum,

> [guilty plea] may encompass negotiation over the reduction of a sentence, dropping some or all of the charges or reducing the charges in return for admitting guilt, conceding certain facts, foregoing an appeal or providing cooperation in another criminal case.[193]

Plea bargaining is especially used in countries governed by the opportunity principle such as the United States, where it is theoretically less controversial than in countries with the legality principle.[194] In fact, the

---

[187] See Bryan A. Garner (ed.), *Black's Law Dictionary*, 10th ed., Thomson/West, St. Paul, 2014, p. 1338; for more detail, see Roza Pati, "The ICC and the Case of Sudan's Omar al Bashir: Is Plea-Bargaining a Valid Option?", in *UC Davis Journal of International Law and Policy*, 2009, vol. 15, no. 2, p. 282. For a definition from a comparative perspective see Carol A. Brook, Bruno Fiannaca, David Harvey, Paul Marcus and Jenny McEwan, "A Comparative Look at Plea Bargaining in Australia, Canada, England, New Zealand, and the United States", in *William & Mary Law Review*, 2016, vol. 57, no. 4, pp. 1147, 1152 ff.

[188] A plea bargain is where a prosecutor agrees to drop some of the counts or reduce the charge to a less serious offence in exchange for a plea of either guilty or no contest from the defendant, see Garner, 2014, p. 1338, *supra* note 187.

[189] For more detailed observations on charge bargaining and sentence bargaining, see Barry Boss and Nicole L. Angarella, "Negotiating Federal Plea Agreements Post-*Booker*", in *Criminal Justice*, 2006, vol. 21, no. 2, pp. 22 ff. See also McCleery, 2016, p. 1104, *supra* note 66.

[190] See Tulkens, 2002, p. 662, *supra* note 180.

[191] *Ibid.*

[192] Maffei, 2004, p. 1061, see *supra* note 183.

[193] Malcolm M. Feeley, "Perspectives on Plea Bargaining", in *Law and Society Review*, 1979, vol. 13, no. 2, pp. 199–200; see also, for example, Fed. R. Crim. para. 11(e).

[194] Jenia Iontcheva Turner, "Plea Bargaining", in Linda Carter and Fausto Pocar (eds.), *International Criminal Procedure*, Edward Elgar, Cheltenham, 2013, pp. 34, 36, 38; Kuczyńska, 2015, p. 96, see *supra* note 27. Norway, albeit following the opportunity principle, generally disfavours the plea-bargaining procedure. A similar situation may be found

latter is, at least as a matter of principle, incompatible with the practice of bargaining between the prosecutor and the accused as this "might purport to alter – to either a greater or lesser extent – the nature of the allegation or surrounding facts".[195] It comes, therefore, as no surprise that the first attempts of using guilty pleas in order to expedite trials occurred in the legal systems of the United States and England/Wales.[196] A special case is Italy, where elements of negotiated justice were inserted "into an inquisitorial legal culture"[197] with probably the "biggest backlog and the slowest pace of litigation" in all Western jurisdictions.[198] Thus, Italy "may then serve as a model country in an attempt to test the resistance of continental systems of criminal procedure against market-oriented ideas and contract-like relations".[199] In 1990 the Italian Supreme Court argued that the prosecution is exempted from the burden of proving guilt beyond reasonable doubt if the accused voluntarily accepts to be sanctioned with a specified sentence.[200] Yet, the judgment itself, as the Supreme Court's reasoning went on, ought to be considered "hypothetical" in nature since it only establishes a hypothesis of responsibility and not its positive ascertainment.[201] In contrast, commentators have long argued that a judgment that serves a penalty on the defendant can be nothing other than an ordinary conviction,[202] since the judge is entitled or even obliged to acquit the defendant when the sentence lacks an adequate factual basis. Otherwise the principle of legality may be violated.[203] In the same vein, the Italian Constitutional Court stated that a judge who rejects a request for a bargained penalty at the pre-trial stage

---

in South Africa. Although France has acknowledged the opportunity principle for a long time, it was a great opponent of plea bargaining until 2004; see Thaman, 2007, p. 3, fn. 10, *supra* note 62.

[195] Inchausti and López, 2003, p. 558, see *supra* note 90. However, see Bachmaier, 2015, p. 105, *supra* note 36: "The plea agreements of the Spanish criminal procedure have no effect on the principle of mandatory investigation and prosecution".

[196] Damaška, 2004, p. 1022, see *supra* note 183; Michael P. Scharf, "Trading Justice for Efficiency", in *Journal of International Criminal Justice*, 2004, vol. 2, no. 4, p. 1071.

[197] Maffei, 2004, p. 1051, see *supra* note 183.

[198] Marco W. Fabri, "Theory versus Practice of Italian Criminal Justice Reform", in *Judicature*, 1994, vol. 77, no. 4, p. 211.

[199] *Ibid.*

[200] Corte Cass., 19 February 1990, in Cass. Pen., 1990, p. 44.

[201] *Ibid.*

[202] Franco Cordero, *Procedura Penale*, 5th ed., Giuffrè, Milan, 2000, p. 972.

[203] Maffei, 2004, p. 1063, see *supra* note 183.

cannot serve as a trial judge, precisely because the early assessment goes to the merits of the case.[204] Apart from these rather principled considerations, a more important practical reason why guilty pleas are more likely to be used in common than in civil law countries seems to be the length of the final public hearing. As stated by John R. Spencer, in England the Crown Court "might take only thirty minutes to deal with a murder case in which the defendant pleaded guilty; in continental Europe this would be considered quite indecent haste".[205]

Notwithstanding the theoretical objections and controversy, plea bargaining is widely practised also in civil law systems and has also been incorporated in the procedural laws.[206] Yet, due to different procedural traditions and concepts, plea bargaining mechanisms have not been introduced identically into the criminal process of "civil law" countries. Thus, for example, the Italian, Argentinian and French plea bargain systems vary substantially due to the differing ways in which the practice has been introduced, and the resistance it has generated.[207] Each European jurisdiction has adopted its own procedure different from the others, "either because of decisions by the legal reformers [...] or because of structural differences between American criminal procedure and the criminal procedures of the civil law tradition".[208]

Probably the most significant difference to plea bargaining as practised in the United States is the French model, which was introduced at the end of June 1999 (Articles 41(2) and 41(3) CPP)[209] with the goal of reduc-

---

[204] Corte Cost., Judgment No. 186/1992, in Ind. Pen., 1994, p. 126.

[205] Spencer, 2002, p. 28, see *supra* note 50.

[206] Turner, 2013, p. 38, see *supra* note 194; Thaman, 2007, pp. 20 ff., see *supra* note 62. See also Tulkens, 2002, pp. 645–49, *supra* note 180. On France, see Jean Cedras, "L'hypothèse de l'américanisation du droit pénal français", in *Archives de Philosophie du Droit*, 2001, vol. 45, p. 156; concerning Italy, see, for example, Paolo Ferrua, "La giustizia negoziata nella crisi della funzione cognitiva del processo penale", in *Studii Sul Processo Penale*, 1997, vol. 3, p. 134.

[207] Máximo Langer, "From Legal Transplants to Legal Translations: The Globalization of Plea Bargaining and the Americanization Thesis in Criminal Procedure", in *Harvard International Law Journal*, 2004, vol. 45, p. 4.

[208] *Ibid.*, p. 3.

[209] Law No. 99–515 of 23 June 1999; J.O., 24 June 1999, p. 9207.

ing the caseload of the courts.[210] While in the United States a plea bargaining shortens the regular criminal proceedings so that a trial is not necessary to determine guilt or innocence, the French *composition* avoids such proceedings in the first place.[211] Furthermore, in US plea bargaining the prosecutor is understood to be in an equal bargaining position with the defence; in France the prosecutor does not negotiate as an equal part but is more akin to a diversion officer to exert control over a person who has broken the law and may commit new offences in the future.[212] Thus, the defendant must accept the prosecutor's offer and admit guilt, not as a party who can end the dispute with his consent but rather as part of his own process of neutralisation, rehabilitation and reparation to the victim.[213] Thus, French plea bargaining very much fits into the definition of consensual justice while US plea bargaining must be seen in the context of negotiated justice. Another form of plea bargaining in France is a proceeding that was introduced in 2004 called *comparution sur reconnaissance préalable de culpabilité* ('CRPC'), which "permits the procureur and the accused to agree on a reduced sentence of up to one year's imprisonment in exchange for a formal admission, avoiding the need for a trial".[214]

A plea bargaining model, which is rather similar to the US model (more specifically, to US sentencing bargaining[215]), is the Argentinian one.

---

[210] See Philippe Conte and Patrick Maistre du Chambon, *Procédure pénale*, 3rd ed., A. Colin, Paris, 2001, pp. 3–4; Roger Merle and André Vitu, *Traité de droit criminel*, vol. 2: *Procedure pénale*, 5th ed., Cujas, Paris, 2001, p. 396.

[211] Merle and Vitu, 2001, p. 396, see *supra* note 210.

[212] Cf. Langer, 2004, p. 60, see *supra* note 207; Verena and Brutaru, 2014, p. 106, *supra* note 66: "[A]s there is no such thing as an agreement between the prosecution and the defense, as result of a negotiation, the effects occur by acceptance of the proposed penalty followed by approval of the judge".

[213] The admission of guilt by the defendant has a pedagogic character. See Ministère de la Justice, "Circulaires de la direction des Affaires criminelles et des Grâces, 3 Présentation des dispositions concernant la composition pénale issues de la loi du 23 juin 1999 renforçant l'efficacité de la procédure pénale et du décret du 29 janvier 2001", in *Bulletin Officiel du Ministére de la Justice*, 2001, vol. 83.

[214] Hodgson, 2005, p. 104 with fn. 11, see *supra* note 143. Concretely speaking, the CRPC law docs not contain a provision on a negotiation of the sentence (Articles 495 ff.). Nevertheless, in practice CRPC sentences are in fact negotiated. See in more detail Hodgson, 2006, p. 224 with fn. 6, *supra* note 7; Erik Luna and Marianne Wade, "Prosecutors as Judges", in *Washington and Lee Law Review*, 2010, vol. 67, no. 4, pp. 1413, 1452; Baele, 2015, p. 43, see *supra* note 33.

[215] See Luis F. Niño, "Causa no. 454, Miguel Ángel Wasylyszyn", in *Cuadernos de Doctrina y Jurisprudencia Penal*, 1998, pp. 628–29.

According to the *procedimiento abreviado*, the prosecution and the defence can reach an agreement about the sentence at any time between the indictment at the end of the pre-trial phase and the determination of the date for trial.[216] The prosecution and the defence have active roles in the negotiations about the sentence and the admission of guilt, while the tribunal's role is basically limited to that of formal control.[217]

The German plea bargaining model, called *Verständigung*, is particularly interesting to consider in this discussion since it was only introduced into the German Code of Criminal Procedure in 2009: § 257c StPO.[218] The astonishing antagonism is that the German Criminal Procedure does, as a matter of principle, apart from some exceptions like §§ 265a, 391, 402, 405, 470(2) StPO, prohibit any form of negotiated justice[219] since the (inquisito-

---

[216] Article 431, Código Procesal Penal ('CPP').

[217] Cf. Langer, 2004, p. 55, see *supra* note 207.

[218] Jenia Iontcheva Turner, "Plea Bargaining and Disclosure in Germany and the United States: Comparative Lessons", in *William & Mary Law Review*, 2016, vol. 57, no. 4, pp. 1549, 1573. As a matter of fact, plea bargaining has been used in Germany since the 1980s, albeit informally; see Turner, 2013, p. 36, *supra* note 194; Kai Ambos and Pamela Ziehn, "§ 257c StPO", in Henning Radtke and Olaf Hohmann (eds.), *Strafprozessordnung*, Franz Vahlen, Munich, 2011, mn. 9 ff. The words "*Absprache*" or "*Vereinbarung*" are wilfully avoided by the German legislator in order to not make the impression that a quasi-contractual agreement, and not the guilt of the accused, is the basis of the judgment. Cf. the explanations given by the German government, BT-Drs. 16/12310, p. 8. See also McCleery, 2016, pp. 1112–13, *supra* note 66, who translates "*Absprachen*" as "agreements" (p. 1112).

[219] Ambos and Ziehn, 2011, mn. 1, see *supra* note 218; Gunnar Duttge, "Möglichkeiten eines Konsensualprozesses nach deutschem Strafprozeßrecht", in *Zeitschrift für die Gesamte Strafrechtswissenschaft*, 2003, vol. 115, no. 3, pp. 542 ff.; Jürgen Seier, "Der strafprozessuale Vergleich im Lichte des § 136a StPO", in Juristenzeitung, 1988, vol. 43, no. 14, p. 684 shows that, in comparison to American law, German law does not allow "plea bargaining" as negotiated justice. Cf. also Heinz J. Dielmann, "'Guilty Plea' und 'Plea Bargaining' im amerikanischen Strafverfahren – Möglichkeiten für den deutschen Strafprozeß?", in *Goltdammer's Archiv für Strafrecht*, 1981, pp. 558 ff.; Claus Kreß, "Absprachen im Rechtsvergleich", in *Zeitschrift für die Gesamte Strafrechtswissenschaft*, 2004, vol. 116, no. 1, pp. 172–87; Andreas Ransiek, "Zur Urteilsabsprache im Strafprozess: ein amerikanischer Fall", in *Zeitschrift für Internationale Strafrechtsdogmatik*, 2008, vol. 3, pp. 116–22; Edda Weßlau, "Absprachen in Strafverfahren", in *Zeitschrift für die Gesamte Strafrechtswissenschaft*, 2004, vol. 116, p. 169. For a differentiated approach see Werner Schmidt-Hieber, "Der strafprozessuale 'Vergleich' – eine illegale Kungelei?", in *Strafverteidiger*, 1986, p. 357; Dominik Brodowski, "Die verfassungsrechtliche Legitimation des US-amerikanischen 'plea bargaining' – Lehren für Verfahrensabsprachen nach § 257 c StPO?", in *Zeitschrift für die gesamte Strafrechtswissenschaft*, 2012, vol. 124, p. 733, comparing the German *Verständigung* and plea bargaining in the USA with a view to constitutional restraints.

rial[220]) German criminal process is governed by both the duty to clarify the facts (§ 244(2) StPO) and the principle of culpability (§ 46 (1) clause 1 StGB).[221] There are elements of consensual justice in the German criminal procedure,[222] though most prominently in § 153a StPO.[223] Most interestingly, § 257c (1) clause 2 StPO unambiguously confirms that the duty to clarify the facts (*Aufklärungspflicht*, § 244 (2) StPO) is still the central aim of the trial that cannot be negotiated away.[224] The same applies to the Spanish *conformidad*.[225] As a consequence, in Germany the basis of a judgment must not be a *Verständigung*.[226] Thus, the German approach to plea bar-

---

[220] For an explanation from the perspective of legal history and comparative law, see Kai Ambos, "Zum heutigen Verständnis von Akkusationsprinzip und – verfahren aus historischer Sicht", in *Jura*, 2008, vol. 30, no. 8, p. 593. See also Michael Hettinger, "Die Absprache im Strafverfahren als rechtsstaatliches Problem", in *Juristenzeitung*, 2011, vol. 66, pp. 292, 294–95.

[221] Bernd Schünemann, *Absprachen im Strafverfahren? Grundlagen, Gegenstände und Grenzen: Gutachten zum 58. Deutschen Juristentag*, Beck, Munich, 1990, pp. 80 ff. (the *Deutscher Juristentag* ['DJT'] is both a registered association and legal congress of its members; it takes place every second year). Cf. also Bernd Schünemann and Judith Hauer, "Absprachen im Strafverfahren, Zentrale Probleme einer künftigen gesetzlichen Regelung", in *Anwaltsblatt*, 2006, pp. 440 ff; Thomas Weigend, "Eine Prozeßordnung für abgesprochene Urteile?", in *Neue Zeitschrift für Strafrecht*, 1999, vol. 57, p. 58; Felix Herzog, "'Dealen' im Strafverfahren: Wahrheit, Schuld – richterliche Berufsethik", in *Goltdammer's Archiv für Strafrecht*, 2014, vol. 161, pp. 688, 691 ff.

[222] Ambos and Ziehn, 2011, mn. 2, see *supra* note 218; Judgment of the German Federal Court, ('BGHSt 43'), p. 195, para. 203; BHG, in *Neue Zeitschrift für Strafrecht*, 1998, p. 32. See also Hans Dahs, "Absprachen im Strafprozeß, Chancen und Risiken", in *Neue Zeitschrift für Strafrecht*, 1988, p. 154; Ernst-Walter Hanack, "Vereinbarungen im Strafprozeß, ein besseres Mittel zur Bewältigung von Großverfahren", in *Strafverteidiger*, 1987, p. 502.

[223] § 153 (1) StPO: "In a case involving a less serious criminal offense, the public prosecution office may, with the consent of the court competent to order the opening of the main proceedings and with the consent of the accused, dispense with preferment of public charges and concurrently impose a condition upon the accused" (translation by Brian Duffett and Monika Ebinger, authorised by the German Federal Ministry of Justice). See also Rainer Hamm, "Wie kann das Strafverfahren jenseits der Verständigung künftig praxisgerechter gestaltet werden – sind Reformen des Strafprozesses erforderlich?: Vorgeschichte und Folgen der BVerfG-Entscheidung zu § 257c StPO", in *Strafverteidiger*, 2013, vol. 33, pp. 652, 653, who refers to § 153a StPO as a "gateway drug for deals" (translation by the authors).

[224] Federal Constitutional Court of Germany ('BVerfG'), in *Neue Zeitschrift für Strafrecht*, 1987, p. 419; BGHSt 43, see *supra* note 222.

[225] Bachmaier, 2015, p. 96, see *supra* note 36.

[226] See *Begründung zum Gesetzesentwurf der Bundesregierung*, BT-Drs. 16/12310, p. 13; Ambos and Ziehn, 2011, mn. 18, 27, see *supra* note 218.

---

gaining pretends to square the circle: on the one hand, the trial shall be expedited and costs lowered, while on the other hand, the inquisitorial principles governing the German criminal process shall not be disposed of and the creation of a "new 'consensual' procedural tool"[227] is not an option, as the Federal Constitutional Court of Germany ruled in 2013. It will be seen whether these conflicting interests can be reconciled in practice.[228]

---

[227] Federal Constitutional Court of Germany, Judgment of 19 March 2013, No. 2 BvR 2628/10, 2 BvR 2883/10, 2 BvR 2155/11, in *Decisions of the Federal Constitutional Court of Germany*, vol. 133, pp. 168, 206 and in *Neue Juristische Wochenschrift*, 2013, p. 1058, 1062 mn. 67; in more detail and with a differentiated view Martin Niemöller, "Anmerkung zu Verfassungsmäßigkeit des Verständigungsgesetzes", in *Strafverteidiger*, 2013, vol. 33, pp. 419, 421. Kubiciel opines that the judgment of the Constitutional Court did not change the situation, i.e., the German legislator is still entitled to create new tools to end proceedings by way of consent; see Michael Kubiciel, "Zwischen Effektivität und Legitimität: Zum Handlungsspielraum des Gesetzgebers nach der 'Deal'-Entscheidung des BVerfG", in *Onlinezeitschrift für Höchstrichterliche Rechtsprechung zum Strafrecht*, 2014, vol. 15, no. 6, pp. 204, 207. About a possible reform and/or amendment of § 257c StPO see also Eberhard Kempf, "Das Absprachen-Urteil des Bundesverfassungsgerichts und die Aktualität legislatorischer Entscheidungen", in *Strafverteidiger Forum*, 2014, pp. 105, 107 ff.; Frank Meyer, "Praxis und Reform der Absprache im Strafverfahren", in *Strafverteidiger*, 2015, pp. 790, 792 ff.

[228] Critically, see Klaus Leipold, "Die gesetzliche Regelung der Verständigung im Strafverfahren", in *Neue Juristische Wochenschrift – Spezial*, 2009, p. 521, regarding the wording of the code as "*bloße Farce*", since the purpose of plea bargaining is to dispense with the further investigation of the case; see also Uwe Murmann, "Reform ohne Wiederkehr? – Die gesetzliche Regelung der Absprachen im Strafverfahren", in *Zeitschrift für Internationale Strafrechtsdogmatik*, 2009, vol. 10, pp. 534 and 538: "Aushöhlung der Prozessmaximen bei deren gleichzeitiger verbaler Aufrechterhaltung" [Erosion of the procedural principles while they are at the same time rethorically upheld] (translation by the authors); Uwe Murmann, "Probleme der gesetzlichen Regelung der Absprachen im Strafverfahren", in Manfred Heinrich, Christian Jäger and Bernd Schünemann (eds.), *Strafrecht als Scientia Universalis. Festschrift für Claus Roxin zum 80. Geburtstag am 15. Mai 2011*, vol. 2, De Gruyter, Berlin, 2011, pp. 1385, 1389–90; Gunnar Duttge, "Die Urteilsabsprachen als Signum einer rechtlichen Steuerungskrise", in Roland Hefendehl, Tatjana Hörnle and Luis Greco, *Streitbare Strafrechtswissenschaft. Festschrift für Bernd Schünemann zum 70. Geburtstag am 1. November 2014*, De Gruyter, Berlin, 2014, pp. 875, 884: "performative[r] Selbstwiderspruch" (performative self-contradiction, translation by the authors); Christoph Knauer and Andreas Lickleder, "Die obergerichtliche Rechtsprechung zu Verfahrensabsprachen nach der gesetzlichen Regelung – ein kritischer Überblick", in *Neue Zeitschrift für Strafrecht*, 2012, vol. 32, pp. 366, 367: "Mogelpackung" (sham package, translation by the authors); Kyriakos N. Kotsoglou, "Über die 'Verständigung' im Strafverfahren als Aussageerpressung: Eine materiell-rechtliche Studie zu §257c StPO", in *Zeitschrift für international Strafrechtsdogmatik*, 2015, vol. 10, pp. 175, 185: § 257c Abs. 1 S. 2 as *petitio principii*; crit. also Karl Heinz Gössel, "Über den unaufhebbaren Gegensatz zwischen Wahrheitsermittlungspflicht (§ 244 Abs. 2 StPO) und verfahrensverkürzenden Abreden (§ 257c StPO) im Strafprozess. Auch: Über mögliche Gründe einer unzulänglichen verfas-

3.4.3.2. Advantages and Disadvantages of Negotiated Justice

The remaining contention between supporters and objectors of plea bargaining refers to the principle of legality as opposed to the principle of opportunity. On the one hand, those who strongly support plea bargaining stress its advantages for all persons involved in the criminal process.

First, the prosecution saves the time and expense of a trial (and appeal),[229] thus being able to maintain control over their caseloads by reducing enforcement costs per case[230] and by minimising the risk of an acquittal.[231] In fact, plea bargains pave the way for increasing the overall number of prosecuted offenders,[232] thereby enabling the prosecution to further its goals of deterrence, incapacitation and retribution.[233] Last but not

---

sungsrechtlichen Argumentation", in Christian Fahl, Eckhart Müller, Helmut Satzger and Sabine Swoboda (eds.), *Festschrift für Werner Beulke zum 70. Geburtstag*, C.F.Müller, Heidelberg, 2015, p. 737.

[229] Maffei, 2004, p. 1064, see *supra* note 183. As of 2006, about 94 per cent of all federal criminal cases in the USA were settled by plea bargaining; see Steven G. Calabresi, "The Comparative Constitutional Law Scholarship of Professor Mirjan Damaška: A Tribute", in Bruce Ackerman, Kai Ambos and Hrvoje Sikirić (eds.), *Visions of Justice – Liber Amicorum Mirjan Damaška*, Duncker & Humblot, Berlin, 2016, pp. 96, 109; in a similar vein Turner, 2013, p. 36, see *supra* note 194; Stephanos Bibas, "Designing Plea Bargaining from the Ground Up: Accuracy and Fairness Without Trials as Backstops", in *William & Mary Law Review*, 2016, vol. 57, no. 4, pp. 1055, 1058; Darryl K. Brown, "Judicial Power to Regulate Plea Bargaining", in *William & Mary Law Review*, 2016, vol. 57, no. 4, p. 1225, 1228 (95 per cent); McCleery, 2016, p. 1110 (90 per cent), *supra* note 66. In 2009–2010, in the Crown Court of England '73.5 percent of charged defendants pled guilty, and 91 percent of convictions occurred through guilty pleas' (*ibid.*, p. 1267). See also Brian D. Johnson, Ryan D. King and Cassia Spohn, "Sociolegal Approaches to the Study of Guilty Pleas and Prosecution", in *Annual Review of Law and Social Science*, (2016), vol. 12, pp. 479, 480–81 with figure 1.

[230] See Frank H. Easterbrook, "Criminal Procedure as a Market System", in *Journal of Legal Studies*, 1983, vol. 12, no. 2, p. 299; Turner, 2013, p. 36, see *supra* note 194.

[231] Jacqueline E. Ross, "Criminal Law and Procedure: The Entrenched Position of Plea Bargaining in United States Legal Practice", in *American Journal of Comparative Law*, 2006, vol. 54, p. 717, claiming that plea bargaining allows the prosecution to dispose cases efficiently.

[232] F. Andrew Hessick III and Reshma Saujani, "Plea Bargaining and Convicting the Innocent: The Role of the Prosecutor, the Defense Counsel, and the Judge", in *BYU Journal of Public Law*, 2002, vol. 16, no. 2, p. 191.

[233] Crit. Christopher Slobogin, "Plea Bargaining and the Substance and Procedural Goals of Criminal Justice: From Retribution and Adversarialism to Preventive Justice and Hybrid-Inquisitorialism", in *William & Mary Law Review*, 2016, vol. 57, no. 4, pp. 1505, 1509–16.

---

least, plea bargains shorten the period of time between the criminal incident and the act of punishment.[234]

Second, the defendant can reduce the overall costs he faces.[235] In the United States these costs include both the criminal punishment and its accompanying trial costs. While criminal punishment comprises both the formal legal sanction imposed on the defendant (for example, years of imprisonment and/or fines) and reputation and opportunity costs (such as loss of income),[236] the trial costs encompass monetary and emotional resources, the time spent in conducting a full trial, and the cost of facing uncertainty (for risk-averse defendants).[237] By negotiating a plea bargain, the defendant can acquire a "discount" in the criminal sanction (conviction for a lesser crime or a lighter sentence), and avoid the accompanying trial costs.[238] Thus, in Germany the accused can gain a chance for a reduced sentence and avoid long public trials that may infringe his privacy.[239] Indeed, the avoidance of a sensational appearance in court is an important incentive to submit to a bargaining procedure. In Italy, for instance, when an application for a bargained penalty is accepted by the court, the judgment is drafted immediately and no public appearance of the defendant in the courtroom is necessary.[240] This is a significant difference from the procedure adopted in England or the United States, where the defendant is required to appear in court, listen to the public arraignment and admit that he or she is

---

[234] See John G. Douglass, "Fatal Attraction? The Uneasy Courtship of *Brady* and Plea Bargaining", in *Emory Law Journal*, 2001, vol. 50, no. 2, p. 439, fn. 6, quoting Santobello, 404 U.S. 257 (1971).

[235] Talia Fisher, "The Boundaries of Plea Bargaining: Negotiating the Standard of Proof", in *Journal of Criminal Law and Criminology*, 2007, vol. 97, no. 4, p. 953. For an economic analysis of plea bargaining in detail, see Russell D. Covey, "Plea Bargaining and Price Theory", in *George Washington Law Review*, 2016, vol. 84, no. 4, pp. 920, 923 ff.

[236] See Shanya M. Sigman, "Comment: An Analysis of Rule 11 Plea Bargain Options", in *University of Chicago Law Review*, 1999, vol. 66, no. 4, p. 1322.

[237] See John P. Gould, "The Economics of Legal Conflicts", in *Journal of Legal Studies*, 1973, vol. 2, no. 2, p. 281, discussing the effect of the defendant's attitude toward risk on the unexpected cost of the trial option.

[238] Fisher, 2007, p. 954, see *supra* note 235.

[239] Stefan Braun, "Gründe für das Auftreten von Absprachen im Strafverfahren", in *Anwaltsblatt*, 2000, p. 226; especially about plea bargaining in criminal trials relating to economic offences, see Kai-D. Bussmann and Christian Lüdemann, "Rechtsbeugung oder rationale Verfahrenspraxis? Über informelle Absprachen in Wirtschaftsstrafver-fahren", in *Monatsschrift für Kriminologie und Strafreform*, 1988, p. 84.

[240] Maffei, 2004, p. 1064, see *supra* note 183.

"guilty".[241] Furthermore, in Italy the judgment served as a result of an application for a negotiated penalty has no effect in related civil or disciplinary proceedings.[242] In other words, in such proceedings, the defendant may still claim innocence or contest the findings of the criminal judgment. Last but not least, defendants will have the conviction expunged from their record after a few years if, in the meantime, they are not convicted for an offence of a similar nature.

Third, other persons involved in the proceedings also benefit from plea bargaining. The defence counsel saves time for other activities and increases the chance of getting new mandates by defending the client successfully.[243] Furthermore, plea bargaining may protect witnesses by lifting psychological pressure.[244]

On the other hand, critics of plea bargaining point to its negative side effects. Interestingly, these objectors come especially from the home country of plea bargaining, the United States.[245] Calabresi even opines that the existence of plea bargaining – giving prosecutors a "huge discretion to be lenient or harsh unguided by any truly constraining rules" – gives the US federal criminal procedure an inquisitorial undertone.[246] There are, first, some courts stating that as a result of plea bargaining the sentencing discounts offered in exchange for guilty pleas can pressure defendants to waive their right to trial.[247] Although this is, to some extent, accepted as a legitimate and inevitable part of plea bargaining, the US Supreme Court has warned: "[C]onfronting a defendant with the risk of more severe punishment clearly may have a discouraging effect on the defendant's assertion of his trial rights".[248] Furthermore, in condoning these pressures of plea bargaining, courts have noted that the criminal justice system has many fea-

---

[241] *Ibid.*

[242] *Ibid.*, p. 1065.

[243] Stefan Braun, "Gründe für das Auftreten von Absprachen im Strafverfahren", in *Anwaltsblatt*, 2000, p. 226.

[244] BGHSt 43, p. 203, see *supra* note 222.

[245] Cf. Pati, 2009, see *supra* note 187.

[246] Calabresi, 2016, p. 109, see *supra* note 229. In the same vein very plainly Slobogin, 2016, p. 1516, see *supra* note 233: "Plea bargaining also makes a mockery of our procedural traditions".

[247] Turner, 2013, p. 37, see *supra* note 194.

[248] *United States v. Mezzanatto*, 513 U.S. 196, 1995, pp. 209–10; Gwladys Gilliéron, "Wrongful Convictions in Switzerland: A Problem of Summary Proceedings", in *University of Cincinnati Law Review*, 2012, vol. 80, no. 4, pp. 1145, 1155.

tures that are coercive. For example, the existence of the indictment alone might pressure some accused to plead guilty.[249] Even worse, neither the US Constitution nor the Bill of Rights include references to the constitutionality of plea bargaining while the accused is brought to waive guarantees enshrined in the Fifth, Sixth and Fourteenth Amendments that have always been seen by the US Supreme Court as the basis of the American adversarial system.[250]

Second, scholars maintain that plea bargaining entails the potential risk of producing unfair and inaccurate results,[251] for example, a lack of reliable information about the strength of the evidence and about the expected post-trial versus post-plea sentence could prevent the defendant from making an intelligent choice to waive his right to trial. Moreover, the lack of information may produce sentences that are too high or too low in relation to the defendant's blameworthiness.[252] Some even draw parallels to the medieval European judicial torture, stating, *inter alia*, that both laws focus on inducing the accused to confess guilt, rather than having the accusers prove it, taking into account the "illusory safeguard of voluntarism".[253] Thus, some strongly demand the prohibition of plea bargaining,[254] partly with the additional statement to replace it "with a system that permits a defendant to elect a judicially administered, nonadversary, expeditious alternative to the traditional Anglo-Saxon trial".[255]

---

[249] *Brady v. United States*, 397 U.S. 742, 1970, p. 750.

[250] See *Nix v. Willams*, 467 U.S. 431, 1984, p. 453.

[251] Wayne R. LaFave, Jerold H. Israel and Nancy J. King, *Criminal Procedure*, vol. 5, 2nd ed., West Group, St Paul, 1999, p. 10; Turner, 2013, p. 37, see *supra* note 194.

[252] Jenia Iontcheva Turner, "Judicial Participation in Plea Negotiations", in *American Journal of Comparative Law*, 2006, vol. 54, no. 1, p. 207.

[253] See John H. Langbein, "Torture and Plea Bargaining", in Joel Feinberg and Hyman Gross (eds.), *Philosophy of Law*, 7th ed., Thomson/Wadsworth, Belmont, CA, 2004, p. 338. See also Donald A. Dripps, "Guilt, Innocence, And Due Process of Plea Bargaining", in *William & Mary Law Review*, 2016, vol. 57, no. 4, pp. 1343, 1364 ff.

[254] See National Advisory Commission on Criminal Justice Standards and Goals, *The Courts*, US Government Printing Office, Washington, DC, 1973, § 3.1; Moise Berger, "The Case against Plea Bargaining", in *American Bar Association Journal*, 1976, vol. 62, no. 5, p. 621; Raymond I. Parnas and Riley J. Atkins, "Abolishing Plea Bargaining: A Proposal", in *Criminal Law Bulletin*, 1978, vol. 14, no. 2, p. 101.

[255] George W. Pugh and Dallis W. Radamaker, "A Plea for Greater Judicial Control over Sentencing and Abolition of the Present Plea Bargaining System", in *Louisiana Law Review*, 1981, vol. 42, no. 1, p. 80. For further discussion on the advantages and disad-

Objections against plea bargaining in German criminal procedure are above all principled, arguing that the inquisitorial, judge-led and truth-driven German criminal process does not allow for elements of negotiations of this kind. Similar concerns have been expressed as to the Spanish *conformidad*.[256] The accused may become an "object of the trial" who, surrounded by professional lawyers, may incriminate himself ignoring the *nemo tenetur* principle.[257] Moreover, it is said that the prosecution violates the principle of legality while the judge violates the principle of an oral and public trial when plea bargaining is allowed.[258]

3.4.3.3. Conditions for Plea Bargaining

After measuring the advantages and disadvantages of plea bargaining, we conclude that the use of plea bargaining is more disputed in countries governed by the legality principle than in those with the opportunity principle. Be that as it may, there is no disagreement as to the necessity of strict conditions to be imposed on the use of plea bargaining. Needless to say, those conditions depend on many factors which vary from country to country[259] and they are very much dependant on the legal tradition of a country. Thus, rules referring to plea bargaining are much easier to grasp in continental Europe than in common law countries like England or the United States since there are generally fewer rules in continental procedure than in common law procedure. The reason for this difference is taken up by Pizzi, who compares the (alleged) common law–continental law antagonism with the difference between the American and European versions of football. While the former has "many, often extremely complicated, rules", in the latter there are "comparatively few rules and most are rather easy to express".[260] Furthermore, while a professional American football game "requires many

---

vantages of plea bargaining in the United States, see LaFave *et al.*, 1999, p. 10 ff., *supra* note 251.

[256] Bachmaier, 2015, pp. 107–8, see *supra* note 36.

[257] Ambos and Ziehn, 2011, mn. 3, see *supra* note 218; Winfried Hassemer, "Pacta sunt servanda – auch im Strafprozeß? – BGH, NJW 1989, 2270", in *Juristische Schulung*, 1989, p. 892; Weigend, 1999, p. 57, see *supra* note 221; cf. also Bernd Schünemann, "Die Verständigung im Strafprozeß – Wunderwaffe oder Bankrotterklärung der Verteidigung?", in *Neue Juristische Wochenschrift*, 1989, p. 1899 ff.: "point of no return" of the defence counsel.

[258] Schünemann, 1990, B84 ff., see *supra* note 221; also Hassemer, 1989, see *supra* note 257.

[259] Thaman, 2007, p. 22 ff., see *supra* note 62.

[260] Pizzi, 1999, p. 8, see *supra* note 41.

---

officials and many whistles on the field", there is only one referee (and two assistants) in a soccer game.[261] Those contrasts have strong parallels when one compares American and European criminal trials.[262]

3.4.3.3.1. Crimes and Maximum Sentences

The first – and one of the most important – conditions on plea bargaining is which crimes allow for a plea. On the one hand, as for the common law countries where plea bargaining is theoretically less controversial than in countries with a legality principle, the United States does not restrict plea bargaining with regard to the nature of the crime, that is, it is admitted with regard to any criminal charge.[263] In Argentina, whose plea bargaining model is based on the US model,[264] the *procedimiento abreviado* can be applied to some, though not all, serious offences; it can be applied, for instance, to manslaughter, rape and aggravated robbery.[265]

On the other hand, civil law countries are still reluctant to allow plea bargaining for most serious cases.[266] A country where the jurisdiction has gone farther than any other civil law country with regard to the forms of Anglo-American criminal procedure is Italy.[267] However, the Italian model does not adopt the US model in an identical fashion, but primarily takes the nature of the crime and the character of the defendant into account. As to the former, a *patteggiamento* cannot be used in the case of crimes related to pornography, paedophilia and sexual harassment or for habitual professional criminals.[268] In 2003 an extended form of *patteggiamento allargato* was introduced by statute,[269] moving the legal threshold up to offences punishable by less than seven and a half years in prison (the old form was only five years). However, the extended *patteggiamento* does not apply if (a) the

---

[261] *Ibid.*

[262] See further *ibid.*

[263] Thaman, 2007, p. 22, see *supra* note 62.

[264] See Niño, 1998, pp. 628–29, *supra* note 215.

[265] Cf. Langer, 2004, p. 55, see *supra* note 207.

[266] Damaška, 2004, p. 1025, see *supra* note 183.

[267] *Ibid.*

[268] Thomas Weigend, "Die Reform des Strafverfahrens", in *Zeitschrift für die Gesamte Strafrechtswissenschaft*, 1992, vol. 104, p. 493; Thaman, 2007, p. 40, see *supra* note 62.

[269] Legge 12 giugno 2003, n.134, *Modifiche al codice di procedura penale in materia di applicazione della pena su richiesta delle parti* (GU no. 136 del 14-6-2003); McCleery, 2016, p. 1115, see *supra* note 66; Verena and Brutaru, 2014, p. 102, see *supra* note 66.

offence relates to the area of organised crime or (b) the suspect is of "bad character". Commentators acknowledge that the 2003 reform has enormously broadened the area of negotiation; offences such as sexual assault, assisting suicide and corruption of judges may now be disposed of through bargains between defence and prosecution. Moreover, since the threshold of seven and a half years refers to the penalty after the reduction for any mitigating factor that may be relevant, crimes such as manslaughter or even homicide may sometimes fall within the ambit of the *patteggiamento allargato*.[270] In case an agreement between the parties is reached at early stages, informally, an informal, non-codified way of "charge" bargaining may still take place to "under-qualify" the charges to make them *patteggiamento* eligible.[271]

In France the law establishes a procedure of initial appearance upon prior admission of guilt (Article 495(7)–(16) CPP) which is quite different from the US-influenced *patteggiamento* of Italy.[272] Such a procedure may only be used for offences punishable by fines or imprisonment not exceeding five years but not for minors under the age of 18, for offences concerning the media, political offences, "involuntary" homicide and offences of which the prosecution falls under a specific law (Article 495–16 CPP). In Spain the *conformidad* may usually be applied for crimes sentenced by no more than six years.[273] However, the introduction of fast-track proceedings in 2002 into Spanish law has made it possible for a defendant to enunciate his or her *conformidad* in any case in which the public prosecutor is requesting a sentence up to 10 years. Last but not least, juvenile cases are excluded from a *Verständigung* in Germany because of the special character of those cases and proceedings.[274]

---

[270] For further discussion, see Maffei, 2004, pp. 1062–63, see *supra* note 183.

[271] *Ibid.*, pp. 1061–62.

[272] Henri-D. Bosly, "Admission of Guilt before the ICC and in Continental Systems", in *Journal of International Criminal Justice*, 2004, vol. 2, no. 4, p. 1045.

[273] Bachmaier, 2015, p. 98, see *supra* note 36. About the 2013 proposal for a new Code of Criminal Procedure in Spain, which provided, *inter alia*, for plea bargaining, see Lorenzo M. Bujosa Vadell, "Discretionary Justice at the Initiation of a Criminal Investigation", in Michele Caianiello and Jacqueline S. Hodgson (eds), *Discretionary Criminal Justice in a Comparative Context*, Carolina Academic Press, Durham, 2015, pp. 13, 20.

[274] Ambos and Ziehn, 2011, mn. 15, see *supra* note 218; Christian Fahl, "Der Deal im Jugendstrafverfahren und das sog. Schlechterstellungsverbot", in *Neue Zeitschrift für Strafrecht*, 2009, vol. 29, no. 11, p. 615, arguing that criminal law relating to juveniles should be kept free from negotiated justice. Against a complete exclusion of plea bargain-

3.4.3.3.2. Admission of Guilt Required?

As we can see, the different procedural traditions leave little room for academic consensus when it comes to the introduction or application of plea bargaining. The existing diversity between civil law and common law countries persists in respect of the question whether an admission of guilt by the defendant or a confession is required.[275] Importantly, it must be stressed that an admission of guilt has to be distinguished from guilty plea in the American system. In the case of the former the court is, despite the confession, still obliged to determine whether the confession is credible and supported by corroborating evidence.[276] In general terms, the difference between common and civil law countries regarding the confession of the accused is that in the former he has to confess his guilt while in the latter he has only to confess the incriminating evidence – whether he is guilty or not is a matter for the court to decide.[277] In the words of Antonio Cassese, the admission of guilt in civil law countries is "simply a part of the evidence to be considered and evaluated by the court".[278]

In Italy the term *applicazione della pena sulla richieste delle parte* (application of penalty upon the request of party) already indicates that only a request for punishment and not an admission of guilt or a confession is

---

ing: Michael Lindemann, "Zu der Wirksamkeit der Absprachen im Strafprozess", in *Juristische Rundschau*, 2009, pp. 82 ff. For a differentiating view: Torsten Noak, "Urteilsabsprachen im Jugendstrafrecht", in *Strafverteidiger*, 2002, p. 449: no plea bargaining should be used in case of educational measures, means of correction and juvenile punishment because of harmful habits; however, plea bargaining is possible in case of a juvenile punishment because of the gravity of the guilt.

[275] McCleery, 2016, p. 1117, see *supra* note 66. A confession is regarded as an admission of guilt made by the accused during the investigation or the trial; see Anna Petrig, "Negotiated Justice and the goals of International Criminal Tribunals", in *Chicago-Kent Journal of International and Comparative Law*, 2008, vol. 8, p. 6.

[276] Michael Bohlander, "Plea-Bargaining before the ICTY", in Richard May, David Tolbert, John Hocking, Ken Roberts, JIA Bing Bing, Daryl Mundis and Gabriël Oosthuizen (eds.), *Essays on ICTY Procedure and Evidence: In Honour of Gabrielle Kirk McDonald*, Kluwer, The Hague, 2001, p. 151.

[277] Damaška, 2004, p. 1025, see *supra* note 183; Turner, 2013, p. 37, see *supra* note 194. For an instructive distinction between plea bargains and confessions, see Brandon L. Garrett, "Why Plea Bargains are not Confessions", in *William & Mary Law Review*, 2016, vol. 57, no. 4, pp. 1415 ff.

[278] International Criminal Tribunal for the former Yugoslavia, *Prosecutor v. Dražen Erdemović*, Appeals Chamber, Separate and Dissenting Opinion of Judge Cassese, IT-96-22-A, 7 October 1997, para. 7 (http://www.legal-tools.org/doc/a7dff6/).

---

required.[279] Similarly, an explicit admission of guilt is not presupposed by the Spanish *conformidad* procedure.[280] However, the defendant must concede that he or she is the accused who has been charged.[281] In civil law countries the lack of an admission of guilt and the fact that the responsibility of the accused is not entirely established by the court mean that the ensuing criminal conviction is considered flawed, since a full conviction requires the full clarification of the facts and the accused's criminal responsibility and a declaration of the legal consequences emanating from such an ascertainment.[282] Thus, a further clarification of the facts can only be dispensed of if an admission of guilt exists. For this reason, in France the law establishes a procedure of initial appearance upon prior admission of guilt (Article 495(7)–(16) CPP).[283] The same applies in Germany, where even a partial guilty plea *shall* be part of a *Verständigung*.[284] This differs from the hitherto existing jurisdiction that qualified guilty plea as a centrepiece of every *Absprache*. The word "shall" now suggests that other procedural conduct of the accused, by which he expresses his goodwill (for example, the consent of the accused to submit evidence), may have the same effect as a guilty plea.[285] However, a *Verständigung* about the guilty verdict,[286] a

---

[279] See Astolfo Di Amato, "Italy", in Roger Blanpain (ed.), *International Encyclopaedia of Laws: Criminal Law*, vol. 3, no. 1, Kluwer Law, The Hague, 2008, p. 159; Rachel A. Van Cleave, "An Offer You Can't Refuse? Punishment Without Trial in Italy and the United States: The Search for Truth and an Efficient Criminal Justice System", in *Emory International Law Review*, 1997, vol. 11, p. 442.

[280] For a detailed description of the Spanish *conformidad* procedure see Verena and Brutaru, 2014, p. 110, *supra* note 66.

[281] Bachmaier, 2015, p. 98, see *supra* note 36 ("The guilty plea is a formal procedural act, which means that it must be expressed at the moment provided for it").

[282] Maffei, 2004, p. 1063, see *supra* note 183. In Germany, for instance, the reasons for the judgment must show the facts deemed to be proven and establishing the statutory elements of the criminal offence (§ 267 StPO). On the contrary, in the United States the content of a criminal conviction consists of the facts inherent in a jury's verdict or embraced by a defendant's plea and prohibited courts from enhancing or aggravating this content through factual findings at sentencing; see *Apprendi v. New Jersey*, 530 U.S. 2000, p. 490; and *Blakely v. Washington*, 542 U.S., 2005, p. 296.

[283] Bosly, 2004, p. 1045, see *supra* note 272.

[284] § 257c(2) clause 2 StPO; Ambos and Ziehn, 2011, mn. 25, see *supra* note 218.

[285] Crit. Lutz Meyer-Goßner, "§ 257c StPO", in Lutz Meyer-Goßner and Bertram Schmitt (eds.), *Strafprozessordnung*, 58th ed., C.H. Beck, Munich, 2015, mn. 16, who requires a guilty plea (vis-à-vis other procedural conduct) for *Verständigungen* related to certain legal consequences; see also Julia Peters, *Urteilsabsprachen im Strafprozess. Die deutsche Regelung im Vergleich mit Entwicklungen in England & Wales, Frankreich und Polen*, Universitätsverlag Göttingen, Göttingen, 2011, pp. 200–1; Uwe Murmann, "Probleme der ge-

Verständigung about measures of reform and prevention (*Maßregeln der Besserung und Sicherung*, § 61 StGB)[287] – even when the courts have discretion to impose them[288] – and a waiver to file an appeal (*Rechtsmittelverzicht*)[289] are inadmissible. In Romania, although the accused is only required to admit the relevant factual circumstances, "including those that *lead* to the determination of guilt", this can certainly be viewed as an "implicit acknowledgment of guilt".[290]

In the United States there is no consistent legal practice the question of whether an admission of guilt by the defendant is required. First, in some courts, it is up to the defendant to accept a plea bargaining or to only enter a plea of *nolo contendere*. In this context, *nolo contendere* means intent to "not contest" the charges, and does not necessitate an explicit admission of guilt. In the German system, such a *nolo contendere* would be insufficient

---

setzlichen Regelung der Absprachen im Strafverfahren", in Manfred Heinrich, Christian Jäger and Bernd Schünemann (eds.), *Strafrecht als Scientia Universalis. Festschrift für Claus Roxin zum 80. Geburtstag am 15. Mai 2011*, vol. 2, De Gruyter, Berlin, 2011, pp. 1385, 1393, who opines that a procedural conduct of the accused that leads to an abbreviated procedure should not be relevant for sentencing.

[286] BGHSt 43, p. 204, see *supra* note 222, reprinted in *Neue Zeitschrift für Strafrecht*, 1998, p. 33; Carl-Friedrich Stuckenberg, "§ 257c StPO", in Volker Erb, Robert Esser, Ulrich Franke, Kirsten Graalmann-Scheerer, Hans Hilger and Alexander Ignor, *Löwe-Rosenberg: Die Strafprozessordnung und das Gerichtsverfassungsgesetz*, vol. 6/2, 26th ed., De Gruyter, Berlin, 2013, mn. 29 and Federal Constitutional Court of Germany, Judgment of 19 March 2013, No. 2 BvR 2628/10, 2 BvR 2883/10, 2 BvR 2155/11, in *Decisions of the Federal Constitutional Court of Germany*, vol. 133, pp. 168, 227.

[287] BGH, NStZ-RR 2005, p. 39, about the imposition of preventive detention; Ambos and Ziehn, 2011, mn. 18, see *supra* note 218.

[288] Stefan König and Stefan Harrendorf, "§ 257c StPO", in Dieter Dölling, Gunnar Duttge and Dieter Rössner (eds.), *Handkommentar – Gesamtes Strafrecht*, 3rd ed., Nomos, Baden-Baden, 2013, mn. 9; in more detail Hans-Joachim Weidner, "Das Verbot der Verständigung über Maßregeln der Besserung und Sicherung – § 257c Abs. 2 Satz 3 StPO", in Klaus Bernsmann and Thomas Fischer (eds.), *Festschrift für Ruth Rissing-van Saan zum 65. Geburtstag am 25. Januar 2011*, De Gruyter, Berlin, 2011, pp. 731, 733 ff.; crit. Gerhard Altvater, "Kann nach der gesetzlichen Regelung der Verständigung im Strafverfahren noch auf die bisherige Rechtsprechung des Bundesgerichtshofs zur Urteilsabsprache zurückgegriffen werden?", in Klaus Bernsmann and Thomas Fischer (eds.), *Festschrift für Ruth Rissing-van Saan zum 65. Geburtstag am 25. Januar 2011*, De Gruyter, Berlin, 2011, pp. 1, 5.

[289] § 302(1) clause 2, StPO.

[290] Article 320 of the Criminal Procedure Code of Romania. See in more detail Verena and Brutaru, 2014, p. 97, *supra* note 66 (emphasis added).

---

to trigger a *Verständigung*.[291] Second, in other courts, judges only accept the plea following an admission of guilt. Third, and most interestingly, it may be even possible that the guilty plea will be accepted where the defendant in fact denied the commitment of the offence charged; this practice was regarded by the Supreme Court as lawful as long as the judge made sure there was a factual basis for the finding of guilty,[292] although this issue was highly disputed among state and lower federal courts.[293]

In Argentina, as part of the agreement, the defendant must admit to the offence and his participation in it as described in the indictment.[294] Fur-

---

[291] Federal Constitutional Court of Germany, Judgment of 19 March 2013, No. 2 BvR 2628/10, 2 BvR 2883/10, 2 BvR 2155/11, in *Decisions of the Federal Constitutional Court of Germany*, vol. 133, p. 209, and in *Neue Juristische Wochenschrift*, 2013, p. 1058, 1063, mn. 70; Martin Heger and Robert Pest, "Verständigungen im Strafverfahren nach dem Urteil des Bundesverfassungsgerichts", in *Zeitschrift für die gesamte Strafrechtswissenschaft*, 2014, vol. 126, p. 457; Knauer and Lickleder, 2012, p. 372, see *supra* note 228; Herbert Landau, "Das Urteil des Zweiten Senats des BVerfG zu den Absprachen im Strafprozess vom 19. März 2013", in *Neue Zeitschrift für Strafrecht*, 2014, vol. 34, p. 430; Hartmut Schneider, "Überblick über die höchstrichterliche Rechtsprechung zur Verfahrensverständigung im Anschluss an das Urteil des BverfG vom 19. März 2013 – Teil 1", in *Neue Zeitschrift für Strafrecht*, 2014, vol. 34, p. 193.

[292] *North Carolina v. Alford*, 400 U.S., 1970, p. 25, at 91; S.Ct. (1970), p. 160. In this case, the accused was indicted for first-degree murder. His attorney questioned all but one of the various witnesses who appellee said would substantiate his claim of innocence. The witnesses, however, did not support the accused's story but gave statements that strongly indicated his guilt. Faced with strong evidence of guilt and no substantial evidentiary support for the claim of innocence, the accused's attorney recommended that he plead guilty, but left the ultimate decision to the accused himself. The prosecutor agreed to accept a plea of guilty to a charge of second-degree murder, and thus the accused pleaded guilty to the reduced charge. The Supreme Court stated:

> That [the accused] would not have pleaded except for the opportunity to limit the possible penalty does not necessarily demonstrate that the plea of guilty was not the product of a free and rational choice, especially where the defendant was represented by competent counsel whose advice was that the plea would be to the defendant's advantage.

[293] On the one hand, for example, *Harris v. State*, 76 Tex.Cr.R., 1915, p. 131; 172 S.W., 1915, p. 977, requires that trial judges reject such pleas. On the other hand, in *Tremblay v. Overholser*, 199 F.Supp., 1961, p. 570, the court concluded that they should not "force any defense on a defendant in a criminal case", particularly when advancement of the defence might "end in disaster", arguing that, since "guilt, or the degree of guilt, is at times uncertain and elusive",

> (a)n accused, though believing in or entertaining doubts respecting his innocence, might reasonably conclude a jury would be convinced of his guilt and that he would fare better in the sentence by pleading guilty.

[294] Article 431*bis*(2) CPP.

---

thermore, the *procedimiento abreviado* includes an admission of guilt by the defendant similar to a guilty plea.[295] However, this admission of guilt is not understood exactly as a guilty plea in the United States, but rather as a confession that may be disregarded by the court, exemplifying the influence of the pre-existing inquisitorial structure on the practice.[296]

3.4.3.4. Plea Bargaining Procedure

As to procedure, the questions of who negotiates, when this negotiation takes place and how it is to be done are answered differently in every legal system.

In Spain the prosecution submits a sentencing request. If such a request does not exceed the maximum sentence of six years and the accused agrees to it, the court may adopt the prosecution's proposal as accepted by the accused without further hearings.[297] Italian law is silent as to the mode of the negotiations. There are no formalities governing the matter and no court supervision is provided for at this stage.[298] In practice, the defence counsel would approach the public prosecutor to draft an agreement, which is followed by a written request with the pre-trial judge in case the agreement contains a specific penalty. In addition, this agreement must be reached before closing speeches start at the committal hearing to ensure procedural economy.[299]

In Germany a *Verständigung* has to take place during the main proceedings,[300] which is different from Spanish law, where a *conformidad* may take place in the intermediate trial stage.[301] However, the possibility of a

---

[295] Cf. Langer, 2004, p. 55, see *supra* note 207.

[296] *Ibid.*

[297] See Gimeno Sendra, V. Moreno Catena and V. Cortes Dominguez, *Lecciones de derecho procesal penal*, E. Colex, Madrid, 2001, pp. 340–44; Jean Pradel, *Droit pénal comparé*, 2nd ed., Dalloz, Paris, 2002, pp. 611–12; Bachmaier, 2015, p. 98–99, see *supra* note 36.

[298] Maffei, 2004, p. 1062, see *supra* note 183.

[299] *Ibid.* When no committal hearing is held, the agreement must be reached before the formal opening of the trial.

[300] Emphasised by the Federal Constitutional Court of Germany, Judgment of 19 March 2013, No. 2 BvR 2628/10, 2 BvR 2883/10, 2 BvR 2155/11, in *Decisions of the Federal Constitutional Court of Germany*, vol. 133, p. 168, 217, and in *Neue Juristische Wochenschrift*, 2013, pp. 1058, 1065, mn. 86. See already German Federal Court of Justice, Judgment of 28 August 1997, No. 4 StR 240/97, in *Decisions of the German Federal Court of Justice*, vol. 43, pp. 195, 204 ff., and in *Neue Zeitschrift für Strafrecht*, 1998, pp. 31, 33–34.

[301] Bosly, 2004, p. 1044, see *supra* note 272.

Verständigung shall be "discussed" (*erörtert*) before the actual hearing (§§ 202a, 212 StPO), albeit not necessarily with all trial participants.[302] In that case the presiding judge is obliged to inform all trial participants that an *Erörterung* (discussion) took place.[303] In essence, plea bargaining in Germany is governed by an urge for transparency, demonstrated by the fact that the (non)-existence and actual substance of the *Verständigung*, its result and even the information about and the substance of an *Erörterung* have to be put in the court record[304] in order to strengthen the trust in transparency[305] and to assure that the *Verständigung* can be fully revised.[306]

A *Verständigung* may encompass either the legal consequences of the judgment/decisions,[307] procedural measures during the investigation stage or the procedural conduct of the parties. More specifically, while "procedural measures during the investigation stage" (*sonstige verfahrensbezogenen Maßnahmen im zugrundeliegenden Erkenntnisverfahren*) include, *inter alia*, decisions on the dismissal of the proceedings and eviden-

---

[302] German Federal Court of Justice, Judgment of 5 October 2010, No. 3 StR 287/10, in *Strafverteidiger*, 2011, pp. 72, 73; German Federal Court of Justice, Judgment of 2 October 2013, No. 1 StR 386/13, in *Neue Zeitschrift für Strafrecht*, 2014, p. 168.

[303] § 243(4) StPO.

[304] § 273(1a) clauses 1 and 2 StPO.

[305] Federal Constitutional Court of Germany, Judgment of 19 March 2013, No. 2 BvR 2628/10, 2 BvR 2883/10, 2 BvR 2155/11, in *Decisions of the Federal Constitutional Court of Germany*, vol. 133, pp. 168, 218, and in *Neue Juristische Wochenschrift*, 2013, pp. 1058, 1065 mn. 89; see also already BGHSt 43, see *supra* note 222.

[306] Begründung zum Gesetzesentwurf der Bundesregierung, BT-Drs. 16/12310, p. 15; Reinhold Schlothauer and Hans-Joachim Weider, "Das 'Gesetz zur Regelung der Verständigung im Strafverfahren' vom 3. August 2009", in *Strafverteidiger*, 2009, pp. 601, 605; crit., since this entails additional work for the courts, Christopher Erhard, "Sind aus Sicht der Praxis nach dem Verständigungsurteil des BVerfG Reformen des Strafprozesses erforderlich?: Anmerkungen eines Tatrichters", in *Strafverteidiger*, 2013, vol. 33, p. 655, 656.

[307] Ambos and Ziehn, 2011, mn. 19, see *supra* note 218. As an exception, compulsory legal consequences can not be subject of a *Verständigung* since the judge has no discretion in that case; see Martin Niemöller, "Urteilsabsprachen im Strafprozess – noch ein Regelungsvorschlag", in *Goltdammer's Archiv für Strafrecht*, 2009, p. 181; Schlothauer and Weider, 2009, p. 602, see *supra* note 306; Ralf Eschelbach, "§ 257c StPO", in Jürgen-Peter Graf (ed.), *Beck'scher Online-Kommentar StPO mit RiStBV und MiStra*, 26th ed.., C.H. Beck, Munich, 2016, mn. 11; Gerwin Moldenhauer and Marc Wenske, "§ 257c stop", in Rolf Hannich (ed.), *Karlsruher Kommentar zur Strafprozessordnung*, 7th ed., C.H. Beck, Munich, 2013, mn. 15. About decisions, see Alexander Ignor, "§ 257c StPO", in Helmut Satzger and Wilhelm Schluckebier (eds.), *Strafprozessordnung*, 2nd ed., Carl Heymanns, Cologne, 2016, mn. 44.

---

tiary matters,[308] "procedural conduct of the persons involved in the proceedings" (*Prozessverhalten der Verfahrensbeteiligten*) refers, for instance, to a guilty plea by the accused (§ 257c (2) clause 2), further clarification of the circumstances of the crime, a victim-offender conciliation and so on. However, the procedural conduct of the accused must be related (*innerer Zusammenhang*) to the crime he is charged with.[309] Furthermore, while an upper limit of a sentence (*Strafobergrenze*) cannot be agreed on,[310] a *Verständigung* about the suspension of a sentence on probation (*Bewährung*) is admissible.[311]

3.4.3.5. Participation of the Judge

In a nutshell, it is fair to say that in both in common and civil law countries the judge is allowed to disregard plea bargaining agreements.[312] However, while common law judges treat bargaining as a contract between the parties, most civil law judges regard it as a rather informal gentlemen's agreement.[313] As a result, if the prosecution violates the terms of the arrangement or the judges disapproves of it, in common law countries the judge will let the defendant revoke the plea while in civil law countries the confession remains valid.[314] An exception may be Germany, where plea bargaining

---

[308] Begründung zum Gesetzesentwurf der Bundesregierung, BT-Drs. 16/12310, p. 13; see also Bertram Schmitt, "Die Verständigung in der Revision – eine Zwischenbilanz", in *Strafverteidiger Forum*, 2012, vol. 17, pp. 386, 387. Other procedural measures are, for instance, those that direct or stay the proceedings, see Stuckenberg, 2013, mn. 34, *supra* note 286.

[309] Cf. BGH, in *Neue Zeitschrift für Strafrecht*, 2004, 338 (339) with a comment by Hans-Joachim Weider; Werner Beulke and Sabine Swoboda, "Zur Verletzung des Fair-trial-Grundsatzes bei Absprachen im Strafprozess", in *Juristenzeitung*, 2005, pp. 71 ff.; Gabriele Schöch, "Konnexität und Vertrauensschutz bei versuchter Verständigung im Strafverfahren", in *Neue Juristische Wochenschrift*, 2004, pp. 3463 ff.; Ignor, 2016, mn. 44, see *supra* note 307; Matthias Jahn and Hans Kudlich, "§ 257c StPO", in Hartmut Schneider (ed.), *Münchener Kommentar zur Strafprozessordnung*, vol. 2, C.H. Beck, Munich, 2016, mn. 106; König and Harrendorf, 2013, mn. 14, see *supra* note 288.

[310] Siehe auch Altvater, 2011, p. 4, see *supra* note 288; Eschelbach, 2016, mn. 12, see *supra* note 307.

[311] Meyer-Goßner, 2015, mn. 12, see *supra* note 285; crit. Stuckenberg, 2013, mn. 32, see *supra* note 286.

[312] Damaška, 2004, p. 1026, see *supra* note 183.

[313] *Ibid.*

[314] *Ibid.*

---

leads to a quasi-contractual agreement[315] and where the result of the *Verständigung* may lose its binding effect and must not be used against the accused (§ 257c (4) StPO).[316]

Thus, it is clear that the legal classification of plea bargaining very much influences the role of the judge during this procedure. If plea bargaining is regarded as a contract between the parties, it ensues that the role of the judge, as in the United States, is essentially passive since he only reviews the formalities of the bargain once it is presented.[317] Many jurisdictions, including US federal courts, even expressly prohibit judges from participating in or commenting on the plea negotiations.[318] It is argued that "greater involvement could interfere with the judge's impartiality and place undue pressure on a defendant to accept a plea deal and concern is magnified when the same judge who participates in unsuccessful plea negotiations also presides over the defendant's later trial and sentencing".[319] In this sense, Rule 11(c) of the Federal Rules of Criminal Procedure provides that the judge may not participate in negotiations in the US federal courts; some US states have already followed this model. In contrast, other US jurisdictions, such as California, permit direct participation of the judge in charge and sentence bargaining. Another matter is the judge's reasoning of the judgment. As a general common law rule, the judge (jury) is not obliged to reason his judgment, even if it is a judgment made by a single judge.[320] Interestingly, the same applies in the United States in relation to guilty plea

---

[315] See Klaus Leipold, "Die gesetzliche Regelung der Verständigung im Strafverfahren", in *Neue Juristische Wochenschrift-Spezial*, 2009, p. 521, who considers the requirement of consent by the prosecution as violation of Article 92 of the Constitution: "The judicial power shall be vested in the judges", and Article 97(1): "Judges shall be independent and subject only to the law". Crit. Lorenz Leitmeier, "§ 257c I 2 i.V.m. § 244 II StPO?!", in *Onlinezeitschrift für Höchstrichterliche Rechtsprechung zum Strafrecht*, 2013, vol. 14, pp. 362, 365, who challenges the notion of freedom as a necessary precondition for a quasi-contractual agreement on the part of the accused.

[316] However, a *Verständigung* only loses its binding effect by a court decision and not by law, German Federal Court of Justice, Judgment of 21 June 2012, No. 4 StR 623/11, in *Decisions of the German Federal Court of Justice*, vol. 57, pp. 273, 278, and in *Neue Zeitschrift für Strafrecht*, 2013, pp. 51, 52, mn. 14; see also Jahn and Kudlich, 2016, mn. 163, *supra* note 309; Stuckenberg, 2013, mn. 62, *supra* note 286.

[317] Cf. Abraham S. Goldstein, *The Passive Judiciary. Prosecutorial Discretion and the Guilty Plea*, Louisiana State University Press, Baton Rouge, 1981, p. 4.

[318] Turner, 2006, p. 199, see *supra* note 252.

[319] *Ibid.*

[320] Thaman, 2007, p. 33, see *supra* note 62.

proceedings since the guilty plea itself is considered a sufficient reason for the respective ruling. This is even more surprising in light of the fact that in the United States, as opposed to traditional common law, the judge occasionally gives reasons for his decision.

In contrast, in civil law countries the judge has a much more active role in the course of plea bargaining. In France, for instance, after reviewing the alleged facts and their legal qualification, the judge may decide to accept the proposed sentence or refuse it.[321] The same applies in Argentina, where the trial court can reject the agreement if it considers the production of additional evidence necessary, or if it fundamentally disagrees with the charges (Article 431 CPP), and Spain.[322] However, if the trial court accepts the agreement, it must reach a verdict based on the evidence collected in the written *dossier*. The trial court can still acquit the defendant, but if convicted, the defendant's sentence cannot exceed the length agreed to by the parties. In Germany either the judge or lay judges are involved in the *Verständigung*.[323] § 257c (1) clause 1 provides that in an "appropriate case" (*geeigneter Fall*) the judge is entitled to bargain for the progress and result of the trial with the parties.[324] The judge has to take into account both the interest in a speedy trial and the interest of the accused and the defence in a good outcome of the trial.[325] A *Verständigung* comes into effect when the accused and the prosecution agree upon the proposal of the judge (§ 257c (2) clause 4 StPO). Therefore, it is in fact the judge who promotes and shapes the bargaining process. A similar picture exists in Italy. There the judge may even ignore the fulfilment of all plea bargaining requirements and take a different decision if he is of the opinion that "an acquittal judgment has to be issued" or "the punishment agreed (by the public prosecutor and the defendant) is not adequate to the charges".[326]

---

[321] Bosly, 2004, p. 1045, see *supra* note 272.

[322] Bachmaier, 2015, pp. 100–1, see *supra* note 36.

[323] This follows from § 30(1) of the German Law on the Organisation of the Judiciary (*Gerichtsverfassungsgesetz*, 'GVG'); clarifying: BGHSt 43, p. 33, see *supra* note 222.

[324] "Parties" in this sense ('*Verfahrensbeteiligte*') are those persons with own procedural rights like the accused, his or her defence counsel, the prosecution, the joint plaintiff, the plaintiff in a private prosecution and so forth.

[325] Cf. Begründung zum Gesetzesentwurf der Bundesregierung, BT-Drs. 16/12310, p. 7; Uwe Murmann, "Reform ohne Wiederkehr? – Die gesetzliche Regelung der Absprachen im Strafverfahren", in *Zeitschrift für Internationale Strafrechtsdogmatik*, 2009, vol. 121, pp. 534 ff.

[326] See Di Amato, 2008, p. 159, *supra* note 279.

3.4.3.6. (Legal) Consequences of Plea Bargaining

Plea bargaining usually leads to a reduction of punishment in most jurisdictions.[327] However, while civil law systems (mainly) offer a reduction of punishment, in common law systems the charges may also be altered or even partially dismissed.[328] Italian courts, for instance, may reduce the sanction up to a third or apply an alternative sanction, that is a punishment other than imprisonment,[329] by delivering a *sui generis* judgment, which is different from that of a conviction.[330] In France, if the defendant fulfils the conditions of the agreement, the prosecution is conditionally suspended (Article 41–42 CPP). In Spain, if the defendant pleads guilty (and therefore avoids the trial) in cases of crimes punished with no more than three years' imprisonment, he will automatically benefit from a one third reduction of the penalty.[331] Last but not least, Switzerland grants a sentence reduction up to 30 per cent.[332]

Another matter of interest is the question of whether the judge is bound to a result that was agreed upon by plea bargaining. Unfortunately, notwithstanding the importance of that question, definite statements can only be found in Germany, Spain and Italy. In Germany, § 257c (4) clause 1 StPO indicates that the judge is, in principle, bound to the content of the *Verständigung*.[333] However, this does not apply to the court of appeal or the court remand.[334] Furthermore, the prosecution is not bound to the consent

---

[327] Damaška, 2004, p. 1026, see *supra* note 183.

[328] *Ibid.* See section 3.5.3.; Langer, 2004, p. 60, see *supra* note 207.

[329] However, alternative sanctions are only available for very minor offences. For a discussion, see Van Cleave, 1997, pp. 430–40, *supra* note 279; Rosanna Gambini Musso, *Il "Plea Bargaining" tra Common Law e Civil Law*, Giuffrè, Milan, 1985, p. 113.

[330] See article 445 CPP on the legal effects of a penalty requested by a party.

[331] Article 801.2 CPP; see also Lorena Bachmaier Winter and Antonio del Moral García, "Spain", in Roger Blanpain (ed.), *International Encyclopaedia of Laws: Criminal Law*, vol. 4, Kluwer Law, The Hague, 2009, p. 226.

[332] See Petrig, 2008, p. 6, fn. 11, *supra* note 275.

[333] § 257c (4) clause 1 and 2 StPO provide for exceptions; Ambos and Ziehn, 2011, mn. 1, see *supra* note 218; German Federal Court of Justice, Judgment of 7 October 2014, No. 1 StR 182/14, in *Strafverteidiger*, 2015, p. 277, 278; Mohamad El-Ghazi, "Auswirkungen einer konsensualen Verfahrensbeendigung auf das Berufungsverfahren", in *Juristische Rundschau*, 2012, pp. 406, 407.

[334] Begründung zum Gesetzesentwurf der Bundesregierung, BT-Drs. 16/12310, p. 15; Schlothauer and Weider, 2009, p. 605, see *supra* note 306; German Federal Court of Justice,

he or she made according to § 154 StPO.[335] Essentially, the same applies in Spain and Italy. While in Spain the guilty plea is subject to judicial control and the trial court must check that the legal assessment is accurate and that the penalty requested corresponds to the offence,[336] the court is bound by the plea and must render its decision on that basis.[337] In Italy, since the judge has the sole discretion to accept or refuse the *patteggiamento*, he will be bound by the bargained penalty if he decides to accept the parties' request.[338]

3.5. Diversion

So far, we have described and compared measures that help to expedite and simplify the criminal process. However, a watchful reader will have realised that the naming of the outlined sub-themes may be controversial since every sub-theme relates to others. In other words, 'summary proceedings' contain elements of 'negotiated justice', and forms of 'negotiated justice' may, in turn, be categorised as 'diversion'. Thus, it is unavoidable that certain aspects will be repeated if we now treat 'diversion' in criminal proceedings. Diversion in pure terminological terms is understood as "[a] deviation or alteration from the natural course of things".[339] Under this heading, we observe methods to completely or partly avoid a charge or a criminal trial, being aware that diversion is a broadly used and interpreted term whose use is more common in civil law countries than in common law countries.

Judgment of 28 February 2013, No. 4 StR 537/12, in *Neue Zeitschrift für Strafrecht – Rechtsprechungsreport*, 2013, p. 373.

[335] Begründung zum Gesetzesentwurf der Bundesregierung, BT-Drs. 16/12310, p. 13. This, however, does not mean that the prosecution can one-sidedly abandon the agreement. If it is of the view that the preconditions are met that the agreement loses its binding effect, it could only appeal the judgment, cf. German Federal Court of Justice, Judgment of 21 June 2012, No. 4 StR 623/11, in *Decisions of the German Federal Court of Justice*, vol. 57, pp. 273, 278–79.

[336] See generally M. Aguilera Morales, *El principio del consenso: La conformidad en el proceso penal espanol*, Cedecs, Barcelona, 2000, pp. 207 ff.

[337] Bachmaier Winter and del Moral García, 2009, p. 227, see *supra* note 331.

[338] Antoinette Perrodet, "The Italian System", in Delmas-Marty and Spencer, 2002, p. 372, see *supra* note 50; Denis Salas, "The Role of the Judge", in Delmas-Marty and Spencer, 2002, p. 511, see *supra* note 50.

[339] Garner, 2014, p. 579, see *supra* note 187. On the meaning of diversion, see Udo Dirnaichner, *Der nordamerikanische Diversionsansatz und rechtliche Grenzen seiner Rezeption im bundesdeutschen Jugendstrafrecht*, Peter Lang, Frankfurt am Main, 1990, pp. 17 ff.

3.5.1. Legal Meaning

In legal terms, some describe diversion as "the collection of enforcement strategies outside the boundaries of conventional and formal criminal procedure".[340] The concept goes back to the diversion movement in the United States that was initiated by the reports of two US government commissions in 1967 and 1973. It has been discussed in Europe since the end of the 1970s.[341] In fact, diversion exists at different stages of the criminal process, from *notitia criminis* to the sentencing.[342] It has a confusing number of definitions, sometimes even within the same legal system. For example, as in the case of English criminal procedure, diversion can be "informal justice",[343] "gatekeeping",[344] "cautioning" and/or "mediation". Diversion is typically admitted in cases of less serious offences, for example offences punishable by less than five years' imprisonment (France),[345] three years' imprisonment (Poland),[346] two years' imprisonment (Belgium)[347] or less than 60 days of imprisonment (Scotland).[348] In all these cases, certain conditions are imposed on the defendant which, if complied with, will result in a dismissal of the prosecution and the absence of any conviction.[349] Usually the following conditions are imposed: total withdrawal from further criminal conduct,[350] restitution,[351] payment of money to public institutions,[352] a

---

[340] Dingwall and Harding, 1998, see *supra* note 30.

[341] See Dirnaichner, 1990, p. 19, see *supra* note 339.

[342] Dingwall and Harding, 1998, p. 4, see *supra* note 30.

[343] Roger Matthews, *Informal Justice?*, Sage, London, 1988.

[344] Andrew Ashworth, "Prosecution, Police and Public – A Guide to Good Gatekeeping", in *Howard Journal of Criminal Justice*, vol. 23, no. 2, 1984, p. 65.

[345] Jacques Borricand and Anne-Marie Simon, *Droit pénal, procédure pénale*, 5th ed., Sirey, Paris, 2006, p. 258.

[346] In the case of Article 66 § 3 KK (Polish Criminal Code) even up to five years, Jan Grajewski, *Przebieg procesu karnego*, 4th ed., C.H. Beck, Warsaw, 2008, p. 87.

[347] See Chapter III of the Belgium CIC.

[348] Albert V. Sheehan and David Dickson, *Criminal Procedure*, 2nd ed., LexisNexis, Edinburgh, 2003, pp. 641 ff.

[349] Thaman, 2007, p. 13, see *supra* note 62.

[350] *Ibid.*

[351] For example, in the Netherlands, Norway, Bulgaria, Brazil and Germany; cf. Thaman, 2007, p. 13, fn. 84, see *supra* note 62; also in France, Claire Saas, "De la composition pénale au plaider-coupable: le pouvoir de sanction du procureur", in *Revue de science criminelle et de droit pénal comparé*, 2004, no. 4, p. 829.

[352] For example, in Croatia, cf. Thaman, 2007, p. 13, fn. 86, see *supra* note 62.

fine,[353] community service work,[354] drug or alcohol treatment[355] or making support payments.[356] As an overall procedural condition, the defendant usually[357] has to agree to these conditions after a form of negotiation between the prosecution and the defence as to the appropriateness of the diversion and the time and conditions it will be subject to.[358]

3.5.2. Procedure

One has to distinguish between forms of diversion provided for by law (formal diversion, for example referral to a hospital) and other not 'formally' contained in law (informal diversion, for example, victim waiver). Informal diversion entails a lack of transparency and therefore definitional difficulties. Thus, in sum, diversion may take the following forms.[359]

- The victim of the offence decides not to press charges ("victim waiver" or resolution of the issue by his or her own action).

- The offending conduct is dealt with alternatively by another agency (for instance, a professional body or association, an educational institution, within a family).

---

[353] For example, in Scotland the "fiscal fines" were originally restricted to £25, but they may now reach £200; see Robert Shiels, Iain Bradley, Peter W. Ferguson and Alastair N. Brown, *Criminal Procedure (Scotland) Act 1995*, 15th ed., W. Green, London, 2016, p. 793; in the Netherlands it is up to €350; Bulgaria from US$250 to US$500; for Denmark, see Thaman, 2007, p. 13, fn. 87, *supra* note 62; for France, see Saas, 2004, p. 830, *supra* note 351.

[354] For example, in France the amount of hours of social work is limited to 60 within six months; see Saas, 2004, *supra* note 351; Borricand and Simon, 2006, p. 259, see *supra* note 345; in the Netherlands and Croatia, see Thaman, 2007, p. 13, fn. 88, *supra* note 62.

[355] For example, in the Netherlands, Denmark, Croatia and Nicaragua; see Thaman, 2007, p. 13, fn. 89, *supra* note 62.

[356] For example, in Croatia; see *ibid.*, pp. 1, 13, fn. 90.

[357] In Poland, the diversion does not depend on the consent of the defendant. In fact, it may be used even despite her or his objection. The diversion is considered in Poland as a punitive measure; see Andrzej Zoll and Grzegorz Bogdan (eds.), *Kodeks Karny: Część Ogólna*, 3rd ed., LEX, Warsaw, 2007, pp. 836 and 826 ff.

[358] For example, in Germany and in Brazil, where the amount of restitution is sometimes negotiated. In the Netherlands, in white-collar crime cases prosecutors have to bargain with defendants who have powerful lawyers representing them; see Thaman, 2007, pp. 13, 14, fn. 93, *supra* note 62, with further references. With regard to the French *composition pénal*, see Langer, 2004, p. 59, *supra* note 207.

[359] See Dingwall and Harding, 1998, p. 5, *supra* note 30; see also Dirnaichner, 1990, p. 43 ff., *supra* note 339.

- Police diversion (that is the diversion of mainly low-level cases out of the criminal process by the administration of an informal warning or a police caution).[360]

- The prosecuting authority decides to proceed no further or deals with the matter itself (prosecution waiver, penalty or deal).

- Before the trial, the issue of guilt and the sanction are negotiated and fixed (plea negotiation). In this situation, the offence is diverted from any trial, while the offender remains within the criminal justice process.

- During the course of the trial process a mentally ill offender may be diverted to hospital.

- At the sentencing stage, the offender may be officially diverted from a sentence (discharged) or from a particular type of sentence – typically a custodial measure.

For reasons of space, we only address some of the most important and interesting forms of diversion in the following.

In England, the most informal but highly relevant form of diversion is the *victim waiver*, where the victim decides not to report the matter to any official agency and thus effectively rules out any formal process prosecution.[361] The reasons why victims try to avoid trials are often psychological: using a "cost-benefit metaphor",[362] the crime is very often regarded as being "not serious enough"[363] or a relationship between the victim and the offender turns the balance to refraining from bringing a crime to court.[364]

Apart from those informal forms of diversion that are (partly) "distinct from the legal order of the state",[365] other forms of diversion operate

---

[360] A police caution is "a formal warning given by an officer of the rank of inspector or above to an offender who admits to having committed a criminal offence which could have led to prosecution. [Cautions] can be accompanied by referral to social, health, or welfare agencies better able to deal with the matter". See Rob Allen, "Alternatives to Prosecution", in Mike McConville and Geoffrey Wilson (eds.), *The Handbook of the Criminal Justice Process*, Oxford University Press, Oxford, 2002, p. 170.

[361] Dingwall and Harding, 1998, p. 38, see *supra* note 30.

[362] Wesley G. Skogan, "Reporting Crimes to the Police: The Status of World Research", in *Journal of Research in Crime and Delinquency*, 1984, vol. 21, no. 2, p. 120.

[363] *Ibid.*

[364] *Ibid.*, pp. 126 ff.

[365] Dingwall and Harding, 1998, p. 70, see *supra* note 30.

within the scope of the legal order; for example, diversion that directs the case away from the process of prosecution and trial before a criminal court and that allows it to be resolved instead through a "form of settlement with the prosecuting authority".[366] In countries governed by the opportunity principle, diversion arises from the discretionary nature of the formal decision to prosecute, while in countries with the legality principle diversion by (public) prosecutors is compulsory.[367] Regarding the former, an English prosecutor, for instance, has to distinguish between youths and adults in applying diversion. While youth cases are usually referred to the Crown Prosecution Service "if the youth has already received reprimand and final warning, unless the offence is so serious that neither of these was appropriate or the youth does not admit committing the offence",[368] in respect to adult suspects prosecutors have the choice between simple and conditional caution.[369] While simple caution depends on the public interest, a conditional caution may be appropriate where a prosecutor considers that the interest of the suspect, victim and community may be better served by the suspect complying with suitable conditions aimed at rehabilitation[370] or reparation[371] even though the public interest justifies prosecution.[372] According to Section 1(1) of the Conditional Cautioning Code of Practice,

> [t]he key to determining whether a conditional caution should be given – instead of prosecution or a simple caution – is that the imposition of specified conditions will be an appropriate

---

[366] *Ibid.*

[367] *Ibid.*

[368] Peter Hungerford-Welch, *Criminal Procedure and Sentencing*, 7th ed., Routledge-Cavendish, London, 2009, p. 54.

[369] *Ibid.*

[370] According to Section 5(2) of the Conditional Cautioning Code of Practice, "this might include taking part in treatment for drug or alcohol dependency (for example attendance at self-help groups provided it can be verified, or on a drug awareness and education programme including assessment of personal needs and appropriate onward referral), anger management courses, or driving rectification classes and the like, or involvement in a restorative justice process (which may lead to reparation). The offender would be expected to pay reasonable costs, if there are any, and a requirement to do so should be one of the conditions".

[371] According to Section 5(2) of the Conditional Cautioning Code of Practice, "this might include repairing or otherwise making good any damage caused to property (for example by cleaning graffiti), restoring stolen goods, paying modest financial compensation, or in some cases a simple apology to the victim. Compensation may be paid to an individual or to the community in the form of an appropriate charity".

[372] Hungerford-Welch, 2009, p. 54, see *supra* note 368.

and effective means of addressing an offender's behaviour or making reparation for the effects of the offence on the victim or the community.[373]

In contrast, in Scotland, the procurator fiscal has a far greater range of diversionary options than in England. He can formally warn the person that his behaviour is unacceptable and, if repeated, will result in prosecution.[374] Furthermore, he can "guide the accused away from the prosecution side altogether" and direct an offender to receive help from a voluntary organisation such as Alcoholics Anonymous;[375] he can offer a fixed penalty in case of a minor road traffic offence,[376] and give the offender the opportunity to pay a fine as an alternative to prosecution in cases of offences which could completely be tried before a district court (but excluding those which could be dealt with by a fixed penalty).[377]

Unlike England and Scotland, in other countries the principle of legality entails a compulsory diversion by the (public) prosecutor.[378] In Germany this mainly applies to young offenders falling under the special regime of the Youth Criminal Law (*Jugendstrafrecht*),[379] since in this field the legality principle is restricted by both the opportunity and the subsidiarity principles.[380] The latter means that a prosecution would only be appropriate if the informal conduct of the prosecution is not sufficient and that both a trial and a formal sanction would only be appropriate if inevitable.[381] It is – in case of a felony (not a misdemeanour)[382] – also applied within the measures of §§ 45 and 47 of the Code of Juvenile Criminal Law (*Ju-*

---

[373] Crown Prosecution Service, Conditional Cautioning Code of Practice and Associated Annexes, Criminal Justice Act, Sections 22–27, "Introduction" (https://www.cps.gov.uk/publications/others/conditionalcautioning04.html#intro).

[374] Sheehan and Dickson, 2003, p. 86, see *supra* note 348.

[375] *Ibid.*

[376] §§ 51–90, Road Traffic Offenders Act 1988 (c. 53).

[377] §§ 75–77, Road Traffic Offenders Act 1988 (c. 53), substituted by the Road Traffic Act 1991 (c. 40), § 34; see Sheehan and Dickson, 2003, p. 87, *supra* note 348.

[378] Dingwall and Harding, 1998, p. 70, see *supra* note 30.

[379] In principle, diversion can also be used for adults if the prosecution or the judge apply juvenile criminal law, §§ 105(1), 109(2)(1), 45, 47 JGG.

[380] Franz Streng, *Jugendstrafrecht*, 4th ed., C.F. Müller, Heidelberg, 2016, p. 90.

[381] Cf. Peter-Alexis Albrecht, *Jugendstrafrecht*, 3rd ed., C.H. Beck, Munich, 2000, § 14 B I 2; Rudolf Brunner and Dieter Dölling, *Jugendgerichtsgesetz*, 12th ed., De Gruyter, Berlin, 2010, Einl. II para. 18 ff.

[382] §§ 45, 47 JGG.

gendgerichtsgesetz, 'JGG'), stating that the least interfering measure has to be used.[383] The objective of diversion is for there to be a fast and non-stigmatising reaction to criminal conduct.[384]

One must distinguish between diversion by the prosecution (§ 45 JGG) and diversion by the judge (§ 47 JGG). The former, which requires a co-operation between the prosecutor and the judge but no consent of the latter,[385] exists in three forms: diversion without consequences (§ 45(1) JGG),[386] diversion with an educational measure (§ 45(2) clause 1 JGG),[387] and diversion in co-operation with the judge (§ 45(3) JGG). Last but not least, there is also a form of police diversion by which the police are entitled and encouraged to caution the offender and take educational measures.[388] However, these measures cannot divert from criminal proceedings but are rather used by the prosecution as an indication for applying for a sentence with educational measures.[389] Some federal states in Germany introduced diversion guidelines for the police.[390]

In Belgium diversion from prosecution follows an interesting system of negotiated justice, demonstrated by article 216*ter* CIC: "the *procureur du Roi* also summons the victim and organises a 'mediation' regarding the compensation, as well as how it is to be carried out".[391] Furthermore, the prosecutor is authorised to put forward conditions as the voluntary payment of a sum of money, the reparation of the damage caused by the offence,

---

[383] See Albrecht, 2000, *supra* note 381; Brunner and Dölling, 2010, *supra* note 381.

[384] Michael Walter, "Wandlungen in der Reaktion auf Kriminalität, Zur kriminologischen, kriminalpolitischen und insbesondere dogmatischen Bedeutung von Diversion", in *Zeitschrift für die Gesamte Strafrechtswissenschaft*, 1983, vol. 95, pp. 50 ff.

[385] § 45(3) JGG.

[386] The conditions of § 153 StPO must be fulfilled: The conduct of the offender must be a misdemeanour; the guilt of the offender must be regarded as being little and there must be no public interest in conducting criminal proceedings.

[387] Such as measures of the parents, the school, police, youth welfare office (*Jugendamt*) and so forth. The educational measure must already have been executed or started.

[388] Streng, 2016, pp. 68–69, see *supra* note 380.

[389] Wolfgang Heinz, "Diversion im Jugendstrafrecht und im allgemeinen Strafrecht – Teil 3", in *Deutsche Vereinigung für Jugendgerichte und Jugendgerichtshilfen-Journal*, 1999, pp. 138 ff.; Werner *Gloss*, "Standards in der polizeilichen Jugendarbeit", in *Zeitschrift für Jugendkriminalrecht und Jugendhilfe*, 2007, vol. 3, pp. 280 ff.

[390] Schleswig-Holstein, "Richtlinien zur Förderung der Diversion bei jugendlichen und heranwachsenden Beschuldigten) vom 24.06.1998", in *Deutsche Vereinigung für Jugendgerichte und Jugendgerichtshilfen-Journal*, 1998, p. 260 ff.

[391] Translated by Tulkens, 2002, p. 657, see *supra* note 180.

therapy, necessary medical treatment or community service.[392] The prosecutor may propose one of these measures or combine them.[393] While this procedure is called mediation because of the name of the respective act ("*loi organisant une procedure de mediation pénale*"),[394] some consider this term misleading[395] and prefer to call it "conciliation/reparation",[396] criticising that it is more or less a "mini-trial" where the victim is only sporadically involved.[397]

3.5.3. Prosecutorial Discretion Not to Charge

The prosecutorial discretion not to charge goes to the heart of every legal system and touches upon the antagonism between the principles of legality (mandatory prosecution) and opportunity (discretion).[398] Therefore, there are, of course, countries where strict application of the legality principle leads to a prohibition of prosecutorial discretion not to charge (for example in Poland).[399] As shown by the general analysis of diversion, the prosecutorial discretion not to charge can be based on agreements between the parties and thus involve formal and informal procedures. Seen from this perspective it is a form of negotiated justice.

3.5.3.1. Forms of Prosecutorial Discretion Not to Charge

According to §§ 153, 154 of the German StPO the prosecutor can exercise considerable discretion under certain conditions and terminate the proceedings:

---

[392] See articles 216*bis*, 216*ter* CIC.

[393] Ivo Aertsen and Tony Peters, "Mediation and Restorative Justice in Belgium", in *European Journal on Criminal Policy and Research*, 1998, vol. 6, no. 4, p. 509.

[394] "Law Holding the Regulation of a Procedure for Mediation in Penal Matters", in *Belgisch Staatsblad*, 27 April 1994. This statute goes back to an "experiment" the prosecutor-general set up in 1991 when he used "penal mediation" in seven judicial districts belonging to the court of appeal of Ghent, although it was by no means clear how far a real mediation between the victim and the offender took place.

[395] Aertsen and Peters, 1998, p. 509, see *supra* note 393.

[396] Michel van de Kerchove, "Médiation pénale et travaux d'intérêt general: réflexions et commentaires relatives aux lois du 10 février 1994", in *Journal des Tribunaux*, 1995, p. 64.

[397] Aertsen and Peters, 1998, p. 514, see *supra* note 393.

[398] See also Vadell, 2015, pp. 14–15, see *supra* note 273.

[399] Jehle, 2010, p. 21, see *supra* note 6.

- if the offence is of little importance, the culpability of the offender is minimal and there is no public interest in a prosecution (§§ 153, 153b, 154(I) (1) and (2), 154a);
- if the public interest can be satisfied in a way other than a prosecution (§ 153a; for example by payment of compensation);
- if the prosecution runs contrary to the public interest (§§ 153d (I), 153e (I), 154c, 154d; for example where the prosecution for offences against the state would likely be detrimental to the national interest of Germany or the offender has taken steps to limit the potential damage to the constitutional order of the country after the commission of an offence); or
- if the victim has personally initiated a prosecution (this is possible for certain "private" offences but the prosecutor is always entitled to take over the proceedings).[400]

A similar situation arises in Spain, where, as in Germany, the principle of legality[401] forces the Ministerio Publico to prosecute, as a rule, every criminal act.

The public interest threshold is also a crucial trigger for not pressing a charge in the Netherlands (Articles 167 and 242 *Wetboek van Strafvordering*, 'Sv') and France[402] (Article 40(1) CPP). In the Netherlands, where the prosecution service can be regarded as the "judge before the judge",[403] this even affects police investigations in so far as the police are allowed to deny starting an investigation in the context of certain criminal offences. Therefore, in practice, there are several instruments co-ordinating investigative activities of the police with the general criminal justice policy.[404] In France the prosecution, which is the oldest one in Europe,[405] is entitled not to charge, but there is no real guidance and direction in respect to this discretion.[406] Thus, prosecutorial policies are very different depending on nation-

---

[400] Barbara Huber, in Vogler and Huber, 2008, p. 290, see *supra* note 34.

[401] Bachmaier Winter and del Moral García, 2009, p. 215, see *supra* note 331.

[402] Catherine Elliott, *French Criminal Law*, Willan, Cullompton, 2001, p. 25.

[403] Jehle, 2010, p. 12, see *supra* note 6.

[404] Marc Groenhuijsen and Joep Simmelink, in Vogler and Huber, 2008, p. 393, see *supra* note 34.

[405] Jehle, 2010, p. 12, see *supra* note 6. In more detail Baele, 2015, pp. 38–44, see *supra* note 33 (especially about the law of 25 July 2013 that amended the French Code of Criminal Procedure).

[406] Elliott, 2001, p. 25, see *supra* note 402.

al, regional and local approaches.[407] Given that a decision not to charge requires an agreement between the victim and the offender, a mediation is possible.[408] Yet, notwithstanding the outcome of the agreement, both the possibility of a public prosecution and the victim constituting himself as a civil party remain open.[409] The prosecution may offer the defendant to divert his case from the standard criminal trial in exchange for an admission of guilt and the fulfilment of a condition such as paying a fine, turning over any objects used to commit the offence (or objects obtained in the course of the offence), forfeiting his driving or hunting licence for a certain period of time, doing community service work, and/or repairing the damage done to the victim.[410] If the defendant accepts this offer, the prosecutor requests its validation by the judge.[411] If the defendant does not accept the offer or does not fulfil the conditions of the agreement, the prosecutor can simply initiate formal proceedings.

In England, where the prosecutorial discretion not to charge is part of the adversarial, party-based system,[412] there are two essential preconditions (stages) for the commencement of a prosecution,[413] referred to as the evidentiary and the public interest stage in the Code for Crown Prosecutors.[414] Before looking on those preconditions in more detail, we must draw our attention to several junctions that exist on the path to their application. The

---

[407] *Ibid.*

[408] Mediation may only be envisaged if it can ensure the compensation of damage caused to the victim, facilitate an end to the trouble resulting from the offence and contribute to rehabilitation of the offender; see Tulkens, 2002, p. 660, *supra* note 180.

[409] *Ibid.*

[410] Articles 41–42 CPP. For a detailed analysis of this mechanism, see Ministère de la Justice, 2001, *supra* note 213. The proposal cannot be made when the defendant is under arrest. The prosecutor or his representative has to inform the defendant of his right to be assisted by an attorney.

[411] The defendant and the victim alike can request a hearing from the judge before he decides about the agreement. However, this hearing is not conducted if it is not specifically requested. See articles 41–42 CPP. Because the composition was introduced as a way to deal more effectively with minor crime, it is assumed that a hearing with the defendant and/or the victim before validating the agreement is exceptional. Ministère de la Justice, 2001, p. 96, see *supra* note 213.

[412] John R. Spencer, "The English System", in Delmas-Marty and Spencer, 2002, p. 161, see *supra* note 50; Brown, 2016, pp. 1257 ff., see *supra* note 229.

[413] Jonathan Rogers, "Restructuring the Exercise of Prosecutorial Discretion in England", in *Oxford Journal of Legal Studies*, 2006, vol. 26, no. 4, pp. 775–803.

[414] See Crown Prosecution Service, Conditional Cautioning Code of Practice, *supra* note 371.

first junction is concerned with the two methods of commencing a prosecution. While the first method entitles the police, other prosecuting authorities and private citizens to "lay an information"[415] before the magistrates' court,[416] the second method refers to the institution of criminal proceedings by the public prosecutor.[417] In this context, "public prosecutor" means, *inter alia*, "a police force or a person authorised by a police force to institute criminal proceedings".[418] The next junction can be approached with regard to this second method of commencing a prosecution: the police themselves decide whether a prosecution with a charge is a viable option.[419] If the police opt for prosecution, the papers will go to the Crown Prosecution Service, where a lawyer then reviews the case and may discontinue the proceedings if he considers that the police were wrong to start them in the first place.[420]

Once these two junctions are passed, the two essential preconditions (stages) for the commencement of a prosecution have to be met. Concerning the first, referring to the evidentiary threshold, the prosecution "must be satisfied that there is sufficient evidence to provide a realistic prospect of conviction against each suspect on each charge".[421] The test of a "realistic prospect of conviction" is an objective one, that is, "that an objective, impartial and reasonable jury or bench of magistrates or judge hearing a case alone, properly directed and acting in accordance with the law, is more likely than not to convict the defendant of the charge alleged. This is a different test from the one that the criminal courts themselves must apply. A court may only convict if it is sure that the defendant is guilty" (Section 4.6., Code for Crown Prosecutors). According to Section 4.7. of the Code for

---

[415] To "lay an information" is a very common practice in the charging procedure in England. When a private prosecutor lays an information, he "tells either an individual magistrate, or a magistrate's clerk or a bench of magistrates sitting as an 'applications court' the nature of the allegation and the name and address of the accused". See Sprack, 2015, p. 33, *supra* note 100.

[416] § 30(4), Criminal Justice Act 2003.

[417] See § 29 (1) Criminal Justice Act 2003: "A public prosecutor may institute criminal proceedings against a person by issuing a document (a 'written charge') which charges the person with an offence". § 29 (1) Criminal Justice Act 2003 came fully into force only in March 2012, see Sprack, 2015, p. 66, *supra* note 100.

[418] § 29(5), Criminal Justice Act 2003.

[419] Sprack, 2015, p. 23, *supra* note 100.

[420] *Ibid.*, p. 66.

[421] § 4.5., Code for Crown Prosecutors.

Crown Prosecutors the court must ask itself, *inter alia*, the following questions:

- is it likely that the evidence will be excluded by the court? (for example, because of an impropriety in the way that it was gathered);
- is the evidence reliable (for example, whether identification evidence is likely to be excluded on the basis of the guidelines in *Turnbull*)?[422]

In respect to the second precondition, referring to the public interest test, "prosecutors must go on to consider whether a prosecution is required in the public interest".[423] This goes back to a statement of Lord Shawcross, who said in a House of Commons debate in 1951: "It has never been the rule in this country – I hope it never will be – that suspected criminal offences must automatically be the subject of prosecution". He added that there should be a prosecution "wherever it appears that the offence or the circumstances of its commission is or are of such a character that a prosecution in respect thereof is required in the public interest".[424] The more serious the offence or the offender's record of criminal behaviour, the more likely it is that a prosecution will be required in the public interest.[425]

3.5.3.2. Limitations of the Prosecutorial Discretion Not to Charge

Given the risks and disadvantages of the prosecutorial discretion, it must be controlled and is, in fact, limited in many countries by procedures which

---

[422] *R. v. Turnbull (Raymond)*, QB, 1977, pp. 229 ff. The *Turnbull* guidelines constitute, in part, a mechanism for determining "threshold reliability". See also Andrew J. Roberts, "Identification: Direction to Jury – Weaknesses in Identification Evidence", in *Criminal Law Review*, 2007, p. 644. According to the guidelines, the case is to be withdrawn from the jury if there are serious doubts over the quality of the identification evidence adduced by the prosecution, in the absence of supporting evidence. In other words, there must be sufficient external indicia of reliability (in the form of supporting evidence) to satisfy a minimum threshold of reliability. If the witness lacks credibility in the eyes of the jury his or her evidence may be rejected, notwithstanding a judicial conclusion that the reliability threshold has been satisfied. As the court pointed out, the guidelines "involve only changes of practice, not law" (*R. v. Turnbull (Raymond)*, QB, 1977, p. 231).

[423] § 4.11, Code for Crown Prosecutors.

[424] House of Commons Debates, vol. 483, 29 January 1951.

[425] § 4.12, Code for Crown Prosecutors.

permit the victim either to seek to compel the prosecutor to charge and/or to bring charges themselves independently through private prosecution.[426]

A classical example of the procedure for compelling the prosecution is the German *Klageerzwingungsverfahren* (§§ 172 ff. StPO): it allows the victim to first lodge a complaint against a prosecutorial decision not to charge to the superior of the respective prosecutor and ultimately appeal to a judge to compel the prosecution to file an accusation.[427]

Similar remedies are provided for in Bulgaria, Italy and the Netherlands. Regarding the latter, the "person directly involved" can lodge an appeal with the court against the prosecutor's decision not to prosecute.[428] The "person directly involved" has a twofold meaning, referring both to the victim (the natural person) and the legal person promoting an interest that would be directly affected by the decision not to prosecute.[429] Similar to the situation in England, the prosecutorial decision can be taken by the prosecutor or the police exercising prosecutorial functions.[430] The appeal is also open in circumstances "where the legal action of the public prosecutor office is limited to a minor offence, even though it appears that proceedings for a more serious offence are possible".[431] The court renders an interim judgment, in which it must ensure that the public prosecutor has good policy grounds to prosecute or not to prosecute.[432]

In France, however, there is no right of appeal against the prosecution's decision not to charge since this decision has "no legal effect", that is, there may still be a prosecution in the future.[433]

---

[426] Thaman, 2007, pp. 3–4, see *supra* note 62.

[427] Roxin and Schünemann, 2014, pp. 327–28, see *supra* note 156; Klaus Volk and Armin Engländer, *Grundkurs StPO*, 8th ed., C.H. Beck, Munich, 2013, p. 116.

[428] Groenhuijsen and Simmelink, 2008, p. 462, see *supra* note 404.

[429] For example, an animal protection society who appeals against non-prosecution of a case of cruelty to animals; see *ibid.*

[430] *Ibid.*, a situation "where a public prosecutor decides against bringing a charge in relation to a criminal offence that has come to his attention before the court" and a situation "where the police refrain from performing investigations to clear up a suspicion that is raised".

[431] See HR 25 June 1996, NJ 1996, p. 714; Groenhuijsen and Simmelink, 2008, p. 462, see *supra* note 404.

[432] See also G.J.M. Corstens, *Het Nederlands Strafprocesrecht*, 6th ed., Kluwer, Deventer, 2008, pp. 518–28.

[433] Elliott, 2001, p. 25, see *supra* note 402.

If the judge orders the prosecution to review the case, but maintains its previous non-prosecution decision, the victim may continue proceedings through a private prosecution.[434] Private prosecution means that the aggrieved party may either prosecute minor offences without mandatory participation of the public prosecutor[435] or participate as a kind of auxiliary (second) prosecutor with full procedural rights.[436] In England, while the objective of private prosecution is seen as "securing justice to the individual in cases where the Crown Prosecution Service refuses to act",[437] in *Jones v. Whalley*, Lord Bingham regards the right to bring a private prosecution as "of questionable value and can be exercised in a way damaging to the public interest".[438] The same view is be taken in Scotland, where, while it is theoretically possible for the victim to compel prosecution through private prosecution, this right has only been granted twice in the last century.[439]

Generally speaking, in Western Europe there is no clear "association between the existence of a right to private prosecution and the adoption of either the opportunity or legality principles".[440] While states like England and Wales (generally) and France and Germany (in relation to certain offences) do not have a monopoly over prosecution, states such as the Netherlands and Sweden do.[441]

---

[434] Regarding Poland, see Tomasz Grzegorczyk and Janusz Tylman, *Polskie Postępowanie Karne*, 6th ed., Wydawnictwo Prawnicze Lexis Nexis, Warsaw, 2007, p. 702.

[435] For example, in Germany, see Roxin and Schünemann, 2014, pp. 511 ff., *supra* note 156; in Spain, see Jacobo López Borja de Quiroga, *Tratado de Derecho Procesal Penal*, 3rd ed., Thomson/Aranzadi, Navarra, 2009, pp. 788 ff.; in England and Wales the private prosecution is not limited to minor offences. According to Section 6(2) of the Prosecution of Offences Act 1985 the public prosecutor is allowed to take over the conduct of any criminal proceedings and thereafter to discontinue it, see Hungerford-Welch, 2009, pp. 134 ff., *supra* note 368; in Denmark, Croatia, Norway, Bulgaria and Brazil, see Thaman, 2007, p. 4, fn. 17, *supra* note 62.

[436] For example, in Poland, Germany, Spain, see Thaman, 2007, p. 4, *supra* note 62.

[437] Darbyshire, 2000, p. 89, see *supra* note 105.

[438] *Jones v. Whalley*, 2006, UKHL 74, para. 16.

[439] Sheehan and Dickson, 2003, §§ 119, 82, 84, *supra* note 348.

[440] Vogler and Huber, 2008, p. 26, see *supra* note 34.

[441] Marianne Wade, "The Power to Decide – Prosecutorial Control, Diversion and Punishment in European Criminal Justice Systems Today", in Jehle and Wade, 2010, p. 64, see *supra* note 6. Most surprisingly, Richard Vogler reports almost the complete opposite, stating that states like England and the Netherlands do not have a monopoly over prosecution, while states such as Belgium and France do; see Vogler and Huber, 2008, p. 26, *supra* note 34. This is certainly not totally correct since these latter states allow for private prosecution in the sense of an *actio popularis*. Regarding Belgium, see Kai Ambos, "Prosecuting

3.5.3.3. Participation of a Judge

To counter the criticisms levelled against private prosecutions, many systems provide for a judicial control as to the necessary evidentiary threshold,[442] thereby trying to safeguard both the public and private interest.[443] In inquisitorial systems, this control is exercised by an investigating magistrate,[444] while in other systems it lies in the competence of a pre-trial judge[445] and sometimes of the trial judge in a pre-trial hearing.[446] Once a formal investigation has been initiated, the prosecutor will often be obliged to ask the judge, usually the trial judge, for permission to dismiss the charges.[447] Yet, there are some exceptions to this rule, for example, in Germany for individual charges in multi-count accusatory pleadings[448] and cases subject to victim–offender conciliation and other limited categories of offences, in Denmark for cases punishable by fines, juvenile cases and so forth and in Scotland.[449]

Guantanamo in Europe: Can and Shall the Masterminds of the 'Torture Memos' be Held Criminally Responsible on the Basis of Universal Jurisdiction?", in *Case Western Reserve Journal of International Law*, 2009, vol. 42, nos. 1/2, pp. 409, 410.

[442] Thaman, 2007, p. 4, see *supra* note 62.

[443] For judicial review of prosecution decisions in England see Brown, 2016, p. 1258, see *supra* note 229.

[444] For example, in France, see Serge Guinchard and Jacques Buisson, *Procédure pénale*, 4th ed., LexisNexis Litec, Paris, 2008, p. 206; Stephen C. Thaman, *Comparative Criminal Procedure: A Casebook Approach*, Carolina Academic Press, Durham, NC, 2002, pp. 21 ff.; also in Croatia, Thaman, 2007, p. 4, fn. 19, see *supra* note 62.

[445] In the United States, see Yale Kamisar, Wayne R. LaFave, Jerold H. Israel, Nancy J. King, and Orin S. Kerr, *Basic Criminal Procedure: Cases, Comments and Questions*, 12th ed., Thomson/West, St. Paul, 2008, pp. 13 ff.; in South Africa, Italy (*guidice dell'udienza preliminare*), see Thaman, 2007, p. 4, fn. 20, *supra* note 62.

[446] In Germany, Roxin and Schünemann, 2014, pp. 331 ff., see *supra* note 156; in Poland, see Grajewski, 2008, pp. 162 ff, *supra* note 346; in Brazil, see Thaman, 2007, p. 4, fn. 21, *supra* note 62.

[447] Thaman, 2007, p. 4, see *supra* note 62.

[448] A multiple count accusatory pleading is an indictment, information or complaint by which the government/prosecution authority begins a criminal prosecution and that contains several separate causes of action or charged offenses, see Garner, 2014, pp. 427, 1339, *supra* note 187.

[449] Thaman, 2007, p. 4, fn. 22, see *supra* note 62.

3.6. Guilty Plea and Plea Bargaining at International Criminal Tribunals[450]

At the modern *ad hoc* tribunals,[451] the guilty plea procedure was modelled after the common law approach,[452] giving the accused in her initial appearance the possibility to enter a plea of guilty or not guilty with regard to each count.[453] In case of a valid guilty plea, the proceedings would automatically

---

[450] The following part is mainly taken from Ambos, 2016, pp. 433 ff., see *supra* note 7.

[451] On the new mixed tribunals which either followed the International Criminal Tribunal for the former Yugoslavia ('ICTY') or International Criminal Tribunal for Rwanda ('ICTR') (Special Tribunal for Lebanon ('STL')) or the International Criminal Court ('ICC') (Special Panels for Serious Crimes Dili, East Timor ('SPSC')) or rejected guilty plea altogether (Extraordinary Chambers in the Courts of Cambodia ('ECCC')), see Nancy A. Combs, "Structure of Uncontested Trial", in Göran Sluiter, Håkan Friman, Suzannah Linton, Salvatore Zappala and Sergey Vasiliev (eds.), *International Criminal Procedure: Rules and Principles*, Oxford University Press, Oxford, 2013, pp. 682, 685; Jenia Iontcheva Turner and Thomas Weigend, "Negotiated Justice", in Göran Sluiter, Håkan Friman, Suzannah Linton, Salvatore Zappala and Sergey Vasiliev (eds.), *International Criminal Procedure: Rules and Principles*, Oxford University Press, Oxford, 2013, pp. 1374, 1392–95. About guilty pleas at the *ad hoc* tribunals that are treated as a sign of remorse, see Oliver Diggelmann, "International Criminal Tribunals and Reconciliation: Reflections on the Role of Remorse and Apology", in *Journal of International Criminal Justice*, 2016, vol. 14, no. 5, pp. 1073, 1084–85 (ICTY) and 1085–87 (ICTR).

[452] Christine Schuon, *International Criminal Procedure: A Clash of Legal Cultures*, T.M.C. Asser Press, The Hague, 2010, p. 196; Christoph Safferling, *International Criminal Procedure*, Oxford University Press, Oxford, 2012, p. 438; Turner and Weigend, 2013, p. 1377, see *supra* note 451; Håkan Friman, "Procedures", in Robert Cryer, Håkan Friman, Darryl Robinson and Elizabeth Wilmshurst (eds.), *An Introduction to International Criminal Law and Procedure*, 3rd ed., Cambridge University Press, Cambridge, 2014, p. 470; McCleery, 2016, pp. 1099, 1110–12, *supra* note 66. Generally on guilty plea before the *ad hoc* tribunals, see Kuczyńska, 2015, pp. 266–76, see *supra* note 27.

[453] Cf. Statute of the International Tribunal for the former Yugoslavia, adopted 25 May 1993 by resolution 827, Art. 20(3) ('ICTY Statute') (https://www.legal-tools.org/doc/b4f63b/); and ICTY, Rules of Procedure and Evidence, adopted 11 February 1994, amended 22 May 2013, Rule 62 (A)(iii)–(vi) ('ICTY RPE') (http://www.legal-tools.org/doc/950cb6/); Statute of the International Tribunal for Rwanda, adopted 8 November 1994 by resolution 955, Art. 19(3) ('ICTR Statute') (http://www.legal-tools.org/doc/8732d6/); and ICTR, Rules of Procedure and Evidence, adopted 1995, amended 13 May 2015, Rule 62 (A)(iii)–(v), ('ICTR RPE') (http://www.legal-tools.org/doc/c6a7c6/); Rules of Procedure and Evidence of the Mechanism for International Criminal Tribunals, 8 June 2012, MICT/1, Rule 64 (A)(iii)–(iv), (B) and (C) ('MICT RPE') (http://www.legal-tools.org/doc/cef176/); Special Court for Sierra Leone, Rules of Procedure and Evidence, adopted 16 January 2002, amended 16 November 2011, Rule 61 (iii)–(v) ('SCSL RPE') (http://www.legal-tools.org/doc/b36b82/) (no reference in the SCSL Statute).

be brought to a separate sentencing stage,[454] whose only purpose is to determine the actual sentence of the defendant[455] (now to be considered guilty). If the Chamber considers the plea invalid, it must reject it and allow the accused to re-plea.[456]

In procedural terms, the parties may conclude a plea agreement – normally at the pre-trial stage[457] – which enables the prosecutor "to amend the indictment accordingly" and apply for "a specific sentence or sentencing range", and obliges her to "not oppose" a respective request of the accused.[458] With the introduction of this quite precise framework, the judges considerably restricted the parties' negotiating powers, especially as compared to the broad charge and sentence bargaining practices known from common law systems.[459]

The Trial Chamber is not bound by such an – inter-party – agreement,[460] since "its fundamental obligation is to ensure that there is a sufficient factual basis for the crime and the accused's participation in it".[461] Both ICTY and ICTR Chambers have in some cases, albeit not the majority,[462] imposed

---

[454] Cf. ICTY RPE, Rule 62 (A)(vi) with 62*bis in fine*; ICTR RPE, Rule 62 (A)(v) with 62 (B) *in fine*; SCSL RPE, Rule 61 (v) with 62 (B); MICT RPE, Rule 64 (B) and (C) *in fine*; on the ICTY, see also Combs, 2013, p. 684, *supra* note 451.

[455] Cf. RPE ICTY/ICTR/SCSL RPE, Rule 100, and MICT RPE, Rule 124.

[456] Combs, 2013, p. 684, see *supra* note 451.

[457] But parties are not precluded from concluding them during trial; cf. Turner and Weigend, 2013, p. 1384, see *supra* note 451.

[458] ICTY RPE, Rule 62*ter* (A); ICTR RPE, Rule 62*bis* (A); MICT RPE, Rule 65 (A).

[459] Gideon Boas, James L. Bischoff, Nathalie L. Reid and B. Don Taylor (eds), *International Criminal Law Practitioner Library*, vol. 3, *International Criminal Procedure*, Cambridge University Press, Cambridge, 2011, pp. 221–22; Turner and Weigend, 2013, p. 1385, see *supra* note 451 (especially pointing to the limitation of "fact bargaining"); McCleery, 2016, p. 1102, see *supra* note 66.

[460] ICTY RPE, Rule 62*ter* (B); ICTR RPE, Rule 62*bis* (B); MICT RPE, Rule 65 (B). See also Turner and Weigend, 2013, pp. 1384 ("unlimited discretion"), 138–88, 1397–98, *supra* note 451.

[461] ICTY, *Prosecutor v. Duško Sikirica et al.*, Trial Chamber, Sentencing Judgment, 13 November 2001, IT-95-8-S, para. 48 (http://www.legal-tools.org/doc/682fa0/). See also McCleery, 2016, p. 1104, *supra* note 66.

[462] Cf. James Meernik, "What Kind of Bargain is Plea?", in *International Criminal Law Review*, 2014, vol. 14, no. 1, pp. 200, 203 (defendants "usually" sentenced within expected range); Turner and Weigend, 2013, pp. 1388–89, 1398 (on average one-third reduction), see *supra* note 451; Fabricio Guariglia and Gudrun Hochmayr, "Article 65", in Otto Triffterer and Kai Ambos (eds.), *Rome Statute of the International Criminal Court: A Commentary*, 3rd ed., C.H. Beck, Munich, 2016, mn. 12.

higher sentences than expected (and agreed) by the accused,[463] and it was found, in an empirical study, that "there is a reasonable, if not significant, doubt that plea bargains lead to lighter sentences".[464] At any rate, given the crucial importance of the certainty of sentencing discounts within the framework of negotiated justice,[465] it is not surprising that the countervailing sentencing practice of some (civil law) judges considerably reduced the attractiveness of guilty pleas.[466]

The International Criminal Court ('ICC') law is fundamentally different from the law of the *ad hoc* tribunals in that it does not recognise a "guilty plea" as such,[467] but only an "admission of guilt" which – despite the ter-

---

[463] Cf. Boas *et al.*, 2011, p. 224 with further references, see *supra* note 459; Turner and Weigend, 2013, p. 1378, see *supra* note 451; crit. of this practice of the tribunals, Kuczyńska, 2015, pp. 282–83, see *supra* note 27.

[464] Meernik, 2014, p. 216 (drawing on a nuanced statistical analysis taking into account several variables), see *supra* note 462. On the guilty plea as a mitigating factor within the framework of sentencing, see Kai Ambos, *Treatise on International Criminal Law*, vol. 2: *The Crimes and Sentencing*, Oxford: Oxford University Press, 2014, pp. 298–302 with further references.

[465] Cf. Nancy A. Combs, "Procuring Guilty Pleas for International Crimes: The Limited Influence of Sentence Discounts", in *Vanderbilt Law Review*, 2006, vol. 59, no. 1, pp. 67, 75 ("to induce such a defendant to plead guilty, a prosecutor must be able to offer the defendant a fairly certain sentence reduction in exchange for his guilty plea"), pp. 92–100 (p. 100: "Now that the recommendations no longer provide that certainty, ICTY defendants apparently prefer to take their chances on a trial.'); Nancy A. Combs, *Guilty Pleas in International Criminal Law: Constructing a Restorative Justice Approach*, Stanford University Press, Stanford, 2007, pp. 89–90 ("it is only through the chambers' adherence to the prosecution's recommendations that the promise of a particular recommendation will persuade defendants to plead guilty"); see also Turner and Weigend, 2013, p. 1378, *supra* note 451; Friman, 2014, p. 471, see *supra* note 452.

[466] Thus, the reduction of guilty pleas at the ICTR has been explained with the case of Jean Kambanda who received a life sentence despite his guilty plea and substantial co-operation with the prosecution; cf. Regina E. Rauxloh, "Negotiated History: The Historical Record in International Criminal Law and Plea Bargaining", in *International Criminal Law Review*, 2010, vol. 10, no. 5, pp. 762–763; Boas *et al.*, 2011, p. 224, see *supra* note 459; Lauren Burens, "Plea Bargaining in International Criminal Tribunals: The End of Truth-seeking in International Courts?", in *Zeitschrift für internationale Strafrechtsdogmatik*, 2013, vol. 8, pp. 322, 328; Meernik, 2014, p. 208, see *supra* note 462

[467] See also Boas *et al.*, 2011, p. 225, *supra* note 459; Safferling, 2012, p. 439, see *supra* note 452; Gilbert Bitti, "Article 64", in Otto Triffterer and Kai Ambos (eds.), *Rome Statute of the International Criminal Court: A Commentary*, 3rd ed., C.H. Beck, Munich, 2016, mn. 42; Kuczyńska, 2015, pp. 283–88, see *supra* note 27; for a more nuanced view, see Friman, 2014, p. 471 ("provision does not prevent plea bargaining as such"), *supra* note 452.

minological similarity[468] – rather resembles a (non-binding) "confession"[469] as known from civil law jurisdictions.[470] For, in procedural terms, an accused at the ICC is not asked to plead guilty or not guilty, but only afforded "the opportunity to make an admission of guilt"[471] at the commencement of the trial,[472] that is, once the charges are confirmed.[473] Article 65 of the ICC Statute basically leaves the decision on the acceptance of the accused's admission to the Trial Chamber and thus opts for a cautious judge-led or at least judge-controlled approach.[474] In fact, it is explicitly stated that the "Court" is not in any way bound by "[a]ny discussions" between the parties "regarding modification of the charges, the admission of guilt or the penalty to be imposed".[475] Of course, the very reference to such "discussions" presupposes that negotiations between the prosecutor and the defence are not ruled out.[476]

---

[468] See the definition of "guilty plea" as a "formal admission in court of having committed the charged offense", in Garner, 2014, p. 1337, *supra* note 187.

[469] On the distinction, see Turner and Weigend, 2013, p. 1376 (confession as statement of fact part of the evidence, guilty plea as "procedural declaration without factual content"), similarly p. 1392, see *supra* note 451.

[470] Cf. Safferling, 2012, p. 440 (but see also p. 445: "not a confession in the Continental European sense"), see *supra* note 452; Burens, 2013, p. 332, see *supra* note 466; Friman, 2014, p. 471 ("leaning more towards the civil law"), see *supra* note 452.

[471] The admission has to be made personally; cf. Guariglia and Hochmayr, 2016, mn. 17, see *supra* note 462.

[472] Rome Statute of the International Criminal Court, 17 July 1998, in force 1 July 2001, Art. 64(8)(a) ('ICC Statute') (http://www.legal-tools.org/doc/7b9af9/).

[473] Given the fact that the admission has as its object of reference the charges it would not make sense to admit any charges, which have not yet been confirmed; also, the Pre-Trial Chamber is not competent to receive an admission of guilt since it is not mentioned in Articles 64 (8)(a), 65 (but only the Trial Chamber); on the other hand, it is perfectly possible that the accused admits charges after the commencement of the trial; cf. Safferling, 2012, pp. 443–444, see *supra* note 452; Guariglia and Hochmayr, 2016, mn. 16, 18, see *supra* note 462. On the controversy whether the opportunity to make the admission should already be given at the first status conference before the Trial Chamber, see Bitti, 2016, mn. 42, see *supra* note 467.

[474] See also Turner and Weigend, 2013, p. 1396 ("greater role for judges"), see *supra* note 451; in favour, Safferling, 2012, p. 442 ("luckily a rather cautious approach"), see *supra* note 452; Combs, in Sluiter et al., 2013, p. 688, see *supra* note 451.

[475] ICC Statute, Art. 65(5), see *supra* note 472. This corresponds to the situation in comparative law; see Turner and Weigend, 2013, pp. 1404-1405, see *supra* note 451.

[476] Guariglia and Hochmayr, 2016, mn. 40, see *supra* note 462; conc. Safferling, 2012, p. 442, see *supra* note 452; Turner and Weigend, 2013, p. 1390, see *supra* note 451.

The ICC regime presents a truly mixed picture: on the one hand, the accused may admit guilt and the parties may have "discussions" regarding charges and sentence,[477] on the other hand, victims are encouraged to debate the "historical truth" of events in public proceedings.[478] In fact, the privileged role of victims before the ICC, confirmed by the above discussed reference to the 'interests of the victims' in Article 65 (4) of the ICC Statute,[479] turns them into unpredictable third parties that may well become a spoiler in any adversarial bargaining process,[480] unless they too prefer a negotiated settlement, since it saves them from being called into the witness stand running the risk of being retraumatised or threatened.[481]

The compromise reached demonstrates the civil law influence, where the search for the truth – the cornerstone of the inquisitorial mode – is a key feature of criminal procedure and any negotiation of the truth is considered to undermine the truth-seeking mission of the court.[482] While this view ignores that an admission of guilt may also contribute to the truth, at least regarding the charges it refers to,[483] it leaves little, if any, room for charge bargaining – despite the acknowledgment of the respective "discussions" in Article 65 (5) – since the ensuing omission of complete charges regarding

---

[477] ICC Statute, Art. 65(5), see *supra* note 472.

[478] Stefanie Bock, *Das Opfer vor dem Internationalen Strafgerichtshof*, Berlin: Duncker & Humblot, 2010, pp. 353–54. See generally McCleery, 2016, pp. 1107–8, 1118, *supra* note 66.

[479] See also International Criminal Court, Rules of Procedure and Evidence, 9 September 2002, ICC-ASP/1/3 ('ICC RPE'), Rule 93 (http://www.legal-tools.org/doc/8bcf6f/) allowing the Chamber to seek the views of victims with regard to Rule 139, that is, an admission of guilt.

[480] In a similar vein, Safferling, 2012, pp. 442–43, see *supra* note 452.

[481] On this side of the coin, see Schuon, 2010, pp. 220–21, 240–41 (regarding ICTY practice), *supra* note 452; Turner and Weigend, 2013, pp. 1406, 1408, see *supra* note 451; Guariglia and Hochmayr, 2016, mn. 7, see *supra* note 462.

[482] See also Burens, 2013, pp. 321, 326, 331, *supra* note 466; Turner and Weigend, 2013, p. 1376, see *supra* note 451; Guariglia and Hochmayr, 2016, mn. 5 (plea bargaining as "erosion of fact-finding mission of criminal procedure"), see *supra* note 462.

[483] Cf. Rauxloh, 2010, pp. 767, 769–70 (arguing that plea bargaining, fulfilling certain conditions, can be used "as a mechanism to build the historical record"), see *supra* note 466; Schuon, 2010, pp. 208–20, 224–25, 232–40, 242–43 (critical discussion of ICTY practice), see *supra* note 452; Burens, 2013, pp. 328–29 ("[t]o a certain extent"), 333 (partial truth), see *supra* note 466; Meernik, 2014, pp. 201, 204 (but also pp. 204–5, pointing to the risk of "insincere confessions" and the harm to the historical record by dropping charges), see *supra* note 462.

international core crimes effectively distorts the historical case record[484] In any case, Article 65 of the ICC Statute modifies a crucial structural feature of the adversarial system to an extent that one could speak, from the perspective of procedural expediency, of an "overregulation" of the guilty plea in a manner that undermines its function as a procedural shortcut.

3.7. Conclusion

While practically every criminal justice system has to cope to a greater or lesser extent with an overload of cases entailing considerable delays in the proper administration of justice, the methods and measures to expedite criminal trials differ substantially, in particular if one looks at the details of the respective procedures. Apart from a certain terminological confusion – it is almost impossible to find a uniform and clear definition of terms like "negotiated justice", "plea bargaining" and "consensual procedures"[485] – the main reason for those differences lies in the structural differences between inquisitorial and adversarial procedures repeatedly referred to throughout this chapter. The introduction of the *Verständigung* in Germany shows how difficult it is for a still predominantly inquisitorial system to reconcile inquisitorial principles like the search for the material truth and the (full) judicial clarification of the facts with an essentially party-orientated element of negotiation.[486] Indeed, the introduction of measures to expedite trials, while sticking to the traditional principles of a judge-led inquisitorial process, always means trying to square the circle and running the risk that the new system is neither fish nor fowl, that is, neither purely inquisitorial nor adversarial but an awkward mixture of doubtful efficiency. If one opts for negotiated solutions to judicial systems overload it seems as if the only way forward is a more radical move towards an adversarial procedure as recently realised by traditionally inquisitorial jurisdictions like

---

[484] In a similar vein, Rauxloh, 2010, p. 752 (charge bargaining as main problem regarding historical record), see *supra* note 466; Burens, 2013, p. 328 (exclusion of sex violence at ICTR), pp. 329–30, 332 (considering it inadmissible), see *supra* note 466; Turner and Weigend, 2013, pp. 1406, 1407, see *supra* note 451; with a view to the discussion at the ICTY, see Schuon, 2010, pp. 206–8, 249–54, 269–70, see *supra* note 452.

[485] Regarding the latter, neither the German Federal Court of Justice (*Decisions of the German Federal Court of Justice*, vol. 50, p. 52 merely states that the StPO does not know a "consensual trial") nor the doctrine clarifies what they precisely mean. See Fezer, 2010, p. 183, *supra* note 2.

[486] Cf. Fezer, 2010, p. 181, see *supra* note 2.

Italy.[487] Such negotiated solutions are also the ones applied at the international level, as described above.

Of course, the law in the books on guilty pleas and plea bargaining in International Criminal Justice is one thing, the law in action is another. At the International Military Tribunal ('IMT') and the International Military Tribunal for the Far East ('IMTFE') a guilty plea was possible (Articles 24(b) IMT Statute, 15(b) IMTFE Statute), but never became practical (let alone any plea bargaining).[488] While there have been a series of guilty pleas at the ICTY and – less often – at the ICTR, nobody ever pleaded guilty at the SCSL.[489]

At the ICC, we recently witnessed the first trial where an individual pleaded guilty. The case against Ahmad Al Faqi Al Mahdi dealt with the destruction of 10 sites of historical, religious and cultural significance in Timbuktu, Mali.[490] Al Mahdi was charged under Article

---

[487] On hierarchical problems that prevent a (desirable) turn towards the adversary system, see Klaus Lüderssen, "'Regulierte Selbstregulierung' in der Strafjustiz? Ein unorthodoxer Beitrag zur Frage der Legitimation der 'Absprachen'", in Edda Weßlau and Wolfgang Wohlers (eds.), *Festschrift für Gerhard Fezer zum 70. Geburtstag*, De Gruyter Recht, Berlin, 2008, pp. 538 ff. On the incompatibility of plea bargaining with the inquisitorial system, see Gerson Trüg, "Erkenntnisse aus der Untersuchung des US-amerikanischen plea bargaining-Systems für den deutschen Absprachediskurs", in *Zeitschrift für die gesamte Strafrechtswissenschaft*, 2008, vol. 120, pp. 371 ff.

[488] See Combs, 2013, p. 683, *supra* note 451; Turner and Weigend, 2013, p. 1377, see *supra* note 451.

[489] For a recent empirical analysis, see Meernik, 2014, pp. 200, 206–7, with table 1 showing that as of January 2013, 20 or approximately 17 per cent of the ICTY accused and 9 or approximately 13 per cent of the ICTR accused have pleaded guilty, *supra* note 462. See also Schuon, 2010, pp. 200 ff., *supra* note 452; Boas, *et al.*, 2011, p. 214, see *supra* note 459; see also Safferling, 2012, pp. 440–41 (regarding ICTY), *supra* note 452; Rauxloh, 2010, pp. 739, 746–49, distinguishing three phases at the ICTY, see *supra* note 466; Turner and Weigend, 2013, pp. 1377–78, 1383, see *supra* note 451, referring in fn. 7 to the only guilty plea at the SCSL, but in contempt proceedings; Guariglia and Hochmayr, 2016, mn. 12–13 (ICTY/ICTR), see *supra* note 462.

[490] See generally Paige Casaly, "Al Mahdi Before the ICC: Cultural Property and World Heritage in International Criminal Law", in *Journal of International Criminal Justice*, 2016, vol. 14, no. 5, pp. 1199 ff.; McCleery, 2016, p. 1100, *supra* note 66; Mark V. Vlasic and Helga Turku, "'Blood Antiquities': Protecting Cultural Heritage beyond Criminalization", in *Journal of International Criminal Justice*, 2016, vol. 14, no. 5, p. 1181. For a comprehensive treatment of the protection of cultural property in international law see recently Sabine von Schorlemer, *Gezielte Zerstörung von (Welt-)Kulturerbe in Krisenländern als Herausforderung für die Vereinten Nationen*, Nomos, Baden-Baden, 2016; about the protection of cultural property from a historical perspective, see Vlasic and Turku, 2016, pp. 1184–91, *supra* note 490.

8(2)(e)(iv) of the ICC Statute[491] and expressed during the confirmation of charges proceedings on 1 March 2016 in closed session his intent to enter a guilty plea, what he then officially did before the Trial Chamber on 22 August 2016.[492] As a result, the shortest trial in the history of the ICC produced a judgment of merely 49 pages and the lowest sentence imposed by the ICC thus far (nine years of imprisonment). In its judgment, Trial Chamber VIII treated Al Mahdi's admission of guilt – in the tradition of the civil law system – merely as a mitigating factor, citing ICTY case law.[493] It is striking that the Chamber especially made an effort to emphasise the implications of the admission of guilt on the goals of the Court, thereby legitimising it with the highest possible policy considerations: It "may also further peace and reconciliation in Northern Mali by alleviating the victims' moral suffering through acknowledgement of the significance of the destruction" and "may have a deterrent effect on others tempted to commit similar acts in Mali and elsewhere".[494] Moreover, from a special prevention perspective,[495] Al Mahdi's admission of guilt demonstrated "that he is likely to successfully reintegrate into society".[496] That the Chamber felt obliged to legitimise the admission of guilt with the goals of international criminal justice not only underlines the Janus-faced nature of the proceeding on an admission of guilt between trial economy and search for

---

[491] ICC Statute, Art. 8(2)(e)(iv) criminalises "intentionally directing attacks against buildings dedicated to religion, education, art, science or charitable purposes, historic monuments, hospitals and places where the sick and wounded are collected, provided they are not military objectives", see *supra* note 472. About Article 8(2)(e)(iv) as a "relativist approach" *vis-à-vis* a universalist approach, see Casaly, 2016, pp. 1203–6, *supra* note 490. About the prosecution by the ICTY of attacks against cultural property, see Serge Brammertz, Kevin C. Hughes, Alison Kipp and William B. Tomljanovich, "Attacks against Cultural Heritage as a Weapon of War: Prosecutions at the ICTY", in *Journal of International Criminal Justice*, 2016, vol. 14, no. pp. 1143 ff., and Casaly, *ibid.*, pp. 1206–10.

[492] About the plea itself in more detail, see Casaly, 2016, pp. 1217–18, *supra* note 490.

[493] ICC, Situation in the Republic of Mali, *Prosecutor v. Ahmad Al Faqi Al Mahdi*, Trial Chamber, Judgment and Sentence, 27 September 2016, ICC-01/12-01/15-171, para. 100 ('Al Mahdi Judgment') (http://www.legal-tools.org/doc/042397/).

[494] *Ibid.*

[495] About special prevention as a goal of international criminal justice, see Kai Ambos, *Treatise on International Criminal Law*, vol. 1: *Foundations and General Part*, Oxford University Press, Oxford, 2013, p. 70.

[496] Al Mahdi Judgment, para. 97, see *supra* note 493. About the association of remorse and apology with reconciliation, see Diggelmann, 2016, pp. 1077–80, *supra* note 451.

truth, or – more broadly – between *Realpolitik* and *Idealpolitik*. It also gives a taste of what the Court is determined to do to reduce its case-load and increase its reputation among critics, who regard it as slow and ineffective. By accepting the plea agreement, the Trial Chamber will certainly motivate other accused to avoid lengthy trials and high sentences for an admission of guilt in return.[497] This, of course, pre-supposes unequivocal evidence, a prospect that will rather be the exception than the norm.[498] The Al Mahdi case, however, should not be underestimated in its communicative effect[499] on all those who are willing to reintegrate into society after a life of conflict and atrocities.

---

[497] See Michael G. Karnavas, "Ahmed al Faqi al Mahdi's Trial or Slow Change of Plea Hearing at the ICC?", in *International Criminal Law Blog*, 30 August 2016, available at http://michaelgkarnavas.net/blog/2016/08/30/al-mahdi-trial-or-plea/.

[498] Valérie V. Suhr, "The ICC's Al Mahdi Verdict on the Destruction of Cultural Heritage: Two Steps Forward, One Step Back?", *Völkerrechtsblog*, 3 October 2016, available at https://voelkerrechtsblog.org/the-iccs-al-mahdi-verdict-on-the-destruction-of-cultural-heritage-two-steps-forward-one-step-back/.

[499] On the communicative function of punishment in international criminal justice, see Ambos, 2013, pp. 70–72, *supra* note 495.

4
_____

Abbreviated Criminal Procedures for Core International Crimes: The Statistical and Capacity Arguments

Ilia Utmelidze[*]

4.1. Introduction

During the twentieth century, the world has witnessed more than 250 conflicts, resulting in the deaths of an estimated 75 to 170 million people. Considerable victimisation has resulted from the conduct of both state and non-state actors engaging in policies of extrajudicial execution, torture, rape and other atrocities in violation of international humanitarian law and international human rights norms.[1] Despite remarkable efforts during the past few decades, the development of effective mechanisms that can address the legacy of massive victimisation and ensure that "the most serious crimes of concern to the international community as a whole must not go unpunished" are still in the making.[2]

Over the years, the lack of political commitment to accountability processes, often manifested in the unwillingness of states to conduct genuine investigation and prosecution, was rightly seen as a major impediment to "put an end to impunity for the perpetrators of these crimes".[3] However, positive developments during the past two decades have undoubtedly pro-

---

[*] **Ilia Utmelidze** is Director, Case Matrix Network, and Senior Legal Adviser, Norges nasjonale institusjon for menneskerettigheter (Norway's National Institution for Human Rights). He was formerly Legal Adviser, Norwegian Centre for Human Rights, Human Rights Department of the OSCE Mission to Bosnia and Herzegovina, and the Norwegian Refugee Council, Azerbaijan.
[1] M. Cherif Bassiouni, "Combating Impunity for International Crimes", in _University of Colorado Law Review_, 2000, vol. 71, pp. 409–422.
[2] Rome Statute of the International Criminal Court ('ICC Statute'), Preamble, para. 4 (http://www.legal-tools.org/doc/7b9af9/).
[3] _Ibid._, Preamble, para. 5.

vided grounds for optimism and hopes that such political obstacles can be overcome.[4]

Yet the scale and complexities that characterise core international crimes cases can often pose other serious challenges to accountability processes. Dealing with the legacy of mass victimisation in the aftermath of armed conflicts or repressive regimes – that often last for a considerable period of time and affect all segments of society – is not an easy undertaking. It is particularly difficult for societies directly affected by such events to mobilise the necessary material and human resources that would adequately address grave and large-scale abuses in a qualified and effective manner. Against the backdrop of a still volatile political environment, the lack of an efficient mechanism to address consequences of mass atrocities could result in the inability of the legal system of any state to carry out investigations or prosecutions of core international crimes in a meaningful way.

There are two essential factors that fundamentally affect the ability of a legal system to process core international crimes cases: 1) large numbers of cases and many suspects, in the context of limited resources and competing demands; and 2) lack of capacity and technical ability to process large numbers of core international crimes cases, taking into consideration the need for specialised approaches to address these complex crimes.[5] The design of any viable mechanisms for accountability processes must take proper account of both factors.

Territorial states are probably most exposed to these challenges. Generally, it can be anticipated that the highest numbers of perpetrators, victims, witnesses, material and other evidence can be found on the territory of a state where the atrocities have occurred. As the process of transition and post-conflict recovery commences, most of these crimes would routinely be submitted to the jurisdiction of the territorial states. The territo-

---

[4]   Since the 1990s there have been developments such as the opening of special tribunals for armed conflicts in the former Yugoslavia and genocide in Rwanda; internationalised jurisdictions like Sierra Leone, East Timor, Kosovo, Cambodia and Bosnia and Herzegovina; and national prosecution efforts within both territorial States and third party jurisdiction, and establishment of a permanent International Criminal Court.

[5]   See Office of the United Nations High Commissioner for Human Rights, *Rule of Law Tools for Post-Conflict States: Prosecution Initiatives*, United Nations, New York and Geneva, 2006, p. 2.

riality principle[6] is always the element which raises expectations that the affected state should have a lead role in addressing consequences of the mass victimisations.[7]

The permissive or mandatory duty of the state to exercise its jurisdiction over core international crimes[8] converts this expectation into a legal obligation. Furthermore, there are expectations of a more political, social and/or ethical nature that put the territorial state in the spotlight of accountability, as victim groups and the general public are increasingly persistent on the issues of truth-seeking and justice for mass atrocities.

---

[6] This is a principle of jurisdiction which provides that states have the authority to prescribe rules for persons or events present on their territory and to execute these regulations. It is derived from the sovereignty that states possess over their territories.

[7] There are several examples within the past two decades where international mechanisms have stepped in when states are unwilling or unable to address these crimes. However, such international solutions are only temporary or limited in scope.

[8] The legal obligation of states to punish those responsible for committing core international crimes is a complex legal issue. The existence of the duty to punish is a generally accepted legal doctrine. However, discussion is still ongoing with regard to application of this concept to different types of crimes. There is a general agreement that a duty exists to punish crimes of genocide: see Convention on the Prevention and Punishment of the Crime of Genocide ('Genocide Convention'), 9 December 1948, Articles I and VI (http://www.legal-tools.org/doc/498c38/), and International Court of Justice, *Case Concerning Application of the Convention of the Prevention and Punishment of the Crimes of Genocide, Bosnia and Herzegovina v. Yugoslavia (Serbia and Montenegro)*, Judgment, 26 February 2007, para. 442 (http://www.legal-tools.org/doc/5fcd00/); war crimes that amount to grave breaches: Convention (I) for the Amelioration of the Condition of the Wounded and Sick in Armed Forces in the Field, Geneva 12 August 1949, ('Geneva Convention I'), Article 49(2); Convention (II) for the Amelioration of the Condition of the Wounded, Sick and Shipwrecked Members of Armed Forces at Sea, Geneva 12 August 1949, ('Geneva Convention II'), Article 50(2); Convention (III) Relative to the Treatment of Prisoners of War, Geneva, 12 August 1949, ('Geneva Convention III'), Article 129(2); Convention (IV) Relative to the Protection of Civilian Persons in Time of War, Geneva, 12 August 1949, ('Geneva Convention IV'), Article 146(2); Protocol Additional to the Geneva Conventions of 12 August 1949, and Relating to the Protection of Victims of International Armed Conflicts (Protocol I), 8 June 1977 ('Additional Protocol I'), Article 85; and torture: Convention against Torture and Other Cruel, Inhuman or Degrading Treatment or Punishment ('Torture Convention'), Adopted and opened for signature, ratification and accession by General Assembly resolution 39/46 of 10 December 1984, Article 7. Moreover, jurisprudence of the European Court of Human Rights and Inter-American Court of Human Rights has reiterated the duty of the state to prosecute grave violations of human rights affecting life, physical integrity and freedom. The sixth paragraph of the Preamble of the ICC Statute also highlights the "duty of the state to exercise its criminal jurisdiction over those responsible for international crimes".

International jurisdictions are often set up with an intention to deal with the worst of the crimes committed and the most senior leaders suspected of being most responsible for crimes,[9] especially when states are unable or unwilling to address international crimes.[10] This approach restricts the number and types of cases that international tribunals actually have to deal with. The main reasoning behind such limitations is to make it possible for the international tribunals to operate within their respective capacities and material-technical resources, and in some cases, the timeframes involved.

Such controls of the jurisdiction of international tribunals are probably the only realistic way of keeping these courts operational. They help to ensure that international tribunals are not overwhelmed with potentially thousands of individual cases.[11] Although the international jurisdictions have access to much larger and more advanced material and human capacity, this practice serves as a safeguard that helps the tribunals to effectively match their workloads with their respective institutional capacities. Unfortunately, this approach only helps in reducing pressure on the international jurisdictions. By no means does it solve the problem of excessive core international crimes cases *per se*. Practice suggests that most of the remaining cases will be sent back to territorial states for the institution of further proceedings.[12]

Non-territorial states[13] are also exposed to the associated challenges of the scale and complexity of the international crimes cases, but probably

---

[9]   UN Security Council, resolution 1503, 28 August 2003, UN doc. S/RES/1503(2003) (http://www.legal-tools.org/doc/9037f5/), for example, effectively sets limitations on the scope of the International Criminal Tribunal for the former Yugoslavia ('ICTY') through a so-called "completion strategy".

[10] ICC Statute, Article 12, see *supra* note 2.

[11] There are legal mechanisms that provide for the possibility to refer surplus cases back to the territorial states or other states. ICTY, Rules of Procedure and Evidence, created 11 February 1994, amended 8 December 2010, Rule 11*bis* (http://www.legal-tools.org/doc/02712f/) provides for the transfer of cases from the ICTY to the national courts for prosecution. Furthermore, so-called Category 2 cases can be referred at the investigation stage from the ICTY Prosecutor's Office to national counterparts.

[12] UN Security Council, resolution 1503, see *supra* note 9, for example, prescribes precisely the transfer of all responsibilities for prosecution from the ICTY to national justice systems of states in the western Balkan region.

[13] Non-territorial jurisdiction comes into play where states can or must exercise jurisdiction with regard to, for example, core international crimes. Such jurisdiction can be based on an

to a lesser extent than territorial states. The involvement of non-territorial states in processing international crimes cases take a variety of forms and is probably too situation-specific to generalise. In some situations, non-territorial states can receive a single case or a handful of cases through the mechanisms of case transfer of the international tribunals.[14] In other situations, states may be directly involved in the hostilities on the territory of other states. When international crimes have occurred, such states could face the challenge of processing a considerable number of potential suspects and incidents.

Migration – during and in the aftermath of armed conflict – can also bring a considerable number of potential suspects and victims to the territory of third states that have no direct link to the hostilities. Following the armed conflicts in the 1990s in the western Balkans and East Africa, a number of the northern European states, including Norway,[15] had to deal with several dozen suspects and victims of mass atrocities who currently reside in their respective territories.

Despite the specificities of different jurisdictional regimes, any comprehensive effort to deal with the legacy of mass atrocity will not be possible without confronting the two essential above-mentioned factors. The large universe of cases and suspects usually generates a backlog of core international crimes cases (that is, the *statistical challenge*) that would particularly affect the justice systems of territorial states. The lack of requisite capacity and technical ability (that is, the *capacity challenge*) can make such backlogs even more entrenched. In these situations, a variety of measures of institutional, legislative and operational character have to be put in place to help justice systems meet these challenges. If all necessary elements are implemented, abbreviated criminal procedures can also play a crucial part.

---

active or passive personality principle or on the basis of universal jurisdiction, a more controversial legal doctrine in some of its purer forms.

[14] For example, the case referral mechanisms of ICTY, Rules of Procedure and Evidence, Rule 11*bis*, see *supra* note 11.

[15] In January 2010 *Aftenposten* (the main national Norwegian newspaper) published several articles highlighting the difficulties of the justice system in dealing with 114 core international crimes cases that were under investigation in Norway.

4.2. The Backlog of Core International Crimes Cases: The Statistical Challenge

A simple but powerful expression – "from the culture of impunity to accountability" – is probably the most accurate and laconic definition of the complex political, legal and social processes that, among other things, aim to create national and international mechanisms to achieve accountability for mass atrocities. Unfortunately, the path from impunity to accountability for mass atrocities can seldom avoid the obstacles of the large numbers of cases and suspects. The reason lies primarily in the objective realities about how these mass atrocities were committed. The history of the development of existing accountability processes, as well as the applicable framework of international criminal law and human rights are other factors that help institute this reality.

The concept of accountability and justice has been influenced by the aspirations of the post-Second World War international order, which was determined "to save succeeding generations from the scourge of war, which twice in our lifetime has brought untold sorrow to mankind".[16] However, viewed historically, it was probably the "faith in fundamental human rights, in the dignity and worth of the human person"[17] that most influenced the modern concept of justice and accountability.

The establishment of international military tribunals in Nuremberg and Tokyo laid the first foundation for individual criminal responsibility for the most serious crimes of concern to the international community. These developments undoubtedly changed the perspectives of post-conflict justice and accountability. According to this new paradigm, every single criminal act with sufficient supporting evidence could potentially be the subject of a criminal investigation and every single individual responsible for concrete criminal acts could be held responsible for committing these crimes.[18]

However, from the very early stages of development of international criminal law it was evident that these types of mass atrocities, namely those that are serious enough to be a concern to the international community as a whole, cannot be isolated or random events, but rather a large-scale and

---

[16] Charter of the United Nations, San Francisco, 26 June 1945, Preamble ('UN Charter').

[17] *Ibid.*

[18] Although the International Military Tribunal at Nuremberg had a mandate to deal with the major war criminals of the European Axis powers, the trials against many lower-ranked perpetrators continued in the German Federation even after the tribunal was closed.

often organised phenomenon. Interestingly, substantive international criminal law is firmly based on the understanding of this very nature of mass atrocities, including their scale and intensity.

4.2.1. Mass Victimisation in the Context of International Criminal Law and Human Rights

The definition of the crime of genocide, for example, provides that atrocities must be "committed with intent to destroy, *in whole or in part*, a national, ethnical, racial or religious group, as such".[19] Importantly, one of the constituent components of this legal requirement "in whole or in part" makes a direct reference to what can be defined as the scale of intended victimisation. According to William A. Schabas:

> In allowing that genocide could be committed "in whole or in part", the drafters of the Convention definition sought to avoid two consequences. First, it was not intended that the crime of genocide extended to isolated acts of racially motivated violence [...]. Second, however, the expression "in whole or in part" indicates that the offender need not intend to destroy the entire group but only a substantial portion of it.[20]

The jurisprudence of both the ICTR and ICTY suggests there is no numeric threshold of victims and the main requirement is to establish the intent to destroy a substantial part of the group that is more than an imperceptible number of the targeted group.[21] Both the jurisprudence of interna-

---

[19] Both Article 2 of the Genocide Convention, see *supra* note 8, and Article 6 of the ICC Statute, see *supra* note 2, provide almost identical definitions of the crimes of genocide.

[20] William A. Schabas, *The International Criminal Court: A Commentary on the Rome Statute*, Oxford University Press, Oxford, 2010, p. 127.

[21] International Criminal Tribunal for Rwanda ('ICTR'), *Prosecutor v. Juvénal Kajelijeli*, Trial Chamber, Judgment, ICTR-98-44A, 1 December 2003, para. 809 (http://www.legal-tools.org/doc/afa827/); ICTR, *Prosecutor v. Laurent Semanza*, Trial Chamber, Judgment, ICTR-97-20, 15 May 2003, para. 316 (http://www.legal-tools.org/doc/7e668a/); ICTR, *Prosecutor v. Ignace Bagilishema*, Trial Chamber, Judgment, ICTR-95-1A, 7 June 2001, para. 58 (http://www.legal-tools.org/doc/6164a4/); ICTR, *Prosecutor v. Alfred Musema* Trial Chamber, Judgment, ICTR-96-13, 27 January 2000, para. 165 (http://www.legal-tools.org/doc/1fc6ed/); ICTR, *Prosecutor v. Georges Rutaganda*, Trial Chamber, Judgment, ICTR-96-3, 6 December 1999, para. 60; ICTR, *Prosecutor v. Clement Kayishema and Obed Ruzindana*, Trial Chamber, Judgment, ICTR-95-1, 21 May 1999, paras. 95, 96, 98 (http://www.legal-tools.org/doc/0811c9/); ICTR, *Prosecutor v. Jean-Paul Akayesu*, Trial Chamber, Judgment, ICTR-96-4, 2 September 1998, para. 521 ('Akayesu case, Trial Judgment') (http://www.legal-tools.org/doc/b8d7bd/).

---

tional tribunals and scholarly opinion suggest that the intent to destroy a group "in part" requires the intention to destroy a considerable number of individuals or a substantial part, but not necessarily a very important part of the group.[22] Although it is not a mere numerical tabulation that defines the essence of these types of atrocities,[23] it is still sensible to suggest that genocide implies a significant pattern of victimisation.

Crimes against humanity is another category of international crimes that reflects the large-scale nature of mass atrocities. The current legal definition of crimes against humanity suggests that these types of atrocities have to be committed "as part of a widespread or systematic attack directed against any civilian population".[24] Relevant international jurisprudence provides that the concept of "widespread" may be defined as massive, frequent, large-scale action, carried out collectively with considerable seriousness and directed against a multiplicity of victims. The concept of "systematic" may be defined as thoroughly organised and following a regular pattern on the basis of a common policy involving substantial public or private resources. There is no requirement that this policy must be adopted formally as the policy of a state. There must, however, be some kind of preconceived plan or policy.[25]

As stated by the ICTY's *Kunarac* Appeals Chamber, "the phrase 'widespread' refers to the large-scale nature of the attack and the number of

---

[22] See also United Nations, Report of the International Commission of Inquiry on Darfur to the United Nations Secretary-General, Geneva, 25 January 2005, para. 492.

[23] See, for example, ICTY, *Prosecutor v. Radislav Krstić*, Appeals Chamber, Judgment, IT-98-33, 19 April 2004, para. 12 ('Krstić Appeals Judgment') (http://www.legal-tools.org/doc/86a108/): "The numeric size of the targeted part of the group is the necessary and important starting point, though not in all cases the ending point of the inquiry. The number of individuals targeted should be evaluated not only in absolute terms, but also in relation to the overall size of the entire group. In addition to the numeric size of the targeted portion, its prominence within the group can be a useful consideration. If a specific part of the group is emblematic of the overall group, or is essential to its survival".

[24] This position is in accordance with the definition of crimes against humanity under contemporary customary law. See ICTY, *Prosecutor v. Duško Tadić*, Trial Chamber, Judgment, IT-94-1, 7 May 1997, para. 646 (http://www.legal-tools.org/doc/0a90ac/), as well as in accordance with Statute of the International Tribunal for the former Yugoslavia, adopted 25 May 1993 by resolution 827 ('ICTY Statute') (https://www.legal-tools.org/doc/b4f63b/), the Statute of the International Tribunal for Rwanda, adopted 8 November 1994 by resolution 955 ('ICTR Statute') (http://www.legal-tools.org/doc/8732d6/), and the ICC Statute, see *supra* note 2.

[25] Akayesu case, Trial Judgment, para. 579, see *supra* note 21.

---

victims, while the phrase 'systematic' refers to the organised nature of the acts of violence and the improbability of their random occurrence". The Chamber correctly noted that "patterns of crimes – that is, the non-accidental repetition of similar criminal conduct on a regular basis – are a common expression of such systematic occurrence".[26]

In the ICTR's *Nahimana* case, the Appeals Chamber observed that events in Rwanda prior to 1994 did not constitute crimes against humanity. But according to the Chamber,

> at most, the extract from Expert Witness Des Forges' report supports the finding that, while repelling the first RPF [Rwandan Patriotic Front] incursion in 1990, Rwandan forces killed between 500 and 1000 civilians, mostly Bahima, people usually identified with the Tutsi, who were accused of having aided the RPF. However, even if there were indeed 17 attacks on Tutsi civilians between 1990 or 1991 and 1993, this does not support the conclusion that there was an ongoing systematic attack against Tutsi civilians between 1 January and 6 April 1994.[27]

Consistent interpretations of this particular legal requirement for crimes against humanity directly link the term widespread to the large-scale nature of the attack and the number of victims. Moreover, it is the "cumulative effect of a series of inhumane acts or the singular effect of an inhumane act of extraordinary magnitude"[28] that characterised the widespread or systemic nature of this category of crimes. Therefore, it is only logical to expect there will be a large amount of cases and suspects if the baseline of this category of crimes is large-scale victimisation of civilian population.

"War crimes" is the category of crimes that has no implicit reference to the scale of victimisation. Plan, policy and a large-scale commission are by no means prerequisite elements of war crimes. A single and isolated act, such as the killing or torture of a single individual by a single perpetrator, can amount to a war crime. However, there is also nothing in the legal ar-

---

[26] ICTY, *Prosecutor v. Kunarac et al.*, Appeals Chamber, Judgment, IT-96-23 & 23/1, 12 June 2002, paras. 94–95 (http://www.legal-tools.org/doc/029a09/).

[27] ICTR, *Prosecutor v. Ferdinand Nahimana, Jean-Bosco Barayagwiza, Hassan Ngeze*, Appeals Chamber, Judgment, ICTR-99-52, 28 November 2007, para. 931 (http://www.legal-tools.org/doc/4ad5eb/).

[28] International Law Commission, *Yearbook of the International Law Commission 1996*, vol. II, part 2, Report of the Commission to the General Assembly on the work of its forty-eight session, UN doc. A/51/10, p. 47 (http://www.legal-tools.org/doc/f6ff65/).

chitecture of this crime that suggests that such crimes cannot be committed on a large scale and magnitude. For example, paragraph 1 of Article 8 of the ICC Statue provides: "The Court shall have jurisdiction in respect of war crimes in particular when committed as part of a plan or policy or as part of a large-scale commission of such crimes".[29] The primary purpose of the paragraph is perhaps to direct the work of the ICC prosecutors in their selection and prioritisation of cases, taking into consideration the limited resources of the ICC. However, it is also indicative that the large-scale commission of war crimes is both a legal and factual reality within this category of crimes.

The development of human rights within the field of international law has dramatically changed the role of individual victims in the account-ability process. The *human right* with its anthropocentric perspective has empowered victims to seek truth, justice and compensation for atrocities committed against them. Through their respective case law, the Inter-American Court of Human Rights and the European Court of Human Rights clearly established the duty to prosecute grave violations of human rights and the right of victims to participate in this process.[30] The *Velásquez Rodríguez* case of 1988 is considered a landmark decision that brought this new perspective to victims of mass atrocities.[31]

The possibility of addressing every single perpetrator and every sin-gle criminal act, thereby recognising each individual victim, has created a whole new perspective for the accountability process. This has provided hope for many; at the same time, it creates a challenge as to how to manage actual justice mechanisms that would be able to realise these expectations.

The new wave of accountability processes that started in the early 1990s has demonstrated the complexity and magnitude of accountability processes for international crimes. Modern hostilities seem to victimise

---

[29] ICC Statute, Article 8, see *supra* note 2.

[30] See also Inter-American Court of Human Rights ('IACtHR'), *Tibi v. Ecuador*, Judgment, 7 September 2004 (http://www.legal-tools.org/doc/b7446b/); IACtHR, *Miguel Castro-Castro Prison v. Peru*, Judgment, 25 November 2006 (http://www.legal-tools.org/doc/7d2681/); European Court of Human Rights ('ECtHR'), *Makaratzis v. Greece*, Judgment, 50385/99, 20 December 2004 (http://www.legal-tools.org/doc/04463f/); ECtHR, *Nachova and others v. Bulgaria*, Judgment, 43577/98, 43579/98, 26 February 2004 (http://www.legal-tools.org/doc/8baba0/).

[31] IACtHR, *Velásquez Rodríguez v. Honduras*, Judgment, 29 July 1988 (http://www.legal-tools.org/doc/18607f/).

huge parts of the civilian population and leave behind large-scale patterns of crimes. The investigation and prosecution of these crimes in practice mean thousands of individual suspects, and yet more criminal incidents and victims. And if the conflicts last for several years or the crimes are committed on a large scale,[32] the number of suspects, incidents and victims is multiplied.

4.2.2. The Situation in Bosnia and Herzegovina

Bosnia and Herzegovina is an interesting empirical example to understand the realities of large-scale victimisation. To address the consequences of mass atrocities committed during hostilities, complex mechanisms of accountability, truth-seeking and reparation processes have been developed. Several key statistics within the context of this conflict provide fairly good examples as to how the scale of mass victimisation can become an issue for the accountability mechanisms and these other related processes in post-conflict societies.

First, there are the domestic prosecution processes. Based on available information provided by the Bosnia and Herzegovina Prosecutor's Office at the end of 2008, there was a total of 4,990 cases involving 9,879 suspects in the country.[33] With the current capacity of the justice sector institutions of the country to process at most several dozen cases every year, such a large backlog of core international crimes cases is undoubtedly

---

[32] According to different estimates, in Rwanda around 800,000 civilians were killed. The ICTR classified many of the atrocities committed during this period as genocide and crimes against humanity.

[33] Bosnia and Herzegovina, National War Crimes Strategy, December 2008. Figure 1 ("Data on the number of outstanding cases") presents an overview of the situation in war crimes cases in Bosnia and Herzegovina at the end of 2007. The European Commission's "Bosnia and Herzegovina 2016 Report" provides that the "implementation of the national war crimes strategy objectives continued, including through the transfer of less complex cases by the state-level judiciary to other judicial levels and the state-level judiciary taking over the most complex cases from other jurisdictions. The initial deadline of 7 years to have the most complex cases solved by December 2015 was not met and a new revised deadline has yet to be agreed, alongside a reinforcement of the role of the Supervisory Body to ensure the successful implementation of the strategy. As of end December, 335 of the most complex cases were completed, leaving 358 pending. Some 450 less complex cases were completed, 426 of which through transfer to other judicial levels, while 357 remained to be completed", see document SWD(2016) 365 final, Brussels, 9 November 2016.

a fundamental challenge.[34] The large number of missing persons is another challenge, both from the perspectives of truth-seeking and accountability. According to the International Committee of the Red Cross and International Commission on Missing Persons, the number of missing persons in Bosnia and Herzegovina right after the hostilities was up to 27,000.[35] These figures are supported by the findings of the Research and Documentation Centre in Sarajevo that discovered the identities of up to 100,000 people (including missing persons) during the conflicts of the 1990s. A close analysis of this statistical data indicates both an extremely high number of civilian victims as well as the criminal nature of this victimisation.

The work of the Srebrenica Commission is very important to understanding the overall complexities of the accountability processes in Bosnia and Herzegovina. The families of the missing persons of the Srebrenica genocide of 1995, frustrated with the very slow pace of the accountability process, have brought hundreds of individual complaints to the Human Rights Chamber.[36] The court processed these complaints and made a ruling in a lead decision in *Ferida Selimović* and 48 others. Among other remedies, the court ordered the "release [of] all information [...] with respect to the fate and whereabouts of the missing loved ones of the applicants", and "to conduct a full, meaningful, thorough, and detailed investigation into the events giving rise to the established human rights violations".[37] As a consequence of this ruling the Srebrenica Commission of Inquiry was established. One of the outcomes of the Commission's work was a list of possi-

---

[34] See also Morten Bergsmo, Kjetil Helvig, Ilia Utmelidze and Gorana Žagovec, *The Backlog of Core International Crimes Case Files in Bosnia and Herzegovina*, 2nd ed., FICHL Publication Series No. 3, Torkel Opsahl Academic EPublisher, Oslo, 2010, pp. 68–76.

[35] A clear majority of these disappearances were actually killed. During the hostilities, many individuals or groups were executed and hidden in mass or individual graves. The tremendous efforts of several international and domestic agencies have led to the identification of thousands of missing persons. This was possible only with the help of very complex and expansive DNA identification methodologies. Notwithstanding the progress made, there are still several thousand individuals missing.

[36] The Human Rights Chamber is a special human rights court established under Dayton Peace agreement in Bosnia and Herzegovina (see http://www.hrc.ba/).

[37] Human Rights Chamber for Bosnia and Herzegovina, *Ferida Selimović and 48 Others v. Republika Srpska*, Decision on Admissibility and Merits, CH01/8365, 7 March 2003, paras. 7, 212.

ble perpetrators that was sent back to prosecutor's office for further investigation and prosecution.[38]

In addition to the issue of the missing persons, the Human Rights Chamber dealt with over 15,000 individual human rights complaints. The majority of these complaints related to various crimes committed during the conflict. The Chamber's jurisprudence indicated that discrimination in the field of employment, social security and religious freedoms was representative of a pattern of victimisation usually referred to as "ethnic cleansing". A considerable number of complaints also related to claims for the return of property taken from individuals during the hostilities of the 1990s in Bosnia and Herzegovina. Deprivation of property was also part of the policies of ethnic cleansing that aimed to create ethnically "clean" territories within the country. At the end of the 1990s a specially established commission for property repossession processed over 210,000 claims and eventually a substantial part of this property was actually returned.

There are also several statutes in Bosnia and Herzegovina that regulated the issues of compensation and social assistance and other war-related benefits. These very fragmented and complex regulations provide for over 150,000 individual benefits and privileges.[39]

The history of the development of existing accountability processes, the framework of applicable international criminal law and human rights, as well as empirical examples indicate that massive victimisation is often the main characteristic of modern hostilities. Dealing with the consequences of these atrocities often requires addressing large numbers of criminal cases, suspects and individual complaints of victims. Processing this caseload overflow can strongly affect the ability of any justice system to deal with mass atrocities in an effective and meaningful way. Mass atrocities not only affect the criminal justice system but also other institutions within the affected societies that have a remedial function in the context of post-conflict recovery. Although collaboration among different institutions is essential, they can seldom substitute for each other's roles and functions. The expectation that referral of backlogs of unresolved criminal cases outside the

---

[38] The exact numbers of possible perpetrators never became public, but there are several thousands of individuals named in this list.

[39] Most of the beneficiaries are war veterans. For example, in the Federation of Bosnia and Herzegovina (one of two entities in the country), there are up to 100,000 war veterans who receive monthly compensation. The total amount of compensation is around 20 per cent of the entire budget of this entity.

justice system might resolve the problem can be unworkable.[40] It is probably only through strengthening justice sectors and finding innovative solutions within existing institutions that can help to resolve backlogs of core international crimes cases.

4.3. The Lack of Capacity and Technical Ability in Processing Large Numbers of Core International Crimes Cases

In general, during hostilities there is very little done to address these crimes, especially in an objective and effective manner. This is often due to the fact that in some cases the commission of mass atrocities is part of the intentional policy of the responsible parties that excludes any possibility of objective accountability processes. In other extreme situations, there can simply be anarchy in which the failed state cannot exercise any effective authority over individuals who are committing these crimes. Once again, territorial states can be especially unprepared to meet the challenge of large-scale victimisation. The long and intensive hostilities of modern conflicts often lead to the partial or complete failure of democratic institutions and rule of law mechanisms within territorial states. These failures of democracy and rule of law usually lead to dysfunctional or biased criminal justice systems.

The weakened post-conflict justice system, in combination with the large and complex backlog of atrocities, can be viewed as the main reasons for the lack of the necessary capacity and technical abilities of the respective jurisdiction to effectively address core international crimes cases. There are different ways and means as to how the lack of capacity of the justice systems can be identified. The challenges can be legal, institutional as well as financial.

The legal capacity of the relevant jurisdiction to address mass atrocities is defined by laws and regulations applicable in the given countries. The gaps in domestic legislation or their inconsistencies with international accepted norms can be serious challenges for the capacity of the national jurisdiction to process core international crimes cases in a fair and objective manner.

---

[40] The example of the Srebrenica Commission demonstrates that, if true, the desire of the victims' groups is to see justice done; only justice institutions, not any other subsidiary mechanism, can address this.

The institutional capacity of the relevant justice system is probably the most complex and sensitive issue to deal with. First of all, it is an organisational set-up to address mass atrocities. Some jurisdictions are designing specialised mechanisms to address the complexity of large backlogs of core international crimes cases.[41] The design and operation of such specialised bodies also have to take a number of challenges into consideration. Efficiency, cost effectiveness and suitability of overall rule of law building are among those. Another interesting component of the institutional capacity is the issue of human resources. Not many national legal systems have developed specialised expertise in the area of international criminal law. The reason for this is that international criminal law is a relatively new legal discipline and not widely practised. This fact can probably explain why expertise in this field of the law is so scarce. It should be noted that this human resource challenge is in many ways common for both developed and developing counties. However, an urgent need to deploy a high number of relevant experts, on the one hand, and the lack of time and resources to develop the necessary expertise, on the other, makes post-conflict societies especially unprepared to overcome this challenge. The lack of institutional capacity of relevant justice systems can also be manifested in poor co-ordination and co-operation among various institutions of this sector. Special concerns regarding institutional capacity often include an inability of the system to deal with vulnerable victims and witnesses and provide necessary support and protection.

Given the limited resources and competing demands, post-conflict societies usually lack the necessary financial resources to process core international crimes cases. Wider support, both internally and often internationally, is essential to ensure necessary resources for capacity building activities in affected societies.

4.4. Conclusion

The large number of cases as well as the many suspects and individual victims are fundamentally affecting the ability of justice systems of post-conflict societies to deal with the consequences of mass atrocities. Therefore, any efforts to enhance national accountability mechanisms should take

---

[41] For example, a number of special courts have been established in Bosnia and Herzegovina, Kosovo, Cambodia, Indonesia, East Timor and Sierra Leone.

serious account both of qualitative and quantitative aspects of dealing with mass victimisation.

The practices of international jurisdictions have mostly focused on the qualitative aspects of the process. This is due to fact that international tribunals can limit their actual work to only the worst crimes committed and the most senior suspects. It is the national justice systems that are left with the challenge of dealing with the quantitative aspects of the accountability process. In the majority of situations, the possibilities of transferring the large backlog of cases to some other national mechanisms outside the criminal justice system are rather limited. The expectations of victims to see justice done can seriously undermine the legitimacy of any such process. Moreover, this can also be imprudent from the perspective of sustainable development of justice sector institutions and the overall enhancement of the rule of law.

In the context of transitional societies, the perceived inability of the justice system to tackle major consequences arising from mass atrocities can further undermine the trust of the general public in the rule of law mechanisms. Furthermore, it can also redirect crucial financial and material support to capacity-building processes within the justice sector. Delayed or incomplete reform processes might undermine the ability of justice systems in societies in transition, in dealing with past atrocities, as well as the sensitive and complex crimes of the present.

However, to enable institutions of the justice sector to deal with the consequences of mass atrocities, it is essential that new and innovative ways to deal with large backlogs of criminal cases are explored. Developing legal and institutional mechanisms at the national level that would address the quantitative challenges of accountability processes remains paramount. Abbreviated criminal procedures can definitely be an integral part of such innovative mechanisms.[42] Such procedures can provide expeditious ways of resolving certain types of

---

[42] Other important elements of such systems are effective management of the large backlog of cases through case mapping and analysis tools as well as a system of case selection and prioritisation that would provide justice institutions with objective and transparent criteria to address large quantities of cases and suspects. Qualitative capacity building and knowledge transfer are also key aspects of strengthening of national accountability processes.

core international crimes cases that can accelerate overall accountability processes.

5

Abbreviated Criminal Procedures for Serious Human Rights Violations Which May Amount to Core International Crimes

Gorana Žagovec Kustura[*]

5.1. Introduction

5.1.1. The Problem and the Purpose

Armed conflicts result in too many atrocities being committed. Once a conflict is over, the criminal justice system of the affected country should ideally hold accountable those responsible for core international crimes. Often, the number of crimes is so high that the criminal justice system simply cannot address all of them through regular criminal procedure. Ensuring a timely response is even more difficult. The obligation to prosecute and punish those responsible for atrocious crimes is enshrined in international law[1]

---

[*] **Gorana Žagovec Kustura** is a Justice Sector Specialist on USAID Justice Project in Bosnia and Herzegovina. She holds a Bachelor in Law from the University of Sarajevo Law Faculty and an LL.M. degree in Public International Law from the University of Oslo, Norway. She was formerly a Legal Adviser at High Judicial and Prosecutorial Council in BiH (2013–2014) and European Union Police Mission in BiH (2010–2011). Previously she worked as a Research Assistant at the ICC Legal Tools Programme of the Norwegian Centre for Human Rights (2008–9) and as a Rule of Law Monitor at the OSCE Mission to Bosnia and Herzegovina (2007–8). She did her practice in the Legal Department of the Court of Bosnia and Herzegovina, supporting the War Crimes Chambers (2006).

[1] Convention (I) for the Amelioration of the Condition of the Wounded and Sick in Armed Forces in the Field, Geneva 12 August 1949, Article 49 ('Geneva Convention I'); Convention (II) for the Amelioration of the Condition of the Wounded, Sick and Shipwrecked Members of Armed Forces at Sea, Geneva 12 August 1949, Article 50 ('Geneva Convention II'); Convention (III) Relative to the Treatment of Prisoners of War, Geneva, 12 August 1949, Article 129 ('Geneva Convention III'); Convention (IV) Relative to the Protection of Civilian Persons in Time of War, Geneva, 12 August 1949, Article 146 ('Geneva Convention IV'); Convention on the Prevention and Punishment of the Crime of Genocide ('Genocide Convention'), 9 December 1948, Article IV (http://www.legal-tools.org/doc/498c38/); and, most recently, Rome Statute of the International Criminal Court ('ICC Statute'), Preamble, para. 6 (http://www.legal-tools.org/doc/7b9af9/). See also Otto Triffterer (ed.), *Commentary on the Rome Statute of the International Criminal Court*, 2nd ed., C.H. Beck, Hart, Nomos, Munich, 2008, p. 11.

---

and national codes of criminal procedure, alongside the concurrent human rights obligation to afford a fair trial to each defendant.[2] In some countries, particularly those in transition from conflicts,[3] the criminal justice system lacks the capacity to deal with all the cases, quite apart from the question of political will. This results in a backlog of such cases within the system.

The introduction of abbreviated criminal procedures for core international crimes is a new idea first introduced in a publication on the backlog of core international crimes cases in Bosnia and Herzegovina.[4] The purpose of this chapter is to examine this topic and to arrive at a set of components and principles under which potential abbreviated criminal procedures for cases of core international crimes may be developed. It will also raise arguments for and against the introduction of this mechanism in national law.[5] The purpose of this mechanism would be to assist states to fulfil their primary obligation to prosecute such core international crimes without compromising principles of due process.

5.1.2. Outline of the Chapter

In order to fulfil the above-stated purpose, this chapter is organised as follows. Section 5.2. provides a brief overview of main developments that created the need to address the backlog of core international crimes cases at the national level. Presentation of the consequences of backlogs on different processes and expectations within the justice sector, victims' communities and political establishment follows.

Section 5.3. identifies relevant legal procedures and practices to help shed light on the requisite qualities of abbreviated procedures for core international crimes. It starts with consideration of judicial mechanisms de-

---

[2] United Nations General Assembly, International Covenant on Civil and Political Rights ('ICCPR'), adopted 19 December 1966, Article 14; American Convention on Human Rights ('ACHR'), adopted 22 November 1969, Articles 8, 9 and 10; European Convention on Human Rights ('ECHR'), adopted 4 November 1950, Article 6; and African Charter on Human and Peoples' Rights ('ACHPR'), adopted 27 June 1981, Article 7. See also ICC Statute, Articles 55, 63, 66 and 67, *supra* note 1.

[3] For example, in Bosnia and Herzegovina, Colombia and Rwanda.

[4] See Morten Bergsmo, Kjetil Helvig, Ilia Utmelidze and Gorana Žagovec, *The Backlog of Core International Crimes Case Files in Bosnia and Herzegovina*, 2nd ed., FICHL Publication Series No. 3, Torkel Opsahl Academic EPublisher, Oslo, 2010.

[5] The approach is based on the assumption that core international crimes that are being processed at the international level will normally be of such gravity that the abbreviated criminal procedures would not be suitable for them.

---

veloped to expedite international criminal procedures. Processes that cannot properly be referred to as abbreviated criminal procedures, but nevertheless seek to expedite the administrative response to mass-atrocities, are also discussed. These processes often exist because full criminal trials for all core international crimes are beyond the capacity of many legal systems. They include traditional plea negotiations, truth and reconciliation commissions and the *gacaca* system of courts in Rwanda. This section continues by discussing some national legislative models of abbreviated procedures for ordinary criminal offences. These offences, of course, differ significantly from core international crimes, but the procedures used are potentially similar to what may be used in an abbreviated system for processing core international crimes. The chapter includes a look at the Colombian procedure for dealing with core international crimes committed in its internal armed conflict. The final part of section 5.3. spells out some basic features that a potential abbreviated criminal procedure for core international crimes should embody. These procedures should: 1) be prescribed by law and an integral part of the criminal justice system, administered by regular courts without creating extrajudicial mechanisms and additional institutional layers; 2) increase the ability to resolve the large numbers of cases that create backlogs; 3) apply on a voluntary basis and respect basic fair trial principles that cannot be compromised; 4) be transparent and open; 5) be designed as part of the wider transitional justice process which is sensitive to victims' interests; and 6) provide for the variety of sanctions with the necessary degree of flexibility.

Section 5.4. sets forth numerous arguments for and against the introduction of abbreviated criminal procedures for core international crimes, and ends with a list of guidelines for such procedures, based on these arguments. Section 5.5. summarises the content of this chapter and offers some concluding remarks.

5.1.3. Methodological Observations

The present topic is novel and unregulated by law.[6] Literature is scarce regarding abbreviated criminal procedures for core international crimes. The sociology of law does not yet address it. As a result, the methodological approach of this chapter consists of a comparative analysis that exam-

---

[6] It should be noted that Colombia has an abbreviated legal framework to address core international crimes, discussed more thoroughly in section 5.3.5. below.

ines expedited judicial mechanisms in international criminal procedure, certain processes outside the scope of abbreviated criminal procedures as defined herein, domestic legislation for ordinary crimes, and a country-specific approach to core international crimes committed in an internal armed conflict. Deduction from these different approaches will allow for a presentation of what abbreviated criminal procedures for core international crimes may entail. It is therefore a *de lege ferenda* discussion. Arguments for and against the introduction of this new mechanism will allow guiding principles for abbreviated criminal procedures to be formulated.

5.1.4. Technical Clarification of Terms

For the purpose of this chapter, some key terms will be given the following meaning. By the expression "core international crimes" I mean genocide, crimes against humanity and war crimes, such as specified in international legal documents like the Rome Statute of the International Criminal Court ('ICC Statute').[7] The term "serious human rights violations" refers to violations of international human rights and humanitarian law that may amount to core international crimes. "Abbreviated criminal procedures" are procedures within the criminal justice system that entail a significantly shortened approach to the processing of core international crimes cases, as opposed to the regular criminal procedure. It does not include certain other processes, as will be discussed below. The term "case file" means there has been a registration and creation of a criminal file within the prosecutor's office. "Criminal justice system" is defined as collective institutions through which an accused offender passes until the accusations have been disposed of or punishment concluded.[8] Transitional justice is a response to systematic or widespread violations of human rights. It seeks recognition for victims and to promote possibilities for peace, reconciliation and democracy.[9]

5.2. The Background

In order to contextualise the topic, this section gives information about the main developments in international criminal law and procedure that caused

---

[7]   See ICC Statute, Articles 6, 7 and 8, *supra* note 1.

[8]   Bryan A. Garner (ed.), *Black's Law Dictionary*, 8th ed., West Group, St. Paul, 2004, p. 403.

[9]   See International Center for Transitional Justice, "What Is Transitional Justice?", International Center for Transitional Justice, 1 January 2009 (https://www.ictj.org/sites/default/files/ICTJ-Global-Transitional-Justice-2009-English.pdf).

backlogs of core international crimes cases to emerge at the national level
(section 5.2.1.). It further undertakes to present the challenge posed to national criminal justice systems by the high number of core international
crimes committed (section 5.2.2.). In the end, it outlines some of the effects
that backlogs have on different processes and expectations within the justice sector, victims' communities and political establishment (section
5.2.3.).

5.2.1. Developments in International Law

Ever since the First World War there has been a growing acceptance in the
world's legal community of the need for accountability of actors involved
in serious violations of human rights law and international humanitarian
law. After the Second World War statutes were adopted to establish international military tribunals at Nuremberg and Tokyo for the just and prompt
trial and punishment of the major war criminals.[10] During the Cold War
period, although wars were waged and atrocities occurred, no international
tribunals were established.[11] In the 1990s, however, the United Nations
Security Council, acting under Chapter VII of the UN Charter, created two
international criminal tribunals, the International Criminal Tribunal for the
former Yugoslavia ('ICTY') and International Criminal Tribunal for
Rwanda ('ICTR').[12] The perception was that these two *ad hoc* international
tribunals, given the competence and impartiality of their international staff,
were most suited to deal with the crimes committed in these two countries.

As these tribunals developed, they shifted focus from lower- or in-
termediate-level perpetrators up the chain of command to the highest-level

---

[10] Charter of the International Military Tribunal ('IMT Charter'), Part of the London Agreement of 8 August 1945 for the Prosecution and Punishment of the Major War Criminals of
the European Axis, Article 1 (http://www.legal-tools.org/doc/64ffdd/). See also Charter of
the International Military Tribunal for the Far East ('IMTFE Charter'), 19 January 1946,
Article 1 (http://www.legal-tools.org/doc/a3c41c/).

[11] One such conflict was in Cambodia. In 2001 the Cambodian National Assembly passed a
law to create a court to try serious crimes committed during the Khmer Rouge regime during 1975–1979. See Law on the Establishment of the Extraordinary Chambers, with inclusion of amendments as promulgated on 27 October 2004 (NS/RKM/1004/006)
(http://www.legal-tools.org/doc/9b12f0/).

[12] Statute of the International Tribunal for the former Yugoslavia, adopted 25 May 1993 by
resolution 827 ('ICTY Statute') (https://www.legal-tools.org/doc/b4f63b/); Statute of the
International Tribunal for Rwanda, adopted 8 November 1994 by resolution 955 ('ICTR
Statute') (http://www.legal-tools.org/doc/8732d6/).

suspects, to senior leaders suspected of being most responsible for crimes within their jurisdictions. By holding senior military and political leaders accountable for crimes, the tribunals demonstrated that even heads of state were not above the law.[13] Due to this evolutionary process, they only touched the tip of the iceberg when it comes to the number of perpetrators actually processed.

It is warranted to use the experience of the ICTY and ICTR to illustrate the main issues, problems and shortcomings of international procedures. According to Antonio Cassese:

> [The] two Ad Hoc Tribunals [...] were perceived as being marred by four essential flaws: i) their costly nature; ii) the excessive length of their proceedings; iii) their remoteness from the territory where crimes have been perpetrated and consequently the limited impact of their judicial output on the national populations concerned; iv) the unfocused character of the prosecutorial targets resulting in trials of a number of low-ranking defendants.[14]

Cassese goes on to explain the "trend" towards processing the majority of these cases at the national level, based on two grounds. First, national courts in the states concerned have become better equipped to handle such cases without bias. Second, the "completion strategy" adopted by the Security Council intended to close down the two *ad hoc* international tribunals and for national courts to increasingly take over their workload.[15] Further strengthening the trend identified by Cassese is the principle of complementarity, enshrined in the ICC Statute, according to which the International Criminal Court ('ICC') will not exercise its jurisdiction unless states are either unwilling or unable to prosecute.[16] The trend has thus shifted the burden of core international crimes prosecutions to the national level and caused the criminal justice system in affected states to become overwhelmed with this complex type of criminal cases.

---

[13] See International Criminal Tribunal for the former Yugoslavia ('ICTY'), Office of the Prosecutor – an Introduction (http://www.icty.org/sid/287).

[14] Antonio Cassese, *International Criminal Law*, 2nd ed., Oxford University Press, Oxford, 2008, p. 332.

[15] *Ibid.*, p. 341.

[16] See ICC Statute, Preamble, para. 10, and Articles 1 and 17, *supra* note 1.

5.2.2. Challenges of Core International Crimes Prosecutions at the National Level

Violent conflicts usually involve commission of a high number of core international crimes involving many perpetrators and their accomplices. These atrocities result in a large-scale victimisation of civilians. When a territorial state directly affected by the crimes has a functional criminal justice system, the responsible authorities should investigate and prosecute core international crimes cases. Regardless of the universality principle[17] and other grounds of jurisdiction, the investigation and prosecution of core international crimes should primarily be undertaken by the authorities in the country where the crimes were committed. This can lead to the subsequent opening of a significant number of case files within the criminal justice system. At the same time, because almost all national criminal justice systems work with insufficient resources, the ability to process core international crimes cases will be limited. As a result, there may be a considerable discrepancy between the actual number of open core international crimes case files, on the one hand, and the number of cases which the national jurisdiction has the capacity to actually process, on the other. This will in most situations create a backlog of core international crimes cases.

A backlog of cases raises several fundamental concerns. First, it is essential that the criminal justice system keeps a complete overview of the number of cases in the backlog. Second, it is vital for public trust in the core international crimes process that only the best-suited cases[18] are prioritised for full investigation and prosecution. If the cases are selected randomly or without apparent reason, expectations of justice are less likely to be met. Third, in many situations the backlog of cases will be so large that a substantial percentage of the cases cannot go forward through the regular trial procedure. Suspects and witnesses alike may die or become too frail to stand or appear at trial. What should be done with these cases? Should they be removed from the criminal justice system and dealt with through a non-judicial mechanism? Perhaps, one may conceive an

---

[17] Universal jurisdiction is the principle that every country has an interest in bringing to justice the perpetrators of grave crimes, no matter where the crime was committed, and regardless of the nationality of the perpetrators or their victims. See *ibid.*, whereby it was pronounced that it is the duty of every state to exercise its criminal jurisdiction over those responsible for international crimes.

[18] According to the applicable criteria that each country will develop depending upon its unique circumstances.

abbreviated criminal procedure that enables the criminal justice system itself to process core international crimes cases in a more timely and cost-effective manner, as may be required and legitimate.

5.2.3. The Effects of Large Case Backlogs

5.2.3.1. Justice Sector Reform

Core international crimes mostly happen in a situation where countries are in a state of war, where the rule of law and democracy are not functioning, or only partly functioning, resulting in a weak or even politically controlled judiciary, characterised by a loss of or even non-existing capacity. This is also why these countries are labelled 'transitional'. It means that they are trying to deal with the inglorious past and to re-establish the rule of law and respect for human rights principles. At the same time, they struggle to develop or strengthen the entire justice sector, which demands considerable capacity building.[19] Even judges and prosecutors are less confident in their important roles, since they, too, are part of the reform process within the new legal, procedural and institutional set-up. A judiciary going through a reform process, or being newly established after the reform, is more vulnerable to the creation of a backlog of cases.

5.2.3.2. Criminal Justice System

Most legal systems have limited resources available for criminal justice reform and development. Reform and development processes in countries in transition occur concurrently with day-to-day operations of the criminal justice system in question. Thus, there are competing priorities of work in such systems against the background of budgetary limitations and ever-changing expectations of justice among victims and others. If a country suffers from a severe pattern of violent crime or organised crime, it may be difficult to sustain support for investigation and prosecution of war crimes of the past. Conversely, if victims' demands for criminal justice for atrocities are so high that priority is given to such prosecutions, it is likely to lead

---

[19] A comprehensive guidebook in Bosnian details issues related to transition in Bosnia and Herzegovina. The executive summary of the guidebook, in English, is available. See United Nations Development Programme, *Transitional Justices Guidebook for Bosnia and Herzegovina: Executive Summary*, United Nations Development Programme, Sarajevo, 2009.

to fewer resources for other types of criminality and reform of the criminal justice system. A strong demand for war crimes justice that contributes to a large backlog of cases can, therefore, have a negative impact on criminal justice reform and development.

5.2.3.3. Public Trust in the Criminal Justice System

Public trust in a criminal justice system correlates to its ability to deal with the cases within it and keep the public informed.[20] If the impression grows that cases do not move expeditiously and fairly through the criminal justice system, the public will lose confidence. Trust in the criminal justice system is fundamentally important for the public to be willing to fund, co-operate and use it. If there has been a sustained but futile effort to build trust in a criminal justice system, for example in the wake of wars or period of authoritarian rule, then the whole effort to create a functional system that protects human rights and the rule of law may suffer a setback.[21] And if a criminal justice system has an exceptionally large backlog of core international crimes cases that may also affect the overall trust in the ability of the system and undermine the entire transitional process.

5.2.3.4. Victims and the Management of Expectation

The role of victims is very important in the overall dynamics of facing the past and healing the past wounds of atrocities. Victims play a crucial role as direct participants in criminal proceedings and in overall processes of transitional justice. Quite often the complexity of conflict creates different victim groups from different sides, each with its own interests and legitimate rights.[22] In many situations where serious human rights violations occurred, marked by exceptional cruelty and its consequences, and where there is a particularly severe victimisation that must be rectified, interest in criminal justice and judicial truth is extremely high.[23] Balancing general interests of

---

[20] *Ibid.*, pp. 19–20.

[21] *Ibid.*, p. 47.

[22] For example, the right to justice. See Diane Orentlicher, "Independent Study on Best Practices, including Recommendations, to Assist States in Strengthening their Domestic Capacity to Combat All Aspects of Impunity", UN Secretary-General for the Commission on Human Rights, 27 February 2004, UN doc. E/CN.4/2004/88, paras. 24–56.

[23] A process by which a legal and historical record of events and culpability of participants is made for use by the criminal justice system and progeny.

justice and the competing demands of victims and the public is challenging. Often the existing mistrust towards governments and authorities in general, and its judicial branch in particular, only increases the tensions. Confidence building between victim groups and the judicial institutions is vital, however, especially against the background of a large backlog of cases within a judicial system that, from the victims' perspective, is not doing enough to effectively resolve it. Giving false promises to victims can lead to further misunderstanding of the possibilities that exist both within and outside the criminal justice mechanisms. It is important to provide realistic information about the limitations of the existing mechanisms and try to seek innovative solutions to the problem.

5.2.3.5. Political Support and the National Core International Crimes Process

Processing core international crimes cases requires strong political support from the outset, both to ensure that undue political influences do not limit or undermine the process, and that necessary financial and other resources are allocated in a sufficient, timely manner.[24] A large backlog of cases, and the difficulty in showing quantifiable results, can substantially weaken the necessary support of local politicians, the representatives of public opinion. Even international donors supporting the transition process may fall prey to scepticism. This potentiality could subvert the entire prosecution process and bring uncertainty to the prospect of accountability for heinous crimes. Political groups initially seen as pillars of the prosecution process could also turn into sceptics when they see only a limited number of cases find their way from the labyrinths of justice or when there is no visible progress in the matter. The society affected with core international crimes has a fundamental interest in seeing that transitional processes bring measurable progress, as this can eventually lead to reconciliation and restoration of a functioning society. Even if these processes are moving forward, slow progress may cause politicians to feel hostage to the inabilities of the justice system, and consequently increase the temptation to resolve a backlog of cases by political interventions, that, in turn, could negatively affect the overall development of the rule of law.

---

[24] Office of the United Nations High Commissioner for Human Rights, *Rule-of-Law Tools for Post-conflict States: Prosecution Initiatives*, United Nations, New York, 2006, p. 3 (http://www.legal-tools.org/doc/1cce75/).

5.3. The Concept of Abbreviated Criminal Procedures

The purpose of this section is to identify components of a potential abbreviated criminal procedure for core international crimes. It initially describes expedited measures employed in international criminal procedure (section 5.3.1.). It then goes on to address practices that fall outside the scope of abbreviated criminal procedures as defined herein, but are still relevant to the discussion (section 5.3.2.). Some national criminal procedures for ordinary crimes that may have similar characteristics to abbreviated criminal procedures for core international crimes follow (section 5.3.3.). Common features of these procedures are discussed (section 5.3.4.). The model for dealing with core international crimes cases used in Colombia is presented (section 5.3.5.). The section finally specifies the basic features for a potential abbreviated criminal procedure for core international crimes (section 5.3.6.).

5.3.1. Expedited Measures in International Criminal Proceedings

There is no such thing as abbreviated criminal procedures in international criminal law. Nevertheless, noteworthy efforts have been made to develop means to expedite international criminal proceedings without compromising the fair trial rights of the accused.[25] These may serve as an incentive for national actors to understand that innovative approaches may be acceptable and even advisable in dealing with lengthy criminal proceedings for core international crimes.

Because international criminal proceedings are extremely time consuming and expensive, mainly due to evidentiary requirements,[26] judges and prosecutors realised that greater efficiency was imperative. For example, prosecutors in the ICTY pushed for greater use of certain existing mechanisms, and the introduction of new ones, in order to remedy the issue, including, *inter alia*, the dossier approach, proof of fact other than by oral

---

[25] Geoffrey Nice and Philippe Vallières-Roland, "Procedural Innovations in War Crimes Trials", in Hirad Abtahi and Gideon Boas (eds.), *The Dynamics of International Criminal Justice: Essays in Honour of Sir Richard May*, Martinus Nijhoff Publishers, Leiden, 2006.

[26] ICTY, *Prosecutor v. Dražen Erdemović*, Appeals Chamber, Separate and Dissenting Opinion of Judge Cassese, IT-96-22, 7 October 1997, para. 8 (http://www.legal-tools.org/doc/a7dff6/). See also ICTY, *Prosecutor v. Slobodan Milošević*, Partial Dissenting Opinion of Judge Shahabuddeen to the Decision on Admissibility of Prosecution Investigator's Evidence, IT-02-54, 8 October 2002, para. 2 (http://www.legal-tools.org/doc/fb26e4/).

evidence, judicial notice of adjudicated facts, joint hearings, the use of electronic tools for the management of evidence and selection of relevant material at the pre-trial stage.[27] Another example to combat inefficiency rises from the ICTY Statute. Because it contained few provisions of a procedural character, the judges were empowered to draft Rules of Procedure and Evidence governing the conduct of the proceedings, with an aim of safeguarding both fair and expedient trials. As the need for efficiency grew, the Rules were significantly amended.[28]

Some rules are particularly interesting in the context of abbreviated criminal procedures for core international crimes. Rule 89(F) allows for receipt of evidence in written form when this is in the interests of justice. Though the Appeals Chamber made its applicability subject to certain stringent requirements,[29] it could nevertheless considerably shorten the procedure if applied in an abbreviated criminal procedure for core international crimes. Further, Rule 94 does not require proof of facts of common knowledge or of adjudicated facts and documentary evidence from other proceedings of the Tribunal, but allows the taking of "judicial notice" of facts, such as for example those characterising historical and background information not subject to reasonable dispute.[30] In this regard, the Trial Chamber in *Momčilo Perišić* stated:

> [W]hen taking judicial notice, the Trial Chamber must balance such interests [that is judicial economy and harmonisation of the Tribunal's judgments] with the right of the accused to a fair trial.[31]

The lawyers who helped establish the ICC wanted to mitigate the problems of protracted proceedings. Therefore, even before the first judges

---

[27] For a detailed elaboration of such mechanisms, see Nice and Vallières-Roland, 2006, pp. 147 ff., *supra* note 25.

[28] For a detailed elaboration of the relevant rules and their application, see Patrick L. Robinson, "Fair but Expeditious Trials", in Abtahi and Boas, 2006, pp. 176 ff., *supra* note 25.

[29] ICTY, *Prosecutor v. Slobodan Milošević*, Appeals Chamber, Decision on Interlocutory Appeal on the Admissibility of Evidence-in-Chief in the Form of Written Statements, IT-02-54, 30 September 2003 (http://www.legal-tools.org/doc/163d3a/).

[30] ICTY, *Prosecutor v. Slobodan Milošević*, Trial Chamber, Decision on Prosecution Motion for Judicial Notice of Adjudicated Facts, IT-02-54-T, 10 April 2003 (http://www.legal-tools.org/doc/ce8e28/).

[31] ICTY, *Prosecutor v. Momčilo Perišić*, Trial Chamber, Decision on Motion for Judicial Notice of ICTY Convictions, IT-04-81-PT, 25 September 2008, para. 7 (http://www.legal-tools.org/doc/d40a45/).

---

took up their mandate, this group prepared a report that set forth measures to reduce the length of the proceedings.[32] The report covered all aspects of ICC criminal procedure. Some solutions are used extensively in national jurisdictions to promote judicial economy, such as developing prosecution strategy at the outset or opting for concerted rather than fragmented trials. The report also suggested the use of mechanisms provided for in the ICC Statute or Rules of Court Statute previously employed in other international tribunals, such as live witness testimony via video link or making greater use of judicial notice. It encouraged the ICC overall to develop its own interpretation of the existing imprecise rules and make greater use of written statements and testimony in lieu of oral testimony, documentary evidence and unsworn statements of the accused, providing at all times the sufficient protection of due process.

It is significant that international lawyers have acknowledged the pressing need to develop mechanisms for more expedient international criminal proceedings. As Geoffrey Nice and Philippe Vallières-Roland state, in order to achieve this goal,

> there must be a healthy dose of open-mindedness and greater willingness of international criminal lawyers and judges to depart from preconceived ideas based on *either* common *or* civil law systems. Most significantly perhaps, international criminal courts must be prepared to question the assumption that all evidence must be heard orally if there is to be any chance of trials being concluded expeditiously.[33]

5.3.2. Other Relevant Processes

In this section I present several processes not included in the idea of abbreviated criminal procedures for core international crimes. These include traditional plea negotiations (section 5.3.2.1.), truth and reconciliation commissions (section 5.3.2.2.) and *gacaca* courts in Rwanda (section 5.3.2.3.). The extensive use of these processes could be legally, politically and socially acceptable in some countries and situations, particularly where there is

---

[32] Håkan Friman, Fabricio Guariglia, Claus Kress, John Rason Spencer and Vladimir Tochilovsky, "Measures Available to the International Criminal Court to Reduce the Length of the Proceedings", in Morten Bergsmo, Klaus Rackwitz and SONG Tianying (editors): *Historical Origins of International Criminal Law: Volume 5*, Torkel Opsahl Academic EPublisher, Brussels, 2017.

[33] Nice and Vallières-Roland, 2006, p. 144, see *supra* note 25.

no functioning criminal justice system to dictate higher standards of judicial scrutiny. In my opinion, although each reduces the quantum of justice and should not be encouraged in practice except on an exceptional basis, they are important to examine because their objectives are to address backlogs of cases in a qualitatively and institutionally different setting.

5.3.2.1. Traditional Plea Negotiations

Traditional plea negotiations have similarity to the concept of abbreviated criminal procedure because their main purpose is to expedite the criminal procedure and save resources. As Michael P. Scharf notes:

> [W]hile no single definition of the term is universally accept-
> ed, the practice may encompass negotiation over reduction of
> sentence, dropping some or all of the charges, or reducing the
> charges in turn for admitting guilt, conceding certain facts,
> foregoing an appeal or providing cooperation in another crim-
> inal case.[34]

Accordingly, traditional plea negotiations may take the form of a plea bargaining, charge bargaining and fact bargaining between prosecutor and accused, where the latter waives some rights in exchange for a certain benefit, mostly a reduced sentence. In this voluntary procedure the accused must be fully appraised of the consequences. Negotiation results in a plea agreement. The court may accept the agreement, in which case there will be no main trial and the agreed sentence, even below the statutory minimum, will be imposed. If the court rejects the agreement, the main trial takes place with no consequence to the accused, especially with respect to the presumption of innocence.

In an abbreviated criminal procedure for core international crimes context, the features of traditional plea negotiations concerning voluntariness and sentence reduction are worth consideration in order to promote fairness from the perspective of the accused. Traditional plea negotiations, however, may have substantial shortcomings. First, traditional plea negotiations may not contribute sufficiently to the reconciliation process through the complete establishment of historical truth. This is especially so with charge bargaining, where, for example, charges for one crime are dropped in exchange for a plea to a lesser crime. A factual basis for the more serious

---

[34]   Michael P. Scharf, "Trading Justice for Efficiency", in *Journal of International Criminal Justice*, 2004, vol. 2, no. 4, p. 1070.

crime may therefore not emerge. In abbreviated criminal procedures for core international crimes, the judgment would have to involve the judicial determination of all the facts relevant for the case at issue. Furthermore, a traditional plea negotiation always results in conviction, whereas in abbreviated criminal procedures for core international crimes the possibility of acquittal still remains.

The traditional plea negotiations process may not fulfil the interests of victims, particularly if a defendant pleads to a lesser crime. Also, traditional plea negotiations may not fully address victims' needs for reparations or, as indicated above, the creation of an historical record. These are deficiencies that must be avoided for an abbreviated criminal procedure for core international crimes to be successful from the perspective of those most harmed by core international crimes.

Procedurally, traditional plea negotiations may be linked to other problems. This was, for example, the case in Bosnia and Herzegovina. When traditional plea negotiation was first introduced in its civil law-based system, the procedural rights of the accused were not sufficiently safeguarded.[35] Also, in some cases plea agreements were concluded at the end of the main trial.[36] The main function of an abbreviated criminal procedure – abbreviation – was therefore thwarted.

Recently, some writers have tried to introduce the idea of the newly designed plea negotiations so as to include "the three key restorative-justice elements – truth-telling, victim participation and reparation".[37] The term "traditional plea negotiations" was therefore intentionally employed as a means to set apart this old practice from these new ideas that, although not termed "abbreviated criminal procedure", come very close to what this expression is meant to embody.

---

[35] For more details, see OSCE Mission to Bosnia and Herzegovina, *Plea Agreements in Bosnia and Herzegovina: Practices before the Courts and their Compliance with International Human Rights Standards*, 2nd ed., OSCE Mission to Bosnia and Herzegovina, 2006.

[36] A good example of this practice may be found in the case of Court of Bosnia and Herzegovina, *Prosecutor v. Paško Ljubičić*, Trial Chamber, Verdict, KT-RZ-140/06, 29 April 2008 (http://www.legal-tools.org/doc/668bf7/).

[37] Nancy Amoury Combs, *Guilty Pleas in International Criminal Law: Constructing a Restorative Justice Approach*, Stanford University Press, Stanford, CA, 2007.

5.3.2.2. Truth and Reconciliation Commissions

Truth and reconciliation commissions are alternative, non-criminal justice mechanisms. In practice they are bodies set up to establish historical truth about past serious human rights violations occurring over a certain period of time in a given country. According to the definition given by Priscilla B. Hayner, truth and reconciliation commissions do not focus on a specific event, but attempt to paint the overall picture of certain human rights abuses, or violations of international humanitarian law.[38] Consequently, truth and reconciliation commissions may exist alongside criminal prosecutions and even help generate information that may lead to such prosecutions.

Truth and reconciliation commissions are always vested with some sort of authority that allows them greater access to information, greater security or protection to dig into sensitive issues, and a greater impact with its report.[39] However, although they possess some of the qualities inherent to judicial organs, such as impartiality, independence and competence, they are not created as part of the criminal justice system. They cannot pronounce on specific crimes, legally determine the guilt of individual perpetrators or mete out criminal sanctions. This is generally because they do not afford the required degree of due process guarantees that are indispensible in criminal proceedings where verdicts of guilt are made. Therefore, truth and reconciliation commissions do not accomplish one of the main tasks of abbreviated criminal procedures for core international crimes, namely, to actually process core international crimes cases. This does not mean that truth and reconciliation commissions do not serve an important purpose, only that the backlog of open core international crimes case files cannot be resolved by means of truth and reconciliation commissions.

Truth and reconciliation commissions are usually temporary and established for a predefined period of time, ceasing to exist with the submission of a report of its findings.[40] It would be reasonable to ask whether it would be better to invest in already existing permanent institutions inside the criminal justice system that may only need strengthening, rather than

---

[38] Priscilla B. Hayner, "Fifteen Truth Commissions – 1974 to 1994: A Comparative Study', in Neil J. Kritz (ed.), *Transitional Justice: How Emerging Democracies Reckon with Former Regimes*, vol. I: *General Considerations*, United States Institute of Peace Press, Washington, DC, 1995, p. 225.

[39] *Ibid.*

[40] *Ibid.*

invest in *ad hoc* institutions with limited objectives and time frames. In addition, transitional justice countries have limited resources to build their institutional capacity. Parallelism can create unnecessary competition regarding internal resources and potential international donations. Strengthening the ability to achieve a higher output from existing criminal justice system procedures, perhaps by investing in abbreviated criminal procedure mechanisms, might be preferable for society in the long term.

The mandate of a truth and reconciliation commission usually sets its purpose and scope of activities. "Commissions have generally pursued five goals: creating an authoritative record that acknowledges past abuses; providing redress and platform for victims; making recommendations for institutional reform; contributing to accountability of and justice for perpetrators; and promoting national reconciliation".[41] All these goals, except perhaps recommendations for institutional reform, may also be achieved in the course of an abbreviated criminal procedure. Perhaps even more is possible. For example, a truth and reconciliation commission makes a finding in its final report, but its ultimate impact depends on whether it is acknowledged as the truth by the relevant government. Knowledge that is officially sanctioned, and thereby made "part of the public cognitive scene" acquires a mysterious quality that is not there when it is merely "truth". Official acknowledgement at least begins to heal the wounds.[42] As opposed to the truth and reconciliation commission report, a judgment pronounced in an abbreviated criminal procedure does not require such an acknowledgement. Judicial truth simply cannot be disregarded by the government of a state that aspires to demonstrate adherence to the qualities of rule of law democracy.

5.3.2.3. *Gacaca* System of Courts in Rwanda

Gacaca emerged from a resolution of the new Rwandan government to oppose any idea of amnesty and to choose the path of accountability against the background of the patent inability of its regular courts to deal with an extreme caseload (80,000 detainees were awaiting trial in 2005). Although historically it represented the traditional method of community dispute

---

41 Steven R. Ratner, Jason S. Abrams and James L. Bischoff, *Accountability for Human Rights Atrocities in International Law*, 3rd ed., Oxford University Press, Oxford, 2009, p. 263.

42 Hayner, 1995, p. 228, see *supra* note 38.

resolution, *gacaca* for core international crimes is an innovative and considerably shortened approach that embodies elements of both restorative and retributive justice.

Gacaca was set up by the 2001 Organic Law, which was significantly amended in 2004.[43] Its preamble recognises the necessity, in order to achieve reconciliation and justice, to permanently eradicate the culture of impunity and enable prosecutions and trials of perpetrators and accomplices, aiming for simple punishment and reconstitution of the Rwandese society after genocide. An abbreviated criminal procedure for core international crimes should undoubtedly focus on similar goals to those set forth above. *Gacaca* panels are composed of nine persons of integrity and five deputies, of at least 21 years old (Article 14).[44] These are lay judges who receive limited legal training. In total, 170,000 judges sit on approximately 10,000 panels. The scope of the atrocities in Rwanda warrants a dilution of expertise in the composition of panels that cannot be tolerated in an abbreviated criminal procedure for core international crimes, which as an integral part of a criminal justice system would require higher standards of professionalism.

Common features exist for all the hearings before *gacaca* courts. As a rule, the hearings in *gacaca* courts are public. Internal decisions and deliberations of judges, however, are made in secret (Article 21). At the hearing, the defendant will always be made cognizant of the charges. The president of the session will give a summary of the nature of the case and evidence establishing guilt. Defendants who do not confess will be given an opportunity to give their defence. Witnesses will be heard under oath, as well as evidence from the public prosecution if it is summoned to the trial. Any interested person may ask questions and the defendant must answer (Articles 64 ff.). Once hearings are closed, the court retires for deliberations and makes decisions on the same or following day. The judgments or decisions taken are pronounced publicly.

Excluding the judges' deliberations, the *gacaca* procedure is open and transparent, much as any abbreviated criminal procedure for core international crimes should be. The broad participatory nature of *gacaca* will likely be impossible to replicate in the abbreviated criminal procedures for

---

[43] Organic Law No. 40/2000, 26 January 2001; and Organic Law No. 16/2004, 19 June 2004 (http://www.legal-tools.org/doc/eb49aa/).

[44] Citations to specific articles relate to Organic Law No. 16/2004, see *supra* note 43.

core international crimes context where professionals are charged to conduct the proceedings. In addition, certain features of *gacaca* are wholly contrary to fair trial principles that must be embedded in any abbreviated criminal procedure for core international crimes, where, for example, no defendant can ever be compelled to testify or be denied counsel.

Article 51 classifies the accused in three categories. The first and second categories involve high- and medium-level actors, respectively, together with their accomplices, while the third category involves persons who only committed offences against property. The first category of the accused falls outside the competence of the *gacaca* courts. However, the law creates punishments for this category because a determination that a person falls within it can in some cases be made during the information-gathering pre-trial stage. Those individuals shall be entitled to the sentencing scheme established for them by the *gacaca* legislation. The community is involved in developing a list of accused individuals and placing them in the above-mentioned categories. In an abbreviated criminal procedure for core international crimes, as in *gacaca*, it may be advisable and even necessary to adopt a classification scheme for different levels of participation in core international crimes when deciding which cases will be tried in regular procedure and which will go to the abbreviated process.

The *gacaca* law encourages accused persons to make use of the procedure of confessions, guilty pleas, repentance and apologies. Confessions, to be accepted, must give a detailed description of the offence, reveal the co-authors and accomplices, and provide any other information useful to the exercise of the public action. The accused has to apologise to the Rwandan society for the offences that she or he has committed (Article 54). This truth-telling function will serve as a valuable therapeutic modality for those who are damaged by core international crimes, although such damages will forever remain.

All *gacaca* panels apply the same substantive criminal law applied by the national courts. However, the law provides a special sentencing regime. Defendants falling within the first category, who refuse to confess, or whose confessions have been rejected, incur a death penalty or life imprisonment. Those who confess incur sentences ranging from 25 to 30 years of imprisonment (Article 72). Defendants who fall into the second category are entitled to commutation of sentence, depending on whether they confess and, if they do, whether they do so before or after their name appeared on the list of suspected persons. One half of their significantly reduced prison

sentence will be commuted into community service (Article 73). Category three defendants are only responsible for civil reparation (Article 75). Persons convicted of genocide or crimes against humanity are liable to the withdrawal of civil rights (Article 76). The legal remedies available to defendants are opposition, appeal and review of judgment (Article 85). The above provisions illustrate the type of flexible approach to sanctions that an abbreviated criminal procedure for core international crimes may emulate.

Gacaca has been widely criticised by human rights non-governmental organisations such as Amnesty International and Human Rights Watch.[45] The main causes of criticism concern the right to legal defence, competence, independence and impartiality, the search for truth, and Rwanda's commitment to international obligations.[46] William A. Schabas expresses his concerns as follows:

> Yet, the terrible and totally unexpected result of the *gacaca* pilot process was not to provide the fabled "closure" but rather to reveal that the numbers of those responsible for genocide may have exceeded 100,000 by a factor of 10. Rather than resolve the outstanding cases, and end the blight of mass detentions under appalling conditions, the initial *gacaca* hearings appear to have opened a Pandora's box.[47]

In January 2006 it was reported that 4,162 individuals have been adjudged.[48] It seems that if *gacaca* is destined to be successful, the pace of adjudications will have to increase exponentially.

5.3.3. Similar National Criminal Procedures (for Ordinary Crimes)

German, Polish and Italian codes of criminal procedure illustrate different national approaches to abbreviated criminal procedures outside the area of core international crimes. This allows a certain extent of analogy with ab-

---

[45] See, for example, Human Rights Watch, *Law and Reality: Progress in Judicial Reform in Rwanda*, Human Rights Watch, New York, 2008, pp. 70–88; see also Ariel Meyerstein, "Between Law and Culture: Rwanda's *Gacaca* and Postcolonial Legality", in *Law and Social Inquiry*, 2007, vol. 32, no. 2, pp. 467–508.

[46] For details and references, see Henry J. Steiner, Philip Alston and Ryan Goodman, *International Human Rights in Context: Law, Politics, Morals*, 3rd ed., Oxford University Press, Oxford, p. 1323.

[47] William A. Schabas, "Genocide Trials and *Gacaca* Courts", in *Journal of International Criminal Justice*, 2005, vol. 3, no. 4, p. 881.

[48] Mark A. Drumbl, *Atrocity, Punishment, and International Law*, Cambridge University Press, Cambridge, 2007, p. 85.

breviated criminal procedures for core international crimes. The instruments employed in these selected examples may help serve in the development of an eventual abbreviated criminal procedure for core international crimes. The subsequent comparative discussion describes the main features of these selected models.

5.3.3.1. Procedures in German Law

Germany uses two abbreviated criminal procedures: penal order and accelerated procedure. These procedures apply to simple offences and require indisputable clarity of evidence. Since core international crimes cases are much more complex, features of the German models, while illustrative, may not suit an abbreviated criminal procedure for core international crimes without modification.

5.3.3.1.1. Penal Order

A penal order is an order issued by a judge that has the same effect as a judgment of conviction following a trial. The German Code of Criminal Procedure envisages the procedure for penal order where public charges are judicially determined through the use of written proceedings, with no main hearing taking place.[49] If the prosecutor does not consider a main hearing to be necessary, s/he may file a written application to this effect, including the desired legal consequence (§ 407). If the accused objects, or the judge either deviates from the prosecutor's assessment or wishes to impose a different legal consequence, a main hearing will take place. Otherwise, the judge will comply with the prosecutor's application and issue the penal order (§ 408). After a penal order is served, an accused may object within two weeks. Without such objection, the order shall be equivalent to a judgment entered into force following the main hearing (§ 410). If the objection is admissible, a main hearing will be scheduled where the defendant may be represented by counsel (§ 411).

This procedure may be consistent with a potential abbreviated criminal procedure for core international crimes, the specific components of which are set forth below.[50] For example, a brief written procedure in lieu

---

[49] Germany, Criminal Procedure Code (Strafprozeßordnung, StPO), 12 September 1950, pt. 6, ch. I (http://www.legal-tools.org/doc/ef2d9d/).

[50] See section 5.3.6. below. Whenever a potential abbreviated criminal procedure for core international crimes is mentioned, it refers to this section.

of a lengthy hearing based on oral testimony would by definition be "abbreviated", and prone to help resolve large numbers of cases. Also, a defendant's rights to a main hearing and counsel are protected. She or he may choose, however, to waive these rights and shorten the process.[51] On the other hand, penal orders usually involve lesser offences. Their content does not create the type of detailed record necessary in core international crimes cases that are inherently more serious. And even though the judge is acting for the benefit of society, the German penal order procedure seems not to address the rights and expectations of victims, a necessary component for a potential abbreviated criminal procedure for core international crimes.

5.3.3.1.2. Accelerated Procedure

When the factual situation or the clarity of evidence warrant an immediate hearing, the prosecutor will file an application for an accelerated decision, dispensing with intermediary proceedings, and the main hearing shall be held immediately or on short notice (§ 417). The charges may be presented by indictment or orally on the record at the beginning of the main hearing. If it is anticipated that imprisonment of at least six months may be imposed, defence counsel shall be appointed if the accused is not already represented (§ 418). A judge's decision regarding this procedure may only be issued until judgment is pronounced in the main hearing, and may not be contested. On refusal, the court may decide to open main proceedings (§ 419). Oral recitation of charges may be considered unacceptable in a potential abbreviated criminal procedure for core international crimes because the factual basis of the indictment will likely be complex.

> [An] indictment is pleaded with sufficient particularity only if it sets out the material facts of the Prosecution case with enough detail to inform a defendant clearly of the charges

---

[51] To be valid, a waiver should be unequivocal and voluntary. A voluntary waiver should be informed, knowing and intelligent. See Extraordinary Chambers in the Courts of Cambodia ('ECCC'), *Prosecutor v. Nuon Chea*, Pre-Trial Chamber, Decision on Appeal against Provisional Detention Order of Nuon Chea, 002/19-09-2007-ECCC/OCIJ, 20 March 2008, paras. 23–27 (http://www.legal-tools.org/doc/4a7199/). Waiver of trial most often arises in the context of plea agreements, an example of which may be seen in ICTY, *Prosecutor v. Željko Mejakić et al.*, Plea Agreement (Predrag Banović), IT-02-65-PT, 2 June 2003, para. 15(c).

against him or her so that he or she may prepare his or her
defence.[52]

In abbreviated criminal procedures for core international crimes, as a matter
of due process, it stands to reason that the best way to provide the detail
necessary for preparation of an adequate defence is with a written
indictment.

In the German accelerated procedure, records of an earlier examination as well as of documents containing written statements may be used,
so long as the defendant, defendant's counsel and the prosecutor consent,
provided they were present at the main hearing. However, the judge de-
termines the extent to which evidence shall be taken (§ 420). In the context of abbreviated criminal procedures for core international crimes, using this aspect of the German accelerated procedure would be significant
in reducing the time required for adjudication, unless a defendant's due
process rights of cross-examination would be curtailed. Further, when
necessary, a mechanism should be provided to allow either party to offer
additional direct and/or rebuttal evidence when the interests of justice
require.

5.3.3.2. Procedures in Polish Law

The Polish Code of Criminal Procedure[53] has several instruments to simplify criminal procedure. I select two here that might have relevance in the
core international crimes context, and that were not addressed by the German models. They are the motion to convict without a trial and voluntary
submission to a penalty.

Polish criminal procedure provides that the prosecutor, with the consent of the accused, may attach to the indictment a motion that the accused
be convicted without a trial (Article 335). The penalty can be significantly
reduced in this process. Other penal measures may also be imposed: deprivation of public rights; prohibition from exercise of or engagement in
specific posts, professions or economic activities; obligation to redress
damage; and/or supplementary payment to the injured or the public.[54] This

---

[52] ICTR, *Prosecutor v. Ferdinand Nahimana et al.*, Appeals Chamber, Judgment, ICTR-99-
52-A, 28 November 2007, para. 322 (http://www.legal-tools.org/doc/4ad5eb/).

[53] Poland, Code of Criminal Procedure (Kodeks postępowania karnego), 6 June 1997
(http://www.legal-tools.org/doc/df9a97/).

[54] Poland, Penal Code, 6 June 1997, Article 39 (http://www.legal-tools.org/doc/f6cda6/).

procedure is allowed if evidence of guilt is beyond doubt and the accused is sufficiently repentant so that the objectives of the proceedings will be achieved despite lack of a trial.

Certain elements of this model could be included in a potential abbreviated criminal procedure for core international crimes. An unequivocal and voluntary waiver by the accused of the right to trial would satisfy due process. The allowance for imposition of alternative punishment may address the rights of victims, the public, or both. Alternative punishment will reduce the costs of imprisonment.[55]

The Polish procedure also allows for voluntary submission by an accused to a specified penalty or penal measure, without evidentiary proceedings. The accused makes a motion for this to occur, but can only do so until the conclusion of the first examination at the first instance hearing (Article 387). The court may grant the motion only when the circumstances surrounding the offence give no rise to doubt, the state prosecutor and the injured party concur, and the objectives of the proceedings are to be achieved despite the hearing not being conducted in full. When granting the motion the court may regard as admitted the evidence specified in the indictment or documents submitted by a party.

For purposes of a potential abbreviated criminal procedure for core international crimes, having the injured party concur in the foregoing procedure helps establish transparency, openness and legitimacy from the victim's perspective. Provided the requirements are met, both Polish procedures exhibit a flexibility that may reduce backlogs, which is also a major aim of abbreviated criminal procedures for core international crimes.

5.3.3.3. *Giudizio Abbreviato* in Italian Law

The Italian Code of Criminal Procedure[56] has a special procedure in which the preliminary hearing judge, without entering into the main trial phase, delivers a judgment on the basis of the indictment filed by the prosecutor and the material contained in the prosecutor's file. The only necessary requirement for this *giudizio abbreviato* to take place is the request of the

---

[55] United Nations Office on Drugs and Crime ('UNODC'), *Criminal Justice Assessment Toolkit, Custodial and Non-custodial Measures: Alternatives to Incarceration*, United Nations, New York, 2006, p. 2.

[56] Italy, Code of Criminal Procedure (Codice di Procedura Penal), 22 September 1988 (http://www.legal-tools.org/doc/77d222/).

defendant. *Giudizio abbreviato* is an option available for any charge, including those punishable by life imprisonment. The request must be expressed after issuance but before confirmation of the indictment (Article 438). The purpose of this procedure is to avoid often lengthy main trial proceedings and, in particular, the presentation of the evidence at the trial. The defendant, by accepting to be judged without all the guarantees of a fair trial, gets a reduced sentence in return (Article 442).

There are two exceptions to the issuance of a judgment exclusively on the basis of the prosecutor's file, and they reduce the advantages of *giudizio abbreviato* in terms of procedural economy. Either the defendant or the judge may seek acquisition of additional evidence (Articles 438, 441). The prosecutor may then offer evidence in rebuttal or amend the indictment if different facts arise, or a connected crime or aggravated circumstance emerge. If the prosecutor submits new accusations, the accused can ask that the proceedings continue in the ordinary course, including the main trial (Article 441*bis*). In this abbreviated procedure, the right to appeal is limited as well. The accused and the prosecutor cannot appeal an acquittal, and the prosecutor cannot appeal a guilty judgment (Article 443).

The preliminary hearing in *giudizio abbreviato* in effect becomes the hearing in which the criminal responsibility of the defendant is assessed. The preliminary hearing judge may become the one who both acquires the evidence and issues the judgment, thus greatly streamlining the procedure. In other regards, this Italian model offers examples relevant when designing a potential abbreviated criminal procedure for core international crimes. First, reduced penalties may serve as strong incentives for defendants to be willing to make use of an abbreviated criminal procedure for core international crimes, thus increasing the ability to resolve more cases. Second, because the defendant requests such a procedure, the danger of infringement of fair trial principles would be alleviated. Third, while the duration of the procedure would be considerably shortened, the full establishment of facts in the final judicial determination would not be compromised. The possibility remains that the accused, the prosecutor or the court can seek additional evidence. This promotes the truth-telling element of judicial determination, important to the fairness of the process as a whole.

5.3.4. Common Features of the German, Polish and Italian Solutions

Certain common elements that occur in the various models presented above should likely be considered for potential abbreviated criminal procedures for core international crimes. The evidence is mainly presented in written form, but the case could also be decided on hearing. From a practical and realistic standpoint, a hearing is probably more suitable for deciding core international crimes cases because of their nature and scope.[57] However, the length of the procedures is considerably shortened since there are no regular hearings as a general rule, or when written evidence is available and its use is agreed on by the participants. If the consent or the request by the accused for such a procedure is not specifically envisaged, there is always a remedy available, namely, a full trial. The reduction of penalties in some models could also serve as a powerful incentive for an accused to make use of such procedures, especially when the prosecution's case is undoubtedly strong. The possibility of alternative sentences should be available as well to provide an appropriate degree of flexibility.

It would be important that a potential abbreviated criminal procedure for core international crimes be regulated by criminal law and administered within the criminal justice system, such as the case with the presented models. This would ensure that case files remain in the criminal justice system, meaning there will be a judicial or prosecutorial record of the decision that possesses a sufficiently detailed determination of the charges and facts in the case at hand. Finally, the right to appeal should be guaranteed.

5.3.5. The Colombian Experience: Can Abbreviated Criminal Procedures Work for Core International Crimes?

Colombia has developed a form of abbreviated criminal procedure for core international crimes. It did so to address the interests that arose in its unique core international crimes context. An examination of its abbreviated criminal procedure for core international crimes – prior to the 2016 peace agreement with the FARC – reveals that it is designed for use in situations where the defendant does not intend to contest culpability. The Colombian experi-

---

[57] A hearing in a core international crime case should always be open to the public to ensure transparency and openness and to protect a defendant's due process rights. See, generally, ICCPR, Article 14, *supra* note 2.

ence, though born out of its internal conflict, may assist other states that seek to develop their own country-specific abbreviated criminal procedure for core international crimes systems.

5.3.5.1. The Backlog of Core International Crimes Cases in Colombia

During the Colombian armed conflict various actors committed atrocities against the civilian population. More than 100,000 people were victimised by different atrocious crimes, including massacres, forced disappearances, sexual violence, torture and arbitrary detention. Approximately three million victims were internally displaced.[58] Consequently, the state needed to address these matters. Peace negotiations between the government and illegal armed groups,[59] held in 2002, resulted in demobilisation of 35 paramilitary groups and over 30,000 individuals belonging to them.[60] A law was also passed, the Justice and Peace Law,[61] that developed a special framework[62] to provide for the investigation and prosecution of core international crimes perpetrated by demobilised members of illegal armed groups.[63]

The Colombian armed conflict resulted in a large backlog of core international crimes cases, consisting of the cases brought against demobilised members of armed groups under the Justice and Peace Law, outside of it, and cases against non-demobilised individuals to be addressed by

---

[58] Maria Paula Saffon, "Problematic Selection and Lack of Prioritization: The Colombian Experience", in Morten Bergsmo (ed.), *Criteria for Prioritizing and Selecting Core International Crimes Cases*, 2nd ed., Torkel Opsahl Academic EPublisher, Oslo, 2010, p. 130.

[59] The ones ascribed to the United Self-Defence Forces of Colombia, *ibid.*, pp. 131–32.

[60] *Ibid.*, p. 132.

[61] Colombia, Law No. 975, Issuing Provisions for the Reincorporation of Members of Illegal Armed Groups Who Effectively Contribute to the Attainment of National Peace, and Other Provisions for Humanitarian Accords Are Issued ('Justice and Peace Law'), 25 July 2005 (http://www.legal-tools.org/doc/ca98de/).

[62] Discussed in a sub-section 5.3.5.2. below.

[63] It should be noted here that illegal armed groups, as referred to in the Justice and Peace Law, fought on the side of the government, as well as against the government, as guerrillas. The law does not address illegality of membership in these armed groups, *per se*. In this writer's opinion, group membership makes no difference in terms of the government's obligation to equally address all the crimes committed, given the international obligation to prosecute those responsible for core international crimes and Colombia's determination to apply the law in a neutral fashion with respect to individual criminal acts.

ordinary criminal procedure.[64] By January 2007 there were over 100,000 cases before the justice and peace prosecutor.[65]

5.3.5.2. The Colombian Justice and Peace Law Special Procedure

The peace negotiations mentioned above were marked by conflicting interests of different actors. Armed groups were not ready to accept any accountability measures for their criminal acts, threatening to resume violence if such measures were to be imposed. At the same time, national and international non-governmental organisations and victims' organisations were strongly opposed to any solution that might result in the eventual impunity or *de facto* or *de jure* amnesties.[66] The Justice and Peace Law framework sought to address these tensions and incorporated many important elements of an abbreviated criminal procedure for core international crimes. Among other things, these include both the victim's right to truth, justice and reparations, and the requirements of peace and individual or collective reintegration into civilian life of the members of armed groups (Article 1).[67]

Within the framework of a potential abbreviated criminal procedure for core international crimes, when enacting the required legislation one possible solution might be to designate special judicial and prosecutorial units inside the criminal justice system to undertake the corresponding actions to implement the adopted procedure. In Colombia, the Justice and Peace Law created the Superior Judicial District Courts for Justice and Peace Matters (Article 32) and the National Prosecutorial Unit for Justice and Peace (Article 33). It is also important to set criteria for determination whether the case is suitable for an abbreviated criminal procedure. Not every case will be. The Justice and Peace Law set eligibility requirements for

---

[64] This chapter addresses the Justice and Peace Law process only.

[65] Pablo Kalmanovitz, "Introduction: Law and Politics in the Colombian Negotiations with Paramilitary Groups", in Morten Bergsmo and Pablo Kalmanovitz (eds.), *Law in Peace Negotiations*, 2nd ed., Torkel Opsahl Academic EPublisher, Oslo, 2010, p. 23. The number indicated may be deceptive because there may be several cases per one perpetrator.

[66] *Ibid.*

[67] The Justice and Peace Law was significantly amended by the rulings of the Constitutional Court, made upon requests and pressures from the civil society, since its application was still seen to result in the lenient treatment of the paramilitaries.

individuals to avail themselves its benefits according to a list provided by the government (Articles 10 and 11).[68]

The Justice and Peace Law procedure has additional distinctive elements for an abbreviated criminal procedure for core international crimes. First, it has a truth-telling function that is irreplaceable to the victims,[69] commencing with a spontaneous declaration and confession given before the prosecutor delegate. This requires that persons shall describe the circumstances of time, manner and place in which they participated in the criminal acts committed on the occasion of their membership in their armed groups, and for which they avail themselves of this law. To ensure completeness and accuracy, the truthfulness of their confessions is subject to verification.

Second, the Justice and Peace Law entails a simplified procedure that saves time and resources while affording due process. A demobilised person shall immediately be placed at the disposal of the judge who, within 36 hours, shall schedule and hold a hearing (Article 17) during which the prosecutor shall make a factual indictment. The prosecutor then undertakes to investigate and verify the facts admitted by the accused. On completion of these tasks, s/he will ask the judge to schedule an indictment hearing, within 10 days (Article 18). The accused may accept the charges. The determination of whether such acceptance was free, voluntary, spontaneous and assisted by defence counsel will be made in a public, transparent hearing. Upon such determination, a hearing for sentencing and imposition of penalty shall be scheduled within 10 days. If the accused does not accept the charges the case shall be forwarded to the ordinary criminal procedure (Article 19). The right to defence is guaranteed through the mechanisms of the Public Defender Service (Article 34), yet another minimum guarantee of due process that the Justice and Peace Law provides.

Third, the Justice and Peace Law procedure involves victims' participation and attends to their respective interests. During the hearing they can make an express request for an interlocutory proceeding regarding reparations resulting from the criminal conduct. Reparations may include restitu-

---

[68] Eligibility requirements were made stricter by the Constitutional Court ruling; see ruling C-370 as cited by Kalmanovitz, 2010, p. 14, see *supra* note 65.

[69] Orentlicher, 2004, paras. 14–23, see *supra* note 22. See also Yasmin Naqvi, "The Right to the Truth in International Law: Fact or Fiction?", in *International Review of the Red Cross*, vol. 88, no. 862, 2006, pp. 245–73.

tion, compensation, rehabilitation, satisfaction and guarantees of non-repetition. The decision on this request will be incorporated into the verdict (Article 23). The Justice and Peace Law also creates a Fund for the Reparation of Victims, made up of all the assets or resources that may be surrendered by persons or illegal armed groups, resources from the national budget, and donations in cash and in kind, both national and foreign (Article 54). Throughout the Justice and Peace Law process, victims also have a right to be heard, to have legal assistance, and to be informed of the course and outcome of the proceedings (Article 37). In this way, the requirement for transparency and openness of the proceedings is facilitated, more so because the law further contemplates means for conservation of archives for historical purposes. These include the duty of memory and specific measures for preserving the archives and facilitating access thereto (Chapter X).

Finally, the Justice and Peace Law creates a special sentencing regime whereby execution of sentence determined in the respective judgment shall be suspended and replaced with an alternative sentence of imprisonment of at least five years and not greater than eight years, based on the seriousness of the crimes and the defendant's effective collaboration in their clarification (Article 29). The defendant will be required to make a commitment to contribute to her or his resocialisation, to promote activities geared to the demobilisation of the armed group of which she or he was a member, as well as not to commit the crimes for which she or he was convicted. These components of reduced and alternative sentences that deter, but also contribute to reconciliation processes, might be further explored within an abbreviated criminal procedure for core international crimes.

5.3.6. Conclusion: Basic Features for Potential Abbreviated Criminal Procedures for Core International Crimes

Based on the information and analysis provided, it is possible to envisage certain basic features that a potential abbreviated criminal procedure for core international crimes should possess to serve the public's interest that justice be done in a fair and expeditious manner.

First, in order to comply with the principle of legality[70] such procedures should be prescribed by law and made an integral part of the criminal

---

[70] Cassese, 2008, ch. 2, §§ 2.3–2.5, pp. 36–52, see *supra* note 14.

justice system.[71] Being part of the criminal justice system will require that abbreviated criminal procedures be administered by regular courts, without creating extrajudicial mechanisms or additional institutional layers. However, depending on the particular needs of the jurisdiction, some judiciaries may decide to have specially designed panels of judges and/or corresponding prosecutorial units.

There may be differences of opinion regarding the issue of whether abbreviated criminal procedures should apply to all core international crimes, or be restrictively applied. In any event, the legal regulation should specifically elaborate which categories of core international crimes may fall under these proceedings, according to clear criteria. Differences in classification were considered in the *gacaca* process in Rwanda. In an abbreviated criminal procedure for core international crimes it may be appropriate to distinguish between more serious core international crimes cases that violate individual life or physical integrity (murder, extermination, torture, rape) from less serious cases, where the interest violated is property (pillaging or destruction), freedom of movement (displacement of a civilian population or an unlawful deportation) and, maybe, personal liberty (unlawful detention). Furthermore, it is important to distinguish between different modes of individual criminal responsibility of a perpetrator. It may be found that different treatment should be imposed on actors such as masterminds, leaders and superiors, direct perpetrators and those who aided, abetted or induced the commission of these crimes. There is also a spectrum between the different consequences of core international crimes for victims, ranging, for example, from the destruction of the whole group to the destruction of property.

Second, abbreviated criminal procedures for core international crimes should increase the ability of criminal justice systems to resolve large numbers of cases that have created a backlog. This entails that the procedure should be simplified to the extent possible. Actual time used for adjudicating a case should be considerably reduced. One way to accomplish this is by limiting oral presentation of evidence, so long as it is in balance with the fair trial rights of the accused.

---

[71] They may be specifically designed to resolve the particular backlog of cases and therefore be introduced through a special legislation. Alternatively, they may be introduced through amendments to the existing legislation.

Third, abbreviated criminal procedures for core international crimes must be voluntary and non-coercive, based on fundamental fair trial principles of due process. The defendant must have the opportunity to opt out. Nevertheless, certain deviations in the quantum of due process may be permissible. "A defendant is entitled to a fair trial, but not a perfect one".[72]

Fourth, abbreviated criminal procedures for core international crimes should be transparent and open. Unless absolutely necessary to protect the safety of a witness or a similar interest, the public should have access to all proceedings, including the pronouncement of the final judgment. Extensive use of court outreach and similar methods should be made in order to satisfy the public interest in having an appropriate degree of insight into the organisation, the course and the outcome of such procedures.[73] For example, when documentary evidence is used, summaries should be made available for public scrutiny and education.

Fifth, abbreviated criminal procedures for core international crimes should be designed as a part of a wider transitional justice process. Several main issues should be addressed in this context. The purpose of the process, and its details and outcomes, should be explained to victims' groups and the general public. Beyond mere explanation, the procedure should actively address victims' claims for justice, truth, apologies and reparations. From a societal standpoint, the procedure should help establish judicial truth by creating an historical and legal record with judgments containing factual and legal findings that should not be significantly different than those issued in regular criminal procedure.

Sixth, an abbreviated criminal procedure for core international crimes should allow for imposition of a variety of sanctions with the necessary degree of flexibility. There could be the possibility of sentence reduction, alternatives to imprisonment and a combination of sentences and/or sanctions. Flexibility might also include barring certain people from serving in police and security forces for a defined period of time or limiting their participation in the political life of the given country.

---

[72] US Supreme Court, *Lutwak v. United States*, 344 U.S. 604 (1953), 619, decided 9 February 1953.

[73] Office of the United Nations High Commissioner for Human Rights, *Rule of Law Tools for Post-conflict States: Maximizing the Legacy of Hybrid Courts*, United Nations, New York and Geneva, 2008, p. 18.

5.4. Arguments for and against an Abbreviated Criminal Procedure for Core International Crimes

The purpose of this section is to assess the appropriateness of abbreviated criminal procedures for core international crimes. To do so, I commence with arguments in favour (section 5.4.1.) and continue with arguments against (section 5.4.2.).[74] The final aim of this section is to offer some guiding principles that I believe should be considered if an abbreviated criminal procedure for core international crimes, as described in section 5.3.6., is to meet the interest of stakeholders in the core international crimes process (section 5.4.3.).

5.4.1. Arguments in Favour

5.4.1.1. Abbreviated Criminal Procedure for Core International Crimes, within Existing Criminal Justice Systems, Is the Fairest and Most Realistic Way to Address the Obligation to Prosecute and Prevent Impunity

In light of the fact that large-scale conflicts result in tremendous damage and destruction to people and property, it is advisable to keep in mind the scale, gravity and complexity of the atrocities and the identity of victims and perpetrators. Countries have individual statutory obligations to investigate and prosecute all crimes. International instruments such as the 1949 Geneva Conventions, the 1948 Genocide Convention and the 1998 ICC Statute impose on the contracting parties a duty to investigate, prosecute and punish individuals responsible for core international crimes.[75] The principle of universal jurisdiction provides the reinforcing effect to the obligation to prosecute.[76] The inability of a criminal justice system to resolve a backlog of core international crimes cases may cause a failure to fulfil this obligation. Pressure to adequately address the issue may create temptations to use mechanisms outside the existing criminal justice system for dealing

---

[74] Some of the arguments in this section are necessarily policy based.

[75] Geneva Convention I; Geneva Convention II; Geneva Convention III; Geneva Convention IV; Genocide Convention; ICC Statute; see *supra* note 1.

[76] Ilia Utmelidze, "The Time and Resources Required by Criminal Justice for Atrocities and de facto Capacity to Process Large Backlogs of Core International Crimes Cases: The Limits of Prosecutorial Discretion and Independence", in Bergsmo, 2010, p. 184, see *supra* note 58.

with the reported crimes[77] or to grant amnesties. An abbreviated criminal procedure for core international crimes, because it is fair and efficient, can address this serious problem and alleviate concerns that use of such alternative mechanisms might result in factual impunity.

It is very important that these matters be resolved within the criminal justice system. When cases remain in the criminal justice system it helps show that government is willing and capable of dealing with past atrocities. Of course, core international crimes are not the only type of crime amenable to creating extraordinary situations within the criminal justice system. In many countries there is often an accumulation of non-core international crimes cases that overload the criminal justice system and create delays in it. In such situations, legal systems attempt to find alternative solutions to deal with backlogs, such as decriminalisation.[78] Due to the nature and gravity of core international crimes, they cannot be decriminalised like some ordinary offences that are removed from the criminal justice system. An abbreviated criminal procedure for core international crimes within the criminal justice system can be an effective way to address the matter of backlogs and prevent the perception and reality of impunity.

5.4.1.2. Abbreviated Criminal Procedure for Core International Crimes Will Be Trusted by Victims and the General Public

In order to trust their government victims and the general public must perceive accountability as serious and genuine. This may be accomplished by an official body with power to deliver justice and the willingness to deal with, and distance itself from, the past atrocities.[79] There is a high expectation that the government demonstrates it possesses the necessary degree of competence, independence and impartiality. Furthermore, it is important for the victims to have their suffering acknowledged in an independent judicial

---

[77] One example is the Commission for the investigation of the events in and around Srebrenica from 10 and 19 July 1995 as one of the attempts to partly resolve the issue, but where the actual outcome was burdening the system with additional lists of thousands of individuals allegedly involved in those crimes.

[78] Jörg-Martin Jehle and Marianne Wade, *Coping with Overloaded Criminal Justice Systems: The Rise of Prosecutorial Power Across Europe*, Springer, Berlin, 2006, p. 5.

[79] Because the commission of core international crimes is quite often affiliated with the government or authorities that either directly perpetrated or failed to protect their people.

process. It is equally important that they have an ability to fully enforce their rights and obtain redress.

An abbreviated criminal procedure for core international crimes structured along the lines indicated in section 5.3.6. will go far in establishing victims' trust. As mentioned above, when cases remain in the criminal justice system, this prevents sending the wrong signal to victims and the general public that the government is unwilling or incapable of dealing with past atrocities. It may calm their fears that reform processes are ineffective or operating too slowly, or that the government is failing to deliver genuine accountability for the crimes occasioned upon them. A properly designed abbreviated criminal procedure for core international crimes possesses a sufficient degree of quality of judicial determination that would be hard for anyone to deny in the future.

5.4.1.3. Abbreviated Criminal Procedure for Core International Crimes Allows Equitable Sharing of Limited Resources and Increases the Overall Capacity of the Criminal Justice System

The prolonged existence of a large backlog of core international crimes cases can have negative effect on the ability of the criminal justice system to deal with other forms of crime, reform of the justice system and capacity building. Other such crimes that societies must cope with include, but are not limited to, hate crimes, organised crime and corruption. In many transitional countries, the whole justice sector is being reformed. The success of reform is normally evaluated by the progress made on the most sensitive and controversial cases. As a rule, limited or scarce available resources will create an exigency to choose priorities. This translates into a need for reasonable allocation of resources in order to resolve different challenges that justice sector might face.

Core international crimes require a specialised capacity. As seen below, the monetary cost of a fully-blown core international crimes trial is enormous. Additionally, extensive investment will have to be made in human and other resources. It will be essential to train legal professionals to meet all the standards of these lengthy and complicated core international crimes criminal procedures. In addition, these cases often attract the most competent minds. This may result in two layers of professionals within the criminal justice system, one that works on core international crimes and another that deals with the rest of the justice matters. Such a

two-tiered system hinders the ability of the criminal justice system to deliver justice across the system. It cannot reasonably be argued that all resources should be allocated to core international crimes, nor can core international crimes receive unlimited logistical support. An abbreviated criminal procedure for core international crimes, because it is efficient and streamlined to process cases more quickly, will allow for a more equitable sharing of time, human and other capital that will increase the overall capacity of the criminal justice system.

5.4.1.4. Abbreviated Criminal Procedure for Core International Crimes Would Be Faster and More Cost-Effective than Full Criminal Trials

When one considers the costs, length and output of full, non-abbreviated core international crimes trials, there is an inconsistency. A few statistics evidence this fact. At the ICTY, in 2005, it was estimated that the average trial at first instance took about one year. Some lasted as long as three years. In nine years the ICTY completed 35 trials, involving 46 individuals. Out of this number, 17 persons in 15 cases pleaded guilty.[80] In 2009 the staff of the Tribunal numbered 1,118. Its budget grew from US$276,000 in 1993 to US$342,332,300 for the 2008–2009 biennial.[81]

At the national level, the statistics for Bosnia and Herzegovina on the number of started and completed core international crimes cases, between January 2004 and April 2009, processed at the four levels of government,[82] show that 133 cases were started[83] and 91 completed.[84] This makes an average of 18 cases processed per year. Even with a dramatic increase in procedural efficiency, it is doubtful the backlog indicated in the National War Crimes Strategy document (1,781 cases, involving 9,879 perpetrators) can be cleared using existing criminal procedures, particularly while suspects

---

[80] Robinson, 2006, p. 169, see *supra* note 28.

[81] See ICTY, "The Cost of Justice" (http://www.icty.org/sid/325).

[82] Bosnia and Herzegovina has a complex administrative organisation. It comprises the state-level authorities, two entity levels – Federation of Bosnia and Herzegovina and Republika Srpska – and Brčko District. Core international crimes are being processed on all these levels of government.

[83] See the statistics announced by the OSCE Mission to Bosnia and Herzegovina.

[84] See *ibid*.

and witnesses are still alive.[85] The existing pace would require 99 years to complete.

From the above, it follows that at the international level the small overall output is perhaps due to cumbersome and over-complex procedures. On the national level, it appears that the problem with output may be due to lack of capacity. In either event, the concept of abbreviated criminal procedures for core international crimes presented in this chapter may reduce the overall time required to prosecute many core international crimes cases and the backlog that results from conducting full trials.

In an abbreviated criminal procedure, the accused may waive her or his right to a main trial and there is an increased possibility that there will be no appellate proceedings. If so, from a practical standpoint, drafting a judgment may likely be the most time-consuming part of the abbreviated criminal procedure. Logistical problems that often exist, such as the lack of courtrooms or specialised premises, would be considerably alleviated. The need may still arise for witness protection measures, but if written testimony is used there would be a decreased, if any, need for witness hearings during the trial. Moreover, when judges do not speak the same language as a witness, abbreviated criminal procedures would save time over simultaneous translations as well as translations of transcripts.

Abbreviated criminal procedures for core international crimes will allow for advances at the sentencing stage, too. The relatively few sentences meted out by the ICTY and ICTR are served abroad on the basis of special agreements with the host countries, but the situation is different when it comes to national jurisdictions where countries might still be badly affected by economic problems. The prison sentences in such core international crimes cases might overstretch the prison capacities.[86] Imprisonment costs will be shifted to the society. Arguably, there might not be enough money for the victims' claims. Studies have shown that alternative mechanisms of punishment can be much less costly than imprisonment.[87] Thus, use of an

---

[85] OSCE Mission to Bosnia and Herzegovina, "Accountability for War Crimes" (http://www.oscebih.org/Default.aspx?id=70&lang=EN).

[86] This was the case in Rwanda; a similar problem exists in Bosnia and Herzegovina. See UK Department for International Development, *Final Report: Examination of the Effectiveness and Efficiency of the Execution of Criminal Sanctions in Bosnia and Herzegovina*, Department for International Development, April 2006.

[87] UNODC, 2006, see *supra* note 55.

abbreviated criminal procedure for core international crimes, if it reduces rates and costs of incarceration, may provide long-term benefits for victims.

5.4.1.5. Abbreviated Criminal Procedure for Core International Crimes May Overcome Public Scepticism

Once a state chooses to implement its obligation to prosecute individuals for alleged core international crimes, it would represent a defeat if the criminal justice system cannot manage to process such cases. It would also create scepticism regarding its general ability to process all cases. This scepticism can come from the general public, victims or donors interested in building capacity in transitional countries. The slow pace of resolving backlogs of cases and the overall low number of judgments rendered can also build scepticism, not to mention speculation regarding the independence of the justice sector from political influences, or its outright willingness to address the issue in a serious manner. The general competence to deal with this complex field of law and the ability to organise the work efficiently and effectively may also come into question. In addition, lawyers may feel they lack competence to handle issues with larger social and political implications, and thus be adversely affected.

If the criminal justice system introduces mechanisms, such as a functioning abbreviated criminal procedure for core international crimes, this will likely increase the output of its work and begin to tangibly resolve the backlog of core international crimes cases. The above-mentioned problems and attitude of sceptics can be managed. Overall progress and the ability to demonstrate visible and realistic ways of resolving the issue motivate the support of the public, political and donor communities, both to the criminal justice system in general and prosecution in particular.

5.4.1.6. Abbreviated Criminal Procedure for Core International Crimes May Decrease the Chances for Impunity

If core international crimes case files cannot be dealt with inside the criminal justice system, due to lack of capacity, but are given to other mechanisms such as truth and reconciliation commissions or general amnesties, the chances for impunity will arise. There will likely be a temptation when dealing with large backlogs of core international crimes cases to argue that alternative mechanisms will better resolve the issues and lessen pressure on the criminal justice system. However, processing core international crimes

cases outside the criminal justice system would be problematic in relation to the principle of individual criminal responsibility. Furthermore, there are strong arguments from the victims concerning their right to justice and legal redress for victimisation and suffering.

Alternative mechanisms may prove disadvantageous in other ways. Even if political considerations result in their use, backlogs may still remain. Such mechanisms may face similar problems to those of the judiciary. These include the lack of capacity, resources and inability to address large number of issues during their limited existence. Their methodologies do not involve processing of individual cases or pronouncements of individual criminal responsibility. Since they will not be able to process the judicial backlog and may even generate their own, they may foreseeably apply amnesties to close backlogs, and impunity will result. With regard to amnesties, Carsten Stahn notes that "there is growing support for the position that amnesties for the core crimes [...] are generally incompatible with international law".[88] In short, alternative mechanisms may not avoid impunity. Because of the capacity of abbreviated criminal procedures for core international crimes to deal with backlogs in a fair manner, the potential for impunity will be decreased.

5.4.1.7. Abbreviated Criminal Procedure for Core International Crimes Will Contribute to Truth-Telling and Creation of a Judicial and Historical Record

It is generally recognised that judicial decisions create an accurate and undeniable historical record of the factual basis of crimes that were committed during a conflict.[89] It establishes, according to the highest judicial standards, the role and involvement of the individuals and organisations in the events. In comparison with any other form of written or oral decisions, a judgment gives the highest degree of attention to important details of atrocities and how they occurred. One decision that clearly established an undeniable factual basis is the ICTY judgment delivered in *Kvočka et al.* regarding the facts and circumstances surrounding the establishment of Omarska,

---

[88] Carsten Stahn, "Complementarity, Amnesties and Alternative Forms of Justice: Some Interpretative Guidelines for the International Criminal Court", in *Journal of International Criminal Justice*, 2005, vol. 3, no. 3, p. 701.

[89] Minna Schrag, "Lessons Learned from ICTY Experience", in *Journal of International Criminal Justice*, 2004, vol. 2, no. 2, p. 428.

Keraterm and Trnopolje concentration camps.[90] Even the genocide in Srebrenica was denied by a certain part of the population on the perpetrators' side. Such denial is absurd after the ICTY judgment in *Krstić* case or the ICJ judgment in the case of *Bosnia and Herzegovina v. Yugoslavia (Serbia and Montenegro).*[91]

An abbreviated criminal procedure for core international crimes preserves the unique and crucially important role of judicial determination and provides a written record of the past, with the highest standard of proof, for generations to come. This is perhaps the main difference between the abbreviated criminal procedure and other alternative mechanisms.

5.4.2. Arguments Against

5.4.2.1. Abbreviated Criminal Procedure for Core International Crimes Might Not Meet Important Fair Trial Standards

No one should be punished for core international crimes without a fair hearing, as a matter of due process. This is a fundamental consideration of human rights and criminal procedure. Although the interrelated right to be tried without undue delay is significant, particularly to the incarcerated, a rush to an abbreviated trial has several important shortcomings. It follows that fairness should not be compromised on account of expediency. For example, if an abbreviated criminal procedure uses previous statements or testimony of a witness, where the defendant or counsel were unable to cross-examine, then the defendant's right to examine witnesses is denied. Also, in the haste to process cases, where often the prosecutor has had months or years to accumulate evidence, there is a question concerning the defendant's right to have adequate time and facilities to prepare a defence.[92] Defence counsel in ordinary criminal proceedings complain that "equality

---

[90] ICTY, *Prosecutor v. Miroslav Kvočka et al.*, Trial Chamber, Judgment, IT-98-30/1-T, 2 November 2001 (http://www.legal-tools.org/doc/34428a/).

[91] Krstić Appeals Judgment, see *supra* note 23. See also ICJ, *Bosnia and Herzegovina v. Yugoslavia (Serbia and Montenegro), Case Concerning the Application of the Convention on the Prevention and Punishment of the Crime of Genocide*, Judgment, 26 February 2007 (http://www.legal-tools.org/doc/5fcd00/).

[92] ICCPR, Article 14; ACHR, Articles 8, 9 and 10; ECHR, Article 6; ACHPR, Article 7; see *supra* note 2. See also ICC Statute, Articles 55, 63, 66 and 67, *supra* note 1.

of arms" slants towards the prosecution.[93] In an abbreviated procedure, these shortcomings will most likely be even more pronounced. Unless these rights can be sufficiently safeguarded, the defendant must receive a full trial.

5.4.2.2. Abbreviated Criminal Procedure for Core International Crimes Are Not Suitable because the Crimes Are Too Serious

No crimes are as serious as core international crimes from an individual and societal point of view. One need only look at a few of these crimes or the acts that constitute them: genocide, extermination, torture, enslavement, biological experiments.[94] These are acts of depravity. It might therefore be very difficult and even unpopular to argue for the application of abbreviated criminal procedures to crimes placed in the core international crimes category. Many in society, not to mention victims, will oppose the concept of abbreviated criminal procedures for core international crimes on this basis alone. This is so, even if, as stated in section 5.3.6. above, certain lines can be drawn to establish sub-categories according to specific criteria. Overall, it is a matter of morality and ethics, and, for this reason, such argument may have merit.

5.4.2.3. Abbreviated Criminal Procedure for Core International Crimes Might Create a Discriminatory Sentencing Regime Causing Adverse Consequences

One of the requirements for a potential abbreviated criminal procedure for core international crimes is an introduction of a special sentencing regime as incentive for defendants to participate and to make the process practicable. However, the imposition of reduced or alternative sentences for core international crimes may be seen as inappropriate and unjust. In this regard, such punishment, considering the seriousness and consequences of core international crimes, could create a perception of insufficiency and cause a strong negative reaction in the public. Opposition from the victims' com-

---

[93] On equality of arms principle see ICTY, *Prosecutor v. Dario Kordić and Mario Čerkez*, Appeals Chamber, Judgment, IT-95-14/2, 17 December 2004, paras. 175–77 (http://www.legal-tools.org/doc/738211/). On defence counsel's claims of inequality see Mark S. Ellis, "Achieving Justice before the International War Crimes Tribunal", in *Duke Journal of Comparative and International Law*, 1997, vol. 7, no. 5, p. 533.

[94] See the ICC Statute for the most comprehensive list of core international crimes, *supra* note 1.

munity might be the most powerful. Politicians, as creatures of public opinion, may feel reluctance to undertake steps needed for legalisation of alternative forms of punishment or abbreviated criminal procedures for core international crimes in general.

Additionally, introduction of a specialised sentencing regime for core international crimes cases will in most situations create a vacuum between the sentencing regime for ordinary crimes and core international crimes. In other words, the murderer in time of peace might get a much harsher sentence than a wartime murderer. If core international crimes are handled so differently, a paradoxical situation will occur that undermines the logic of the whole criminal justice system. It would be extremely difficult to explain to the victims why certain interests are being protected and valued more in peacetime than in war.

5.4.2.4. Abbreviated Criminal Procedure for Core International Crimes Might Not Meet Expectations of Victims

When it comes to the processing of and accountability for core international crimes, victims' expectations could arguably be placed in two categories, one involving process and the other involving punishment. Research conducted in post-conflict or conflict regions reflects the preferences of victims:

> The statistics on what victims view as the main purposes of taking action against offenders are fascinating. Sixty-nine percent said that establishing the truth about what happened is a main purpose – in fact, this is the most frequently identified purpose. A further 25 percent answered that enabling people to live together was a main purpose; the same percentage indicated that taking revenge on the perpetrators was a main purpose (again researchers permitted multiple responses by victim interviewees).[95]

The same study also notes: "Overall, in terms of sanction, 42 percent of victims supported imprisonment and 39 percent payment of money to the victims".[96]

Besides the views supporting the victims' right to truth, trial, justice and punishment, there are others who maintain that, for example, a judicial

---

[95] Drumbl, 2007, p. 43, see *supra* note 48.
[96] *Ibid.*, p. 42.

pronouncement of guilt with all its implications is sufficient for the rein-statement of the victim, regardless of the enforcement of punishment. Some other views profess that one cannot talk about victims before the occurrence of a trial wherein their victimhood is established. Until then, one can only speak about the 'alleged' victims and the 'alleged' perpetrators.[97]

Moreover, because an abbreviated criminal procedure for core international crimes does not provide a full trial, some victims may feel they are treated like they have suffered less. They might think that justice is biased and that certain crimes are accorded preferential treatment through prioritisation. Indeed, the family of a murdered person cares little about how their loved one was killed or about the legal classification of the act; in either event a member of the family is forever gone. However, legal classification could cause some of these crimes to be prioritised for full trial while others may be directed into an abbreviated procedure. Victims may feel neglected if perpetrated crimes qualify for an abbreviated criminal procedure. The potential for differentiation in the treatment and punishment of perpetrators for their crimes makes abbreviated criminal procedures for core international crimes both difficult to administer and insufficient to satisfy the needs and expectations of victims.

5.4.2.5. Abbreviated Criminal Procedure for Core International Crimes Might Lack Consensus or Face Significant Resistance

It may be an extraordinary task for the main actors of the criminal justice system to agree on the application of an abbreviated criminal procedure for core international crimes. A large number of lawyers may be keen to preserve the traditional legal thinking that the main effect of criminal law is deterrence and retribution. These lawyers will most likely be oriented towards making perpetrators face full trials and receive maximum sentences. Much effort and debate may be necessary to persuade lawyers to acknowledge that the legal system they belong to and trust is not always able to cope with the challenges before it in a fair, efficient and productive manner.

In post-conflict countries, the debate on abbreviated criminal procedures for core international crimes might easily become a political discus-

---

[97] For more on all the above views, see Jesús-María Silva Sánchez, "Doctrines Regarding 'The Fight Against Impunity' and 'The Victim's Right for the Perpetrator to be Punished'", in *Pace Law Review*, 2008, vol. 28, no. 4, pp. 865–84.

sion where it will not be easy to secure necessary support. Many political actors may fear that such an approach will be perceived as a lenient criminal policy towards perpetrators. Their main concern is how to formally end the process of transition while serving the interests of victims, the general public and the rule of law, and the conflicts that often arise between them. Since an abbreviated criminal procedure for core international crimes may prove controversial from the point of view of these different groups and interests, politicians may choose not to take a clear position in the matter. However, their need not to be seen as 'soft' towards those whose behaviour is condemned by the public creates a paralysing effect that causes inaction rather than action that may undermine necessary political support. Despite their motivations, delay exacerbates the problem of dealing with core international crimes overall, not to mention completing the transition process.

More than constituting an argument against abbreviated criminal procedures for core international crimes, this phenomenon is an explanation as to why abbreviated criminal procedures for core international crimes may not occur. Without leadership from the relevant actors, public support cannot be generated and reform will most likely never get off the ground.

5.4.2.6. Abbreviated Criminal Procedure for Core International Crimes Will Require Amendments to Both Substantive and Procedural Law

Substantial changes of law and the introduction of new institutions are a challenging exercise that requires effort and consensus at the legislative, executive and judicial levels. The introduction of an abbreviated criminal procedure for core international crimes will require significant changes in very sensitive areas of criminal procedure and sentencing policy. If special court panels and prosecutorial units are to be designated solely for the application of abbreviated criminal procedures, then laws on courts and prosecutors' offices might also require amendments. Very few jurisdictions presently allow for some sort of accelerated procedure even for ordinary crimes. Although not largely perceived as controversial, the majority of the civil law countries do not even see a need for the introduction of a plea negotiations procedure. It would not be surprising, therefore, to see these same countries oppose an abbreviated criminal procedure for core international crimes with its innovative features.

However, even if the legal community accepts the possibility as such, the introduction of an abbreviated criminal procedure for core international crimes might encounter further obstacles at the political level. Some prominent members of political parties in countries in transition, associated with various groups in the former conflict, may pursue a negative agenda when it comes to formulating and implementing an abbreviated criminal procedure for core international crimes. In other words, they might apply pressure to create a watered-down procedure in which it is difficult to obtain full accountability for criminal behaviour, in order to protect their favoured group. There is also a more negative possibility that these same individuals find themselves sitting in a parliament.

Once more, this is not a substantive legal argument against an abbreviated criminal procedure for core international crimes, but rather it constitutes a political obstacle that cannot be ignored with respect to prospects for its implementation.

5.4.2.7.   Abbreviated Criminal Procedure for Core International Crimes Is Uncertain to Actually Work in Practice

Abbreviated criminal procedures for core international crimes are untested and unproven. The absence of precedent makes it more difficult to know if they will work in practice. Under the best of circumstances it will be a challenge to make them function. Legal professionals will have to be trained in order to deliver positive results. This may not be an easy task. First, it is a foreign concept to the majority of criminal justice systems and may therefore breed scepticism among practitioners, and an unwillingness to use it. Second, to implement change in an institutional system that was functioning in the same constant mode for many years may take too much time. Assuming the resistance to change outweighs other variables, an abbreviated criminal procedure for core international crimes may never get off the ground.

5.4.2.8.   Abbreviated Criminal Procedure for Core International Crimes Might Not Be Capable of Resolving the Backlog

The possibility exists that, even with an abbreviated criminal procedure for core international crimes, some situations will entail a scale of victimisation so large, like in Rwanda, that the number of perpetrators overwhelms the ability of the criminal justice system to address this issue in its totality. Ev-

en with the procedure in place and all the will needed, the lack of adequate participation by perpetrators (described below) or the simple weight of too many cases will prove that the mechanism is ineffective or has little effect on actually solving the backlog. In such a situation, no system within the criminal justice system will work. As previously discussed, it would not serve the public interest to create a system that will not remedy the problem.

5.4.2.9 Abbreviated Criminal Procedure for Core International Crimes Might Be Rejected by Perpetrators

The political and ideological context may cause perpetrators to reject abbreviated criminal procedures for core international crimes. In some cases, suspects for core international crimes might find themselves going to trial as heroes in the eyes of their governments, political factions, religious or ethnic groups. The possibility that these suspects will actively participate in the abbreviated criminal procedure can be perceived as treason. They may not regret the crimes they have committed. If they admit the facts, they are betraying their cause. They may also fear that they or their family will be persecuted on account of their admission, especially in places where there is still strong political support for the ideology or political system that stood behind or benefited from perpetration of these crimes. Mark Drumbl catches the spirit of this mentality quite well in the Rwandan context, through interviews conducted with genocide suspects in the central prison of Kigali:

> Nearly every interviewee did not believe he or she had done anything "wrong", or that anything really "wrong" had happened, in the summer of 1994. Detainees who acknowledged that violence had occurred generally believed it was necessary out of self-defence. These detainees did not perceive the massacres as genocidal or in any way manifestly illegal. They saw themselves as honourable citizens tasked to do the dirty work of furthering the interests of the state. Even after years in jail, these detainees had not been disabused of the propaganda fed to them by extremist Hutu leaders, according to which the Tutsi were out to attack them, so, therefore this attack had to be pre-empted by killing all the Tutsi. This violence therefore became legitimized as a preemptive war of survival, not condemned as genocide. Unsurprisingly, then, many detainees

saw themselves as prisoners of war, simply ending up on the
losing side.[98]

It is ironic, however, that these suspects, with their skewed visions
of reality, by rejecting the potential benefits of an abbreviated criminal
procedure for core international crimes, may thereby subject themselves
to a less forgiving outcome of a regular criminal procedure.

5.4.3. Conclusion: Observations on the Arguments and Positions – Guiding Principles

As seen above, reasonably compelling arguments can be made on both
sides of the issue concerning abbreviated criminal procedures for core international crimes, depending on one's perspective. In attempting to synthe-
sise the positions surrounding this matter, I believe a system that addresses
the basic features described in section 5.3.6. would create an effective, efficient and fair mechanism. In addition, I believe the following guiding principles for an abbreviated criminal procedure for core international crimes
might be helpful in addressing and serving the interests of the stakeholders,
and increase the prospects for its success.

First, the system must be flexible. This will allow the judge, sometimes in consultation with the parties, to fashion the process in a way that
best serves the dictates of justice. In other words, one size does not fit all.
Flexibility will protect fundamental human rights standards for fair proceedings in a process tailored to meet the requirements of each particular
case. For example, in a relatively simple, straightforward matter, the parties
may agree that all evidence is submitted in writing. In a more complex case,
the judge may decide or a party may request that written evidence be supplemented by oral testimony. The overarching aim is to make the criminal
justice system work.

Second, the system should effectively process large backlogs of cases
without violating precepts of due process. It must indeed provide more
cost-effective and faster justice than the normal procedure while also allowing for the interests of victims to be respected and the historical record to be
preserved by detailed, reasoned judicial decisions.

Third, it must be administered within the criminal justice system, that
is, the case files must remain within the prosecution service and the judici-

---

[98] Drumbl, 2007, p. 97, see *supra* note 48.

ary until they are closed, while not dismissing alternative mechanisms in the most extreme cases.

Fourth, it may be necessary to distinguish between the most serious and less serious core international crimes, and the levels of participation in their commission, without a discriminatory effect.

Fifth, there must be a real risk of normal criminal justice accountability for a suspect to be willing to make use of an abbreviated criminal procedure for core international crimes while at the same time providing an incentive to choose the process, perhaps by offering reduced punishments.

Sixth, it must generate sufficient support in the political, legal and other communities of interest in society. To do so, an abbreviated criminal procedure for core international crimes must be clearly and precisely defined, predictable and practical, attending to requirements of legitimacy, efficiency and fairness.

5.5. Concluding Remarks

The ultimate purpose of a criminal justice system is to promote the rule of law and thereby further the interests of society. Without the rule of law, citizens can lose faith in their government and political institutions, even in each other. When this happens, the climate ripens for conflict and strife that may in the most extreme circumstances result in the commission of core international crimes. This is the sad legacy of history. When core international crimes occur, calls for accountability arise in the aftermath. It is therefore important to create mechanisms that are consistent with the maintenance of the principle of individual criminal responsibility, especially when criminal conduct shocks the conscience. Out of the international resolve to prosecute individuals responsible for these crimes, international tribunals emerged, from Nuremberg to the more recent *ad hoc* tribunals for Yugoslavia and Rwanda, to the ICC.

As seen in this chapter, these recent *ad hoc* tribunals did not cope with the large number of core international crimes cases within their jurisdiction, and over time prioritised prosecutions of those involving the highest-level suspects, the senior leaders suspected of being most responsible for crimes. Over time, a general shift of the duty to prosecute core international crimes cases occurred from international tribunals to the countries where crimes were committed. Many of these states, however, are in the process of transition from conflict and lack adequate capacity to address the

issue of core international crimes through criminal prosecutions. They must therefore make important and difficult decisions as to whether they will deal with these heinous crimes within their criminal justice system or outside of it.

States ideally will choose a path where core international crimes are processed inside the criminal justice system but, depending upon the circumstances, this may not be possible. Individual conflicts and the ramifications that result are never the same in their nature and scale. Each country in conflict has its unique history, circumstances and internal pressures. Different interest groups, such as victims, perpetrators, lawyers, politicians and others, have different agendas and expectations. There is an ongoing competition for capacity and resources available to address societal demands. Core international crimes are but one such instance. As a result, some states may choose alternative mechanisms, such as truth and reconciliation commissions, to move their process of transition and rehabilitation of society forward towards completion. These alternative methods are not without shortcomings. This chapter does not deliver judgment about which path is the right one for an individual state to choose for itself. Rather it acknowledges the many factors involved in these determinations.

In states that choose to fulfil the international obligation to prosecute core international crimes and address them within their criminal justice system, the need to develop the capacity of the criminal justice system is paramount. Most likely, an extreme number of cases will create backlogs. The criminal justice system will therefore have to be nurtured and strengthened to combat backlogs. One means to accomplish this purpose, described here, may be through the adoption of an abbreviated criminal procedure for core international crimes which include procedures that entail a significantly shortened approach to the processing of core international crimes cases, as opposed to the regular criminal procedure of a full trial. Their primary aim is to increase the ability of the criminal justice system to resolve large number of cases that create backlogs, while respecting basic fair trial principles. This latter feature cannot be compromised. In order to achieve the desired aim, these procedures should be prescribed by law and administered by regular courts in a flexible manner, without creating additional institutional layers that can further impede the system. To build public confidence, the process must be transparent and open, serving not only to mete out justice and address the needs of victims but also to educate and assist societies in transition to become whole. The abbreviated criminal procedure

for core international crimes mechanism must provide for a variety of sanctions with a necessary degree of flexibility. The component of general flexibility is essential throughout the system to deal with peculiarities that will invariably arise in the facts, circumstances, contexts and evidentiary needs of case files. An abbreviated criminal procedure for core international crimes must function under the principle that not one size fits all.

There will be arguments in favour and against an abbreviated criminal procedure for core international crimes, some strictly legal while others overlap into the political. None should be overlooked or dismissed outright. This chapter examined certain arguments and culled from them guiding principles that may be indispensable in the development of an abbreviated criminal procedure for core international crimes. The guiding principles assume that the features for an abbreviated criminal procedure for core international crimes, set forth in section 5.3.6., would apply. Perhaps the overarching principle is that the procedure must be flexible and tailored to meet the requirements of each particular case for the purpose of resolving backlogs of cases expeditiously, yet not ignore the rights of defendants or the interests of victims or the society at large. It must garner support of the stakeholders within the criminal justice system and other interested parties, and be seen as a reliable tool of the criminal justice system. In exceptional circumstances, alternative mechanisms such as truth and reconciliations commissions may be appropriate in conjunction therewith. An abbreviated criminal procedure for core international crimes must be responsive to different classifications of core international crimes cases, but not arbitrary. Finally, the procedure must incentivise its use by defendants while maintaining a tangible risk of normal criminal justice accountability.

Design and implementation of abbreviated criminal procedures for core international crimes will not be an easy task. Each country that creates an abbreviated criminal procedure for core international crimes will have to mould it according to its needs. The Colombian peace and justice process is a good example of a state that did so. This chapter did not seek to provide concrete answers and solutions for a system that does not yet exist, but set forth to raise issues for consideration when and if that time comes. It would be gratifying to have a world without core international crimes, but that is not the reality. When these crimes occur, generally on a large scale, they should not go unaddressed simply because a criminal justice system cannot deal with their number. Core international crimes cases cannot be ignored, even if they must be dealt with outside the crimi-

nal justice system. Otherwise, impunity and a potential breakdown of society may loom. If we desire to live in a civilised world, giving respect to principles of international law, the laws of humanity and the requirements of the public conscience, this is a true test of our character.[99]

---

[99] For a discussion of the principles underlying the Martens Clause as it developed from the 1899 Hague Convention II with Respect to the Laws and Customs of War on Land, then restated in the 1907 Hague Convention IV on the same matter, see Antonio Cassese, "The Martens Clause: Half a Loaf or Simply Pie in the Sky?", in *European Journal of International Law*, 2000, vol. 11, no. 1, pp. 187–286.

6

The Colombian Peace and Justice Law: An Adequate Abbreviated Procedure for Core International Crimes?

Maria Paula Saffon*

In recent years, Colombia has become fashionable in discussions about transitional justice as an example of the possibility to prosecute core international crimes at the national level.[1] This is in part due to the implementa-

---

* **Maria Paula Saffon** holds a bachelor (Magna Cum Laude) in law and an LL.M. degree of Universidad de Los Andes (Bogota, Colombia). She is a researcher of the Colombian Center for the Study of Law, Justice and Society (DeJusticia). For several years, she was a law lecturer at Universidad de Los Andes and Universidad Nacional de Colombia. She does research on transitional justice, the rights of victims of atrocities, internal forced displacement and international human rights, among others. She has published several articles on the subjects, as well as a co-authored book titled *Transitional Justice without Transition? Truth, Justice and Reparations for Colombia* (DeJusticia, 2006). This text was written in 2010 in connection with the original FICHL-conference on the topic. It has not been updated since then and, consequently, it only refers to the very early implementation years of the Justice and Peace law. It does not discuss special justice procedures in the context of the 2016 peace agreement signed by the Colombian government and Fuerzas Armadas Revolucionarias de Colombia ('FARC', Revolutionary Armed Forces of Colombia).

[1] I use the notion of 'core international crimes' to refer to genocide, crimes against humanity and war crimes, which are the crimes with respect to which states' international legal duty to investigate, prosecute and punish has been most clearly established, as recognised in special treaties. As noted in a working paper with Morten Bergsmo, the term 'international' used in this notion refers to the proscription of core crimes by international law, but does not restrict their jurisdiction to international courts. This is so given the applicability of international law in national jurisdictions, as well as the states' duty to establish mechanisms for guaranteeing the efficacy of the duty to investigate, prosecute and punish. On the latter, see Convention on the Prevention and Punishment of the Crime of Genocide ('Genocide Convention'), adopted by General Assembly resolution 260, 9 December 1948, Articles 1, 5 and 7 (http://www.legal-tools.org/doc/498c38/); Convention on the Non-Applicability of Statutory Limitations to War Crimes and Crimes Against Humanity, adopted by General Assembly resolution 2391, 26 November 1968, Articles 1, 3 and 4 (http://www.legal-tools.org/doc/4bd593/); Convention against Torture and Other Cruel, Inhuman or Degrading Treatment or Punishment ('Torture Convention'), adopted by General Assembly resolution 39/46, 10 December 1984, Articles 4, 5, 8 (http://www.legal-tools.org/doc/326294/).

tion of the Justice and Peace Law in the country,[2] aimed at dealing with the massive demobilisation of right-wing paramilitary groups by establishing special criminal procedures for the prosecution of the demobilised individuals who have committed core international crimes. However, it is important to make a cautious analysis of the Colombian case in order to avoid romantic interpretations and problematic transplants of its novel legal framework. Indeed, the Justice and Peace Law has been a very contested law in both its content and implications. Moreover, there exists a stark difference between the law and its implementation, which has made the latter even more contested and problematic. In spite of these shortcomings, there are still some relevant features of the Justice and Peace Law that can be useful for thinking about abbreviated criminal procedures as an alternative for dealing with core international crimes in transitional contexts.

The purpose of this chapter is to offer a cautious analysis along these lines, which can contribute to a clear understanding of the Justice and Peace Law's potentialities and limitations, and thus frame the discussion about the extent to which it can be considered a pertinent and replicable example in the discussion about abbreviated procedures. To do so, in the first section I present a succinct account of the Colombian armed conflict, so as to identify the context in which the Justice and Peace Law is to operate, and to highlight the complexities of the criminal cases under consideration. In the second section, I refer to the innovations introduced by the Justice and Peace Law, and particularly to the special criminal procedure it created. In the third section, I summarise the main modifications that such procedure has suffered in the implementation phase of the Justice and Peace Law. In the fourth and final section, I report the main outcomes that the justice and peace processes have produced so far, which can give some hints about the risks and potentialities of its use as a model for other transitional justice criminal processes.

---

[2]   Colombia, Law No. 975, Issuing Provisions for the Reincorporation of Members of Illegal Armed Groups Who Effectively Contribute to the Attainment of National Peace, and Other Provisions for Humanitarian Accords Are Issued ('Justice and Peace Law'), 25 July 2005 (http://www.legal-tools.org/doc/ca98de/).

6.1. The Context of the Justice and Peace Law: Complexities of the Colombian Case[3]

The investigation and prosecution of core international crimes is a particularly difficult task in Colombia, in great part as a result of several traits of the armed conflict. Along with the Palestinian–Israeli and the Indian–Pakistani conflicts, the Colombian case is one of the longest armed conflicts in the world.[4] The conflict includes various actors: subversive guerrilla groups,[5] the state[6] and right-wing paramilitary groups,[7] all of whom have

---

[3] This section of the chapter is based on Maria Paula Saffon, "Problematic Selection and Lack of Clear Prioritization: The Colombian Experience", in Morten Bergsmo (ed.), *Criteria for Prioritizing and Selecting Core International Crimes Cases*, 2nd ed., Torkel Opsahl Academic EPublisher, Oslo, 2010, pp. 127–41. In turn, the latter draws extensively from Maria Paula Saffon and Rodrigo Uprimny, "Uses and Abuses of Transitional Justice in Colombia", in Morten Bergsmo and Pablo Kalmanovitz (eds.), *Law in Peace Negotiations*, 2nd ed., Torkel Opsahl Academic EPublisher, Oslo, 2010, pp. 354–400.

[4] See Comisión Nacional de Reparación y Reconciliación ('CNRR', Colombian National Commission for Reparations and Reconciliation), *Hoja de Ruta* [Road Map], 17 January 2006. The most cautious analysts point to 1964 as the contemporary origin of the Colombian conflict, since this was the year in which FARC – the strongest guerrilla group in the country – took arms. See CNRR, *Fundamentos filosóficos y operativos. Definiciones estratégicas de la Comisión Nacional de Reparación y Reconciliación* [Philosophical and Operational Foundations. Strategic Definitions of the National Commission for Reparations and Reconciliation], 2006. However, many other analysts point to the period of violence between the liberal and conservative political parties in the 1940s as the origin of the conflict as we know it today. See Gonzalo Sánchez and Ricardo Peñaranda (eds.), *Pasado y presente de la violencia en Colombia* [Past and Present of Violence in Colombia], IE-PRI-CEREC, Bogota, 1991. The length and perpetuation of the conflict can be partially explained by the strong links between illegal armed groups and drug trafficking, as the latter constitutes an almost unlimited source of war finance. For the relationship between conflict and drug trafficking in Colombia, see Andrés López Restrepo, "Narcotráfico, ilegalidad y conflicto en Colombia" [Drug Trafficking, Illegality and Conflict in Colombia], in Francisco Gutiérrez, María Emma Wills and Gonzalo Sánchez (eds.) *Nuestra guerra sin nombre: Transformaciones del conflicto en Colombia*, Instituto de Estudios Políticos y Relaciones Internacionales (IEPRI), Bogota, 2006, pp. 405–39.

[5] Today, only two subversive guerrilla groups confronting the Colombian state's authority are still active: Ejército de Liberación Nacional ('ELN', National Liberation Army), which is currently at the first stages of peace negotiation with the government, but still with uncertain results, and FARC, which concluded a peace agreement with the government in late 2016. However, several other subversive guerrilla groups confronted the state in earlier times, such as the April 19 Movement ('M-19'), Ejército Popular de Liberación ('EPL', Popular Liberation Army), the indigenous guerrilla group Quintín Lame, Partido Revolucionario de los Trabajadores de Colombia ('PRT', Workers' Revolutionary Party of Colombia), and Corriente de Renovación Socialista ('CRS', Current of Socialist Renewal). The latter groups received amnesties in the 1990s. At varying magnitudes, all these groups

committed atrocities against the civil population on a significant scale. So far, the conflict has produced more than three million victims of internal forced displacement (equivalent to around 7 per cent of the Colombian

---

have committed atrocities against the civil population, particularly killings and kidnappings.

[6] It is a notorious fact that the state, through its armed forces, participates in the armed conflict combating guerrilla groups and more recently paramilitary groups. Paradoxically, the government has denied the existence of an armed conflict in Colombia and instead talked about a terrorist threat, apparently with the objective of impeding the international political recognition of guerrilla groups as organized armed groups. See R. Uprimny, "¿Existe o no conflicto armado en Colombia?" [Is There or Is There Not an Armed Conflict in Colombia?], in Plataforma Colombiana Democracia, Derechos Humanos y Desarrollo (ed.), *Más allá del embrujo: Tercer año de gobierno de Álvaro Uribe Vélez?* [Beyond Enchantment: Third Year of Alvaro Uribe Vélez's Government], Plataforma Colombiana Democracia, Derechos Humanos y Desarrollo, Bogota, 2005. It has also been judicially proven (both at the national and the international levels) that agents of the Colombian state have been responsible for international human rights and humanitarian law violations either by commission or omission. See, for instance, the cases that have been decided by the Inter-American Court of Human Rights ('IACtHR') against the Colombian state, regarding atrocities committed by paramilitaries with the collaboration or omission of agents of the public force. IACtHR, *Case of the 19 merchants v. Colombia*, Judgment, 5 July 2004, Series C No. 109 (http://www.legal-tools.org/doc/f93718/); IACtHR, *Case of the Mapiripán Massacre v. Colombia*, Judgment, 15 September 2005, Series C No. 134 (http://www.legal-tools.org/doc/5830c0/); IACtHR, *Case of the Pueblo Bello Massacre v. Colombia*, Judgment, 31 January 2006, Series C No. 140 (http://www.legal-tools.org/doc/cb12ef/); IACtHR, *Case of the Ituango Massacres v. Colombia*, Judgment, 1 July 2006, Series C No. 149 (http://www.legal-tools.org/doc/df6c7c/); and IACtHR, *Caso of the La Rochela Massacre v. Colombia*, Judgment, 11 May 2007, Series C No. 163 (http://www.legal-tools.org/doc/0c7f35/).

[7] In the 1980s right-wing paramilitary groups appeared with the justification of the need to combat guerrilla groups in a stronger way. However, since the very beginning, paramilitaries committed heinous crimes against civilians, including massacres and forced disappearances. There have been more than 30 paramilitary groups in the country. See Oficina Alto Comisionado para la Paz [Office of the High Commissioner for Peace], "Proceso de Paz con las Autodefensas: Informe Ejecutivo" [Peace Process with the Self-Defence Forces: Executive Report], Bogota, December 2006. Although paramilitary groups are not organised hierarchically and do not have a united or centralised mandate, in 1997 most of them joined to create the Autodefensas Unidas de Colombia ('AUC', United Self-Defence Forces of Colombia). The leaders of most of the groups included in AUC participated in the peace negotiations with the government in 2002, and their members demobilised in the following years. However, quite a few of these groups refused demobilisation and took up arms again. Moreover, since the demobilisations, many new paramilitary groups – commonly known as emergent bands or "black eagles" – have been created, composed of both demobilised and non-demobilised paramilitaries.

---

population),[8] and more than 100,000 victims of other atrocious core international crimes, including massacres, forced disappearances, kidnappings, sexual violence, torture and arbitrary detentions, among others.[9] In general, these victims pertained to the least favourable sectors of society before the commission of atrocities, and most of them are under conditions of severe deprivation.[10]

In the contemporary developments of the conflict, there have been partial negotiations between the state and some armed groups.[11] Therefore,

---

[8] Official sources currently talk about 3,303,979 forcedly displaced persons in the country. See Acción Social, *Estadísticas de la población desplazada* [Statistics of the Displaced Population], 2009. This is, however, a disguised figure that only takes into account the number of persons who are officially registered in the government's Registro Único de Población Desplazada ('RUPD', Single Displaced Persons Register) and, thus, excludes displaced people who have not been able to register. That is why already by 2006 other sources like the United Nations High Commissioner for Refugees referred to around three million forcedly displaced people. See United Nations High Commissioner for Refugees, *2006 Global Trends: Refugees, Asylum-seekers, Returnees, Internally Displaced and Stateless Persons*, Geneva, UNHCR, 2007.

[9] For some preliminary calculations of the total amount of victims in Colombia and the cost of their reparation, see Camilo González, "Prólogo" [Prologue], in Diego Otero Prada (ed.), *Las cifras del conflicto* [The Ciphers of the Conflict], Indepaz, Bogota, 2007; Mark Richards, *Quantification of the Financial Resources Required to Repair Victims of the Colombian Conflict in Accordance with the Justice and Peace Law*, Centro de Recursos para el Análisis de Conflictos (CERAC), Bogota, 2007.

[10] This is so, perhaps with the exception of some victims of extortion kidnapping. In this, the Colombian situation is similar to that of Guatemala (where the majority of victims belonged to Mayan ethnic groups) and Peru (where the majority of victims were rural), and very different to that of Argentina and Chile (where victims were mostly from the middle classes).

[11] There were general peace agreements and consequent amnesties during the period of violence between the liberal and conservative political parties from the 1940s to 1960s. See Colectivo de Abogados José Alvear Restrepo, *¿Terrorismo o rebelión? Propuestas de regulación del conflicto armado* [Terrorism or Rebellion? Proposals for the Regulation of the Armed Conflict], Colectivo de Abogados José Alvear Restrepo, Bogota, 2001; Gonzalo Sánchez and Donny Meertens, *Bandits, Peasants, and Politics: The Case of "La Violencia" in Colombia*, University of Texas Press, Austin, 2001. However, in the contemporary developments of the conflict, apart from the FARC, there have only been partial peace negotiations with some factions of the conflict, notably with the M-19, EPL, Quintín Lame, PRT and CRS guerrilla groups during the 1990s, and with paramilitary groups in 2002. See Iván Cepeda Castro, "Pacto de lealtades e impunidad" [Loyalty Pacts and Impunity], 23 December 2003 (http://www.derechos.org/nizkor/colombia/doc/cepeda9.html). Many have argued that negotiations with paramilitary groups should not be considered a peace agreement, due to the fact that these groups never confronted or even opposed the government. On this, see Cepeda, *idem*.

these negotiations have taken place in the middle of conflict, and have not brought about a real or complete transition from war to peace. The negotiations held in 2002 between the Colombian government and most paramilitary groups affiliated to the Autodefensas Unidas de Colombia ('AUC', United Self-Defence Forces of Colombia), resulted in the demobilisation of 35 paramilitary groups and over 30,000 individuals belonging to them.[12] These have been the first negotiations that have led to the development of a special legal framework intended to investigate and prosecute the crimes perpetrated by demobilised individuals.[13] However, for various reasons, the nature of paramilitary groups imposes difficult challenges to the investigation and prosecution of their crimes. On the one hand, paramilitary groups are pro-systemic, not anti-systemic actors.[14] They never intended to overthrow the government or to defeat the army, but rather to support the state's struggle against guerrilla groups through illegal means. Moreover, for many years the state did not persecute them, and even benefited from their support.[15] On the other hand, paramilitary groups have created strong economic and political power structures. In fact, since their origins, they have held strong ties with economic elites and with drug lords, which have allowed them to amass substantial fortunes and to accumulate great tracts of land.[16]

---

[12] According to the Oficina Alto Comisionado para la Paz, 2007, see *supra* note 7, the number of collectively demobilised paramilitaries was 31,671.

[13] Indeed, the peace agreements with guerrilla groups in the 1990s brought about individual pardons or the ceasing of criminal procedures for the members of these groups, but excluded from these benefits those individuals who had committed certain atrocious crimes and crimes without a political intention. However, no special criminal procedures were established for the purpose of prosecuting the excluded individuals, who were therefore submitted to the ordinary criminal laws. See Cepeda, 2003, *supra* note 11; Colectivo de Abogados José Alvear Restrepo, 2001, *supra* note 11.

[14] For this distinction see Leopoldo Múnera, "Proceso de paz con actores armados ilegales y parasistémicos (los paramilitares y las políticas de reconciliación en Colombia)" [Peace Process with Illegal and Para-systemic Armed Actors (Paramilitaries and Reconciliation Policies in Colombia)], in *Revista Pensamiento Jurídico*, 2006, no. 17.

[15] For an analysis of the Colombian legal framework, on the base of which many paramilitary groups were created, see the cases that have been decided by the Inter-American Court of Human Rights against the Colombian state, regarding atrocities committed by paramilitaries with the collaboration or omission of agents of the public force, *supra* note 7.

[16] See Mauricio Romero, *Paramilitares y autodefensas, 1982–2003* [Paramilitaries and Self-defences Forces, 1998–2003], IEPRI-Planeta, Bogota, 2003; Gustavo Duncan, *Los señores de la guerra: de paramilitares, mafiosos y autodefensas en Colombia* [The Warlords: Of Paramilitaries, Mafias and Self-defence Forces], Planeta, Bogota, 2006; Maria Paula Saffon, 2006, "Poder paramilitar y debilidad institucional. El paramilitarismo en Colombia: un caso complejo de incumplimiento de normas" [Paramilitary Power and Institutional

Furthermore, paramilitary groups have established strong relations of collaboration and complicity with state agents, which not only include members of the public forces[17] but also intelligence agents, local politicians and many national congressmen.[18] Finally, paramilitary groups are not organised hierarchically and do not have a united or centralised mandate, but rather function as semi-autonomous cells belonging to a nodal structure.[19]

These features of the Colombian situation make the criminal investigation and prosecution of core international crimes committed an especially complex endeavour. In effect, it implies carrying out, in the midst of the armed conflict, criminal processes against a great number of perpetrators belonging to different groups with complex political, economic and military structures, who have committed innumerable crimes, many of them of a systematic nature, over quite a long period of time.

6.2. The Justice and Peace Law: The Establishment of a Special Criminal Procedure[20]

In spite of these difficulties, a special legal framework has been developed with the purpose of dealing with atrocities committed by members of armed groups who decide to demobilise either individually or collectively. This legal framework is based on Laws 782 of 2002 and 975 of 2005 (commonly known as the Justice and Peace Law). Although it was formulated as a response to the negotiations with paramilitary groups, the framework is also applicable to members of guerrilla groups who decide

---

Weakness. Paramilitarism in Colombia: A Complex Case of Disobedience to the Law], M.A. thesis, Los Andes University, Bogota.

[17] On this also see the five cases decided by the Inter-American Court of Human Rights about the State's responsibility in relation to paramilitary crimes, *supra* note 7.

[18] See Duncan, 2006, *supra* note 16; Saffon, 2006, *supra* note 16. By 2010, criminal investigations for links with paramilitaries had been opened against 65 congressmen, which represented 23 per cent of the total of members of the legislature. See "Cifras del escándalo de la parapolítica dejan al descubierto su dimension" [Ciphers of the Parapolitics Scandal Expose its Dimension], in *El Tiempo*, 26 April 2008.

[19] On this, see Manuel A. Alonso Espinal, Jorge Giraldo Ramírez and Diego Jorge Sierra, "Medellín: El complejo camino de la competencia armada" [Medellin: The Complex Way of Armed Competition], in *Diálogo mayor: Memoria colectiva, reparación, justicia y democracia: el conflicto colombiano y la paz a la luz de experiencias internacionales* [Major Dialogue: Collective Memory, Reparations, Justice and Democracy: The Colombian Conflict and Peace in Light of International Experiences], Universidad del Rosario, Bogota, 2005.

[20] The first part of this section of the also draws greatly on Saffon, 2010, see *supra* note 3.

to demobilise. However, it excludes state agents, who have to be investigated and prosecuted through pre-existing criminal laws that regulate the prosecution of public servants.[21]

This legal framework constitutes an innovation in the Colombian context for various reasons. On the one hand, it sharply contrasts with the country's historic tendency to confer amnesties or individual pardons to the actors of conflict,[22] since it implies that demobilised individuals can receive legal pardons unless they have committed atrocious crimes.[23] On the other hand, instead of leaving the task of dealing with such crimes to the ordinary criminal jurisdiction,[24] it creates a special jurisdiction for the investigation, prosecution and judgment of core international crimes committed by demobilised individuals. Such jurisdiction is mainly composed by the special Justice and Peace Unit of the General Prosecutor's Office, the Superior Tribunals of Justice and Peace, and the Peace and Justice second instance jurisdiction of the Supreme Court of Justice's Criminal Chamber.[25]

Finally, but most importantly, the framework establishes a special criminal procedure for dealing with those crimes, known as the justice and peace procedure. The main objective of the procedure is to grant a substantial reduction of the criminal sentence (a minimum of five and a maximum of eight years, regardless of the quantity and gravity of the crimes committed) to those demobilised individuals who cease their illegal activities, fully and trustworthily confess the crimes in which they participated, and offer assets for the reparation of their victims.[26] In order to

---

[21] Justice and Peace Law, Article 2, see *supra* note 2.

[22] González, 2007, see *supra* note 9. As already noted, this historic tradition started to break in the amnesty processes carried out in the 1990s in relation to some guerrilla groups, which imposed certain conditions to the concession of pardons and the ceasing of criminal procedures.

[23] Literally, the law refers to "atrocious acts of ferocity or barbarianism, terrorism, kidnapping, genocide, non-combat homicide or homicide against victims in a state of defencelessness". Colombia, Law 782, 23 December 2002, Article 5 (http://www.legal-tools.org/doc/9e9c84/).

[24] As did the legal framework that regulated the negotiation processes carried out in the 1990s, by contemplating the possibility of prosecution of demobilised individuals who had committed certain atrocious crimes, but not instituting special criminal laws for that purpose.

[25] Justice and Peace Law, Articles 16, 26, 33 and 34, see *supra* note 2.

[26] *Ibid.*, Article 11.

fulfil that objective, the law foresaw that the government should submit to the Justice and Peace Unit a list of those collectively demobilised individuals who have committed core international crimes.[27] Apart from the list, individually demobilised armed actors could voluntarily submit to the justice and peace procedure at any time, under the condition that they fulfil the same requirements mentioned in the case of collectively demobilised individuals, as well as the requirement to deliver information about the armed group to which they belonged.[28]

According to the law, in both cases the Justice and Peace Unit is supposed to verify the satisfaction of those requirements, by carrying out public hearings, called "free version" hearings, in which each demobilised individual delivers his or her confession.[29] After each free version hearing, the Justice and Peace Unit must determine if and which charges can be pressed, and consequently press them in a public hearing for that purpose.[30] After this public hearing, the Unit must undertake a two-month to four-month investigation aimed at verifying the confessed facts and at investigating others that might be relevant.[31] After this investigation, the Justice and Peace Unit must convoke an indictment public hearing, in which the demobilised can either accept or reject the charges.[32] In case he or she does not accept, the justice and peace procedure will be considered terminated and the crimes will be investigated by the ordinary jurisdiction. The process will continue with respect to all the charges he or she accepts, and will pass to the judgment stage, under the responsibility of the Superior Tribunals of Justice and Peace.[33] This stage will start with a judicial hearing in which the voluntary and free character of confession will be verified. In case it is confirmed, the process will continue with a reparations incidental hearing, in which conciliation between the demobilised individual and his/her victims will try to be reached regarding the reparations owed to the latter.[34] Subsequently, the competent justice will issue the criminal sentence, which will also contain either the reparations

---

[27]   *Ibid.*, Article 10.
[28]   *Ibid.*, Article 11.
[29]   *Ibid.*, Article 17.
[30]   *Ibid.*, Articles 17 and 18.
[31]   *Ibid.*, Article 18.
[32]   *Ibid.*.
[33]   *Ibid.*, Article 68.
[34]   *Ibid.*, Article 23.

agreement – if reached – or an order to repair based on the justice's discretion.[35] The sentence may be appealed before the Criminal Chamber of the Supreme Court of Justice.[36]

6.3. The Implementation of the Justice and Peace Law: Modifications of the Special Criminal Procedure

The justice and peace procedure has suffered significant changes after the issuance of the Justice and Peace Law, as a result of the interpretations given to it by the Constitutional Court in charge of assessing the constitutionality of its dispositions, and by the government and the judicial agents in charge of applying them.

To begin with, the government issued a decree in which it offered a lax interpretation of the legal disposition according to which demobilised individuals who have committed core international crimes cannot receive legal pardons and must therefore appear before criminal justice. In the framework of the justice and peace procedures, the result of this interpretation was that by 2008 the government excluded from the list that it submitted to the Justice and Peace Unit more than 90 per cent (28,544) of the demobilised paramilitaries.[37] These individuals have benefited from legal pardons, even though it is likely that they participated in the commission of atrocities but did not have any open processes against them, as a result of the country's exceptionally high rate of impunity.[38] It is true that the pardoned individuals are not entirely shielded from criminal justice since they could eventually be prosecuted if a criminal investigation proved their participation in an atrocious crime. However, it is highly unlikely that this will happen, given that the Prosecutor's Office is already overloaded with the task of investigating the several thousand who have entered the peace and law procedure (the majority of whom are paramilitar-

---

[35] *Ibid.*, Article 24.

[36] *Ibid.*, Article 26.

[37] See the 2008 report elaborated by a group of human rights organizations on the Colombian state's compliance with human rights standards: VV.AA., "Informe para el examen periódico universal de Colombia" [Report for the Universal Periodic Review of Colombia], July 2008; See also Saffon, 2006, *supra* note 16.

[38] For the different ways in which such rate has been calculated, see Elvira María Restrepo and Mariana Martínez Cuéllar, "Impunidad penal: mitos y realidades" [Criminal Impunity: Myths and Realities"], in *Documentos Cede*, no. 24, 2004.

ies).[39] So it will probably not have the time and resources necessary to investigate the other more than 28,000 perpetrated atrocities. For that reason, this interpretation has been criticised as a veiled amnesty, which brings about impunity under the appearance of accountability.[40]

On the other hand, when analysing the constitutionality of the Justice and Peace Law dispositions, the Constitutional Court modified the justice and peace procedure in at least three fundamental ways.[41] First, it stated that confessions made by demobilised actors in public hearings must be complete and truthful, lest they do not receive the substantive reduction of the criminal sentence foreseen in the law.[42] Thus, in contrast with initial interpretations of the law made by the government and the Prosecutor's Office, the Constitutional Court determined that demobilised actors could not recognise in later stages of the process that they lied or omitted facts in their confessions and still receive the benefit of a reduced sentence. In that way, the Constitutional Court's decision created a strong incentive for demobilised actors to confess, as it made it clear that they could lose the benefit of sentence reduction at any stage of the process if such confessions were not complete and truthful. Moreover, the Constitutional Court's decision implies that it is the duty of the Justice and Peace Unit to verify the confessed facts and to investigate if others were committed. It also implies that if the Justice and Peace Unit establishes that the concerned individual lied or omitted crimes, the indictment will only cover the confessed crimes, and the rest will have to be prosecuted and judged through the ordinary criminal process.[43]

---

[39] This information was supplied by Luis González, the Chief of the Peace and Justice Unit of the Colombian National Prosecutor's Office, in a written response to an information petition that the Colombian Commission of Jurists presented, on 19 June 2009. See also Colombian Commission of Jurists, "Un balance de la aplicación de la Ley de Justicia y Paz" [Evaluation of the Application of the Justice and Peace Law], 2009 (Preliminary Manuscript).

[40] *Ibid.* See also Gustavo Gallón, "La CNRR: ¿Dr. Jekyll o Mr. Hyde?" [The CNRR: Dr. Jekyll or Mr. Hyde?], in Guillermo Hoyos Vásquez (ed.), *Las víctimas frente a la búsqueda de la verdad y la reparación en Colombia* [Victims in Search of the Truth and Reparations in Colombia], Pontificia Universidad Javeriana, Bogota, 2007, pp. 127–49.

[41] See especially Colombian Constitutional Court, Decision C-360 of 2006, in which the Court analysed most of the Justice and Peace Law's dispositions and declared a great part of them unconstitutional or constitutional under the condition that they satisfy certain requirements.

[42] *Ibid.*

[43] *Ibid.*

Second, the Constitutional Court established that the criminal sentence resulting from a justice and peace procedure should include both the reduced sentence as an alternative sentence, and the real sentence the individual would receive if he or she were not the beneficiary of the alternative sentence.[44] In so doing, once again the Constitutional Court created a stronger incentive for demobilised individuals to comply with the requirements of the Justice and Peace Law both during and after criminal processes. Indeed, it follows from the Constitutional Court's decisions that individuals can lose the benefits of the alternative sentence not only if they lie or omit facts from their confessions but also if they do not concede adequate reparations to victims, and if they continue committing crimes after the sentence.[45] In all those scenarios, individuals would be condemned to serve the real or principal sentence included in the initial ruling.

Third, the Constitutional Court determined that, in order to verify the truthfulness and completeness of confessions, the Prosecutor's Office must have reasonable terms to develop its investigations. In particular, it indicated that indictments cannot be made immediately after free version hearings, but must be preceded by the formulation and fulfilment of a methodological programme aimed at verifying confessions as well as at investigating other facts that might have been committed by the ex-combatants under process.[46] The Constitutional Court also noted that the two-to-four months foreseen by the law for the investigation subsequent to the provisional formulation of indictments are reasonable terms of investigation,[47] but this is so only under the condition that they are preceded by a methodological plan it required.

On the basis of the Constitutional Court's decision, the Prosecutor's Office developed a preliminary investigation strategy with the purpose of preparing the grounds for designing the methodological investigation plan required by the court in each case. This strategy consists in the gathering of information about the contexts of operation, structure, logic and patterns of action of the armed groups to which demobilised individuals be-

---

[44] *Ibid.*
[45] *Ibid.*
[46] *Ibid.*
[47] *Ibid.*

longed before the free version public hearings take place.[48] The strategy has been developed in a way that each of the prosecutors that comprise the Justice and Peace Unit is in charge of one or two of the demobilised paramilitary groups, and has the responsibility of documenting their "origins, structure, areas of influence, financial sources, assets, imputable facts and victims".[49] Each of these prosecutors is then in charge of developing the public hearings, investigation and prosecution of all individuals belonging to the group(s) of which they are in charge. Following the ordinary criminal law on preliminary investigation terms – which, according to the Supreme Court of Justice should be observed in this matter – this preliminary investigation should last not longer than six months.[50]

The Supreme Court of Justice has reinforced the importance of investigations that give account of the relationship between individual crimes and the armed groups' structure and logic of operation. Indeed, in exercising its role of appeals tribunal, it established that all indictments in the justice and peace processes must include the crime of "conspiracy", which proves the participation of individuals in the armed group.[51] And it has also indicated that the Prosecutor's Office should always determine if the different crimes under investigation correspond to systematic patterns of crime commission, by relating such crimes to the armed actors' logic of operation and to the general context of victimisation.[52]

Figure 1 illustrates the general scheme of the first instance justice and peace procedure, including the modifications it has undergone since the issuance of the Justice and Peace Law.

---

[48] This information was supplied by Luis González, the Chief of the Peace and Justice Unit, in a written response to an information petition that I presented, on 28 July 2008.

[49] *Ibid.*

[50] See Colombian Supreme Court of Justice, Criminal Chamber, Decision, 31 July 2009, Judge Rapporteur Augusto J. Ibáñez, p. 19.

[51] *Ibid.*

[52] *Ibid.*

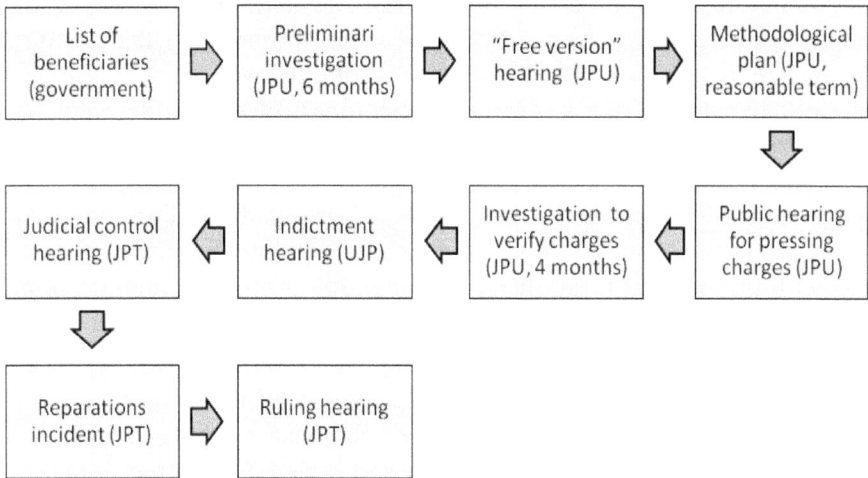

Figure 1: General scheme of the first instance justice and peace procedure.

6.4. The Outcomes of the Justice and Peace Law: An Adequate Abbreviated Procedure?

As described in the previous section, the Colombian justice and peace procedure can be understood as an abbreviated criminal procedure. Indeed, it largely relies on confessions made by demobilised individuals in such a way that, if confessions worked adequately and were actually complete and truthful, the investigation process would be less burdensome than ordinarily, as prosecutors would mainly have to verify the confessed facts and to check them against those confessed by other group members. This is so because the main purpose of confessions is, so to speak, to reverse the burden of fact gathering in exchange of substantive criminal benefits. Moreover, the terms for the investigation and prosecution of core international crimes are such that, if these activities could be adequately and strategically developed, procedures would not last very long.

Now, the outcomes that the Justice and Peace Law has so far produced leave much to be desired in terms of the abbreviated nature of the procedure and of its capacity to guarantee accountability and impede impunity. Indeed, four years after the issuance of the Justice and Peace Law, of the 31,671 demobilised paramilitaries, only 3,635 were candidates for the

peace and law procedure, which certainly suggests that the law is operating as a *de facto* amnesty mechanism.[53]

What is more, of those 3,625 individuals, by June 2009 some 2,149 of them had been summoned for a free version public hearing and 1,836 of such audiences had begun.[54] But only 1,210 individuals had ratified their will to participate in the process and only 621 had confirmed this decision.[55] These numbers can be explained as a result of the fact that several demobilised individuals had not even been properly identified by the Prosecutor's Office (which in many cases only had their names or aliases), while others either did not show up to the free version hearings after summoned, or decided not to participate in the justice and peace procedure.[56] In spite of this, only one of those individuals was excluded from the special procedure, even though the lack of attendance is a sufficient reason for losing the criminal benefits of the Justice and Peace Law.[57] As has been recognised and criticised by the Supreme Court of Justice, the failure to exclude these individuals from the procedure greatly reduces the efficacy of the incentive to confess,[58] as it gives the impression that individuals will not be sanctioned with the loss of criminal benefits if they do not attend the confession hearings. However, even if these individuals were indeed excluded from the procedure, it is very likely that many would still not be prosecuted through the ordinary process, since in many cases there probably does not exist any evidence against them as a result of the structural problem of impunity in the country and of the lack of information about crimes commission that it entails.

On the other hand, many of the individuals who have actually assisted the free version public hearings have not confessed many facts, and yet have not been excluded from the justice and peace procedure.[59] This might be the result of 'silence agreements' made among members of paramilitary groups to only confess what is already known by the Prosecutor's Office and to hide all other facts, under the assumption that the latter will have a

---

53 Response by Luis González, 19 June 2009, see *supra* note 39; Colombian Commission of Jurists, 2009, see *supra* note 39.

54 Response by Luis González, 19 June 2009, see *supra* note 39.

55 *Ibid.*

56 Colombian Commission of Jurists, 2009, see *supra* note 39.

57 *Ibid.*

58 Colombian Supreme Court of Justice, see *supra* note 50.

59 Colombian Commission of Jurists, 2009, see *supra* note 39.

very hard time finding evidence elsewhere. Again, as the Supreme Court has also recognised, the failure to exclude these individuals from the procedure undermines the incentives to confess.[60] However, at the same time, such exclusion would probably not be a strong enough incentive, given the lack of information and evidence of the Prosecutor's Office.

In spite of the former constraints, many facts have nevertheless been confessed in free version public hearings. Given the Prosecutor's Office's limitations in terms of available information and material and human resources, it is still not clear whether all those facts can be verified in a timely manner, and especially if the Office will have the time and resources to investigate non-confessed facts. Since there exists considerable pressure for it to produce outcomes, these limitations can force the Office to make decisions about pressing charges and indicting demobilised individuals, which are rather poor in content and potential impact. The outcomes that the Justice and Peace Unit has so far produced suggest that this might be happening to some extent.

In fact, by June 2009 charges had only been pressed against 85 demobilised individuals and only 13 persons had been indicted.[61] Further, the Supreme Court of Justice annulled the first ruling for not involving the crime of "conspiracy".[62] In these few cases, charges and indictments have not included many facts, as is best illustrated by the first case for which a ruling was issued (and later annulled), which condemned the concerned individual, alias "El Loro" (The Parrot), for just three crimes, even though he is a paramilitary commander with an important degree of responsibility.[63]

This brief account shows that there exist crucial drawbacks that seriously undermine the possibility of the justice and peace criminal processes' capacity to guarantee timely justice with significant results. Now, despite the limitations, a few lessons can still be drawn from the implementation of these processes, especially thanks to the intervention of higher courts to assure a better interpretation of the Justice and Peace Law, and to the good practices of some prosecutors. These lessons include: the importance of generating strong incentives to confess whenever

---

[60] Colombian Supreme Court of Justice, 2009, see *supra* note 50.

[61] Response by Luis González, 19 June 2009, see *supra* note 39.

[62] Colombian Supreme Court of Justice, see *supra* note 50.

[63] *Ibid.*

confessions are used as a strategy in abbreviated procedures; the strong potential of linking the investigation and prosecution of core international crimes committed in a conflict situation to the wider context of the violations, and to the armed groups' organisational structure and patterns of operation; and, the relevance of developing an investigation strategy and a methodological plan for adequately addressing the commission of multiple, complex and systematic crimes.

7

The *Gacaca* Courts and Abbreviated Criminal Procedure for Genocide Crimes in Rwanda

Phil Clark[*]

7.1. Introduction

Following the 1994 genocide in Rwanda, during which approximately 800,000 people were killed, many by their own neighbours and friends, the country embarked on one of the most comprehensive justice programmes attempted anywhere in the world. Whereas most post-conflict societies limit prosecutions to a handful of ringleaders of mass crimes, Rwanda sought to bring hundreds of thousands of everyday genocide suspects to justice. Central to Rwanda's post-genocide justice structure have been the *gacaca* community courts, which between 2002 and 2012 comprised 11,000 jurisdictions across the country, overseen by locally elected lay judges. Over that decade, *gacaca* prosecuted around 400,000 suspects. Because of *gacaca*'s plea-bargaining scheme, the vast majority of those convicted by *gacaca* either had their sentences commuted to community service or, if they were imprisoned, have now been reintegrated into the same communities where they committed crimes during the genocide.

This chapter explores the function and efficacy of the *gacaca* courts, focusing on their attempts to expedite the process of hearing such an enormous caseload of genocide suspects. Based on the author's research into *gacaca*, which covered the entire lifespan of the process and involved more than 600 interviews with participants in *gacaca* and relevant Rwandan and international political and judicial officials, this chapter argues that *gacaca* has produced variable results, especially in terms of justice and truth, but

---

[*]   **Phil Clark** is Reader in Comparative and International Politics at SOAS University of London, Department of Politics and International Studies. Previously, he was a Research Fellow in Courts and Public Policy at the Centre for Socio-Legal Studies, University of Oxford, a Golding Research Fellow at Brasenose College, and co-founder and convenor of Oxford Transitional Justice Research. He has a D.Phil. in Politics from Balliol College, University of Oxford, where he studied as a Rhodes Scholar. His latest book is *The Gacaca Courts, Post-Genocide Justice and Reconciliation in Rwanda: Justice without Lawyers* (Cambridge University Press, 2010).

overall has generated crucial benefits for the post-genocide society. The chapter proceeds in five sections: a brief background to the Rwandan genocide; the history and modalities of *gacaca*; the virtues of *gacaca*'s use of abbreviated criminal procedure; the problems associated with this approach; and some concluding remarks regarding the relevance of the *gacaca* experience for more general considerations of expedited methods of post-conflict accountability.

7.2. Background to the Rwandan Genocide

Between April and July 1994, Rwanda experienced one of the most devastating waves of mass killing in modern history. In around 100 days, nearly three-quarters of the Tutsi population (which constituted around 11 per cent of the overall population of Rwanda in 1994, while Hutu constituted nearly 84 per cent) were murdered and hundreds of thousands more exiled to neighbouring countries.[1] What distinguishes the Rwandan genocide from other cases of mass murder in the twentieth century, and in particular from the genocide of Jews during the Second World War, is the use of low-technology weaponry, the mass involvement of the Hutu population in the killings, the social and cultural similarities of the perpetrators and victims, and the astonishing speed of the genocide. The majority of murders were carried out brutally with basic instruments such as machetes, spears and spiked clubs and often near victims' homes.[2]

Events in the early 1990s are important for our understanding of the genocide.[3] On 1 October 1990 the Rwandan Patriotic Front ('RPF'), comprising mainly descendants of Tutsi refugees who fled Hutu violence in the 1960s, invaded Rwanda from Uganda.[4] Government forces repelled the RPF and a guerrilla war broke out in the north-east of the country. After

---

[1] Gérard Prunier, *The Rwanda Crisis: History of a Genocide*, Hurst, London, 1998, pp. 264–68.

[2] See, for example, Alison Des Forges, *Leave None to Tell the Story: Genocide in Rwanda*, Human Rights Watch, New York, 1999, pp. 209–12; African Rights, *Rwanda: Death, Despair and Defiance*, rev. ed., African Rights, London, 1995, ch. 9; Roméo Dallaire, *Shake Hands with the Devil: The Failure of Humanity in Rwanda*, Random House Canada, Toronto, 2003, ch. 11.

[3] For a useful account of the flurry of key events in 1990, see Peter Uvin, *Aiding Violence: The Development Enterprise in Rwanda*, Kumarian Press, West Hartford, CT, 1998, pp. 60–65.

[4] Prunier, 1998, p. 72 and ch. 3, see *supra* note 1.

nearly three years of fighting, the government and the RPF signed the United Nations ('UN')-brokered Arusha Peace Accords in August 1993.

Important dynamics both within and outside of Rwanda exacerbated ethnic tensions during this period. The assassination on 21 October 1993 of the Burundian President Melchior Ndadaye, a Hutu, by members of the Tutsi-led army, led to mass killings of Burundian Hutu and the exodus of thousands of refugees to Rwanda, sparking fears among Rwandan Hutu that the violence would spill across the border. Many Hutu politicians – aided by extremist media sources such as the Hutu newspaper *Kangura* and the country's largest radio station Radio-Télévision Libre des Mille Collines ('RTLM') – used the violence in Burundi as justification to call for greater suppression of Tutsi in Rwanda.[5] Meanwhile, the Rwandan President Juvénal Habyarimana, supported by the French government,[6] was training Hutu youth militias called *interahamwe* – Kinyarwanda for "those who stand together" or "those who fight together" – to attack Tutsi.[7] As Alison Des Forges explains, before the genocide "[m]assacres of Tutsis and other crimes by the Interahamwe went unpunished, as did some attacks by other groups thus fostering a sense that violence for political ends was 'normal'".[8]

On the night of 6 April 1994, President Habyarimana and the Burundian President Cyprien Ntaryamira were returning from regional talks in Tanzania. At around 20.30, as their plane neared Kayibanda airport in Kigali, two missiles fired from near the airport's perimeter struck the aircraft, which crashed into the garden of the presidential palace, killing everyone on board. Within an hour of the crash, government roadblocks were set up across Kigali and troops and *interahamwe* began stopping vehicles and checking identity papers. Shots rang out across the city as killings began at the roadblocks and Presidential Guards and militiamen went house-to-house, killing Tutsi and Hutu accused of collaborating with Tutsi.[9]

---

[5] See, for example, African Rights, 1995, pp. 36–45, *supra* note 2; Jean-Pierre Chrétien, "Un génocide africain: de l'idéologie à la propagande", in Raymond Verdier, Emmanuel Décaux, and Jean-Pierre Chrétien (eds.), *Rwanda: un génocide du XXème siècle*, Harmattan, Paris, 1995, pp. 45–55.

[6] Andrew Wallis, *Silent Accomplice: The Untold Story of France's Role in the Rwandan Genocide*, I.B. Tauris, London, 2007, pp. 51–78.

[7] Des Forges, 1999, p. 4, see *supra* note 2.

[8] *Ibid.*

[9] Dallaire, 2003, ch. 10, see *supra* note 2.

The killing spree spread rapidly beyond Kigali into towns and villages across Rwanda. In the following weeks, government leaders fanned out from the capital to incite the entire Hutu population to murder Tutsi, backed by messages of hate on RTLM. By most estimates, around 250,000 Tutsi were killed in the first two weeks of the genocide.[10]

The killing of Tutsi was far from spontaneous or indiscriminate and not, as the government tried to tell foreign diplomats and the international media both at the time and after the genocide, merely a proportional military response to the RPF invasion.[11] The violence was the result of long-term planning and systematic implementation by the Hutu regime. One source of evidence of the planning behind the government's campaign of violence was the extent to which the orchestrators of the genocide targeted key Tutsi and Hutu moderate political leaders in the immediate aftermath of Habyarimana's death. Their aim was to wipe out any semblance of political opposition before launching wider attacks against Tutsi.[12]

On 21 April, the UN Security Council determined that the rapidly deteriorating situation posed a major threat to its personnel on the ground. It passed a resolution to reduce the number of UNAMIR troops from approximately 2,000 to 270.[13] While the UN debated the nature of its intervention in the genocide, the RPF swept through the countryside, capturing Kigali on 4 July. Two weeks later the RPF gained control of the entire country, in the process halting the genocide. Thousands of predominantly Hutu refugees fled into Zaire, among them many of the main organisers of the genocide.[14]

---

[10] African Rights, 1995, p. 258, see *supra* note 2; Des Forges, 1999, p. 770, see *supra* note 2; Alan J. Kuperman, *The Limits of Humanitarian Intervention: Genocide in Rwanda*, Brookings Institution Press, Washington, DC, 2001, p. 16.

[11] Linda Melvern, *A People Betrayed: The Role of the West in Rwanda's Genocide*, Zed Books, London, 2000, chs. 11–13; Linda Melvern, *A Conspiracy to Murder: The Rwanda Genocide and the International Community*, Verso, New York, 2004, ch. 10.

[12] African Rights, 1995, p. 177, see *supra* note 2.

[13] United Nations Security Council, Adjustment of the Mandate of the UN Assistance Mission for Rwanda Due to the Current Situation in Rwanda and Settlement of the Rwandan Conflict, 21 April 1994, UN doc. S/RES/912.

[14] Gérard Prunier, "Opération Turquoise: A Humanitarian Escape from a Political Dead End", in Howard Adelman and Astri Suhrke (eds.), *The Path of a Genocide: The Rwanda Crisis from Uganda to Zaire*, Transaction Publishers, New Brunswick, 1999, pp. 294–301.

7.3. History and Modalities of *Gacaca*

In the months following the genocide in Rwanda, around 120,000 genocide suspects, mostly Hutu, were rounded up by the new RPF-led government and transported to jails around the country built to hold only 45,000 inmates.[15] Most detainees were never formally charged with any crime and were forced to live in hellish conditions: underfed, drinking dirty water and crammed into tiny rooms where they were often made to sleep in lattice-work formations for lack of space.[16] During the genocide the Rwandan judicial system – which manifested signs of debilitation before 1994 – was nearly destroyed completely, as the infrastructure of the national courts was decimated, and many judges and lawyers were killed or fled the country.[17] With the existing judicial system incapable of dealing with massive numbers of suspects, the government sought new mechanisms to hear genocide cases. As the then Vice President and now President Paul Kagame said in 1998: "Presently, the maintenance of 120,000 prisoners costs US$20 million per year, for which we receive assistance from the international community. This cannot continue in the long-term: we have to find other solutions".[18]

In response to the social, political, economic and legal problems created by the overcrowded prisons, the Rwandan government in 2001 instituted *gacaca* to hasten the prosecution of lower-level genocide suspects, most of whom had been imprisoned for more than six years. In March 2005 *gacaca* entered its most crucial phase, as it expanded nationwide and in some communities began judging and sentencing the first wave of genocide suspects, some of whom, as a result of their conviction at *gacaca*, have now been sentenced to new prison terms. In the later years of *gacaca* identified and prosecuted many new suspects who were not rounded up during the initial incarceration process.[19]

---

[15] International Centre for Prison Studies, "Prison Brief for Rwanda", King's College, ICPS, London, 2002.

[16] Author's Fieldnotes, Butare Central Prison, 4 February 2003.

[17] Amnesty International, "Rwanda: Gacaca: A Question of Justice", AI doc. AFR 47/007/2002, December 2002, pp. 12–13.

[18] Paul Kagame, quoted in Stef Vandeginste, "A Truth and Reconciliation Approach to the Genocide and Crimes against Humanity in Rwanda", Working Paper 1998/1, Centre for the Study of the Great Lakes Region of Africa, University of Antwerp, May 1998, p. 45.

[19] There is considerable debate about exactly how many new genocide suspects *gacaca* has identified. The Rwandan government estimates that up to one million genocide suspects

Following the enactment of the Gacaca Law in January 2001,[20] the Rwandan government stated that *gacaca* was designed to expedite justice

have been prosecuted, after *gacaca* has unearthed hundreds of thousands of new cases since 2002. (Author's Government Interviews, Domitilla Mukantaganzwa, Executive Secretary, National Service of Gacaca Jurisdictions, Kigali, 24 April 2009.) There is little evidence so far to suggest that so many new cases – approximately an increase of 800 per cent to the initial number of genocide suspects – have been identified. Interviews at *gacaca* provincial offices and at the community level suggest that the numbers are likely to be considerably lower than the government claims. National Service of Gacaca Jurisdictions officials in the Northern and Southern provinces reported approximately 300 per cent and 400 per cent increases respectively in the number of genocide suspects identified by *gacaca*. At the community level, Alphonse and Cypriet, two detainees who had confessed to committing crimes during the genocide and whom I interviewed on several occasions in 2003 and again in 2006, 2008 and 2009, claimed that in their local jurisdictions, *gacaca* had led to roughly a 100 per cent increase in the number of genocide suspects identified. In Alphonse's community, around 50 individuals had confessed to genocide crimes while in prison after the 1994 round-up of suspects, and *gacaca* had subsequently identified 65 new suspects; in Cypriet's community, 55 new suspects had been identified, alongside the 40 who had initially confessed. (Author's Detainee Follow-up Interviews, Alphonse, Nyamata, Kigali Ngali, 11 June 2006; Cypriet, Nyamata, Kigali Ngali, 11 June 2006.) Based on these findings, it is more likely that *gacaca* has dealt with around one million *cases* rather than *suspects*, as many suspects are accused of committing multiple crimes and many crimes were committed by groups.

20 Republic of Rwanda, Organic Law 40/2000 of 26/01/2001 Setting Up Gacaca Jurisdictions and Organising Prosecutions for Offences Constituting the Crime of Genocide or Crimes against Humanity Committed Between 1 October 1993 and 31 December 1994, in *Official Gazette of the Republic of Rwanda*, October 2000, Article 13 ('Gacaca Law'). The Gacaca Law has been modified five times, as explored in greater detail below. The five documents that comprise these modifications are: Republic of Rwanda, Loi Organique No. 33/2001 du 22/6/2001 Modifiant et Completant Loi Organique No. 40/2000 du 26 Janvier 2001 Portant Creation des "Juridictions Gacaca" et Organisation des Poursuite des Infractions Constitutives du Crime de Genocide ou de Crimes contre l'Humanité, Commises entre le 1 Octobre 1990 et 31 Decembre 1994, in *Official Gazette of the Republic of* Rwanda, 22 June 2001 ('*Gacaca* Law (Modified 2001)'); Republic of Rwanda, Organic Law No. 16/2004 of 19/6/2004 Establishing the Organisation, Competence and Functioning of Gacaca Courts Charged with Prosecuting and Trying the Perpetrators of the Crime of Genocide and other Crimes against Humanity, Committed between 1 October 1990 and 31 December 1994, in *Official Gazette of the Republic of Rwanda*, 19 June 2004 ('Gacaca Law (Modified 2004)'); Republic of Rwanda, Organic Law No. 28/2006 of 27/06/2006 Modifying and Complementing Organic Law No. 16/2004 of 19/06/2004 Establishing the Organisation, Competence and Functioning of Gacaca Courts Charged with Prosecuting and Trying the Perpetrators of the Crime of Genocide and Other Crimes against Humanity, Committed between 1 October 1990 and 31 December 1994, in *Official Gazette of the Republic of Rwanda*, 27 June 2006 ('Gacaca Law (Modified 2006)'); Republic of Rwanda, Organic Law No. 10/2007 of 01/03/2007 Modifying and Complementing Organic Law No. 16/2004 of 19/6/2004 Establishing the Organisation, Competence and Functioning of Gacaca Courts Charged with Prosecuting and Trying the Perpetrators of the Crime of Gen-

for genocide crimes, while pursuing more subtle social goals such as reconciliation by encouraging direct community participation in genocide prosecutions. *Gacaca* was not intended to replace the national courts in the hearing of genocide cases, but rather to relieve the immense pressure on the national system by addressing the vast numbers of low-level suspects, while leaving more senior accused to the national courts and the UN International Criminal Tribunal for Rwanda ('ICTR').[21]

Two legal documents establish the modalities of *gacaca*: the Organic Law of 1996 and the Gacaca Law of 2001, with the latter modified five times, minimally in June 2001, June 2006 and March 2007, and more substantially in June 2004 and June 2008. The Organic Law is organised to prosecute "the crime of genocide or crimes against humanity" or "offences […] committed in connection with the events surrounding genocide and crimes against humanity".[22] The Organic Law defines "genocide" and "crimes against humanity" in accordance with three international conventions, to which Rwanda is a signatory: the 1948 United Nations Convention on the Prevention and Punishment of the Crime of Genocide, the 1949 Geneva Convention on the Protection of Civilian Persons in Time of War, and the 1968 Convention on the Non-Applicability of Statutory Limitations to War Crimes and Crimes against Humanity.[23] The Organic Law, and subsequently the Gacaca Law of 2001, divides genocide suspects into four categories of crimes committed between 1 October 1990 and 31 December

---

ocide and Other Crimes against Humanity, Committed between 1 October 1990 and 31 December 1994, as Modified and Complemented to Date, in *Official Gazette of the Republic of Rwanda*, 3 January 2007 ('Gacaca Law (Modified 2007)'); and Republic of Rwanda, Organic Law No. 13/2008 of 19/05/2008 Modifying and Complementing Organic Law No. 16/2004 of 19/6/2004 Establishing the Organisation, Competence and Functioning of Gacaca Courts Charged with Prosecuting and Trying the Perpetrators of the Crime of Genocide and Other Crimes against Humanity, Committed between 1 October 1990 and 31 December 1994, as Modified and Complemented to Date, in *Official Gazette of the Republic of Rwanda*, 19 May 2008 ('Gacaca Law (Modified 2008)'). Gacaca Law (Modified 2004) and Gacaca Law (Modified 2008) constitute a more significant rewriting of parts of the original Gacaca Law than do the other modified laws. The 2001, 2006 and 2007 revised document are concerned primarily with minor changes to the wording of several sections of the Gacaca Law, while the 2004 and 2008 versions comprise several important reforms of the *gacaca* process, outlined later in this chapter.

21 See, for example, Charles Murigande, "Report on Urugwiro Talks from May 1998 to March 1999", in *Report on the National Summit of Unity and Reconciliation*, Kigali, NURC, 18–20 October 2000, pp. 30–33.

22 Republic of Rwanda, Organic Law No. 08/96, 30 August 1996, Article 1 ('Organic Law').

23 *Ibid.*

1994. When the Gacaca Law was modified in 2004, a key change was the merging of the old second and third categories[24] to form a synthesised second category, thus reducing the overall number of categories to three, which by the 2008 version of the Gacaca Law were organised as follows:

First category:

a) any person who committed or was an accomplice in the commission of an offence that puts him or her in the category of planners or organisers of the genocide or crimes against humanity;

b) any person who was at a national leadership level and that of the prefecture level: public administration, political parties, army, gendarmerie, religious denominations or in a militia group, and committed crimes of genocide or crimes against humanity or encouraged others to participate in such crimes, together with his or her accomplice;

c) any person who committed or was an accomplice in the commission of an offence that puts him or her among the category of people who incited, supervised and ringleaders of the genocide or crimes against humanity;

d) any person who was at the leadership level at the sub-prefecture and commune: public administration, political parties, army, gendarmerie, communal police, religious denominations or in a militia, who committed any crimes of genocide or other crimes against humanity or encouraged others to commit similar offences, together with his or her accomplice;

e) any person who committed the offence of rape or sexual torture, together with his or her accomplice.

Second Category:

---

[24] In the original categorisation of crimes detailed in the Organic Law and the Gacaca Law of 2001, the second category comprised "persons whose criminal acts or whose acts of criminal participation place them among perpetrators, conspirators or accomplices of intentional homicide or of serious assault against the person causing death", while the third category comprised "persons whose criminal acts or whose acts of criminal participation make them guilty of other serious assaults against the person". (Organic Law, Article 2, see *supra* note 24; Gacaca Law, Article 51, see *supra* note 22) In Gacaca Law (Modified 2004), these two categories are merged to create a new second category, while the old fourth category, which deals with individuals charged with property-related crimes, is now rendered as category 3 (Gacaca Law (Modified 2004), Article 51, see *supra* note 22).

a) a notorious murderer who distinguished himself or herself in
   his or her location or wherever he or she passed due to the
   zeal and cruelty employed, together with his or her accomplice;

b) any person who tortured another even though such torture
   did not result in death, together with his or her accomplice;

c) any person who committed a dehumanising act on a dead
   body, together with his or her accomplice;

d) any person who committed or is an accomplice in the commission of an offence that puts him or her on the list of people who killed or attacked others resulting into death, together with his or her accomplice;

e) any person who injured or attacked another with the intention to kill but such intention was not fulfilled, together with
   his or her accomplice;

f) any person who committed or aided another to commit an
   offence against another without intention to kill, together
   with his or her accomplice.

Third Category:

A person who only committed an offence related to property.
However, when the offender and the victim come to a settlement by themselves, settle the matter before the authorities or
before the witnesses before commencement of this law, the offender shall not be prosecuted.[25]

Until 2008 *gacaca* had jurisdiction only over suspects in the second
and third categories, while the first category cases were referred to the national court system and the ICTR. The 2008 modifications to the Gacaca
Law, however, shifted a range of first category cases to *gacaca*, including
those of suspected orchestrators of the genocide at the sub-prefecture and
commune levels and suspected perpetrators of rape or sexual torture. The
outstanding first category cases concerning national or prefecture-level
planners of the genocide remain solely the jurisdiction of the national courts
and the ICTR.[26] Although no explicit principles existed for the distribution
of suspects between the ICTR and the national courts, an unofficial division

---

[25] Gacaca Law (Modified 2008), Article 9, see *supra* note 22.
[26] *Ibid.*, Articles 5–7.

assumed that the ICTR would hear the cases of suspects considered to be among the most important planners and perpetrators of the genocide.[27]

For those suspects over whom *gacaca* had jurisdiction, the Gacaca Law divided the hearing of their cases, according to category, among the approximately 11,000 jurisdictions at two administrative levels. Each of these levels carried out a different task in the *gacaca* process. The cell was charged with the investigation of crimes committed within the cell during the specified period and with the production of four lists: first, of all those who lived in the cell before 1 October 1990; second, of all those who were killed in the cell during the specified period; third, of the damage to individuals or property inflicted during this time; finally, of suspects and their category of alleged crimes. The cell heard cases only of suspects in the third category. Cases of suspects in the first and second categories were heard at the sector level. The sector also functioned as the jurisdiction for the appeal of all cases heard in gacaca and the point from which certain first category cases were forwarded to the national courts.[28]

A crucial issue for the effective running of *gacaca* was the election of judges. *Gacaca* was unique among post-conflict judicial structures around the world in its mass involvement of the population in the delivery of justice. Over the decade of trials, nearly every Rwandan adult attended *gacaca* at some stage, including hundreds of thousands who provided eyewitness testimony. *Gacaca* judges were required to be Rwandan nationals over the age of 21 years, without any previous criminal convictions or having ever been considered a genocide suspect (except in relation to property crimes), and an honest, trustworthy person, "free from the spirit of sectarianism" but "characterised by a spirit of speech sharing".[29] Judges could not at any time have been an elected official, government or non-governmental organisation employee, trained judge or lawyer, or a member of the police, armed services or clergy. The stated motivation for this exclusion was to ensure

---

[27] The *ad hoc* division of jurisdiction between the ICTR and the national courts has on occasion created major tensions when the two bodies have sought jurisdiction over the same genocide suspects. See, for example, Philip Gourevitch, "Justice in Exile", in *New York Times*, 24 June 1996, A15; and Frédéric Mutagwera, "Détentions et poursuites judiciaires au Rwanda", in Jean-François Dupaquier (ed.), *La Justice internationale face au drame rwandais*, Karthala, Paris, 1996, pp. 17–36.

[28] Gacaca Law (Modified 2008), Articles 5–7, see *supra* note 22.

[29] *Ibid.*, Article 14. The phrase "speech sharing" appears to entail that judges should be capable of encouraging the community to participate in *gacaca* hearings and of facilitating peaceful, productive discussions in the General Assembly.

that *gacaca* was a popular process, run by citizens at the local level and free from actual or perceived political or legal interference.

Both levels of *gacaca* – cell and sector – consisted of a General Assembly, a bench of judges, a president and a co-ordinating committee. At the cell level, the General Assembly constituted every resident of the cell over the age of 18 years. In October 2001, General Assemblies across the country elected 19 judges to form cell-level benches of *inyangamugayo* (in Kinyarwanda, "a person of integrity" or "wise and respected elder") while also nominating five representatives to form the General Assembly at the sector level. The revised Gacaca Law in 2004 reduced the number of judges at both levels of jurisdiction to nine, with five deputies also nominated who could substitute for any of the nine judges if they were absent.[30] In July 2004, the *gacaca* judges who were elected in 2001 decided among themselves which individuals would stay on as either judges or deputies, thus reducing the number of judges nationwide from approximately 250,000 to around 170,000.[31] Surveys into the make-up of benches of *gacaca* judges across Rwanda show that most judges were middle-aged, professional, educated members of the community, with women constituting around 35 per cent of all *inyangamugayo* at the cell level, and judges with higher education usually nominated to the sector level of *gacaca*.[32]

Gacaca judges were empowered to carry out various tasks, including summoning witnesses to testify at hearings, issuing search warrants and imposing punishments on those found guilty. Judges usually sat once a week before a required quorum of 100 members of the General Assembly. In phase one of a *gacaca* jurisdiction, which ideally comprised six weekly meetings (but invariably took much longer), the Assembly gathered to determine a schedule of hearings and to begin compiling the four lists mentioned above. In phase two, which comprised the seventh meeting, the General Assembly gathered to produce a detailed dossier of evidence on each individual accused of a crime and listed during the sixth meeting of phase one. The accused then had the opportunity to respond to the evidence brought against them during phase three of *gacaca*, after which in phase

---

[30] *Ibid.*, Articles 13 and 23.

[31] IRIN News, "Rwanda: Plans to Reform Traditional Courts", 16 June 2004 (http://www.irinnews.org/report/50257/rwanda-plans-to-reform-traditional-courts).

[32] Penal Reform International, "Interim Report on Research on Gacaca Jurisdictions and its Preparations (July–December 2001)", PRI, Kigali, January 2002, p. 32; African Rights, 1995, "Gacaca Justice", p. 6, see *supra* note 2.

four the judges weighed all of the evidence they had heard and passed judgment on defendants.[33] The president of the judges bench chaired all meetings and was responsible for leading an orderly, directed discussion that encouraged truthful testimony and created a space for victims and survivors to describe their personal pain and loss.

A key role of the president in this scenario was to maintain order within the Assembly, especially as the discussion could become emotionally charged and testimonies may diverge. The Ministry of the Interior was tasked with guaranteeing the security of judges, suspects and the community at large during *gacaca* hearings, usually by providing one or two armed security guards for all sessions.[34] The president also had to encourage those who were reluctant to speak – especially women and the young – to testify. In particularly emotional or complex cases where witnesses were unwilling to testify in front of a large gathering, judges (or in cases involving sexual violence, a single judge) could convene *in camera* with a witness to hear evidence. Lawyers were forbidden from assisting either suspects or witnesses at any stage of a hearing as their involvement was seen as a potential threat to the open, non-adversarial approach of *gacaca*. *Gacaca*'s insistence on delivering justice without lawyers constituted one of the primary reasons legal critics and human rights groups have been so hostile toward the institution.

After hearing evidence against a suspect, judges retired *in camera* to consider the individual's guilt, before which judges were expected to recuse themselves from any cases involving friends or family members to the second degree of relation. The president would attempt to reach a consensus among the judges before deciding on the person's guilt. However, in cases where consensus was impossible, a majority decision by the nine judges sufficed. The bench then announced its decision concerning a suspect's guilt to the General Assembly, either at the same meeting or the next, at which point those convicted of crimes were entitled to appeal the bench's decision first to the *gacaca* jurisdiction that initially heard their case or, if

---

[33] In very few *gacaca* jurisdictions do the three phases occur as quickly as originally planned. For example, by June 2003 only 16 of the 73 pilot *gacaca* jurisdictions inaugurated in June 2002 had completed both phases one and two of the *gacaca* process and none had yet begun phase three. Republic of Rwanda, "La situation actuelle des juridictions gacaca", Kigali, Supreme Court of Rwanda, 6th Chamber, 25 June 2003, pp. 1–2.

[34] Republic of Rwanda, "Les parténaires du processus gacaca", Official Rwandan Government website (http://www.inkiko-gacaca.gov.rw/Fr/Partenaires.htm).

they remained dissatisfied with this judgment, to the sector level of *gacaca* and upward.[35]

The Gacaca Law dictated that punishment should be meted out in various ways. Individuals who refused to testify at *gacaca* or were found to have provided false testimony were subject to a prison term of three to six months.[36] The centrepiece of the *gacaca* judicial structure was a pre-determined matrix of sentences that incorporated a system of confession and plea bargaining that is foreign to the European judicial system but finds a place in some jurisdictions in the United States. According to this matrix, suspects could decrease their sentences by at least half if they confessed their crimes. Another important feature of the *gacaca* sentencing mechanism was the combination of prison terms and community service. Most community service was carried out in *travaux d'intérêt général* ('TIG') camps, administered by Rwanda Correctional Services, and involved convicted perpetrators in community work programmes such as road building, clearing ground, making bricks and rebuilding houses for genocide survivors. The sentencing structure, as established by the Gacaca Law, operates as shown in Table 1 in the annex to this chapter.[37]

7.4. Virtues of *Gacaca*'s Abbreviated Criminal Procedure for Genocide Crimes

This chapter turns now to analyse the efficacy and impact of *gacaca*'s use of abbreviated criminal procedure for genocide crimes. This section highlights two principal virtues of this aspect of *gacaca*, namely its capacity to deliver accountability for everyday genocide perpetrators while also reintegrating them into their home communities, and the important forms of post-genocide truth that have emerged through *gacaca*'s emphasis on plea-bargaining and popular participation during hearings.

First, *gacaca* has proven remarkably successful at expediting the post-genocide justice process, delivering accountability for hundreds of thousands of genocide perpetrators. It has also commuted many convicted perpetrators' sentences to overcome the problem of overcrowded prisons and facilitated the reintegration of most detainees into everyday society. By mid-2012, *gacaca* had completed the backlog of genocide cases, including

---

[35] Gacaca Law (Modified 2008), Articles 7, 23 and 24, see *supra* note 22.

[36] Gacaca Law (Modified 2004), Article 29, see *supra* note 22.

[37] *Ibid.*, Articles 72–81; Gacaca Law (Modified 2008), Articles 17–22, see *supra* note 22.

the multitude of new suspects that the population identified since *gacaca* began and the hundreds of first category cases transferred from the national courts to *gacaca* since 2008. Thus, the Rwandan government delivered on its promise of comprehensive prosecutions of those responsible for committing genocide crimes, but without recreating the problem of overcrowded jails that necessitated *gacaca* in the first place. It also completed the genocide caseload in the relatively short period of 10 years at a cost of only USD 40 million.[38] *Gacaca* therefore proved substantially cheaper to run than more conventional justice institutions, especially when compared to the immense costs involved with the running of the ICTR, which cost more than USD 1 billion.[39]

By clearing the backlog of genocide cases, *gacaca* also improved living conditions in Rwandan prisons and saved government resources necessary to sustain such a large prison population. *Gacaca*'s ability to release detainees more rapidly created more living space for the detainees who remain. In October 2008, the International Centre for Prison Studies stated that 59,311 prisoners remained in Rwanda's jails, which had a capacity of 46,700, although this figure has not been updated since 2002 and does not account for the construction of new prisons around Rwanda.[40] These statistics indicate the significant decrease in the overall prison population, which stood at around 120,000 at the beginning of *gacaca*. The problem of overcrowded prisons in Rwanda has therefore generally been overcome.

Second, empirical research shows that *gacaca*'s emphasis on popular participation during hearings – a key feature of its abbreviated procedure – has yielded significant dividends in terms of truth. In particular, much of the Rwandan population argues that *gacaca* has been important for recovering truth in the form of legal facts regarding the genocide and therapeutic truth in terms of allowing individuals to tell and hear personal narratives of the genocide that may allow them to deal emotionally and psychologically with the past. Regarding legal truth, many survivors argue that they partici-

---

[38] Republic of Rwanda, "Ministry of Finance and Economic Planning Budgets, 2002–2009", Ministry of Finance and Economic Planning. It should be noted, however, that this figure does not include *gacaca*-related expenditure by other government bodies such as the National Unity and Reconciliation Commission, the Ministry of Justice and the Rwanda Correctional Services.

[39] Hirondelle News Agency, "Cost of the ICTR to Reach $1 Billion by the End of 2007", 12 May 2006 (http://allafrica.com/stories/200605120745.html).

[40] International Centre for Prison Studies, 2002, see *supra* note 17.

pated readily in legal truth-telling at *gacaca*, for example by giving eyewitness testimony concerning genocide crimes and by helping construct the four lists of evidence discussed above. Patrice, a 62-year-old survivor in Ruhengeri, whose wife, two sons and one daughter were killed during the genocide, said:

> I hope that we [survivors] will be allowed to speak freely at gacaca. I have much to tell about what I saw during the genocide. [...] I saw many crimes with my own eyes and I want to tell what I know at *gacaca*.[41]

Gacaca's compilation of testimony from 11,000 communities today provides a rich, diverse reservoir of historical material regarding genocide crimes.

At the same time, many suspects were very aware that their truth-telling at *gacaca*, particularly as it incorporated public confession and apology, would lead to their exoneration if they were innocent of crimes or allow them to benefit from *gacaca*'s plea-bargaining system if they were guilty. Richard, a suspect in Butare, who argued that he had been unjustly accused of complicity in murder during the genocide, said: "The community will definitely accept what I say at *gacaca*. I will stand up and tell them everything I saw when these killings occurred and they will agree that I am telling the truth".[42] More than half of the approximately 300 individuals interviewed in the general community between 2003 and 2012, who themselves were neither survivors nor suspects but had relatives who were accused of genocide crimes, described the primary function of *gacaca* as the potential for truth-telling to exonerate their loved ones, whose innocence they maintained. All of these individuals said that they would testify or had already testified at *gacaca* to clear their loved ones' names.[43] "*Gacaca* is a source of light that brings the truth", said Agathe, a 46-year-old widow in Nyamata, whose parents and three siblings were accused of genocide crimes and were still in prison. "It will allow us to see who is guilty and who is innocent".[44]

---

[41] Author's Survivor Interviews, Patrice, Ruhengeri (author's translation).

[42] Author's Solidarity Camp Interviews, Butare (no. 15) (author's translation).

[43] Author's Fieldnotes, 2003–2009.

[44] Author's General Population Interviews, Agathe, Kigali Ngali, Nyamata, 19 May 2003 (author's translation).

Many popular sources also argued that truth-telling at *gacaca* served an important therapeutic function. Both suspects and survivors argued that the opportunity to speak openly at *gacaca* about events and emotions concerning the genocide contributed to their personal healing. Many guilty suspects claimed to have gained a sense of release from feelings of shame and dislocation by confessing to, and apologising for, their crimes in front of their victims and the General Assembly at *gacaca*. Many survivors meanwhile claimed to have overcome feelings of loneliness by publicly describing the personal impact of genocide crimes and receiving communal acknowledgement of their pain. As Paul, a survivor whose father, two brothers and one sister were killed during the genocide, said after a gacaca hearing in Ruhengeri:

> *Gacaca* is important for us survivors because it helps us live and work in the community again. […] All the survivors come together and talk about what has happened. We realise that we are in the same situation, that we have all had family who were killed. We understand each other and we realise that we are not alone.[45]

7.5. Challenges of *Gacaca*'s Abbreviated Criminal Procedure for Genocide Crimes

While the previous section highlighted important virtues of *gacaca* in terms of accountability and truth recovery, this section argues that *gacaca*'s use of abbreviated criminal procedure also produced significant problems on these same two fronts. Regarding justice through *gacaca*, many survivors increasingly criticised the lenient sentences handed down to many convicted *génocidaires*. In particular, many survivors perceived community service as insufficient punishment, given the gravity of crimes committed during the genocide. Chantal, a survivor in Bugesera, recognised that many detainees had already spent years in jail and that there were understandable pragmatic reasons for not returning perpetrators to prison *en masse*. She argued, however, that the community service demanded of some perpetrators – "you kill six or seven people and you spend only six or seven months doing TIG" – was inadequate.[46] Many survivors argued that convicted perpetrators have in the main benefited from the government's need to rapidly empty the

---

[45] Author's Gacaca Interviews, Paul, Ruhengeri, Buhoma, 4 May 2003 (author's translation).
[46] Author's Survivor Interviews, Chantal, Kigali Ngali, Bugesera, 9 September 2008.

prisons and thus *gacaca*'s tendency toward lenient sentencing. It appears that some perpetrators and their families share this view. Alphonse, a convicted *génocidaire* in Bugesera, said: "*Gacaca* has been good here because most of the detainees are now back with their families. Some have gone back to jail but most are here now and working on their farms again".[47]

Second, while the degree and types of truth that have emerged through *gacaca* have provided the benefits discussed in the previous section, significant truth-related problems also developed. *Gacaca*'s attempt to deal with the massive backlog of genocide cases involved weekly hearings over 10 years in many communities. For many Rwandans, this meant hearing repeatedly highly emotive testimony concerning genocide crimes, with the result that *gacaca* increased levels of trauma among many of its participants. The retraumatisation of many individuals who are still dealing with the emotional and psychological legacies of the genocide is one of the major costs of *gacaca*'s truth process.

Furthermore, the truth component of *gacaca* itself suffered from many participants' instrumental calculations based on the plea-bargaining scheme. In particular, many genocide suspects had a major incentive to confess falsely to crimes in order to benefit from *gacaca*'s predetermined system of sentencing. A case in Bugesera district of Kigali Ngali province amply illustrates this point. At a *gacaca* hearing by a small banana frond-encircled lake in June 2006, a suspect came from a nearby prison to confess to his genocide crimes. Standing in front of around 200 people in the General Assembly, he admitted to looting some property from a house on the edge of the community, near the main road leading to Nyamata. When the suspect finished speaking, the judges highlighted for the audience's benefit that he had admitted to committing third category crimes involving property and that, if found guilty, he would need to give the same amount of goods or the financial equivalent to the victims of his crimes and perhaps perform some community service. The judges asked if anyone in the General Assembly wished to respond to the suspect's confession. After a lengthy silence, an elderly lady stood at the back of the gathering and asked permission to speak. When this was granted, she launched into a searing tirade: "This man is lying and you judges are not doing your job because you should know that he is lying". The judges were visibly shocked and

---

[47] Author's Detainee Follow-Up Interviews, Alphonse, Kigali Ngali, Bugesera, 9 September 2008 (author's translation).

asked the woman to explain herself. She said that she knew the suspect was lying because the house from which he claimed to have looted property was her house, and the judges should have known this because, six months earlier, they had convicted a different man for these same crimes.

The woman sat down and the judges conferred. After they had deliberated, they asked several questions of others sitting in the General Assembly, then announced that the woman was correct that this case had already been completed at an earlier hearing. After asking several questions of the suspect, they stated that he had clearly provided a false confession. The suspect initially protested but soon admitted that this was true. It emerged that he was in fact innocent of all genocide crimes. After spending many years in prison, however, he had deemed it preferable to fabricate a confession to a low category of genocide crime, which would bring a minimal sentence, rather than spend further years in jail, with no immediate prospect of release. On this basis, the *gacaca* judges found the detainee guilty of perjury and sentenced him to two years in jail. In short, the suspect had gambled on *gacaca*'s plea-bargaining system and lost.[48] Such cases confirm the fears expressed by many genocide survivors that *gacaca*'s use of plea bargaining to extract confessions from suspects and thus expedite the judicial process would lead to a spate of false confessions.

7.6. Conclusion: General Lessons from the *Gacaca* Experience

Rwanda has attempted to deliver justice on a scale unimaginable in most countries, seeking to involve such large swathes of the population in the prosecution of hundreds of thousands of genocide suspects. The use of the community-based *gacaca* jurisdictions to abbreviate the criminal procedure for the prosecution of genocide crimes stemmed from drastic resource constraints, as well as the belief that only face-to-face engagement among suspects, survivors and the general population during hearings could facilitate reconciliation and other important social goals. The experience of *gacaca* shows that it is possible to deliver accountability to rank-and-file perpetrators of mass crimes such as genocide and to do so in a way that involves the population most directly affected by conflict, thus maximising the societal impact of justice. For many Rwandans, that impact has been the rapid reintegration of their loved ones into the community after their trials and/or time spent in prison. In interviews, many Rwandans state that the country

---

[48] Author's Gacaca Observations, Kigali Ngali, Bugesera, 12 June 2006.

will benefit from having delivered accountability and thus sanctioning the crimes of even low-level perpetrators, but without strict punitive measures, including lengthy prison terms. For others, however, *gacaca* has been too lenient in decreasing prison terms and employing community service as punishment for individuals found guilty of crimes as grave as murder. Such disagreements point less to fundamental flaws in the *gacaca* process than to the impossible balancing act required in the post-genocide society – namely, the need for acknowledgement of crimes and for justice alongside the need to reintegrate perpetrators into their towns and villages to help rebuild the social and economic foundations of the country.

7.7. Annex

Table 1: *Gacaca* sentencing scheme.

Judgment Category	Guilty with no confession	Guilty with confession during trial	Guilty with confession before trial	Minors (14 to 18 years old) when offence committed[*]
1	Life imprisonment with special provisions	25–30-year prison term; possibility of commuting half to community service	20–24-year prison term; possibility of commuting half to community service	10–20-year prison term if guilty without confession; 8–9-year prison term following confession during trial or 6.5–7.5-year prison term following confession before trial
2 (a–e) (judged at sector level; appeals to sector level)	10–15-year prison term	6.5–7.5-year prison term; possibility of commuting half to community service and having one-third suspended	6–7-year prison term; possibility of commuting half to community service and having one-third suspended	10–15-year prison term if guilty without confession; otherwise, half of adult sentence; possibility of commuting half to community service and having one-third suspended, except when no confession is made
2 (f) (judged at sector level; appeals to sector level)	5–7-year prison term; possibility of commuting half to community service	3–5-year prison term; possibility of commuting half to community service and having one-third suspended	1–3-year prison term; possibility of commuting half to community service and having one-third suspended	Half of adult sentence; possibility of commuting half to community service
3 (judged at cell level; appeals to sector level)	Reparations for damage caused or equivalent community service			

---

[*] Minors who were less than 14 years old at the time of the offence cannot be prosecuted at *gacaca* but instead are placed in special solidarity camps (Gacaca Law (Modified 2008), Article 20).

8

Key Elements of Possible Abbreviated Criminal Procedures for Core International Crimes

Gilbert Bitti[*]

Abbreviated criminal procedures tend to develop in all legal systems: the constant development of criminality makes it more and more difficult for judges and prosecutors to deal with all cases. What applies for 'common criminality' applies equally for core international crimes where possible cases raise to the thousands. In response to the development of criminality, prosecutors in many countries have created some informal mechanisms by which they have tried to tackle a (big) part of the criminality they are confronted with (and which could be qualified as mid- or low-level criminality). Informal mechanisms mean that prosecutors will not follow a formal judicial process, prosecutors being more and more selective in the cases they choose to follow such a long and arduous process.

This has resulted in a phenomenon which sociologists have qualified as 'dejudiciarisation of criminality', a lot of crimes simply escaping the judicial arena. This has, in turn, created a sense of impunity in society and a high level of frustration for victims of crimes. The use of abbreviated criminal procedures is an interesting solution to 'rejudiciarise' criminality, that is, to make criminality re-enter the arena of judicial proceedings. It is therefore interesting to see how abbreviated criminal procedures could satisfy the victims' rights (section 8.1.) and which could be the elements of such a process (section 8.2.).

8.1. Victims' Rights and Abbreviated Criminal Procedures

The idea of trying to avoid criminality going out of the judicial system is of course linked to the rights of victims, which are:

1) the right to know the truth: one of the main reasons victims resort to judicial mechanisms which are available to them against those who

---

[*]   **Gilbert Bitti**, Senior Legal Adviser, Pre-Trial Division, International Criminal Court. The opinions expressed are solely those of the author.

victimised them is to have a declaration of the truth by the competent body;[1]

2) the right to justice: victims have the right to have those who victimised them prosecuted, tried and convicted, and subjected to a certain punishment;[2]

3) the right to reparation: victims are entitled to reparations for the harm they have suffered including restitution, compensation, rehabilitation, satisfaction and guarantees of non-repetition.[3]

According to paragraph 19 of the Basic Principles and Guidelines for Reparations to Victims, *restitution* should, whenever possible, restore the victim to the original situation before the gross violations of international human rights law or serious violations of international humanitarian law occurred. Restitution includes, as appropriate: restoration of liberty, enjoyment of human rights, identity, family life and citizenship, return to one's place of residence, restoration of employment and return of property.

According to paragraph 20 of the Basic Principles and Guidelines for Reparations to Victims, *compensation* should be provided for any economically assessable damage, as appropriate and proportional to the gravity of

---

[1] International Criminal Court ('ICC'), Situation in the Democratic Republic of Congo, *Prosecutor v. Germain Katanga and Mathieu Ngudjolo Chui*, Pre-Trial Chamber I, Decision on the Set of Procedural Rights Attached to Procedural Status of Victim at the Pre-Trial Stage of the Case, ICC-01/04-01/07-474, 13 May 2008, paras. 31–36 (http://www.legal-tools.org/doc/285b52/); see also, *inter alia*, Inter-American Court of Human Rights ('IACtHR'), *Bámaca Velásquez v. Guatemala*, Judgment, Series C no. 70, 25 November 2000, para. 201 (http://www.legal-tools.org/doc/e1f6bb/); IACtHR, *Barrios Altos v. Peru*, Judgment, Series C no. 75, 14 March 2001, para. 48 (http://www.legal-tools.org/doc/f1439e/).

[2] ICC, Situation in the Democratic Republic of the Congo, Pre-Trial Chamber I, Decision on the Applications for Participation in the Proceedings of VPRS 1, VPRS 2, VPRS 3, VPRS 4, VPRS 5 and VPRS 6, ICC-01/04-101-Corr, 17 January 2006, para. 53 (http://www.legal-tools.org/doc/2fe2fc/); IACtHR, *Villagrán-Morales et al. v. Guatemala*, Judgment, Series C no. 63, 19 November 1999, para. 227 (http://www.legal-tools.org/doc/32ef2e/); see also, Raquel Aldana-Pindell, "An Emerging Universality of Justiciable Victims' Rights in the Criminal Process to Curtail Impunity for State-sponsored Crimes", in *Human Rights Quarterly*, 2004, vol. 26, no. 3, p. 605.

[3] See United Nations General Assembly, Basic Principles and Guidelines on the Right to a Remedy and Reparation for Victims of Gross Violations of International Human Rights Law and Serious Violations of International Humanitarian Law, resolution 60/147, adopted 16 December 2005, UN doc. A/RES/60/147 ('Basic Principles and Guidelines for Reparations to Victims'); see also Rome Statute of the International Criminal Court ('ICC Statute'), Article 75 (http://www.legal-tools.org/doc/7b9af9/).

the violation and the circumstances of each case, resulting from gross violations of international human rights law and serious violations of international humanitarian law, such as: a) physical or mental harm; b) lost opportunities, including employment, education and social benefits; c) material
damages and loss of earnings, including loss of earning potential; d) moral
damage; and e) costs required for legal or expert assistance, medicine and
medical services, and psychological and social services.

According to paragraph 21 of the Basic Principles and Guidelines for
Reparations to Victims, *rehabilitation* should include medical and psychological care as well as legal and social services.

According to paragraph 22 of the Basic Principles and Guidelines for
Reparations to Victims, *satisfaction* should include, where applicable, any
or all of the following: a) effective measures aimed at the cessation of con-
tinuing violations; b) verification of the facts and full and public disclosure
of the truth to the extent that such disclosure does not cause further harm or
threaten the safety and interests of the victim, the victim's relatives, witnesses or persons who have intervened to assist the victim or prevent the
occurrence of further violations; c) the search for the whereabouts of the
disappeared, for the identities of the children abducted, and for the bodies
of those killed, and assistance in the recovery, identification and reburial of
the bodies in accordance with the expressed or presumed wish of the victims, or the cultural practices of the families and communities; d) an official
declaration or a judicial decision restoring the dignity, the reputation and
the rights of the victim and of persons closely connected with the victim; e)
public apology, including acknowledgement of the facts and acceptance of
responsibility; f) judicial and administrative sanctions against persons liable
for the violations; g) commemorations and tributes to the victims; and h)
inclusion of an accurate account of the violations that occurred in international human rights law and international humanitarian law training and in
educational material at all levels.

According to paragraph 23 of the Basic Principles and Guidelines for
Reparations to Victims, *guarantees of non-repetition* should include, where
applicable, any or all of the following measures, which will also contribute
to prevention: a) ensuring effective civilian control of military and security
forces; b) ensuring that all civilian and military proceedings abide by international standards of due process, fairness and impartiality; c) strengthening
the independence of the judiciary; d) protecting persons in the legal, medical and healthcare professions, the media and other related professions, and

human rights defenders; e) providing, on a priority and continued basis, human rights and international humanitarian law education to all sectors of society and training for law enforcement officials as well as military and security forces; f) promoting the observance of codes of conduct and ethical norms, in particular international standards, by public servants, including law enforcement, correctional, media, medical, psychological, social service and military personnel, as well as by economic enterprises; g) promoting mechanisms for preventing and monitoring social conflicts and their resolution; and h) reviewing and reforming laws contributing to or allowing gross violations of international human rights law and serious violations of international humanitarian law.

The victims' rights, especially the victims' right to justice, makes it doubtful that alternatives to justice such as truth and reconciliation commissions, which are not meant to establish the criminal responsibility of the offenders and to punish them for the crimes committed, could be seen as being in conformity with international law.

Abbreviated criminal procedures involve different actors and need to find a balance between those different actors in order to be successful. This may include delicate compromises between the rights of the accused, the necessity to avoid impunity especially for heinous crimes but also the perception of justice by victims.

Such procedures do not necessarily need to follow the US model of plea bargaining, which may be difficult to accept in legal cultures different from the American one. Indeed, plea bargaining entails an agreement between the prosecutor and the defendant whereby the latter renounces to the guarantees of a fair trial and confesses guilt and the former agrees to dismiss charges or make favourable sentence recommendations to the court. Most often, however, prosecutors, in order to avoid the burden of a trial, will renounce the pursuit of the most serious charges,[4] which is in direct violation of the victims' right to know the truth. Plea bargaining has been so criticised that different models have been proposed in Canada[5] and the

---

[4] Robert E. Scott and William J. Stuntz, "Plea Bargaining as a Contract", in *Yale Law Journal*, 1992, vol. 101, p. 1909.

[5] Simon N. Verdun-Jones and Adamira A. Tijerino, "Four Models of Victim Involvement during Plea Negotiations: Bridging the Gap between Legal Reforms and Current Legal Practice", in *Canadian Journal of Criminology and Criminal Justice*, 2004, vol. 46, no. 4, p. 471.

United States[6] in order to associate victims to the process of plea bargaining. However, the process of plea bargaining is still being heavily criticised by victims because it entails three different categories of promises that may be made by the prosecutor:

1) promises relating to the nature of the charges to be laid (charge bargaining);

2) promises relating to the ultimate sentence that may be meted out by the court (sentence bargaining);

3) promises relating to the facts that the prosecutor may bring to the attention of the trial judge (fact bargaining).

This has very serious consequences for the victims of crimes who could be seriously affected by any plea bargaining. Indeed, it may be of extraordinary significance to the victim of a crime whether the charge laid accurately reflects what has really happened rather than a watered-down version of the events that effectively denies the reality of the victims' suffering.

This is even more so with core international crimes which affect entire communities and where the establishment of an accurate historical record and the search for the truth are of crucial importance for the victims.[7] Bargaining on charges and facts may precisely prevent the victims from reaching such goals and should therefore be avoided.

8.2. Key Elements for Abbreviated Criminal Procedures

Taking into consideration that abbreviated criminal procedures presuppose the agreement of the person prosecuted, the incentives (section 8.2.1.) the law is going to offer to the accused to give his or her consent to this kind of

---

[6] In Indiana, for example, a prosecutor must notify the victim of a felony of negotiations with the defendant or the defendant's attorney concerning a recommendation that the prosecutor may make to the court. If an agreement is reached, the prosecutor must show the agreement to the victim, and the victim may give a statement to the court at the sentencing hearing (Indiana Code, 1996, para. 35-35-3-2).

[7] This is a crucial aspect in relation to prosecution of core international crimes whether at the national or international levels; in this respect it is important to underline this comment made during the negotiations of the ICC Statute: "Delegations should bear in mind the additional historical dimension and truth-finding mission of the Court". See Preparatory Committee on the Establishment of an International Criminal Court, Report of the Working Group on Procedural Matters, Addendum, Revised Abbreviated Compilation, 11 December 1997, A/AC.249/1997/WG.4/CRP.11/Add.2 (http://www.legal-tools.org/doc/9c6e14/).

procedure are essential, but so too is the scope of those abbreviated criminal procedures (section 8.2.2.) and their procedural aspects (section 8.2.3.), especially in relation to the specific role of the different actors involved in such process.

8.2.1. Incentives for the Accused

Although it may be difficult in certain legal cultures for prosecutors to accept the very idea of negotiating with the persons prosecuted, the basis for abbreviated criminal procedures is the agreement of the person prosecuted to recognise the facts for which he or she is prosecuted; and it is difficult to imagine people recognising facts if they do not have an incentive to do that.

In order to avoid discrepancies on the different agreements reached depending on the prosecutor and the person involved, it could be suggested that the incentives be determined by law instead of being the result of a negotiation between the accused and the prosecutor. For example, it could be established by law in a uniform way that the maximum penalty for a certain offence be half of what it is in the criminal code for the crime in question in a case of the accused recognising the facts. Concerning the kind of sanction, in cases of offences against property or even in cases of offences against individual liberty of limited duration and not accompanied with offences against personal integrity, it may be an important incentive for the accused to accept abbreviated criminal procedures if alternatives to imprisonment are proposed to the accused, especially if measures to compensate victims are available and agreed to by the accused.[8]

Other incentives may certainly be proposed to the accused. For somebody convicted, his or her criminal record may be a serious problem for his or her future, especially if such a record is accessible to the public. The accused may be willing to confess guilt in order to avoid such problems.

It is, for example, possible to establish two parts in the criminal record: one confidential and one public. If the accused recognises the facts, the penalty would go to the confidential part of the record which would only be accessible to judges in case he or she commits another crime within a certain period of time, but that confidential part of the record would not be

---

[8] Consideration should be given in this respect to the agreed contribution of the accused to the forms of reparation provided for in the Basic Principles and Guidelines for Reparations to Victims, paras. 19 to 23, see *supra* note 3.

accessible to the public. This would make it difficult for the public to trace those who have been convicted for core international crimes. It may be an important advantage for those prosecuted. If, however, the accused does not recognise the facts, the eventual conviction pronounced would go to the public part of the record, accessible to the public, thus making it more difficult for the person convicted to, for example, find a job. Another interesting option would be simply not to have at all the conviction in the criminal record in case the accused recognises the facts.

8.2.2. The Scope of Abbreviated Criminal Procedures for Core International Crimes

The incentives in order for the person prosecuted to accept abbreviated criminal procedures for core international crimes are not the only problem to tackle. One of the essential problems is certainly the scope of those abbreviated criminal procedures. It may not be possible or advisable to have abbreviated criminal procedures for all types of crimes, especially with regard to core international crimes.

Victims may find it absolutely unacceptable to offer any kind of incentive to people prosecuted for crimes against life or personal integrity. It may be easier for victims to accept abbreviated criminal procedures for crimes against property and eventually for those in relation to personal liberty, in cases where the restriction to personal liberty was of limited duration and was not accompanied by other offences against personal integrity. It may, however, be possible to leave some flexibility to judges in relation to the scope of abbreviated criminal procedures for core international crimes, especially if all participants to the proceedings, including victims, accept such proceedings. Such acceptance may in turn depend on the incentives given to the accused but also on procedural aspects of those proceedings.

The determination of the scope of application of abbreviated criminal procedures presupposes a clear overview of the pending cases concerning core international crimes in a particular situation. It should be determined as much as possible in advance to how many cases those procedures could apply, depending on the scope adopted. It is important to emphasise that in the conduct of such abbreviated criminal procedures, it may be more efficient to try to group all similar cases for crimes committed in the same area.

8.2.3. The Procedural Aspects of Abbreviated Criminal Procedures for Core International Crimes

The role and guarantees accorded to the different actors in the proceedings – victims, prosecutors, judges, accused – should be carefully thought through in order to reach the best possible implementation of those procedures with the full agreement of all actors involved.

8.2.3.1. The Victims

Taking into consideration that core international crimes produce mass victimisation, the first issue is to make sure that all victims are properly involved, as the exclusion of some of them may lead to further trauma. Mechanisms should be established to eventually ensure the collective participation of victims[9] and to take into consideration possible disagreements among them.

The first crucial issue is the necessity to inform victims before any kind of decision is made on the process to follow: it will not be acceptable to victims to be presented with an agreement already reached between the prosecutor and the accused. As described above, even in the process of plea bargaining victims are more and more often informed before an agreement is reached between the prosecutor and the accused. Proper information for the victims presupposes, of course, their identification and thus a thorough investigation.

Concerning the involvement of victims, after the proper disclosure of information it could be the case that a veto power is given to the victims who have the procedural standing to block any proposal made by the prosecutor to the accused by bringing the case to an investigating judge through the normal criminal procedure. This is the case in France.[10]

At least victims should be associated with the initiation of those abbreviated criminal procedures. Where they disagree they should be able to present their views to the trial chamber, which will decide whether or not to accept the agreement reached between the prosecutor and the accused and

---

[9] It should be possible to have one common legal representative for an entire community; see in this regard ICC, Rules of Procedure and Evidence, adopted by the Assembly of States Parties, 3–10 September 2002, ICC-ASP/1/3, Rule 90 (http://www.legal-tools.org/doc/8bcf6f/).

[10] See, France, Code of Criminal Procedural, inserted by Law no. 2000-516 of 15 June 2000, Article 85 (http://www.legal-tools.org/doc/32fb10/).

therefore to follow such abbreviated criminal procedures. The law should state that the trial chamber may order that the criminal proceedings will follow their normal course if the victims disagree with abbreviated criminal procedures. The trial chamber should also be in a position to order at least a partial presentation of the evidence if it considers that necessary for the interests of victims or at least an oral presentation of victims' views in relation to the case at stake.

What is important for victims in a criminal trial is the establishment of the truth: there should be no bargain on the facts, which must all be recognised by the accused.

Of course, one crucial aspect for the victims will be the reparations that they may receive. In this respect, what should be proposed to the accused is an agreement which consists of three parts which he or she has to accept in order to benefit from a reduced sentence and other benefits resulting from an abbreviated criminal procedure:

1) the first part of the document to be presented to the accused is actually a description of the facts;

2) the second part is the applicable law (legal qualification of crimes and mode of liability), the corresponding penalty provided by law for those crimes and the penalty proposed;

3) the third part is the measures of reparations for the victims, which should be previously discussed with the identified victims; in case the prosecutor who is to present the agreement to the accused is of the view that the amount of reparations requested by the victims is not reasonable, he or she may leave that third part to be solved by the trial chamber, while informing the accused that he or she will have to respect that part of the decision by the trial chamber otherwise the entire agreement would be null and void.

A problem may arise when the accused accepts the first and the second parts but not the third. This may be solved according to two options: a) informing the accused that he or she has to accept in totality the agreement proposed; or b) give an opportunity to the accused to refuse that part only of the agreement but with the proviso that reparations will be decided by the trial chamber, after having listened to the accused and the victims. If the accused would fail to execute the part of the judgment relating to reparations to the victims, the agreement on the penalty would be declared null and void, something the accused should know in advance.

One has to think also of incentives for victims to accept or at least adhere to this kind of abbreviated criminal procedure: the incentive could be that that the accused accepts the reparations part of the agreement and that reparations have to be enforced immediately. This may allow victims to get reparations more rapidly than after a full regular trial.

8.2.3.2. Judges and Prosecutors

One important point in relation to abbreviated criminal procedures for core international crimes is certainly the division of powers between judges and prosecutors in this kind of proceedings. Prosecutors alone cannot conduct such abbreviated proceedings, as they end with a criminal sanction which could represent years of imprisonment, a sanction which can only be pronounced by a judge, not by a prosecutor.

Prosecutors may only initiate those abbreviated proceedings and present a proposal to the accused. The agreement of the accused shall be given before the prosecutor first, and then reiterated before the judge. The agreement of the accused may only be final after it is reiterated before the judge. The decision to accept or decline the agreement should be in the hands of the judges as there should be a separation between the authorities in charge of prosecution and the authorities in charge of conviction and sentencing.[11]

In instances in which the law only sets the maximum penalty when the accused accepts the proposal made by the prosecutor (for example, half of what can be imposed normally for the crimes committed), but still leaves some discretion to the prosecutor for the actual proposal, in order to avoid discrepancies and inequalities between accused and also to avoid judges refusing the agreements presented to them, it may be interesting to have a precise scale of penalties for each particular type of facts that could be prosecuted, as is the practice in France.[12] This scale would be agreed in advance between the prosecutors and the judges in charge of those proceedings. This also could reduce the length of those abbreviated criminal procedures.

---

[11] See in this regard, the decision issued by the Constitutional Court in France, 2 February 1995 (95–360 DC).

[12] See Philip Milburn, Christian Mouhanna and Vanessa Perrocheau, "Controverses et compromis dans la mise en place de la composition pénale", in *Archives de politique criminelle*, 2005, no. 27, p. 151.

There could be, at the initiative of the judge or at the request of the victims, an intervention by the victims or a limited presentation of some crucial evidence, during a 'short' trial. This may be of importance to the victims and the option should not be either a full trial with all evidence presented or no evidence presented at all; some leeway should be left to the judge in order to organise those proceedings and to allow for some interventions or some presentation of evidence.[13]

The role of the judge should not simply be to witness the consent of the accused and then to pronounce a sanction. In addition to verifying the informed character of the consent given by the accused, the judge has a role in the sanction to be pronounced for which he or she could have some discretion within the limits of the maximum provided by law in case of abbreviated criminal procedures or within the limits of the maximum agreed by the prosecutor and the judges for this type of case. Another important role for the judge would be to decide on the reparations for victims, taking into consideration paragraphs 19 to 23 of the Basic Principles and Guidelines for Reparations to Victims, especially in cases where the accused has not accepted the proposal presented to him or her in this respect or if the victims or some of them disagree with the proposal made to the accused. This part of the proceedings, which should be an integral part of the abbreviated criminal procedure, could also be the occasion to allow the victims to present some observations or to call some evidence on the particular issue of reparations.

8.2.3.3. The Accused

Another crucial aspect in abbreviated criminal procedures for core international crimes are the rights of the accused. The accused should be presented with a proposal which he can accept or refused but which is not open to discussions. As explained above, it is of the utmost importance to avoid any

---

[13] See, in this regard, ICC Statute, Article 65, para. 4, *supra* note 3, which states:

> Where the Trial Chamber is of the opinion that a more complete presentation of the facts of the case is required in the interests of justice, in particular the interests of victims, the Trial Chamber may: (a) Request the Prosecutor to present additional evidence, including the testimony of witnesses; or (b) Order that the trial be continued under the ordinary trial procedures provided in this Statute, in which case it shall consider the admission of guilt as not having been made and may remit the case to another Trial Chamber.

kind of bargain on the facts or on the charges, as these are crucial aspects for victims which could otherwise result in victims objecting the entire proceedings.

The proposal, which is to be presented by the prosecutor, should be accepted by the accused after consultation with his or her defence counsel. The defence counsel must have access to the case file established by the prosecutor. The entire proceedings presuppose a comprehensive investigation on the facts. Abbreviated criminal proceedings could be very effective in reducing the time of the judicial process in general as they avoid most if not all presentations of evidence during trial, and are in addition generally not followed by an appeal. However, they are not meant to reduce the time necessary for a comprehensive investigation which must be done in order to establish the facts and the criminal responsibility for those facts.

This aspect of the process is of utmost importance as any renunciation to the rights of the accused must be explicit. Indeed the European Court of Human Rights ('ECtHR') has made clear that if neither the spirit nor the letter of Article 6, paragraph 1 of the European Convention on Human Rights on the right to a fair trial would prevent an accused from waiving such right, this presupposes that the accused is acting on his own free will and in an unequivocal manner.[14] According to the ECtHR, in order to be effective for the purposes of the Convention, a waiver in relation to the entitlement to the guarantees of a fair trial must also be attended by a minimum of safeguards commensurate with its importance.[15] The person must reasonably foresee the consequences of his waiver.[16] This means that the consent of the accused can only be given after consultation with a defence counsel and after having declared in writing by signing the agreement presented by the prosecutor and orally before the judge that he or she fully understands the consequences of his or her consent to follow an abbreviated criminal procedure.

If the accused agrees to follow an abbreviated criminal procedure, there must be a public hearing before a judge, with the presence of the

---

[14] European Court of Human Rights ('ECtHR'), *Case of Albert and Le Compte v. Belgium*, Plenary of the Court, Judgment, Applications nos. 7299/75 and 7496/76, 10 February 1983, para. 35 (http://www.legal-tools.org/doc/1e16ee/).

[15] ECtHR, *Case of Hermi v. Italy*, Grand Chamber, Judgment, Application no. 18114/02, 18 October 2006, para. 73.

[16] ECtHR, *Case of Anthony Jones v. United Kingdom*, Decision as to the admissibility of Application no. 30900/02, 9 September 2003, p. 8.

prosecutor and the victims. The publicity of the proceedings may be of utmost importance for the victims. This hearing also ensures the solemnity of the judicial process which could otherwise be seen as a simple bargain between the prosecutor and the accused that may not have much to do with a judicial process. It would also be important to have the facts exposed during this public hearing, together with the charges, so that it is clear to the victims and the public that no bargain on the charges or on the facts has been made.

The accused, in the presence of counsel, should reiterate his or her consent in relation to the facts as exposed before the judge, so that the judges may verify if he or she understands the consequences of his or her acceptance to be tried through abbreviated proceedings and that the consent covers all facts.

The last issue in relation to the rights of the accused which has to be considered is the right to appeal the decision of the first instance judge after the consent given by the accused. Such an appeal should not be prohibited but should mainly be limited to procedural issues, especially to make sure that the consent given by the accused was informed, genuine and offered freely. The accused of course shall be informed of this fundamental aspect of his or her agreement: as long as it was informed, genuine and given freely, it is irreversible.

8.3. Conclusion

In conclusion, an abbreviated criminal procedure requires serious follow up in order to have meaning for victims, especially if obligations are imposed on the person convicted in relation to reparations to victims. There must be supervision of the implementation of the agreement and in case of non-compliance there must be a mechanism to go back to the 'original track' for the prosecution of those crimes through normal criminal proceedings. The use of abbreviated procedures for core international crimes may assist in ensuring credibility for the judicial system in the country, especially in the eyes of the victims, as it will demonstrate its ability to provide a judicial answer to the serious crimes committed. This will contribute to strengthening the judicial system and its independence, which could be seen as a guarantee of non-repetition for the victims, in the sense of paragraph 23 of the Basic Principles and Guidelines for Reparations to Victims.

How to Deal with Backlog in Trials of International Crimes: Are Abbreviated Criminal Proceedings the Answer?

Marieke Wierda[*]

9.1. Introduction

Crimes designated for prosecution under international law, such as war crimes, crimes against humanity or genocide, usually involve atrocities of scale, with numerous perpetrators and victims. At the same time, criminal proceedings are generally designed to deal with breaches of law as an exceptional circumstance rather than as a widespread occurrence. In situations where such breaches are frequent, such as during armed conflict, trials in the aftermath can create an enormous burden on the criminal justice system. In addition, it is now well known that such trials are time-consuming and expensive.[1] The time occupied by criminal proceedings dealing with serious crimes can create serious challenges, including exceeding time limits allowed for pre-trial detention; erosion of evidence of older cases; frustra-

---

[*] **Marieke Wierda** is an international expert on transitional justice and international criminal law. A Dutch national born and raised in the Republic of Yemen, Marieke Wierda earned an LL.B. at the University of Edinburgh, Scotland, and an LL.M. at New York University, specialising in international law and human rights. She has been Director of the Criminal Justice Program at the International Center for Transitional Justice, and has worked with the United Nations ('UN'), including as an associate legal officer for the International Criminal Tribunal for the former Yugoslavia ('ICTY') from 1997 to 2000. Prior to this, she volunteered with the Office of the Legal Counsel at the UN in New York, the UN High Commissioner for Refugees in London and Interights in London. She is a member of the New York Bar and has taught international criminal law at the University of Richmond. She is the co-author (with Richard May) of *International Criminal Evidence* (Transnational Publishers, 2002). The views given are those of the author and not the organisations. This article was written in 2009.

[1] For an interesting discussion on this, see Alex Whiting, "In International Criminal Prosecutions, Justice Delayed Can Be Justice Delivered", in *Harvard International Law Journal*, 2009, vol. 50, no. 2, p. 323.

tion of victims; and the closing of the "politically acceptable timeframe" within which to conduct these trials.[2]

Backlog is a particularly serious problem especially in pure civil law systems, where there is no strict equivalent to the common law prosecutorial discretion, and where there is a presumption that if there is evidence of a crime, it ought to be prosecuted (the principle of legality). If files are opened they cannot subsequently just be closed. This has created backlog in diverse situations such as Argentina,[3] Colombia[4] and Bosnia and Herzegovina,[5] all of which are dealing with trials in the aftermath of mass atrocities. Bosnia and Herzegovina in particular still strives to conduct trials of hundreds of perpetrators, dealing with thousands of open case files.

Several ways have been proposed internationally to deal with these problems, including expediting trials (section 9.2.), making adjustments in the prosecutorial strategy to prioritise cases (section 9.3.) and diverting cases to other mechanisms in a comprehensive approach (section 9.4.). The experiences of Colombia, Argentina and Timor-Leste are considered below (section 9.5.). These lessons remain relevant, particularly since it is doubtful to what extent one can truly abbreviate criminal proceedings for serious crimes. "Abbreviated criminal proceedings" is an unfavourable term, as it can be seen as suggesting a summary procedure which risks undermining the rights of the accused, and the right to equal treatment of similar cases.

---

[2]   The concept of "politically acceptable time frame" was used in Sierra Leone.

[3]   Argentina has been retrying cases stemming from the period when the military junta ruled for seven years from 1976 to 1983. During that time, there were thousands of arrests and killings as well as widespread torture. Up to 30,0000 people disappeared. Starting in March 2001, a series of judgments and new laws invalidated the Full Stop and Due Obedience laws which had been instituted after the first round of trials in Argentina, in 1986 and 1987. More than 650 accused have either been charged or are on trial. As of late 2009, over 60 had been sentenced. See ICTJ Briefing Note, "Criminal Prosecutions for Human Rights Violations in Argentina", International Center for Transitional Justice, New York, November 2009 (https://www.ictj.org/sites/default/files/ICTJ-Argentina-Prosecutions-Briefing-2009-English.pdf).

[4]   Colombia is holding trials for demobilised paramilitaries under Law No. 975, Issuing Provisions for the Reincorporation of Members of Illegal Armed Groups Who Effectively Contribute to the Attainment of National Peace, and Other Provisions for Humanitarian Accords Are Issued ('Justice and Peace Law'), 25 July 2005 (http://www.legal-tools.org/doc/ca98de/). This process is further described below.

[5]   See Bogdan Ivanišević, *The War Crimes Chamber in Bosnia and Herzegovina: From Hybrid to Domestic*, International Center for Transitional Justice, New York, 2008.

In any case, certain parameters would need to apply to abbreviated criminal proceedings which may diminish their practicality (section 9.6.).

9.2. Expediting International Criminal Trials

It is important to remember that international criminal proceedings in themselves are a relatively recent phenomenon (except the trials after the Second World War, many of which applied abbreviated procedures akin to military commissions, some of which are considered unfair under current standards). International criminal procedures lack the breadth of procedure found in more developed systems of law. One of the main developments in the area of international criminal law has been a constant evolution of international criminal procedure, including attempts to expedite the trials in a variety of ways. In addition, each new tribunal is building on the experiences of those that have come before it to improve the procedure. Slowly but surely the international justice sector is arriving at the 'prototype' of an international criminal trial that blends civil and common law traditions to arrive at a state of optimum efficiency and fairness.

Expedition of trials, rather than "abbreviated proceedings", has long been emphasised in international criminal proceedings. The Charter of the International Military Tribunal at Nuremberg provided that the "Tribunal would confine trial strictly to an expeditious hearing of the crimes raised by the charges [...] take any strict measures to prevent any action which will cause unreasonable delay".[6] A more recent tribunal, the Special Tribunal for Lebanon ('STL'), has a very similar provision in its Statute, which states that the STL "shall confine the trial, appellate and review proceedings strictly to an expeditions hearing of all the issues raised by the charges [...] it shall take strict measures to prevent any action that may cause unreasonable delay".[7]

As of 8 December 2010, the International Criminal Tribunal for the former Yugoslavia's ('ICTY') Rules of Procedure and Evidence had gone through 45 sets of revisions, a number of which are meant to deal with expediting trials. Many of these revisions were intended to assist trial man-

---

[6] Charter of the International Military Tribunal, Part of the London Agreement of 8 August 1945, Article 18 ('IMT Charter') (https://www.legaltools.org/doc/64ffdd/),

[7] Statute of the Special Tribunal for Lebanon, attached to UN Security Council resolution 1757, 30 May 2007, UN doc. S/RES/1757, Article 21(2), ('STL Statute') (https://www.legaltools.org/doc/da0bbb/).

agement and the expedition of proceedings. First, there has been a notable shift away from the "principle of orality" and towards documentary sources of evidence, especially when dealing with so-called "crime-based evidence" rather than evidence on the guilt or innocence of the particular accused.[8] The most notable development in this regard has been Rule 92*bis*, but there are other examples, such as the use of transcripts from other trials and the filing of written testimony by experts. A second strategy is to hold multiple defendant trials. These may, however, only save time if there is confluence, rather than conflict, in the interests of the accused. Many rules also deal with trial management and regulation intended to identify and narrow the scope of what is in dispute, including advance disclosure to the trial chamber, the conducting of pre-trial conferences, monitoring of witness lists, time limits on witness testimony and so forth. Judicial notice has been useful insofar as it concerns adjudicated facts accepted under stringent conditions.[9] A final area where time is saved is through finding common ground between the parties before trial, either through the use of admissions or through plea agreements.

The quest for efficiency has long formed a battleground between lawyers from common and civil law systems, and is also responsible for a shift towards civil law procedure in international criminal proceedings. In the latest of the international tribunals, the STL, several of these approaches for expediting trials are contained in the Rules of Procedure and Evidence.[10] The STL is the international tribunal with the narrowest mandate to date: it exists to bring to justice those "responsible for the attack of 14 February 2005 that resulted in the death of former Lebanese Prime Minister Rafiq Hariri and in the death or injury of other persons" as well as connected cas-

---

[8] ICTY, Rules of Procedure and Evidence, 8 December 2010, IT/32/Rev.45 ('ICTY Rules') (http://www.legal-tools.org/doc/02712f/). See Marieke Wierda, "International Criminal Evidence: New Directions", in *The Law and Practice of International Courts and Tribunals*, 2003, vol. 2, no. 3, pp. 369–72.

[9] ICTY, *Prosecutor v. Hadžihasanović and Kubara*, Trial Chamber, Décision finale relative au constat judiciaire de faits admis dans d'autres affaires, IT-01-47-T, 20 April 2004 (http://www.legal-tools.org/doc/ae3cbb/).

[10] STL, Rules of Procedure and Evidence, 10 June 2009, STL/BD/2009/01/Rev.1 ('STL Rules') (http://www.legal-tools.org/doc/3773bf/). See Matthew Gillet and Matthias Schuster, "The Special Tribunal for Lebanon Swiftly Adopts its Rules of Procedure and Evidence", in *Journal of International Criminal Justice*, 2009, vol. 7, no. 5, pp. 855–909; International Center for Transitional Justice, *Handbook on the Special Tribunal for Lebanon*, International Center for Transitional Justice, New York, 2008.

es.[11] The STL Statute and its Rules of Procedure and Evidence represent an attempt to curb some of the time-consuming tendencies of adversarial trials by giving the judge increased powers to control the proceedings as a "truth-seeker". The pre-trial judge has an expanded role in that he serves separately from any of the chambers, sits alone, reviews and confirms indictments, deals with disclosure issues and can take steps to preserve evidence. He compiles a file and gives it to the trial chamber. He may also issue other orders for the conduct of the investigation and preparation of a fair and expeditious trial, ensuring that the proceedings are not unduly delayed.[12] It is also anticipated that the judges will question the witnesses first.[13] The establishment of the STL was preceded by a full-scale and lengthy investigation, with mechanisms to share its evidence with the tribunal.[14]

However, overall the international experience shows some of the limitations in expediting trials. The problem is not always that the procedure is complicated, but that the factual patterns for the trial are very complicated and that it takes time to present and understand the cases.

9.3. Impact of Prosecutorial Strategy

The challenge of dealing with large numbers of perpetrators and victims makes it essential to devise a targeted prosecutorial strategy. This is particularly true within national systems, where there are many competing priorities, such as dealing with current crimes. The implementation of a targeted prosecution strategy can be achieved through means such as mapping the universe of cases, to form rational hypotheses for investigation and to assist in case selection.[15] The strategy needs clear communication and outreach, which seek to explain to victims and affected communities the choices that have been made.[16] The strategy can be reflected not only in case selection but also in narrowing the charges against a particular accused. For instance, in Sierra Leone it was practice to bring more limited charges against the

---

[11] STL Statute, Article 1, see *supra* note 7.

[12] *Ibid.*, Article 18. See also STL Rules, Rules 88–97, *supra* note 10.

[13] STL Statute, Article 20(3), see *supra* note 7.

[14] *Ibid.*, Article 19.

[15] The Bosnian National War Crimes Strategy, adopted December 2008, is an example of an elaborate strategy, which has been studied elsewhere, including in Colombia.

[16] Office of the United Nations High Commissioner for Human Rights ('OHCHR') *Rule-of-Law Tools for Post-Conflict States: Prosecution Initiatives*, United Nations, New York and Geneva, 2006, p. 5 (http://www.legal-tools.org/doc/1cce75/).

accused than had been the case at the ICTY. The indictment against Radovan Karadžić was amended to drastically reduce the number of municipalities of Bosnia and Herzegovina, in an attempt to expedite the trial and to ensure its completion. In civil law systems, it may be more complicated to implement a strategy due to limitations on prosecutorial discretion, but investigations can still focus on patterns of crimes rather than individual incidents, and cases can still be collapsed through different theories of responsibility, or indeed prioritised.

In international criminal tribunals it is increasingly accepted that trials should focus on "those bearing the greatest responsibility". This concept has eliminated the issue of backlog in many of the international systems, including the ICTY,[17] the Special Court for Sierra Leone and the International Criminal Court. The irony in this is that national systems are often expected to do more than international systems, but with fewer resources. But in any scenario, massive crimes will still leave an "impunity gap" which will need to be dealt with in other ways.

9.4. A Comprehensive Approach to Justice Issues

The existence of an impunity gap points to the need for other measures to deal with perpetrators and victims of mass atrocities. Transitional justice seeks to address legacies of human rights abuses through multiple mechanisms, including criminal justice, truth commissions, reparations or institutional reform. These measures should not be viewed as alternatives, but should be combined into a comprehensive approach which ought to apply in the aftermath of conflict or other circumstances in which abuses were rife. Many countries are now applying such a comprehensive approach to the aftermath of massive atrocities, including recently Peru, Sierra Leone and Timor-Leste. The UN Secretary-General, in his Report on Transitional Justice and the Rule of Law in Conflict and Post-conflict Societies in 2004, also endorsed a comprehensive approach:

> The international community must see transitional justice in a
> way that extends well beyond courts and tribunals. The chal-
> lenges of post-conflict environments necessitate an approach
> that balances a variety of goals, including the pursuit of ac-

---

[17] The ICTY started out by prosecuting low-level perpetrators when it was difficult to get anybody into custody, but after United Nations Security Council resolution 1534, 26 March 2004, UN doc. S/RES/1534 (2004) (http://www.legal-tools.org/doc/e331ed/), it changed course to focus on high-level perpetrators while referring less important cases back to national jurisdictions through ICTY Rules, Rule 11*bis*, see *supra* note 8.

countability, truth and reparation, the preservation of peace and the building of democracy and the rule of law. A comprehensive strategy should also pay special attention to abuses committed against groups most affected by conflict, such as minorities, the elderly, children, women, prisoners, displaced persons and refugees, and establish particular measures for their protection and redress in judicial and reconciliation processes.[18]

A comprehensive approach is also reflected in the UN Updated Set for the Protection and Promotion of Human Rights through Action to Combat Impunity.[19] But it is not just UN Policy. Comprehensive approaches to these questions are found in various other important policy documents such as the Agreement on Accountability and Reconciliation signed by the Government of Uganda and the Lord's Resistance Army on 29 June 2007;[20] the Report of the African Union High-Level Panel on Darfur, presented to the African Unions's Peace and Security Council on 29 October 2009;[21] and the Action Plan on Peace, Justice and Reconciliation, approved by the Government of Afghanistan in December 2006.[22]

Part of the premise of transitional justice is that it will be impossible to try all the perpetrators of massive atrocities, or for that matter to deal with all the victims. As mentioned, countries that have attempted to prosecute large numbers of perpetrators (such as Rwanda) show the pitfalls of

---

[18] United Nations Security Council, Report of the Secretary-General, The Rule of Law and Transitional Justice in Conflict and Post-conflict Societies, 23 August 2004, UN doc. S/2004/616, para. 25.

[19] United Nations Economic and Security Council, Commission on Human Rights, Updated Set of Principles for the Protection and Promotion of Human Rights through Action to Combat Impunity, 8 February 2005, E/CN.4/2005/102/Add.1, principle 1: "Impunity arises from a failure by States to meet their obligations to investigate violations; to take appropriate measures in respect of the perpetrators, particularly in the area of justice, by ensuring that those suspected of criminal responsibility are prosecuted, tried and duly punished; to provide victims with effective remedies and to ensure that they receive reparation for the injuries suffered; to ensure the inalienable right to know the truth about violations; and to take other necessary steps to prevent a recurrence of violations".

[20] "Agreement on Accountability and Reconciliation between the Government of Uganda and the Lord's Resistance Army/Movement", Juba, Sudan, 29 June 2007.

[21] Report of the African Union High-Level Panel, "Darfur: The Quest for Peace, Justice and Reconciliation", presented to the African Unions's Peace and Security Council, 29 October 2009, AU doc. PSC/AHG/2(CCVII).

[22] Afghanistan, "Action Plan of the Government of the Islamic Republic of Afghanistan on Peace, Justice and Reconciliation", December 2006.

that approach. Attempts to try large numbers can lead to new human rights violations as accused await trial. But it is not just the impossibility of holding many criminal trials that causes societies to explore a comprehensive approach involving other mechanisms. It is also the recognition that different mechanisms are needed to satisfy the different justice demands in a society. The crimes to which these mechanisms respond are complex in nature: hence the response must also be appropriately complex.

International experience over the last decade indicates that victim expectations differ both between and within societies. The clamour for criminal justice may be strong in Bosnia and Herzegovina but varies according to the context. The International Center for Transitional Justice ('ICTJ') participated in surveys among affected populations in contexts as diverse as Afghanistan and Uganda. In Afghanistan, the call for criminal justice was very strong, with more than 90 per cent of those surveyed demanding it.[23] In Uganda, views were more divided. In a survey called "Forgotten Voices", which was conducted by Berkeley–Tulane and ICTJ in 2005, a majority of respondents (66 per cent) said they favoured "hard options" in dealing with Lord's Resistance Army leaders, including trials, punishment or imprisonment. Only 22 per cent preferred options such as forgiveness, reconciliation and reintegration.[24] The survey was repeated in 2007 in a report entitled "When the War Ends", at the height of the Juba peace process.[25] At that time, 54 per cent preferred soft options and 41 per cent preferred hard options: the views had reversed. This also demonstrates that the views of victims change over time.

There is some danger in linking the expectation of the fulfilment of victims' rights to truth or reparations directly to the ability of the criminal justice system to deliver. This can erode the credibility of the system as

---

[23] See Afghan Independent Human Rights Commission, *A Call for Justice: A National Consultation on Past Human Rights Violations in Afghanistan*, Afghan Independent Human Rights Commission, Kabul, 2005.

[24] Phuong Pham, Patrick Vinck, Marieke Wierda, Eric Stover and Adrian di Giovanni, "Forgotten Voices: A Population-Based Survey of Attitudes about Peace and Justice in Northern Uganda", International Center for Transitional Justice and Human Rights Center, University of California, Berkeley, July 2005.

[25] Phuong Pham, Patrick Vinck, Eric Stover, Andrew Moss, Marieke Wierda and Richard Bailey, "When the War Ends: A Population-Based Survey on Attitudes about Peace, Justice and Social Reconstruction in Northern Uganda", International Center for Transitional Justice, Human Rights Center, University of California, Berkeley, and Payson Center for International Development, December 2007.

victims wait for these various demands to be delivered. The case study of Colombia, given below, demonstrates this to some extent. There is also a danger in overstating the case for criminal justice or romanticising legal solutions. For instance, Geoffrey Robertson said in Sierra Leone when deciding a dispute with the Truth and Reconciliation Commission: "Criminal courts offer the most effective remedy: a trial, followed by punishment for those who are found guilty".[26] This may be overstating the case.

An historical record of the conflict requires more than criminal investigation. Historical truth must be compiled in a variety of ways. For instance, truth commissions can give a valuable perspective of the context in which the crimes occurred. They also give more leeway for victims to tell their stories without having to confine themselves to the contours of a criminal proceeding. In fact, capturing the "subjective" experience of victims of particular violations can provide an important complement to the more objective and forensic exercise of finding someone guilty beyond reasonable doubt in a court of law. After all, the outcome of any litigation depends on a variety of factors that can serve to prevent a conviction, as shown in the case of *Slobodan Milošević*.

A truth commission can constitute an investigation that can help to pave the way for trials. It can compile evidence against individuals. The link between truth commissions and amnesties is often misunderstood. In recent years, the South African formula of individualised amnesty for truth has not been followed by other commissions, many of which leave the door open to prosecutions.[27] In fact, in places such as Chile and Argentina the information gathered by each respective truth commission fed directly into criminal investigations.[28] In Sierra Leone, a Truth and Reconciliation

---

[26] Special Court for Sierra Leone ('SCSL'), *Prosecutor v. Moinina Fofana, Allieu Kondewa and Sam Hinga Norman*, Trial Chamber, Decision on Request by the Truth and Reconciliation Commission of Sierra Leone to Conduct a Public Hearing with Samuel Hinga Norman, SCSL-2004-14, 30 October 2003 ('Fofana case') (http://www.legal-tools.org/doc/df2bb5/).

[27] In fact, in South Africa most applicants for amnesty were denied it and many prominent apartheid-era figures, including senior politicians and military leaders, never applied. Post-apartheid prosecutions are still being pursued today.

[28] In Argentina, the report of the Comisión Nacional sobre la Desaparición de Personas ('CONADEP', National Commission on Disappeared Persons), *Nunca Más* [Never Again], 1984, was used in the trials of nine former members of the military junta held in 1985. The vast majority of witnesses appearing in the trial were taken from the CONADEP case files. ICTJ Briefing Note, 2009, see *supra* note 3.

Commission and Special Court functioned simultaneously for a number of years, in relative harmony.[29] Reparations provide an essential guarantee that acknowledgement of responsibility either through truth-seeking or trials is not just about empty words, but that society is willing to take measures to restore the dignity of victims in concrete ways. A comprehensive approach is essential to dealing with the impunity gap.

9.5. International Experiences with Criminal Trials

Aside from a comprehensive approach, international experience also indicates that on occasion streamlined criminal processes have been pursued to deal with large numbers of cases. The key that has allowed for streamlining is to entice co-operation from the accused, not through an amnesty as was the case in South Africa, but through suspended or reduced sentences. But this has not been done everywhere: for instance, in Argentina the emphasis remains on trials.

9.5.1. Argentina

In Argentina, the "second round" of trials has also given rise to backlog. At the time of the Sarajevo conference in October 2009, there were around 670 cases from Argentina's Dirty War still being prosecuted, including military personnel, but also civilians, including priests, judges and former ministers.[30] The prosecutorial strategy followed the conclusions of the Trial of the Juntas conducted in 1985 and resulting in the convictions of the leaders of the junta, including two former presidents, Jorge Rafael Videla and Roberto Eduardo Viola. But there was resistance to adopting any special rules to deal with the proceedings precisely because a lot of legitimacy is garnered from using the ordinary justice system. As eloquently articulated by the renowned Argentinian scholar, Carlos Santiago Nino, in *Radical Evil on Trial*:

> When trials take place before impartial courts, with ample opportunity for the accused to be heard, thorough consideration of defenses, and adherence to the procedures governing evi-

---

[29] The one dispute between the institutions concerned the question whether those accused before the Special Court for Sierra Leone could still give public testimony to the Truth and Reconciliation Commission. This was not allowed by the Special Court; see SCSL, Fofana case, *supra* note 26.

[30] ICTJ Briefing Note, 2009, see *supra* note 3.

dence and the imposition of punishment, the benefits of the rule of law are showcased. In a trial setting, the value of the rule of law is further highlighted when the meticulous procedures of the court are juxtaposed – as prosecutors repeatedly did in Argentina – with the lawless conduct of the defendants.[31]

Special procedures in Argentina were associated with the military junta, which widely used summary proceedings and unfair trials against its opponents. At the same time, the general prosecutor set a target of achieving the highest number of "significant trials" in the shortest period of time possible. "Significant trials" are interpreted as those that involve a high number of crimes committed by one person, or ones that involve multiple accused and victims. Prosecutors sought to group cases together as far as possible. A Coordination Unit assisted in linking connected cases that may arise from as many as 13 federal districts, and further such mechanisms have been put in place to try to streamline the caseload.[32] Nonetheless, the pace of trials dealing with events of many years ago has put some political pressure on the system. Argentina therefore remains a powerful historical and current example of successfully implementing justice through the full criminal trial at the domestic level.

9.5.2. Colombia's Justice and Peace Law

Colombia has suffered a longstanding conflict between left-wing guerrilla fighters of Fuerzas Armadas Revolucionarias de Colombia ('FARC', Revolutionary Armed Forces of Colombia) and Ejército de Liberación Nacional ('ELN', National Liberation Army) and the state's armed forces and right-wing paramilitary groups. President Álvaro Uribe came to power in 2002 on an election promise to return security and sovereignty to Colombia. He introduced legislation known as the Justice and Peace Law (Law No. 975).[33] The law provided for reduced sentences for ex-paramilitaries, the Autodefensas Unidas de Colombia ('AUC', United Self-Defence Forces of

---

[31] Carlos Santiago Nino, *Radical Evil on Trial*, Yale University Press, New Haven, 1996, p. 146.

[32] ICTJ Briefing Note, 2009, see *supra* note 3.

[33] Colombia, Law No. 975, Issuing Provisions for the Reincorporation of Members of Illegal Armed Groups Who Effectively Contribute to the Attainment of National Peace, and Other Provisions for Humanitarian Accords Are Issued, 25 July 2005 ('Justice and Peace Law'), (http://www.legal-tools.org/doc/ca98de/).

Colombia, in exchange of a full, complete and genuine disclosure of crimes given by way of deposition (the "*version libre*"). A previous version of the law suggested a range of penalties that formed alternatives to incarceration, including temporal disqualification for public duty, prohibition on carrying weapons, prohibition on living in or visiting certain places where the crimes were committed or where the victims reside, and restricted geographic movement, for instance to agricultural estates.

The original intention of the government was to offer demobilised paramilitary combatants alternative, non-custodial sentences within the context of a specialised criminal justice procedure. The initial law adopted by Congress in 2005 reflected this intention and was heavily criticised by victims' groups, human rights organisations and the Office of the United Nations High Commissioner for Human Rights ('OHCHR'). The Constitutional Court ruled on 18 May 2006 that some of the law's main provisions were incompatible with both constitutional and international law. But the Constitutional Court in general terms approved the law as an instrument for achieving peace as a fundamental right, holding that it introduced a new balance between benefits for former combatants and victims' rights to truth, justice and reparations. The court ruling improved the law regarding reparations to victims, and stated that all benefits of the law are forfeited if ex-paramilitaries do not confess the whole truth as part of the *version libre*.[34] Regarding the provision for reduced sentences, the Constitutional Court held that prison terms should be no fewer than five years and no more than eight. This, it found, does not disproportionately compromise the rights of victims under the Constitution.

The Constitutional Court ruling was generally welcomed by international and local civil society. The law was received as an opportunity to combine criminal justice with truth-seeking, and to bring to light the atrocities in which paramilitaries had been involved.

The reduced sentences created an incentive for paramilitaries to co-operate with the Justice and Peace Law, as they would ordinarily be liable for high sentences for the crimes they had committed. Other motivations included subjecting to the law to escape extraditions to the United States or

---

[34] Other conditions are co-operation with judicial authorities in the demobilisation process and the making of comprehensive reparation to victims, including release of persons, forfeiting of illegally obtained assets, public apologies and promises of non-repetition, and collaboration in locating remains of disappeared persons.

even investigation by the International Criminal Court ('ICC'). (Colombia is currently under preliminary examination at the ICC but the prosecutor has not yet opened an investigation as she is assessing the admissibility of the case due to the presence of national proceedings. And even though a tacit pact was reached that prevented extraditions, the Colombian government has extradited more than 25 paramilitaries since the demobilisation, including a number of commanders.)

However, even though the Justice and Peace Law in Colombia provided for a streamlined procedure, it has not been expeditious. Its implementation took place in a highly politicised and polarised environment, and has given rise to serious concerns. The Justice and Peace Law gave rise to a flood of cases, not all of which have to do with the commission of serious crimes. Selection of those eligible for the process was made by the government rather than by judicial authorities. Prioritisation of cases should have been addressed but backlog remained a serious issue.

By mid-2009, only five depositions had reached the charging stage, and only one case had gone through trial and sentencing, but only on partial charges for four crimes, and that sentence was annulled on appeal.[35] Partial charges, which have been allowed by the courts, threaten to undermine the system as they do not require full disclosures of the crimes. Disclosures have brought to light particular crimes but did not serve to expose criminal structures. Furthermore, the extraditions to the United States contributed to a lack of legal certainty and diminishing incentives for others to co-operate. Some of the paramilitaries confessed having links to senior politicians, and over 80 members of Colombia's Congress are currently under criminal investigation by the Supreme Court for links to paramilitary groups. (This is the Congress that passed the Justice and Peace Law, thus casting further doubts on the law's legitimacy.) The focus remains on perpetrators, as victims' versions of the events were not considered in the proceedings. Moreover, victims have not realised their right to reparations under the law, which is linked to obtaining convictions. Around 120,000 victims filed claims under the Justice and Peace Law. The capacity of the Justice and Peace Unit to conduct complex investigations remains limited, with the disclosures remaining the main source of information that is according to

---

[35] See Cecile Aptel, "Domestic Justice Systems and the Impact of the Rome Statute", Discussion Paper at the Consultative Conference on International Criminal Justice, New York, 9–11 September 2009.

the version presented by the accused. All in all, the system seemed to be failing.

On paper, the Colombian approach seemed to be an important model and one that has been studied in a variety of other contexts. But in practice, the operations of the Justice and Peace Law have demonstrated many pitfalls which would need careful study before any decisions are made to replicate it elsewhere.

9.5.3. Timor-Leste

In the aftermath of the violence following the popular consultation on the status of Timor-Leste, prosecutors of the Serious Crimes Unit established by a UN regulation faced a difficult task of up to 1,400 murders to investigate. With time, a prosecutorial strategy was drawn up that focused on crimes against humanity rather than just cases of murder.

However, apart from conducting cases, the Serious Crimes Unit also had an arrangement with the Commission for Reception, Truth and Reconciliation ('Commission'). This Commission included a novel approach known as a community reconciliation procedure. Through it, people accused of crimes not resulting in death or injury, such as theft, minor assault, arson, the killing of livestock or destruction of crops, could take part in a community reconciliation procedure, which was loosely modelled on the traditional justice system of *adat*.[36] The procedure was designed to have local religious and cultural resonance. At the end of a community reconciliation procedure, which would often involve a public ceremony, a person could be sentenced to community service as a way to contribute to reparations for the harms he had perpetrated. This arrangement was judicially ratified. One of the stated goals of the Commission was to reintegrate former offenders, many of which had fled to West Timor in the aftermath of the violence.

In order to take part in a community reconciliation procedure, a candidate was required to submit a statement disclosing his involvement in crimes, which was forwarded to the Serious Crimes Unit. The latter re-

---

[36] Caitlin Reiger and Marieke Wierda, *The Serious Crimes Process in East Timor: In Retrospect*, International Center for Transitional Justice, New York, 2006, p. 34. This was stipulated in United National Transitional Administration in East Timor ('UNTAET'), Regulation No. 2001/10, 13 July 2001, UNTAET/REG/2001/10, Schedule 1 (http://www.legal-tools.org/doc/afd3d9/).

served the right to prosecute if the crimes fell within its subject-matter jurisdiction. It is interesting to note that, technically speaking, these crimes could have qualified as war crimes or even crimes against humanity, so that the dividing line was not clear. It was clarified further (although not completely) in a subsequent directive which stated that "in principle, serious criminal offences, in particular, murder, torture and rape" would not be dealt with by a community reconciliation procedure.[37] In practice, the Serious Crimes Unit was not able to investigate or prosecute the majority of perpetrators, and up to 800 murders were not investigated at all. This allowed the community reconciliation procedures to fill some the "impunity gap" left by formal prosecutions.

Over 1,400 persons participated in the community reconciliation procedures but there were some drawbacks. Within the Commission, the community reconciliation procedures consumed considerable resources. In addition, people who volunteered to participate in the community reconciliation procedures felt disillusioned when the Serious Crimes Unit failed to prosecute some of the main perpetrators of the violence.

In the context of Uganda, there have been similar debates on the integration of formal and informal justice systems after the conclusion of the Juba Agreement on Accountability and Reconciliation and the establishment of a War Crimes Division (later renamed the International Crimes Division) of its High Court in July 2008.[38] In northern Uganda, traditional ceremonies are still used to reintegrate former rebels. These ceremonies are a part of Acholi traditions, and encompass a wide array of measures, ranging from the simple cleansing ceremonies to the more elaborate ceremony of the *mato oput*. This refers to the "bitter root". It involves an extended negotiation between the clans of the perpetrator and the victim in order to come to a common version of events, followed by an agreed compensation and a reconciliation ceremony which culminates in the mutual drinking of the crushed bitter root. The *mato oput* is much publicised and debated both locally and internationally. While a full-scale integration of these justice systems is not currently being considered, there is significant support for the idea that traditional justice ceremonies would be used for the vast num-

---

[37] UNTAET Directive on Serious Crimes No. 2002/9 of 18 May 2002.

[38] A delegation of the Ugandan War Crimes Division visited the Bosnian War Crimes Chamber in September 2009 to study their practices.

ber of rebels returning from the conflict, whereas criminal justice will be reserved for a few.

9.6. Conclusion: Parameters for Abbreviated Criminal Proceedings

Based on this cumulative experience, it is possible to conclude that a range of measures must be taken to deal with the problem of backlog in international criminal proceedings. This still leaves open the question of abbreviated criminal proceedings and whether these may be appropriate. It may be possible to consider these, but within certain parameters which may make them difficult in practice.

First, trials should form part of a comprehensive approach and should not be expected to deal with all, or even the vast majority, of perpetrators. Second, any criminal trials must respect international standards of fairness as provided for in international human rights law. This includes the right of equality before the law; the right to a public trial; the right of the accused to examine witnesses against him or her; equality of arms; the right to representation; the right to silence and the presumption of innocence. All of these have implications for abbreviated criminal proceedings. Third, sufficient resources should be devoted to investigations. These form the backbone of any criminal justice approach and a necessary complement to the offer of any incentives to perpetrators for co-operation.

Fourth, abbreviated criminal proceedings may be possible where the accused agrees to co-operate. This may involve either the use of admissions or guilty pleas, depending on what the particular legal system in question permits. But in order for this to be feasible, there must be an incentive, such as the possibility of pleading guilty to lesser charges,[39] avoiding public trial,[40] or suspending or reducing sentences. In this regard, in international criminal law the philosophy of punishment is rather underdeveloped and still centres largely on the gravity of the crime, which is linked to retribution or deterrence. Punishment is very culturally variable: for instance, in Uganda it was argued that sending rebel leaders to ICC detention in The

---

[39] Biljana Plavšić pleaded guilty to crimes against humanity before the ICTY to avoid a genocide charge.

[40] For instance, while former President Alberto Fujimori stood trial for crimes such as the Barrios Altos massacre in Peru, he pleaded guilty to corruption charges to avoid public trial.

Hague was a reward, not a punishment. More creativity in this area would be welcome but it remains controversial.[41]

Lastly, public trust is vital to any such strategy. It is worth bearing in mind the general negative reactions by Bosnian victims' groups to the dropping of indictments of lower offenders, plea agreements and the early release of convicted persons at the ICTY.[42] If victims feel that justice has not been rendered or if they feel excluded from the process, this will damage the legitimacy of abbreviated criminal proceedings. However, if communications towards victims are open, honest and clear about both the possibilities and indeed the limitations, it is possible that they will understand and support them.

---

[41] This was a debate during the Ugandan peace talks held at Juba in 2006–2008. Some argued in favour of reduced sentences being promised to the rebels who disarmed, much like in Colombia. But others opposed this approach, pointing to the gravity of the crimes. See for instance Human Rights Watch, "The June 29 Agreement on Accountability and Reconciliation and the Need for Adequate Penalties for the Most Serious Crimes", Briefing Paper, July 2007. Human Rights Watch insisted that the penalties available should be comparable to those of the ICTY.

[42] Refik Hodžić, "Living the Legacy of Mass Atrocities: Victims Perspectives on War Crimes Trials", in *Journal of International Criminal Justice*, 2010, vol. 8, no. 1, p. 9.

10

The Role of Abbreviated of Criminal Proceedings

Hanne Sophie Greve[*]

10.1. Introduction

Abbreviated criminal procedures represent a specific form of legal action. The purpose of this chapter is to examine whether there exist reasons for such action; that is, to see if there are considerations that call for or justify the usage of abbreviated criminal procedure. Are there one or more objective reasons that support this course of action regardless of whether it is realised? Reasons may be matters of fact or value, but values are always relevant. The objective is thus neither to examine *de lege lata* existing abbreviated criminal procedures – that is, positive law – nor to offer a *de lege ferenda* exploration aimed at developing a specific model of abbreviated criminal procedure for core international crimes or the ideal legislation in this respect. In this chapter there are only a few limited comments on abbreviated criminal procedures as such – primarily to highlight that abbreviated criminal procedures are not an anomaly in modern criminal justice systems, and that abbreviated criminal procedures may well be so provided for in the legislation as to meet with all the human rights requirements concerning a fair trial.

In this chapter the approach is more philosophical. Why should society have abbreviated criminal procedures for core international crimes? Or rather, what is the role – the purpose, reason, rationale, motivation – for abbreviated criminal procedures in cases concerning genocide, crimes

---

[*] **Hanne Sophie Greve** is Vice President of the Gulating High Court, Norway, and a member of the International Commission against the Death Penalty. She has previously served, *inter alia*, as an Expert in the UN Commission of Experts for the Former Yugoslavia established pursuant to UN Security Council resolution 780 (1992) (1993–94); and Judge at the European Court of Human Rights (1998–2004). In the United Nations she has, moreover, held office as a UNHCR assistant protection officer (1979–1981, duty station Bangkok) and as a mediator for the UN Transitional Authority in Cambodia (1992–beginning of 1993, duty station Phnom Penh). She has had several consultancies in and lectured extensively on international law (human rights, refugee law and criminal justice).

against humanity and grave breaches of the 1949 Geneva Conventions? As will be explained, there are normative reasons – considerations having ethical force – that call for and justify that the commission of core international crimes should be followed by justice and criminal procedures. Facts – here the crimes – become obligating reasons in conjunction with these normative considerations; they give rise to an obligation to seek justice. Practical needs assign an important role to abbreviated criminal procedures in this context.

10.2. The Rule of Law

Whether it is agreed to measure length in metres or inches or anything else, or not to take advantage of any measurement, there exist dimensions in the physical world. Similarly, where there are human beings there is behaviour and there will be codes of conduct in existence – that is, *de facto* or *de jure* regulations of human behaviour. The main question in every society is who is entitled or allowed – sometimes by default – to decide and establish the codes of conduct, be these *de facto* or *de jure* laws.

10.2.1. A Primordial Stage of Everyone against Everyone

The initial human habitats are sometimes referred to as representing a natural stage of total calm, idyllic and peaceful, where all is well and plentiful and everyone acts towards everyone else in a spirit of loving kindness and where consensus rules supreme. Whether or not this was ever so is of limited significance, as conflicts of interests soon became one of the characteristics within any group of people living together not to speak of the relationship between different groups of people. For this reason it is quite common to speak of a primordial fight of everyone against everyone else.

Being vulnerable is a key element of the human condition. From total helplessness in infancy to the frail phase of old age, the human being is more or less in constant need of protection and support. Even the strongest and most capable of men – mentally and physically – at the zenith of their lives have no chance to protect their interests when outnumbered.

Human nature nevertheless is social. It is only in the interaction with fellow human beings that the individual can develop his or her full potential as a human being and become fully humane.

Another constituent of the human condition is the ability to reason – to learn, invent and create. Human beings soon realised that protection

and respect for the interests of others were useful and valuable, good for barter even. Living together in groups, human beings experienced that they could better provide for their needs – protection not in the least. To live and let live proved a more prosperous approach than to let everything be ultimately settled as a matter of physical strength – individual or in terms of numbers. Reciprocity opened up for development.

Ubi non est lex, ibi non est transgressio quoad mundum (where there is not law, there is not transgression, as far as this world is concerned). Every interest not respected had literally to be fought for, and defended by force. In order to terminate the primordial fight of everyone against everyone else, and transgressions to communities and societies, human beings entered initially *de facto* into some kind of social contracts. People joined together in communities structured internally by some guiding principles to avoid eternal fights among them, and to be better prepared to stand up against other groups.

10.2.2. The Rule of Law as Crucial to a Prosperous State

The rule of law is the largely formal or procedural properties of a well-organised legal system. These properties include in particular: 1) a prohibition of arbitrary power, meaning that no one – not even the lawgiver – is beyond or above the law; 2) laws that are general, prospective, clear and consistent and thus capable of guiding conduct; and 3) tribunals that are accessible and structured to hear and determine legal claims in a fair manner. The law is made by the state and the state by the law: *civitas fundaretur legibus*.[1] A well-ordered community is based on a legal system.

Following the Second World War, some basic principles were singled out as human rights – belonging to every human being in the very capacity of being human. Or, as ascertained in the Preamble to the Universal Declaration of Human Rights ('UDHR'):

> Whereas recognition of the inherent dignity and of the equal and inalienable rights of all members of the human family is the foundation of freedom, justice and peace in the world,
>
> Whereas disregard and contempt for human rights have resulted in barbarous acts which have outraged the conscience of mankind, and the advent of a world in which human beings

---

[1] *Digesta Iustiniani liber primus*, 2.2.4., available as *The Digest of Justinian*, trans. by Charles Henry Monro, vol. 1, Cambridge University Press, Cambridge, 1904.

> shall enjoy freedom of speech and belief and freedom from fear and want has been proclaimed as the highest aspiration of the common people,
>
> Whereas it is essential, if man is not to be compelled to have recourse, as a last resort, to rebellion against tyranny and oppression, that human rights should be protected by the rule of law[.][2]

Democracy is central to the European understanding of both the rule of law and human rights. The three are not only intertwined, but in part also properties of one another. Understood in this context, it may be said that the rule of law is the rationale for building a community in contradistinction to a mere power base. Even the latter will sooner or later wither from within lest the people consider their interests to be provided for by the power structure.

The idea of every society being based on a kind of social contact may emerge as a theoretical construction, but can nevertheless help improve our understanding of communities – small and large. Social cohesion is a complex and multifaceted balance of give and take.

The Council of Europe has proposed defining the social cohesion of a modern society as follows:

> Society's ability to secure the long-term well-being of all its members, including equitable access to available resources, respect for human dignity with due regard for diversity, personal and collective autonomy and responsible participation.[3]

The definition encompasses key aspects of a political strategy for a modern society to enable the strengthening of the bonds between individuals and between them and the community to which they belong. *Salus populi (est) suprema lex* (the welfare of the people is the supreme law). The pursuit of the rule of law is legitimate in every state; it needs no further legitimacy.

---

[2] United Nations General Assembly, Universal Declaration of Human Rights, 10 December 1948, Preamble ('UDHR') (http://www.legal-tools.org/doc/de5d83/).

[3] Council of Europe, *Concerted Development of Social Cohesion Indicators: Methodological Guide*, Council of Europe, Strasbourg, 2005, p. 23.

10.2.3. Arbitrariness versus Equity

A basic feature of the rule of law is that it replaces arbitrary power. No human being shall be beyond or above the law, not even the lawgiver. It provides room for flexibility if a ruler may himself give the laws and let it be at his behest whether the laws are to be followed or not, when and by whom. Laws in this latter context, however, are only one other means of arbitrary power – a sham that can never establish the rule of law. The way Adolf Hitler stood not only above and beyond the law in the Third Reich, but *de facto* also became the law, is but one extreme example.

It is thus no surprise that the revolutionary aspect of human rights is that they belong to *every member of the human family in the mere capacity of being human*. That groups of people had also recognised advanced rights for members of their own group was nothing new – that had been the situation for thousands of years. The United Nations understood the recognition of the inherent dignity and of the equal and inalienable rights of all members of the human family as the *sine qua non* of freedom, justice and peace in the world, as affirmed in the Preamble to the UDHR.

The recognition of the inherent dignity and of the equal and inalienable rights of every human being does not only imply that it is conceded that:

> Article 1
>
> All human beings are born free and equal in dignity and rights. They are endowed with reason and conscience and should act towards one another in a spirit of brotherhood.
>
> Article 2
>
> Everyone is entitled to all the rights and freedoms set forth in this Declaration, without distinction of any kind, such as race, colour, sex, language, religion, political or other opinion, national or social origin, property, birth or other status. [...]

All rights belong to everyone, and no one shall be subjected to out- lawed abuses – all in line with these basic principles:

> Article 6
>
> Everyone has the right to recognition everywhere as a person before the law.
>
> Article 7
>
> All are equal before the law and are entitled without any discrimination to equal protection of the law. All are entitled to

> equal protection against any discrimination in violation of this
> Declaration and against any incitement to such discrimina-
> tion.[4]

Fairness – a core constituent of the rule of law – demands that equal situations are handled in an equal or similar manner regardless of the persons involved. The law is the main equaliser – no one shall be above or beyond the law, and everyone shall have equal standing in front of the law. Equity in contradistinction to arbitrariness was recognised in ancient times as a property of a well-organised legal system. Some of the old Roman law adages illustrate this:

- *Prima pars aequitatis aequalitas* (the first part of equity is equality);
- *ratio in jure aequitas integra* (reason in law is perfect equality);
- *leges suum ligent latorem* (laws should bind their own author); and
- *stare decisis et non quieta movere* (to adhere to precedents and not to leave established principles).

It must be appreciated that *talis non est eadem, nam nullum simile est idem* (such is not the same, for nothing similar is the same thing.) This, however, does not imply that it is impossible to have some agreed and more objective standards for identifying similarity and differences between cases – to avoid arbitrariness and discrimination.

10.2.4. The Rule of Law as an Effective Normative System

Laws are setting standards. Legal provisions thus are normative and intended to regularise the behaviour of people. Ideally, the law in itself suffices to have people behave according to its prescribed standards. When and where this is not the case, the power of the state can be utilised to right the wrongs and establish the rule – the supremacy – of law. Or, as expressed in the Roman law maxim *juris effectus in executione consistit* (the effect of law – or of a right – consists in the execution). Unless the state is willing and able to uphold the law there is no legal system that is really beneficial to the population.

This is of particular significance in the field of criminal law. It is best that the laws as such prevent crime. But every state in times of peace and stability will have to regularly administer criminal justice. Large

---

[4] UDHR, see *supra* note 2.

numbers of crimes may be due to, but are not limited to, wars and armed conflicts, globalisation and mobility, and financial problems. In addition to chastening people to observe and honour their obligations not to commit crimes, the state itself has crucial obligations – obligations to react to crimes and positive obligations to prevent the most significant crimes that concern life and limb and personal integrity in particular. This is a situation in which *lex deficere non potest in justitia exhibenda* (the law cannot fail in dispensing justice). Article 8 of the UDHR states:

> Everyone has the right to an effective remedy by the competent national tribunals for acts violating the fundamental rights granted him by the constitution or by law.[5]

For the state to have an effective criminal law system – normative as it regularises peoples' behaviour – crimes as such are deterred, and when that is not achieved in individual cases the breaches of the criminal law must have consequences. Establishing guilt and responsibility is probably more important than punishing the perpetrators. The latter should, however, in any event be deprived of all unlawful gains and divested of any and all authority and power abused (having proved for the time being that they have not been qualified to handle the trusted authority), for example in the police or security apparatus or in offices of a political nature. It is for the state to balance rights and to somehow restore a broken balance.

In this context, it may prove useful to keep in mind that *omnis exceptio est ipsa quoque regula* (every exception is itself also a rule.) Moreover, even when a political situation in a country is not transitional, all criminal justice is in essence transitional, aimed at recreating a more or less workable moral universe.

10.3. Immediate Implications of Core International Crimes

In this chapter 'core international crimes' signify genocide, crimes against humanity and war crimes such as specified in international legal documents like Articles 6, 7 and 8 of the Rome Statute of the International Criminal Court ('ICC Statute').[6] Core international crimes are the most heinous of crimes – crimes that every state is required to punish and has a positive

---

[5] UDHR, Article 8, see *supra* note 2.

[6] Rome Statute of the International Criminal Court ('ICC Statute'), Articles 6–8 (http://www.legal-tools.org/doc/7b9af9/).

obligation to protect its population against. Core international crimes are moreover crimes *erga omnes*, an affront against humankind as such that may be punished under any jurisdiction regardless of the identity of the perpetrators and the victims and of on what territory the crimes were committed. It follows from the description of the elements of these crimes that they, generally speaking, have much more destructive consequences both for the individual victims and for the collective or the state as such than other less serious crimes, due to their effects and the scale on which they have been committed.

10.3.1. Victimisation on an Individual Level

Core international crimes will more often than not affect the life and limb of the victims. People may, for example, have been killed, tortured and enslaved or any combination of all three of these absolute violations of human dignity. On an individual level this may not be entirely different from what happens in exceptionally gruesome criminal cases that do not as such amount to core international crimes.

Core international crimes do have an added dimension of scale, as they are part of an overall plan, widespread and systematic, or disproportionate and beyond military necessity. In consequence, the number of victims is likely to be high. As every human being has his or her own dignity and worth, and is unique so that no one can ever be replaced (not even cloned to be the same person – already time, place and circumstances will be different), the significance of large-scale crimes lies in the number of individual victims involved. That is, however, not the only distinction between ordinary crimes and core international crimes. One other dissimilarity is that numbers of victims affected by core international crimes are likely to be interrelated in a manner that, generally speaking, will victimise them in more than one respect directly or indirectly or both.

'Ethnic cleansing' may illustrate this. Ethnic cleansing may be organised so that the adult male population is separated from the women, children and elderly to be killed or physically and mentally broken; and the rest of the group is deported. Every woman is not only a victim of deportation with its ensuing deprivation, but she is likely furthermore to have lost more than one male family member – whether a father, husband, brother, brother-in-law or son. The sheer number of losses – more or less

matched by the losses of the other women in the victimised community – will make it far more difficult for her both as a direct and an indirect crime victim to deal with her sorrow and pain, than for a victim of but one serious crime. And her way back to a normal life will become much more thorny if at all accessible for her. Both the family network and the social fabric, that under regular circumstances are crucial for crime victims to stumble back to a normal life, are torn if they function at all. People in old age, children and male survivors face similar difficulties. This is exactly what the masterminds behind the ethnic cleansing intend.

In short, the victimisation on an individual level of core international crimes is likely to represent a complexity making restorative justice equally complicated, and more often than not unachievable.

10.3.2. Victimisation on a Collective or State Level

Core international crimes, being part of an overall plan, widespread and systematic, or disproportionate and beyond military necessity, do not only imply high numbers of individual victims. These crimes are characteristically committed in armed conflicts or other large-scale social upheavals in which commonly not just one core international crime is committed, but multiple such crimes.

In consequence, core international crimes are likely to considerably weaken the social fabric in the community at large if not also at the state level. This is, in particular, the situation when in addition to everything else the core international crimes committed have, in the first place, been aimed at victimising the leadership in the affected community – be it politicians, judges and law enforcement officers, teachers and community leaders of every kind. Even if not intended as genocide, it may have the same extreme consequences for the survival of an ethnic group as such.

In short, there is likely to be victimisation on a collective or state level of core international crimes. This is a kind of victimisation that may impair large parts of the state apparatus – its political, administrative and judicial structures and the state's income-generating ability. For this reason, in the aftermath of core international crimes, the state's ability to assist the individual victims of crimes in overcoming the consequences of these crimes may have been considerably weakened. Large-scale destruction of public and community property will increase these difficulties further.

10.3.3. A Shift of Balance in Favour of Perpetrators

Genocide and crimes against humanity – such as, but not limited to, ethnic cleansing – are intended to shift the social balance in favour of the perpetrators and their group(s) by them taking over the possessions and positions of the victims. That is, these crimes are aimed at creating a void in terms of people in which the culprits and their followers are prepared to more or less replace the victims' group. The *Boden* policy of the Third Reich when it attacked the Soviet Union in 1941 illustrates this. According to this "land only" policy, the Nazis wanted to conquer land only, and to annihilate or evict the people who lived in the area when it was captured. This was in contradistinction to the *Blut und Boden* policy in countries inhabited by so-called Aryan people such as Norway and the Netherlands, where the populations were allowed to remain in place as long as the Nazis thought they could subjugate them to the new Nazi order.

Furthermore, every serious crime affecting life or limb and personal integrity of another person will by necessity enfeeble the victim, and it thereby reduces that person's ability to protect self, kith and kind, possessions and other interests. The crime as such will have a disabling effect on a person's potential for defending his or her own interests. This problem is considerably augmented when more than one family member or member of a specific group is victimised. Any sizeable destruction of a person's property is also likely to have a debilitating effect on a person's possibilities to take care of his or her interests.

In sum, sometimes core international crimes deprive victims of their means in a manner that makes the same means available to the perpetrators for the latter to harvest the future advantage of these means. In other situations, the pre-crime equilibrium or relative strength characterising the relationship between the victims and the perpetrators are shifted simply by the victims being deprived of some of their relative strength regardless of this 'strength' not being made available to the perpetrators. As always, extensive knowledge of the weaknesses of others – which many perpetrators are likely to have after the commission of core international crimes – gives them some kind of an upper hand if the victims and perpetrators are to make up a future society with room for both of them. It is no surprise in this context that former members of security services become organised criminals in countries that have experienced profound changes.

On the other hand, the victims have a right to know the truth about the wounds inflicted on them and a right to know the identity of the perpetrators at the different levels. Lest this information is provided to the victims, the lack of information not only represents an added cruelty to the wounds inflicted by the crimes as such but the victims are also likely to be even more susceptible to future abuses as well.

The legacy of brutality that is likely to follow the commission of core international crimes will, moreover, frequently have a close to crippling effect on the sufferers. For example, the Khmer Rouge legacy long made it unnecessary for the group's former assassins to demonstrate any residual power to have things their way. When aborted, a reign of terror does not instantaneously lose its grip on victims. *Injuria propria non cadet beneficium facientis* (no benefit shall accrue to a person from his own wrongdoing). No one, that is, should be left to benefit from or take ad- vantage from his or her own wrong – and in particular not of core international crimes. This basic principle cannot be effective least any shifted balance in favour of perpetrators is attended to and counteracted.

The no benefit prescription must pertain both to immediate benefits and to benefits in a longer perspective. In no event should crime be permitted to function as *de facto* steps in a career.

10.3.4. A Shattered Moral Universe

The word 'moral' has its roots in the Latin language, *mos*, *moris*, meaning custom or usage. When certain positive standards – value wise – are generally adopted in a community, these standards form the moral code of that society. Being incorporated into the state's criminal law provisions, commonly reinforces the basics from the moral code. *Thou shalt not kill*, and so forth.

In a rule of law situation the state is willing and able to enforce its laws which thus function as normative standards regulating the way the individuals on the state territory behave towards one another. If the laws of the land are not enforced, the regulative force of the legal provisions decreases. As the main provisions of criminal codes in well-functioning legal systems are in harmony with the community's basic understanding of what is right and good and what is wrong and sub-standard, crimes as such also have implications for the community's perception of values and morals. This is particularly so if the most serious of crimes do not have

consequences for the perpetrators – not to say if such crimes prove beneficial to the perpetrators even after the perpetrators' identities have
become known to the state.

Core international crimes do somehow shatter the moral universe in
a community. When the basic standards of what is right and what is
wrong are ignored and broken, the very moral structure in society will be
questioned. That is, standards not abided by give way to new standards,
like water always finds its level. If a state is unwilling or unable to set the
rules that are to govern the relationship between people living on its territory, the standards are set by those who impose their standards by the use
of force, whether criminals from within the state or from outside. There is
no inhabited territory without rules that the inhabitants or a majority of
them will have to accept. The rule of the strongest is a negation of the rule
of law, but it still implies regulations that the inhabitants will have to
follow.

Thus the committing of core international crimes leaves behind a
somehow shattered moral universe, and begs the question of who is entitled to set the standards and the rules according to which life in the affected community will go on also after these crimes have ceased. The rule of
law, human rights and democracy all presuppose that it is the society as
such that adopts and enacts the laws of the land. These laws will have to
meet with the minimum requirements as provided for in human rights,
and will have to promote some kind of a fair social balance as well.

Neither in the life of an individual nor in the life of a community is
it possible just to draw a line and start afresh. Every moment and every
event in history is an end, a beginning and a continuation.

If a state lets something as gruesome as core international crimes be
bypassed in terms of criminal procedures, by regarding these crimes as
belonging to an era that is over, can it then start with criminal procedures
only in relation to far less significant *new* crimes and still be considered a
non-arbitrary society – a society based on the rule of law? And what about
a person serving a prison sentence for an ordinary crime for which he or
she was convicted prior to the commission by others of core international
crimes? Should that person be released before serving his or her sentence
in order not to receive unequal treatment as compared to the treatment of
the perpetrators of the core international crimes? Justice and fairness as
significant concepts contributing to social order are easily undermined if a

community thinks that it can bypass an interregnum of a shattered moral universe by pretending that it never existed. This is even more so when there is also an ensuing shift of balance in favour of perpetrators.

Unumquodque dissolvitur eodem ligamine quo ligature (the same binding by which it is bound together dissolves everything): As much as a functioning state is based on a legal order, the lack of legal order makes a state disintegrate. Telling the truth and distinguishing right from wrong are significant to reconstructing the moral universe.

10.4. Options Following the Commission of Core International Crimes

For a start, as Aristotle said, "Not even God can undo what has been done". Crimes committed are facts – they may be ignored, but cannot be deleted. Following the commission of core international crimes there is, ideally speaking, a need to rectify:

- the shift of balance in the pre-crime equilibrium or relative strength characterising the relationship between the victims and the perpetrators. This is so even if the balance can only be restored to a degree: 1) the dead cannot be summoned back to life; 2) more often than not, health cannot be fully restored; 3) financial deprivation may not be fully compensated for – the perpetrators and society may lack the necessary resources for that. In any event, such repair may take time and there may be at least a *de facto* need for a conviction prior to establishing a legal obligation to compensate. Furthermore, years lost in an individual's life cannot be regained or caught up with;
- the tremendous harm caused to individuals and society at large; and
- the shattered moral universe.

Furthermore, the victims have a right to know the truth about the wounds inflicted on them – and thus a right to know the identity of the perpetrators at the different levels.

Particular challenges occur in respect of those perpetrators that remain within a society following armed conflicts between different groups within one state – fratricide – and in respect of perpetrators who as traitors collaborated with an invading or occupying alien power and took part in core international crimes committed by the aliens. Situations where alien perpetrators can be expelled after an armed conflict are in numerous

respects far easier to manage than when victims and perpetrators are compelled to continue to live side by side in the same state.

10.4.1. Impunity

With impunity the perpetrator is left at large without any punishment for the crimes that have been committed. Guilt is not properly established. The perpetrator may therefore shield him or herself behind such basic general provisions as found in the UDHR:

> Article 11
>
> Everyone charged with a penal offence has the right to be presumed innocent until proved guilty according to law in a public trial at which he has had all the guarantees necessary for his defence.
>
> Article 12
>
> No one shall be subjected to arbitrary interference with his privacy, family, home or correspondence, nor to attacks upon his honour and reputation. Everyone has the right to the protection of the law against such interference or attacks.[7]

Within the human rights regime, the lack of criminal justice may imply that people having committed the most heinous and serious crimes remain in positions of power. This is so also when they have enhanced their actual power base and potential for being able to abuse that base by financial gains and a reputation for brutality in combination with a special insight into the weaknesses of other people and society at large – all of which are acquired by the crimes. If this is allowed, serious crimes are not only not deterred but heinous crimes are *de facto* even encouraged, which is far worse.

Again, this is by no means new insight. The two following adages of Roman law illustrate this: *impunitas semper ad deteriora invitat* (impunity invites [an offender] to ever worse offences); and, *veniae facilitas incentivum est delinquendi* (the ease of winning pardon is an incentive to committing crime). When massive crimes go unpunished it is *de facto* the criminals who are permitted to keep the upper hand – that is, an oppressive upper hand. Neither a tyrannical regime (too much state power) nor

---

[7] UDHR, Articles 11 and 12, see *supra* note 2.

criminals (too little state power) should ever be permitted to set the standards and the rules by which the state is governed.

It was in recognition of the strong need to liberate humankind of the scourge of impunity for core international crimes that first the United Nations *ad hoc* tribunals for the former Yugoslavia and Rwanda and later the ICC were established. However, the international tribunals cannot do all that is needed to remove the plague of impunity. International justice will only be available to some – ideally the principal instigators of core inter- national crimes; the remaining perpetrators will have to be prosecuted within national criminal justice systems. Although it is unrealistic to prosecute every culprit, the point in case is that no major criminal should be able to evade justice. It is particularly difficult to accept impunity as there is no alternative to criminal justice within the context of the rule of law. Impunity is a negation of the rule of law.

Cui bono? The phrase is regularly used to imply that one or more persons guilty of committing a crime may be found among those who have something to gain from it. Here in the context of impunity the following question may be asked: Who will benefit from impunity? The answer in most cases is that impunity will be to the benefit of the perpetrators and to the disadvantage of the victims.

Furthermore, people engaged in organised crimes – and in particular transnational and international organised crimes – look for situations conducive to their destructive activities. Impunity for core international crimes establishes a thriving environment for organised crimes as the perpetrators possess insider knowledge that can be abused for their lucrative benefit. As if this were not enough in terms of potential damage attached to impunity as its shadow, impunity following the commission of core international crimes may endanger vital interests in a state already subjected to these crimes. Perpetrators benefiting from impunity have 'dark secrets' in their portfolio. They are already of ill repute and, as such, marginalised in their own way. The threshold for them trading in their insider knowledge of the state's vulnerability may be quite low. Perpetrators with impunity may become 'useful idiots' who betray the interests of their fellow citizens to the benefit of outside powers. *Realpolitik* in international affairs – that is, arbitrariness ruling supreme – is not yet a phenomenon of the past.

With regard to persons serving prison terms for convictions predating the commission of core international crimes by others in the same

country, impunity for these later and most gruesome crimes is everything but equal treatment under the law.

10.4.2. Truth and Reconciliation

After core international crimes have been committed, there is no doubt a pressing need for the truth concerning these crimes to be established and recorded as accurately as possible. The right to know is part of the human rights of the individual victims. It is also basic for the proper development of a society that it has the fullest possible understanding of its own history and in particular the exact nature of the severe difficulties encountered in the past. The committing of core international crimes is part of the latter. There is, moreover, a strong need for society as such to reconcile itself with its past, meaning to be familiar with it, to acknowledge it and to move on into the future on this basis. Ideally, former perpetrators and victims of their crimes are also reconciled on a personal level. The latter, however, cannot be demanded by society or even expected of it. The relationship between perpetrator and direct and indirect victims of his or her crimes is far too complex for that. Many a time a victim has a basic right to be spared the open-ended experiment of just meeting the perpetrator once again.

Frequently, reconciliation is spoken of as a synonym for forgiveness. That is, reconciliation is but another demand on the victims. First, no one can forgive anyone anything done to others and not to oneself. Any surviving fellow human being cannot forgive a murderer for the crime committed against the dead person. The bereaved individual can at most forgive the murderer for the loss, pain and sorrow caused to that person. Second, reconciliation is not an alternative to justice, is not a managed process and it cannot be unconditional. Whether unconditional forgiveness has a religious role to play is an entirely different issue. Resentment of a crime and all its dire consequences is instrumental to the upkeep of what has been referred to already as the moral universe.

Some countries in South America, Africa and elsewhere have established truth and reconciliation commissions, with or without international involvement and support, in order to secure the need for the truth to be told and for reconciliation – the latter often used as a generalised and rather indeterminate concept. Most probably, each such commission has had some beneficial results.

It is appreciated that it may be easier to confess one's sins in full if no sanctions follow; and, conversely, the perpetrator is commended for having thereby contributed his or her part to reconciliation in its vague and wide sense. There is, on the other hand, reason to believe that the instigators of crimes and the people most responsible for crimes will demonstrate dexterous footwork in order to minimise their involvement and to try to the fullest extent to leave the main responsibility with the actual henchmen. If these efforts are successful, this action also represents injustice. It also distorts any understanding of what happened. In short, it is a means of having people accused of serious crimes speak, but no guarantee that they will speak the truth. As core international crimes represent acts that outrage the human conscience and violate the elementary dictates of humanity, it is still vital to an individual human being's understanding of self to recognise responsibility for such crimes. The perpetrators will face infamy in fact (*infamia facti* despite there being no *infamia juris*) the more crimes they take responsibility for. Some perpetrators may – as another extreme – want to take the opportunity to exaggerate their crimes to enhance their notoriety and reputation for extreme brutality in order to strengthen a continued quest for power.

More often than not, truth and reconciliation commissions have been established to replace criminal justice. Many a time such commissions have been explicitly prevented by their mandate from naming the individuals found to be responsible for the actual crimes. Perpetrators are protected from being embarrassed by their names being revealed – as they have not received due process of law with the privilege of being presumed innocent until guilt has been proved beyond any reasonable doubt. In other cases, the expression of guilt of a perpetrator has been exchanged for an amnesty, such as in South Africa. Whether the South African example – where the truth and reconciliation process has replaced criminal justice almost completely – is a success story can best be judged when one sees how that society evolves after the leading lights of the fight against apartheid are no longer around to ensure calm. Already, the resentment of the amnesty policy and the ensuing injustice run high among previous victims and their descendants, people who still, rightly or wrongly, consider themselves as victimised by the legacy of the apartheid policy.

In short, truth and reconciliation mechanisms as they are known thus far are more or less linked to impunity if they operate to replace criminal justice and not to complement it. On their own, truth and recon-

ciliation mechanisms fall short of securing the rule of law. It should be remembered that in Rwanda a truth and reconciliation commission delivered its report just before the genocide started in April 1994.

In Europe it may be argued that truth and reconciliation mechanisms that operate to the exclusion of criminal justice will be in violation of Article 6 of the European Convention on Human Rights ('ECHR') giving everyone the right to a fair trial:

> In the determination of his civil rights and obligations or of any criminal charge against him, everyone is entitled to a fair and public hearing within a reasonable time by an independent and impartial tribunal established by law.[8]

Almost any negative public sanction linked to a crime committed is considered a situation in which a person is having a criminal charge against him or her with the right to a fair trial and presumption of innocence until proved guilty according to law. Thus, the lack of criminal justice has implications far beyond impunity as such. Traditional means of conflict resolution and reconciliation are not common at the state level in Europe today, and, as with truth and reconciliation mechanisms, will not be able to substitute for criminal justice.

10.4.3. Compensation

In the European legal system, the law has traditionally penalised the conduct of the wrongdoer as well as ensured that the victim is adequately compensated. For example, the law has for at least the last two millennia entitled the victim of theft not only to recover stolen property or its equivalent but also to damages that represent a multiple of the victim's interests; this is in addition to the punishment of the culprit upon conviction.

As far as core international crimes are concerned, the harm inflicted on the victims directly and indirectly can never be fully compensated. Life, limb and physical and mental health can never be subjected to *restitutio in integrum*. The direct losses and other damages are furthermore likely to add up to such amounts of money that perpetrators individually or collectively will be unable to pay any considerable part of the compensation due from them. Even society at large may be unable to compensate the victims enough for them to meet their bare indispensable financial

---

[8]   Council of Europe, European Convention on Human Rights, Rome, 4 November 1950, as amended 1 June 2010, Article 6 (http://www.legal-tools.org/doc/8267cb/).

needs, not to speak of providing assistance to victims to deal with the traumas represented by the core international crimes. The damage and destruction done to society as such may effectively prevent the state from stepping in to replace the lack of compensation from the perpetrators. International aid may not be unconditional and there may be less visible strings attached as well. Not even international aid is likely to ensure full compensation for pecuniary losses alone.

But, and this is significant, compensation as such is not dependent on there being verdicts in criminal cases establishing guilt for individual crimes. For compensation *to be received* – that is, for individual victims to qualify for compensation – it will normally suffice that it can be established that the person has been victimised in the overall events. The degree of proof needed in this respect may not be more than the probability that the person was affected by any one specific instance – such as, but not limited to, a person considered to belong to a persecuted ethnic group being present when his or her village or town was ethnically cleansed. Having been detained in a specific Nazi concentration camp would, for example, qualify for compensation according to the German Law on the Creation of a Foundation "Remembrance, Responsibility and Future".[9]

As the victims as a group are unlikely to receive proper and full compensation from the state and through international aid, it is in their interest – and it is their right as well – to be able to seek compensation from the perpetrators of the crime. This right may nonetheless prove more of a lofty ideal than a reality if there are no criminal proceedings against the alleged culprits. Starting civil proceedings for the victims to pursue their rights may be beyond their financial means. In any event, it will be overly costly and painful as compared to situations where the compensation claims can be linked to criminal justice cases in which the basic facts are established beyond doubt and to a degree that no perpetrator can thenceforth shield him or herself behind the right to be presumed innocent until proven guilty by a criminal court.

On its own compensation goes some way in assisting the victims in overcoming some of the effects of the core international crimes having befallen them. Bare compensation – as understood in Europe today – does

---

9. The Law on the Creation of a Foundation "Remembrance, Responsibility and Future", 2 August 2000.

not ensure the rule of law and it does not give the victims their due in terms of basic human rights.

10.4.4. Full Criminal Procedures

In a modern European democracy with the rule of law and respect for human rights, the *one* general response to the commission of a more or less serious crime is criminal procedures. There is no reason – as opposed to practical resource considerations – why this should be different when the subject matter is core international crimes. A modern European state in fact has no other tool available than criminal procedures if it to obtain a number of core goals: 1) to prevent arbitrariness and re-establish the rule of law; 2) to do justice to the victims – individuals as well as collectivities and the society at large; 3) to even out imbalances caused by the crimes in favour of their perpetrators; and 4) to recreate the shattered moral universe. This does not exclude the possibility of the state establishing special compensation schemes and assistance programmes for victims, or that a conducive atmosphere for reconciliation is sought throughout.

Only through criminal procedures can the law be made to work for everyone. After many cataclysms – including recent ones – there have been total changes in the leadership of many new states. Time and again new leaders have previously been severely victimised. For this reason many have come across as extremely generous if they have pardoned everyone who in the past had committed crimes against them. More or less simultaneously, many of these new leaders have made it known that they would like their forgiveness to serve as an example for all or most other victims as well. It should be appreciated that it is a very far cry between a person showing benevolence when raised to a position of power after a debacle, and the situation of the ordinary citizen who may face a lifelong struggle in a state of deprivation and hardship due to the crimes visited upon him or her.

On the other side, members of the upper echelons of society are more likely than ordinary people to evade anything but proper criminal procedures. When more affluent perpetrators escape justice they may continue to harm not only their former victims but also their previous frontmen, their accomplices in the crimes.

Criminal justice is crucial in securing social cohesion and to prevent fragmentation and a lasting breakdown in social relations. It is no less important in transitional periods of recovery than under normal circumstances to follow basic guidelines found, for example, in the categorical imperatives formulated by Immanuel Kant:

> Act only in accordance with that maxim through which you can at the same time will that it become a universal law (*Handle so, daß die Maxime deines Handelns jederzeit zugleich als Prinzip einer allgemeinen Gesetzgebung gelten könnte*).

> Act in such a way that you always treat humanity, whether in your own person or in the person of any other, never simply as a means but always at the same time as an end (*Handle so, daß die Menschheit, sowohl in deiner Person als in der Person eines jeden anderen jederzeit zugleich als Zweck, niemals bloß als Mittel brauchst*).[10]

The main challenges for a fair justice system remain perpetually the same: to seek a balance between the interests of the victims, the perpetrators and society at large. It is, however, a prerogative for the state to enact the codes of conduct in the society and never to leave this prerogative – not even *de facto* – to any unrepresentative group of citizens and in particular not to criminal groups.

The fundamental reason for every state-organised or international justice system is to break the vicious circles of revenge, and thus to pre-empt and prevent private 'justice'. That is, it is not only the victims of the crimes who are protected by a public criminal justice system; it also clearly works to the advantage of perpetrators, in particular the less protected among them. Street or mob 'justice' is, generally speaking, overly harsh and arbitrary – it may not necessarily be concerned with finding the real perpetrators; a scapegoat may do.

Proper criminal procedures will, furthermore, stand in stark contrast to the negation of the rule of law in the time of the conflict when people who were considered political enemies were not provided with recourse to the protection of the law. After such calamities there is a need to demonstrate that conflicts can be settled properly within the law – as well as

---

10 Immanuel Kant, *Grounding for the Metaphysics of Morals: On a Supposed Right to Lie because of Philanthropic Concern*, trans. by James W. Ellington, 3rd ed., Hackett, Indianapolis, 1993, orig. publ. 1785, pp. 30, 36.

criminal cases. There must be a justice system where defendants are also handled with respect for their human dignity and offered the benefit of legal protection and proper procedures.

A state that has severe unresolved domestic problems almost always becomes a target of meddling, interference and exploitation by other states and outside forces – frequently the least benevolent and organised international criminal groups that are always in search of non-functioning or less well functioning states. Hard-core criminals are, unfortunately, on one level far more flexible than the different justice systems.

The fact that core international crimes will not be time barred also favours these crimes being dealt with within the criminal justice system as soon as possible. It is in the best interest of every state to be able to handle *all* criminal cases within its own criminal justice system. International justice is subsidiary. The rationale for the *ad hoc* tribunals for the former Yugoslavia and Rwanda was *never* that the competence and impartiality of their staff were preferable to local justice.

10.4.5. Abbreviated Criminal Procedures

There are many situations where there are too many criminal cases to bring them all to full trial due to a lack of adequate human or financial resources or both within the relevant criminal justice system. In particular, after armed conflicts or other major upheavals the regular courts may be unable – if the courts are utilising full criminal procedures – to deal with an extreme caseload. After major cataclysms there may be tens of thousands of criminal cases pending.

In civil law systems there is a duty to prosecute all cases that come to the attention of the prosecution. When there is information that gives reason to believe that a crime has been committed, a file has to be opened. The law provides for no discretion in this respect. Prosecution is mandatory. It is not possible for the prosecution to select for prosecution only the number of cases considered tenable under the circumstances.

It is highly unfortunate when many core international crime case files have already been opened within a criminal justice system that is unable to process the cases within a reasonable time. It is equally unfortunate when many core international crimes have been committed but hardly any case files opened. Backlogs of criminal cases – sometimes huge –

are not exclusively a phenomenon after significant debacles. Globalisation and large-scale trafficking in people are some other causes.

For a number of reasons abbreviated criminal procedures have come to represent a main criminal law agenda in most European countries today. There are many national legal systems that have different kinds of abbreviated criminal procedures in other areas than the one represented by core international crimes. Abbreviated criminal procedures are considered one legal tool among several within most European criminal justice systems today. The idea of utilising abbreviated criminal procedures for core international crimes is new. Despite the existence of a new overall concept, core international crimes are primarily compound, utterly complex and multifaceted serious crimes, although not exclusively that complex and serious. Full criminal procedures represent the main or regular norm. Also abbreviated criminal procedures are regular in the sense that they are not irregular.

Proper criminal procedures shall, in the words of the UDHR, secure the following:

> Article 9
>
> No one shall be subjected to arbitrary arrest, detention or exile.
>
> Article 10
>
> Everyone is entitled in full equality to a fair and public hearing by an independent and impartial tribunal, in the determination of his rights and obligations and of any criminal charge against him.
>
> Article 11(1)
>
> Everyone charged with a penal offence has the right to be presumed innocent until proved guilty according to law in a public trial at which he has had all the guarantees necessary for his defence.
>
> Article 11(2)
>
> No one shall be held guilty of any penal offence on account of any act or omission which did not constitute a penal offence, under national or international law, at the time when it was committed. Nor shall a heavier penalty be imposed than the

          one that was applicable at the time the penal offence was committed.[11]

Minimum requirements to criminal procedures are, for example, that prosecutors and judges administer the cases, provisions guaranteeing *ne bis in idem*, and the right to appeal are added in Protocols to the ECHR. Beyond the basics there is nevertheless quite some leverage for states to organise their criminal systems according to their traditions and preferences. Most national criminal justice systems will have room for the possibility of elaborating and enacting abbreviated criminal procedures – entirely within the due process of law requirements – significantly more time- and cost-efficient than regular full criminal procedures.

Abbreviated criminal procedures must be so construed as to secure the interests of the victims. Detailed and reasoned judicial decisions that are needed for the society to obtain accurate historical records form no obstacle to the adoption of abbreviated criminal procedures. The utilisation of abbreviated criminal procedures does not impact on the prioritisation that will have to be made when huge numbers of cases are waiting to be processed. Prioritisation may be based on the seriousness of the crime or the violated interests, and on the degree of the perpetrators' guilt. On a different level, a criterion for priority can be that an alleged perpetrator already has a core international crime case file open when a new crime allegedly has been committed.

The use of abbreviated criminal procedures should reflect the different levels of gravity of the core international crimes. For example, property offences and minor unlawful detention prior to large-scale transfers of whole population groups are offences committed on an immense scale in many armed conflicts. These offences do not as such violate the interests of life or personal integrity and may thus suitably be addressed in abbreviated criminal procedures.

For the purpose of this discussion, it is presupposed that abbreviated criminal procedures are so construed as to meet fair trial standards. Abbreviated criminal procedures will furthermore have to comply with the principle of legality. It is also taken as given that the abbreviated criminal procedures are prescribed by law and made an integral part of the state's criminal justice system. The legality principle may not exclude some kinds of conditional discretion. Extrajudicial mechanisms are not

---

[11]   UDHR, Articles 9–11, see *supra* note 2.

regarded as abbreviated criminal procedures. The many abbreviated criminal procedures in use in Europe presently *do in general meet* the due process requirement; they do not fall short of respecting human rights and the fair trial prerequisites. Abbreviated criminal procedures are intended, however, to provide the minimum needed and to represent accelerated procedures. Thereby the abbreviated criminal procedures are likely to significantly shorten the time and reduce the resources spent to process case files.

Abbreviated criminal procedures can thus have a very significant role to play by helping states to maintain the rule of law and protect fundamental human rights by also being able to prosecute large numbers of core international crimes within their national criminal justice system and with full respect for fair trail principles. The core of the matter is to simplify without compromising due process.

10.5. Concluding Remarks

There are, to summarise, normative reasons – considerations having ethical force – to support the implementation of justice and criminal procedures following the commission of core international crimes. Facts – here, the crimes – become obligating reasons in conjunction with these normative considerations. They give rise to an obligation for the state to seek justice. Abbreviated criminal procedures are *one* tool available in the aftermath of core international crimes for the state to meet its obligation to administer justice and uphold the rule of law. The best can be the enemy of the good. The interests at stake when criminal justice is foregone are highly significant and should never be left unattended to in search for 'perfect' criminal procedures. What matters is to concentrate on what is good. In the secular world only criminal justice can restore the rule of law fully.

There is a false perception that it is only by having a less than perfect criminal justice system that the state can make a serious mistake, and then only *vis-à-vis* the perpetrators. Not administering justice can be more harmful, primarily with regard to victims and the society at large but also in relation to perpetrators. In law, as in medicine, there ought to be a basic *primum non nocere* norm (first, do no harm) based on which societies constantly seek a fair balance between the interests of all those involved – on all sides – in criminal justice cases and without ever sacrificing the human rights of either side. As sang Vera Lynn back in 1942:

> There's a land of begin again
>
> On the other side of the hill
>
> Where we learn to love and live again
>
> When the world is quiet and still

That "land of begin again" is as far as can be seen one of rule of law, human rights and democracy.

INDEX

A

accelerated procedure, 139, 141, 162
adversarial
    adversarial system, 28–32, 34–39, 63,
        86, 96, 97, 200, 227
Afghanistan, 229–30
African Union, 229
Al Mahdi, Ahmad Al Faqi, 98, 99
alternative mechanisms, 6, 152, 155–58,
    166–68
alternative punishment, 142
Ambos, Kai, xi, 2, 10–11, **27–100**
American, 34, 40, 53–57, 60–65, 68–69,
    71, 74–75, 78, 91, 134, 150, 201, 213,
    234–35
Amnesty International, 138, 193
amnesty, 13, 135, 178, 181, 185, 231–32,
    257
Argentina, xvi, 1, 13, 65, 70, 75, 175, 224,
    231–33
Aristotle, 253

B

Basic Principles and Guidelines for
    Reparations to Victims, 210–11, 214,
    219, 221
Belgium, 33, 39, 41, 78, 83–84, 90, 220
Bergsmo, Morten, i, iii, xi, **1–18**, 24, 112,
    120, 131, 145–46, 171, 173
Bitti, Gilbert, **209–21**
Bosnia and Herzegovina, i, iii, iv–vii, ix,
    x, xii, 1, 3–5, 7–11, 14, 16–17, 101–
    103, 111–13, 115, 119–20, 126, 133,
    154–55, 158, 224, 228, 230, 275
Braathu, Jan, i, iii, xi, 8–9

C

capacity building, 115–16, 126, 153
Cardozo, Benjamin, 22
case selection, iv, 22, 116, 227

Cassese, Antonio, 29, 67, 124, 169
Centre for International Law Research
    and Policy, i, iii, 1
China, 34
civil law, 30–31, 55, 65, 67–68, 73, 75–
    77, 94–96, 99, 131, 133, 162, 224,
    226, 228, 262
Clark, Phil, **189–208**
Code for Crown Prosecutors, 86–88
Codice di procedura penale 11, 36
Colombia, i, xiii, xvi, 1–3, 7, 13, 16, 120–
    21, 129, 144–46, 171–76, 178, 180–
    81, 224, 227, 231, 233, 235, 239
Colombian Peace and Justice Law, xv, 12,
    171
common crimes 25
common law, 30, 35, 38, 64–65, 67, 73–
    74, 76–77, 92–93, 224–25
community dispute resolution, 136
community reconciliation procedure, 236
community-based, 206
Comparative Criminal Procedure, 10, 29,
    91
Complementarity and the Exercise of
    Universal Jurisdiction, 3, 276
complementarity, 20, 124
Conditional Cautioning Code of Practice,
    81–82, 86
confession, 39, 48, 67, 71, 73, 95, 147,
    179, 185, 201, 203, 205–6, 208
Consensual Procedures
    constitution, 23
constitutionalisation 23
Council of Europe, 244, 258
Criteria for Prioritizing and Selecting
    Core International Crimes Cases, 4,
    145, 173, 275
Crown Court, 40, 55, 60
Crown Prosecution Service, 81–82, 86–
    87, 90

principle of legality, 7, 32, 33, 54, 60, 64, 82, 85, 148, 224, 264
prioritisation, iv, x, 4, 5, 10, 16, 110, 116, 161, 264
procedural expediency, 97
procedural justice, 52
procedural rights, 45, 75, 90, 133
Prosecutor's Office of Bosnia and Herzegovina, v, 4
prosecutorial discretion, 32–33, 36, 84, 86, 88, 224, 228
prosecutorial strategy, 224, 227, 232, 236
public interest, 17, 34, 81, 83, 85–86, 88, 90, 150, 164
public trial, 64, 238, 254, 263
public trust, 127

R

Radio-Télévision Libre des Mille Collines, 191–92
rank-and-file perpetrators, 206
reconciliation, vi, 9, 20, 99, 121–22, 128, 131–32, 134–36, 148, 156, 167, 195, 206, 212, 229–30, 236–37, 256–58, 260
reduced penalties, 143
regular courts, 12, 121, 135, 149, 167, 262
reintegration, 146, 201, 206, 230
reparations, 133, 146–47, 150, 179, 182, 210, 217–19, 221, 228, 230, 234–36
Robertson, Geoffrey, 231
Robinson, Patrick, iii
Romania, 69
rule of law, vi, 7, 9, 15, 114–16, 126–128, 135, 162, 166, 229, 233, 243–246, 251–52, 255, 258, 260–61, 265–66
Rwanda, i, xiii, xv, 2, 13, 16, 24, 32, 92, 102, 107–9, 111, 120–21, 123, 131, 135–36, 138, 149, 155, 163, 166, 189–195, 198–202, 206, 229, 255, 258, 262
Rwandan Patriotic Front, 109, 190, 192

S

Saffon, Maria Paula, **171–87**
Sarajevo, i, iii, v, ix, 1, 6–7, 16, 24, 112, 119, 126, 232

Schabas, William A., 107, 138
Scharf, Michael P., 54, 132
Scotland, 49, 78–79, 82, 90–91, 223
Security Council, 8, 104, 123–24, 192, 225, 228–29, 241
sentence reduction, 76, 94, 132, 150, 181
sentencing discretion, 45
Sierra Leone, 92, 102, 115, 224, 227–28, 231–32
South Africa, 6, 54, 91, 231–32, 257
Spain, 33, 39, 40, 43, 66, 71, 75, 76, 85, 90
Special Court for Sierra Leone, 92–93, 98, 231–32
Special Tribunal for Lebanon, 92, 225–26
Srebrenica Commission, 112, 114
Stahn, Carsten, 157
State Court of Bosnia and Herzegovina, v, 17
substantive justice, 52
summary proceedings
summary trial, vi, 37, 39, 41, 47, 51, 77, 233
Supreme Court of Justice, 178, 180, 183, 185–86
Sweden, 90
Switzerland, 62, 76

T

territoriality, 2, 103, 125
Timor-Leste, xvi, 224, 228, 236
Tokyo, i, 106, 123
transitional justice, 2, 6, 10, 12–13, 16, 19, 21–25, 121, 127, 135, 150, 171–72, 223, 228–29
transparency, 4, 72, 79, 142, 144, 148
truth and reconciliation commissions, 121, 131, 134, 156, 167, 212, 256–57
truth-telling, 20, 133, 137, 143, 147, 202–3
Tutsi, 109, 164, 190–92

U

Uganda, 190, 192, 229–30, 237–38
undue political influences, 128
United States 34, 53–56, 61–62, 64–65, 69, 71–75, 78, 201, 213, 234–35

TOAEP TEAM

OTHER VOLUMES IN THE
FICHL PUBLICATION SERIES

Morten Bergsmo, Mads Harlem and Nobuo Hayashi (editors):
Importing Core International Crimes into National Law
Torkel Opsahl Academic EPublisher
Oslo, 2010
FICHL Publication Series No. 1 (Second Edition, 2010)
ISBN 978-82-93081-00-5

Nobuo Hayashi (editor):
National Military Manuals on the Law of Armed Conflict
Torkel Opsahl Academic EPublisher
Oslo, 2010
FICHL Publication Series No. 2 (Second Edition, 2010)
ISBN 978-82-93081-02-9

Morten Bergsmo, Kjetil Helvig, Ilia Utmelidze and Gorana Žagovec:
The Backlog of Core International Crimes Case Files in Bosnia and Herzegovina
Torkel Opsahl Academic EPublisher
Oslo, 2010
FICHL Publication Series No. 3 (Second Edition, 2010)
ISBN 978-82-93081-04-3

Morten Bergsmo (editor):
Criteria for Prioritizing and Selecting Core International Crimes Cases
Torkel Opsahl Academic EPublisher
Oslo, 2010
FICHL Publication Series No. 4 (Second Edition, 2010)
ISBN 978-82-93081-06-7

Morten Bergsmo and Pablo Kalmanovitz (editors):
Law in Peace Negotiations
Torkel Opsahl Academic EPublisher
Oslo, 2010
FICHL Publication Series No. 5 (Second Edition, 2010)
ISBN 978-82-93081-08-1

Morten Bergsmo, César Rodríguez Garavito, Pablo Kalmanovitz and Maria Paula Saffon (editors):
Distributive Justice in Transitions
Torkel Opsahl Academic EPublisher
Oslo, 2010
FICHL Publication Series No. 6 (2010)
ISBN 978-82-93081-12-8

Morten Bergsmo, César Rodriguez-Garavito, Pablo Kalmanovitz y Maria Paula Saffon (editors):
Justicia Distributiva en Sociedades en Transición
Torkel Opsahl Academic EPublisher
Oslo, 2012
FICHL Publication Series No. 6 (2012)
ISBN 978-82-93081-10-4

Morten Bergsmo (editor):
Complementarity and the Exercise of Universal Jurisdiction for Core International Crimes
Torkel Opsahl Academic EPublisher
Oslo, 2010
FICHL Publication Series No. 7 (2010)
ISBN 978-82-93081-14-2

Morten Bergsmo (editor):
Active Complementarity: Legal Information Transfer
Torkel Opsahl Academic EPublisher
Oslo, 2011
FICHL Publication Series No. 8 (2011)
ISBN 978-82-93081-55-5 (PDF)
ISBN 978-82-93081-56-2 (print)

Sam Muller, Stavros Zouridis, Morly Frishman and Laura Kistemaker (editors):
The Law of the Future and the Future of Law
Torkel Opsahl Academic EPublisher
Oslo, 2010
FICHL Publication Series No. 11 (2011)
ISBN 978-82-93081-27-2

Morten Bergsmo, Alf Butenschøn Skre and Elisabeth J. Wood (editors):
Understanding and Proving International Sex Crimes
Torkel Opsahl Academic EPublisher
Beijing, 2012
FICHL Publication Series No. 12 (2012)
ISBN 978-82-93081-29-6

Morten Bergsmo (editor):
Thematic Prosecution of International Sex Crimes
Torkel Opsahl Academic EPublisher
Beijing, 2012
FICHL Publication Series No. 13 (2012)
ISBN 978-82-93081-31-9

Terje Einarsen:
The Concept of Universal Crimes in International Law
Torkel Opsahl Academic EPublisher
Oslo, 2012
FICHL Publication Series No. 14 (2012)
ISBN 978-82-93081-33-3

莫滕·伯格斯默 凌岩 （主编）：
国家主权与国际刑法
Torkel Opsahl Academic EPublisher
Beijing, 2012
FICHL Publication Series No. 15 (2012)
ISBN 978-82-93081-58-6

Morten Bergsmo and LING Yan (editors):
State Sovereignty and International Criminal Law
Torkel Opsahl Academic EPublisher
Beijing, 2012
FICHL Publication Series No. 15 (2012)
ISBN 978-82-93081-35-7

Morten Bergsmo and CHEAH Wui Ling (editors):
Old Evidence and Core International Crimes
Torkel Opsahl Academic EPublisher
Beijing, 2012
FICHL Publication Series No. 16 (2012)
ISBN 978-82-93081-60-9

YI Ping:
戦争と平和の間——発足期日本国際法学における「正しい戦争」
の観念とその帰結
Torkel Opsahl Academic EPublisher
Beijing, 2013
FICHL Publication Series No. 17 (2013)
ISBN 978-82-93081-66-1

Morten Bergsmo and SONG Tianying (editors):
On the Proposed Crimes Against Humanity Convention
Torkel Opsahl Academic EPublisher
Brussels, 2014
FICHL Publication Series No. 18 (2014)
ISBN 978-82-93081-96-8

Morten Bergsmo (editor):
Quality Control in Fact-Finding
Torkel Opsahl Academic EPublisher
Florence, 2013
FICHL Publication Series No. 19 (2013)
ISBN 978-82-93081-78-4

Morten Bergsmo, CHEAH Wui Ling and YI Ping (editors):
Historical Origins of International Criminal Law: Volume 1
Torkel Opsahl Academic EPublisher
Brussels, 2014
FICHL Publication Series No. 20 (2014)
ISBN 978-82-93081-11-1

Morten Bergsmo, CHEAH Wui Ling and YI Ping (editors):
Historical Origins of International Criminal Law: Volume 2
Torkel Opsahl Academic EPublisher
Brussels, 2014
FICHL Publication Series No. 21 (2014)
ISBN 978-82-93081-13-5

Morten Bergsmo, CHEAH Wui Ling, SONG Tianying and YI Ping (editors):
Historical Origins of International Criminal Law: Volume 3
Torkel Opsahl Academic EPublisher
Brussels, 2015
FICHL Publication Series No. 22 (2015)
ISBN 978-82-93081-15-3 (print) and ISBN 978-82-93081-14-6 (e-book)

Morten Bergsmo, CHEAH Wui Ling, SONG Tianying and YI Ping (editors):
Historical Origins of International Criminal Law: Volume 4
Torkel Opsahl Academic EPublisher
Brussels, 2015
FICHL Publication Series No. 23 (2015)
ISBN 978-82-93081-17-7 (print) and ISBN 978-82-93081-16-0 (e-book)

Morten Bergsmo, Klaus Rackwitz and SONG Tianying (editors):
Historical Origins of International Criminal Law: Volume 5
Torkel Opsahl Academic EPublisher
Brussels, 2017
FICHL Publication Series No. 24 (2017)
ISBN 978-82-8348-106-8 (print) and 978-82-8348-107-5 (e-book)

Morten Bergsmo and SONG Tianying (editors):
Military Self-Interest in Accountability for Core International Crimes
Torkel Opsahl Academic EPublisher
Brussels, 2015
FICHL Publication Series No. 25 (2015)
ISBN 978-82-93081-61-6 (print) and ISBN 978-82-93081-81-4 (e-book)

Wolfgang Kaleck:
Double Standards: International Criminal Law and the West
Torkel Opsahl Academic EPublisher
Brussels, 2015
FICHL Publication Series No. 26 (2015)
ISBN 978-82-93081-67-8 (print) and 978-82-93081-83-8 (e-book)

LIU Daqun and ZHANG Binxin:
Historical War Crimes Trials in Asia
Torkel Opsahl Academic EPublisher
Brussels, 2016
FICHL Publication Series No. 27 (2016)
ISBN 978-82-8348-055-9 (print) and 978-82-8348-056-6 (e-book)

All volumes are freely available online at http://www.fichl.org/publication-series/.
Printed copies may be ordered from distributors indicated at http://www.fichl.org/
torkel-opsahl-academic-epublisher/distribution/, including from http://www.amazon.
co.uk/. For reviews of earlier books in this Series in academic journals, please see
http://www.fichl.org/torkel-opsahl-academic-epublisher/reviews-of-toaep-books/.